THE
RED MAN'S
BONES

THE RED MAN'S BONES

GEORGE CATLIN, ARTIST AND SHOWMAN

Benita Eisler

W. W. NORTON & COMPANY

New York • London

Excerpt from "Children of Light" from *Collected Poems* by Robert Lowell, copyright ©
2003 by Harriet Lowell and Sheridan Lowell. Reprinted by permission of Farrar, Straus
and Giroux, LLC. Selections from *The Letters of George Catlin and His Family: A Chronicle of
the American West* by Marjorie Catlin Roehm, © 1966 by the Regents of the University of
California. Published by the University of California Press. Reprinted by permission of the
University of California Press.

For information about permission to reproduce selections from this book,
write to Permissions, W. W. Norton & Company, Inc.,
500 Fifth Avenue, New York, NY 10110

For information about special discounts for bulk purchases, please contact
W. W. Norton Special Sales at specialsales@wwnorton.com or 800-233-4830

Manufacturing by Courier Westford
Book design by Chris Welch Design
Production manager: Julia Druskin

Library of Congress Cataloging-in-Publication Data

Eisler, Benita.
The Red Man's Bones : George Catlin, Artist and Showman / Benita Eisler. —
First edition.
pages cm
Includes bibliographical references and index.
ISBN 978-0-393-06616-6 (hardcover)
1. Catlin, George, 1796–1872. 2. Painters—United States—Biography. 3. Indians in art.
4. West (U.S.)—In art. I. Title.
ND237.C35E39 2013
759.13—dc23
[B]
2013013973

W. W. Norton & Company, Inc.
500 Fifth Avenue, New York, N.Y. 10110
www.wwnorton.com

W. W. Norton & Company Ltd.
Castle House, 75/76 Wells Street, London W1T 3QT

1 2 3 4 5 6 7 8 9 0

For Colin and Rachel

CONTENTS

Our fathers wrung their bread from stocks and stones
And fenced their gardens with the Redman's bones

—ROBERT LOWELL,
"Children of Light"

THE
RED MAN'S
BONES

Prologue

OPENING CEREMONY

I t was just daybreak when he seized his sketchbook and made his way, running, from Fort Clark to the nearby cluster of Mandan villages at the mouth of the Knife and Missouri Rivers. He had been at the fort for more than a week now, waiting for the festival called O-kee-pa, to begin, and had learned—only at the last minute—that he would be allowed to witness its mysteries.

In spring 1832 the artist George Catlin, thirty-five years old, felt at the height of his powers. The West and the beauty of its native people had fired his talent with an energy and drive he had never known. He worked like a man possessed. The very hairs on his brush seemed to exude sparks, and his likenesses of chiefs and warriors inspired tribal leaders to call him "'a great *medicine white man,*'" indeed, "the greatest medicine man in the world," Catlin recalled, "for they said I had made *living beings.*"

Earlier in this mythic year, at Fort Union, twelve hundred miles upriver, he had spent a month painting, by some accounts, more than 186 portraits of men and women—Crow, Blackfeet, Mandan, Cheyenne, and other Northern Plains Indians who gathered around the fort to trade.

His fame preceded him downriver to Fort Clark, where he had stopped, held by rumors, on his way back to St. Louis: O-kee-pa would begin any day now. While waiting, Catlin hadn't wasted a moment; he could claim sixteen Mandan portraits, including one of his great friend Mah-to-toh-pa, "Four Bears," retired warrior, fellow artist, and the tribe's beloved second chief.

Now the herald, visible from afar by the dazzling white paint covering his face and body, was seen racing toward the settlements, signaling the start of the four-day celebration. As soon as they sighted Oke-hee-de, "First Man," the native villagers crowded on the roofs of their lodges, screaming—in terror or welcome, it was hard to know.

What Catlin knew at this moment was that he had been doubly chosen: He would be one of the few white men ever to pass through the doors of the great medicine lodge, open only for this ceremony. But a greater distinction was to be his alone. He was the only white artist ever to be invited as an *artist*, to witness and to record all that he saw.

From everywhere and nowhere the sounds of drumming and chanting began, low at first, then, by barely audible degrees, louder. Catlin arrived at the great lodge, escorted by his host, James Kipp, head of the fort and son-in-law of "Four Bears." The two white men were seated upon a raised platform sacred to the tribe's wise men. There, for the next four days—from sunrise to sunset—Catlin took his place of honor and, hardly raising his pencil from the page, he drew.

Drawing, by focusing his mind and hand, also distracted him; his art distanced the artist from the acts of ritualized violence and carnage that unfolded before his eyes. However pagan and "savage," O-kee-pa, he reminded himself, was still a "*Mandan Religious Ceremony*" and George Catlin, a professing Christian, entered the "*medicine house . . . as I would have entered a church . . . little did I expect to see the interior of their holy temple turned into a slaughter-house, and its floor strewed with the blood of its fanatic devotees.*"

His hosts had designated the best seat in the lodge for him; but more, they had set aside a field studio for his use, "an earth-covered wig-wam, with a fine sky-light over my head." There, from dozens of sketches, Catlin made four of his most famous paintings. Together they provide the only surviving pictorial narrative of O-kee-pa, the Mandan passion play.

Within the shadowy interior of *Mystery Lodge* the stage is set for the first act of the drama. Half-naked players huddle in groups. The pride of Mandan youth, they are among the chosen fifty to be tested through torture. Those who survive will assure the tribe of a new generation of heroic leaders, along with a bountiful hunt and harvest. Each has hung his shield on the wall behind him, a reminder, together with the paired human and cow skulls at his feet, of the trial by agony to come. Deprived of food and water for four days, they sit or lie, waiting. The earthen floor of the great circular space is lit only by a crescent of sky visible through the smoke hole in the roof and the sacred flame which burns in a pit sunk in the center of the space. A medicine man tends the fire; left arm raised, he invokes the Great Spirit with prayers and offerings.

With *The Cutting Scene* the worst has happened: Two at a time, the elect hang from rawhide cords attached to wooden splints driven through their flesh. In this puppet theater of pain, they are manipulated from above by torturers whose heads are visible through the roof opening. Below, designated tormentors prod and turn one of the agonized bodies. The other appears to have lost consciousness; his flayed skin hangs in strips exposing the white flesh beneath. A third victim, freshly cut down, lies propped on his elbows, observing, trance-like, as the skin of his thighs is pulled and torn away by two elders. In the foreground nearest the artist, a band of ecstatic fellow tribesmen drums steadily, while a lone musician, arms raised, shakes his rattles in accompaniment.

Survivors faced further tests. In *The Last Race*, those who crawled from the lodge were held to the ritual amputation of a finger. On reaching the public square, they are goaded into a final frenzied circle dance. Dragging elk skulls skewered to their flayed flesh, the half-dead boys are hauled over stony ground by masked figures, bodies gaily painted vermilion and bright blue, running at top speed.

O-KEE-PA, IN ALL its ambiguities, clung to Catlin like a succubus. For most of his lifetime, the four paintings, *The Cutting Scene* in particular, inspired reactions of disbelief and denial from contemporaries. To his rivals and enemies, these works provided welcome proof of the artist's unreliability; at the least he had exaggerated; at worst, in a spirit of unsavory voyeurism, he had sensationalized, exploited—or invented the whole thing, cooking up for profit a queasy brew of sadism, blood lust, and sexual titillation.

Five years after his visit smallpox swept through the Mandan settlements. Carried by a white trader from a river boat, the disease killed most of this beautiful and mysterious tribe. In their fevered agony, many had leaped from the cliffs into the rushing waters of the Missouri. Among the suicides was said to have been Four Bears, who died cursing the white visitors whom he had trusted—and who had repaid his friendship with death.

1

HOMECOMING

In October 1870, a small gray figure, enveloped in a shabby over-coat, stepped from a ship's gangplank onto a New York dock. He peered into the waiting crowd, searching for familiar faces. Finally, he recognized one figure, a smaller, more threadbare version of himself, but not the three smartly dressed young women accompanying him. Neither would they have known the passenger they had come to meet. They needed their uncle Francis with them to identify their father. George Catlin had not seen his daughters for twenty years. They were little girls when they had been taken from their father's care.

When George Catlin left America for England in 1839, he was at the height of his fame as an artist and explorer. His paintings of Northern Plains Indians had taken him to places few Americans had ever seen. An aura of heroic trailblazer banished any stereotype of effete artist. Catlin was small and wiry, with frank blue eyes and wavy chestnut hair; in his beaded and fringed buckskin jacket, the painter conjured both exotic Indian and rugged mountain man. He packed lecture halls with illustrated talks on the native tribes whose ways he knew intimately; the sheer number of likenesses—610 by Catlin's count—suggested that he had painted an Indian a day. In fact the artist's familiarity with this feared and still-unknown race was unchallenged. Starting in 1831, he had spent the better part of six years living and painting among the tribes whose settlements were scattered along the Mississippi and Missouri Rivers. A decade later, in 1841, he published the best-selling memoir of his adventures, *Letters and Notes on the Manners, Customs, and Conditions of the North American Indians.*

Still, Catlin had never managed to translate his fame into success—or even a decent living. He had no interest in rich patrons; he saw himself as the nation's painter. Despite repeated offers on his part and lobbying by powerful friends in Washington, the artist had failed to sell his collective portrait to the nation. So, in 1839, George Catlin, aged forty-three, with no money and his pride in tatters, left America. He would not return for thirty years.

He saw the future, and it was action. In Catlin's three decades abroad he largely gave up painting for a new, quintessentially American career: showman. Exhibiting "live" troupes of Iowa and Ojibwa to ecstatic audiences in London, Paris, and Brussels, thirty years before William Cody became "Buffalo Bill," George Catlin animated the static images of his Indian Gallery into the first Wild West show.

Nonetheless he would surely have reflected on the irony that continues to deny fame to the artist while his art is hijacked in the service of our collective memory: His craft has become our reality, available to all.

"My life had been a tissue of risks and chances," he once said, and for a brief moment his gambles seem to have paid off. The exile's triumphs abroad redeemed his rejections at home. Then, one by one, the pieces of his enterprise came apart, never to be reconnected.

LONG BEFORE HIS death in 1872, in a Jersey City hotel, obscurity had engulfed his name and art. Not until the 1960s, when the "New Politics" finally addressed "old" crimes of slavery and genocide did George Catlin reemerge.

His years of oblivion also speak to the perils of originality. Until the photographs of Edward S. Curtis—more than sixty years in the future from when Catlin was active—the artist's painted images *were* "the Indian" to his audiences. Over time the hundreds of Native Americans who sat for him merged with their likenesses: They became their portraits. It was easier for the nation to claim these men and women—proud, vibrant, and safely dead—as its own than it was to confront their impoverished and accusing descendants, their traditional tribal life largely destroyed as Catlin foretold. Reproduced everywhere, the iconic painted images have taken on a life of their own. The triumph of his art rendered the artist anonymous. In recent years, however, Catlin's protean talent, including his reissued writings, has emerged from obscurity in all the brilliance of his paint and prose: Exhibited, reproduced, and studied, his works are finally recognized as an achievement unparalled in American art and ethnology.

His diminished reputation mirrored the destruction of the tribal life already under way while he lived. In recent years both have been revived and revitalized.

Now, almost 150 years after his death, George Catlin's work is represented in most major public collections of American art in the United States, starting with the White House; his paintings are the pride of museums dedicated to Western art; and for the last half century, Catlin's portraits, landscapes, and scenes of Indian life have been pursued by private collectors. On the rare occasion that an important picture or album of watercolors comes up for sale, it is the star of any auction of American art, with prices to match.

In the making of *Dances with Wolves* (1990), the award-winning epic Western, filmed in Wyoming and North Dakota, authenticity was established through the use of the Lakota language (with subtitles) and the meticulous re-creation—in motion picture terms—of Catlin's great painting of a buffalo hunt. We can only imagine how the artist would have loved seeing his bison herd thunder across the wide screen (ear-splitting noise provided by Dolby sound). "Mixed media," "happenings," "performance," and "appropriation" art—Catlin deployed all of these, inventing new combinations as he went. He was so far ahead of his time that he disappeared beyond its horizons, like a rocket fired into the future.

ARTISTS BEFORE CATLIN had painted Indians; some, like Charles Bird King, specialized in visiting delegations to Washington and Philadelphia. Others, such as Titian Peale,* were attached to government expeditions charged with exploring unmapped territories, along with their inhabitants. But no artist before Catlin lived among the tribal people he would paint, smoking pipes, sharing meals and ceremonies, and games and hunts with his subjects. No one had rendered their costumes and weapons, the somber reserve and unguarded glimpses of parental love. No one before George Catlin earned the title "First Artist of the West."

His portraits, however, refuse any redemptive happy endings to our history. To stand surrounded by the Indian Gallery is to feel the weight of collective tragedy. Taken together, each presence—fierce chief, proud brave, young mother—constructs a memorial. Catlin's fate is inseparable from theirs. In a strange portrait, painted in England in 1849, Catlin is shadowed by an Indian warrior and his wife. But which ones are the Other, the artist or his subjects?

Pursued by fear of failure, an easy mark for get-rich-quick schemes promising gold and land, forever chasing the all-American chimera of success, George Catlin to this day remains a contentious figure: artist and huckster, celebrity and outlaw, Indian advocate and exploiter, hero and pariah. What remains indisputable are the

* His brothers—named Rembrandt, Raphaelle, and Rubens, reveal the hopes of their father, Charles Willson Peale, for his sons.

unlikely circumstances of his early years—unlikely, that is, to have produced a great artist.

HE WAS BORN in Wilkes-Barre, Pennsylvania, in 1796, a place then so remote from the civilized seaboard outposts of the young Republic that it might as well have been the country west of the Mississippi for which Lewis and Clark would set out seven years later.

Known as "the endless mountains," the region's hilly ridges, tumbling from the Catskills and Alleghenies, were the first landscapes that George Catlin saw. Neither mountainous nor "endless," the terrain suggests a corrugated plateau, which one observer likened to "crumpled paper." But the romantic name stuck, first stamped on eighteenth-century maps of the northeastern corner of Pennsylvania, cradling the Susquehanna River as it loops between that state and New York, including the farms that George's restless father, Putnam Catlin, kept buying and soon selling before moving on.

Like border regions the world over, these valley settlements were a battleground. In one important respect, however, this vast backcountry, barely claimed from wilderness, was different. The Pennamite-Yankee wars, which roiled Pennsylvania's Wyoming Valley between 1769 and 1799, did not pit land claimants from New York State, across the Susquehanna, against the Pennsylvanians. These decades of disputes involved Connecticut and Pennsylvania, hostilities being further complicated by the fact that both sides—older established settlements of New Englanders with royal grants who stayed put and new settlers like Putnam Catlin—almost all had roots in Connecticut. Little actual blood, moreover, was shed in these so-called wars; battles were largely confined to courthouses and corridors, enlisting what we would now define as white-collar warriors—lawyers, judges, legislators, absentee investors, and resident property owners. Descended from "old" Connecticut Yankees but a "new" Pennsylvanian by choice, Putnam Catlin represented both sides of the continuing conflict.

———

THE FIRST OF the family to leave England for the colonies was Thomas Catlin, a scion of minor gentry and royal office holders listed in the Domesday Book, who arrived from Kent, near Tunbridge Wells, to settle in Hartford, Connecticut, in 1645. From there his descendants moved inland; the largest contingent put down roots in Litchfield, thirty-four miles distant, where they prospered as farmers, millers, and merchants.

In 1777, when Litchfield called for volunteers in the war against England, no fewer than twelve Catlins enlisted. These included Eli, the artist's grandfather, and Putnam, his father, then thirteen years old; Eli with a captain's commission, the boy as a regimental fifer. Both returned unscathed. When they were demobilized Eli went back to his farm; his eighteen-year-old son, who showed a marked aptitude for books, read law.

Admitted to the Connecticut bar in 1786, Putnam decided to leave Litchfield. The sleepy farming community had grown into a rich urban center—the fourth largest in the state. New local fortunes were based upon larger enterprises: iron, textiles, and the China trade. Prosperity bred more lawyers, and the competition now included young men from wealthy, well-connected families, whose classical education at Yale, Dartmouth, and Williams colleges burnished their legal training. So, with his cousin Luther Catlin and a group of other restless friends, Putnam set out for a part of Pennsylvania that seemed to offer wide-open opportunity without leaving the bounds of civilization; Philadelphia was only a few days' travel away, while the new frontier itself represented a compromise between unsettled virgin forests and rich valley bottomland, cheap and ideal for farming. And for a farmer who was also a lawyer, the region promised clients, concentrated in the newly established, burgeoning settlement of Wilkes-Barre, named for its two English founders who had supported the War for Independence and made fortunes in their new home. Putnam Catlin could reasonably hope that similar rewards would be his.

Within five years the fledgling attorney, aged twenty-two—one of the first to be admitted to the bar of the recently founded Luzerne County in 1787—had set up a law practice and become a property owner. For ten pounds he purchased from Jacob Dyer, a resident of Windham, Connecticut, one lot and most of the adjoining piece of land in the center of Wilkes-Barre. He also found a wife and started a family. Putnam's nineteen-year-old bride, Mary Sutton, called Polly, was descended from early Quaker settlers of the Wyoming Valley, the area around Wilkes-Barre. Her father owned a prosperous grist-mill, but its location, at the foot of a mountain gorge, was nonetheless described as gloomy and isolated.

In 1778 the military alliance between Tory sympathizers and local Iroquois against "rebel" landowners erupted in the battle known as the Wyoming Valley Massacre. Despite few casualties, the gory name given to the series of raids and skirmishes now appears as evidence of anti-Indian hate propaganda rather than a description of mass kill-ings. That same year seven-year-old Polly Sutton and her mother were captured by Indians. Based upon family accounts, George Catlin later declared that their captors had done more than free his mother and grandmother unharmed: They had "hunted for them and supplied them with food and painted their faces red, calling them 'sisters and children' and treating them with the greatest kindness," adding that such humanity revealed "the honour of the Indian character."

Both women would recall the period of captivity among the Iroquois as "brief," but its actual duration remains unknown. Recent studies, however, have tracked how quickly Anglo-Europeans living among Indians, especially children taken as captives, erased memory of their mother tongue, soon replaced by native languages. For Polly, forget-ting may have been hastened with her "adoption" by the small group with whom she lived. Whether for this reason or the trauma caused by the original seizure, Polly Sutton, at the time of her marriage, was a functional illiterate. She seems to have mastered only the rudiments of reading and writing English when her own children began learning their lessons from the primer. As a measure of the shame her illiteracy caused her, she unfailingly apologized for her ignorance, either in postscripts or entire letters dictated to her husband for the children as they moved away from home. As George would prove the most literate of her brood, his mother never seems to have written to him at all, asking only to be "remembered" in Putnam's letters to their second son.

IN THE DOZEN years before George's birth in 1796, his father had represented his neighbors in cases that were the bread and butter of a backcountry law practice. He pursued debtors or defended the claims of small landowners or would-be buyers in the endless disputes over grants, deeds, and boundaries that filled court dockets everywhere in the still largely rural Republic. His experience in this area of the law did not go unnoticed. In 1798 Putnam Catlin was hired as a local agent by two of the most famous financiers of the period, partners in a vast development scheme whose utopian prospectus concealed the scam of the century.

During the worst days of the Terror in France, just after the Revolution, a group of French royalist émigrés in Philadelphia and their rich planter counterparts in Santo Domingo hatched a plot to establish a refuge for their queen, Marie Antoinette, and her court along the banks of the Susquehanna twenty-five miles north of Wilkes-Barre. "Asylum," as its name suggested, would be a small French city rising from the wilderness, complete with a château for the exiled monarch. Unfortunately the key rescue piece of the plot failed: The tumbrel carrying the queen from the Conciergerie to the guillotine was never diverted to the American brig, *Sally*, rumored to await her off Le Havre. While the disappointed minor émigré nobility tried to replicate life at Versailles in the Pennsylvania backcountry, two other Philadelphians saw Asylum as a great speculative opportunity.

In April 1793 Robert Morris, the financier of the Revolution and a U.S. senator, together with John Nicholson, a rich industrialist and now Pennsylvania comptroller general, established the Asylum and Pennsylvania Land Company. The plan called for the acquisition of more than a million acres, of which the émigré community accounted for a mere sixteen hundred. To finance the projected stock offering, both Morris and Nicholson borrowed heavily against credit to buy out the small parcels of land whose owners were divided between Pennsylvania and Connecticut. With the connivance of a Philadelphia judge, each landowner was led to doubt the legality of his holding, thus assuring his "eagerness" to accept the company's low offer. This seems to have been where Putnam Catlin, a young lawyer known and respected in the region, entered the picture. In 1798, he was engaged to act as Nicholson's agent in the area. (Morris's credit was already overextended, and he would shortly cede his interest in the Asylum Company to his partner; three years later he was in debtor's prison.)

It's impossible to know whether Putnam Catlin was complicit in implementing this strategy of intimidation—or merely credulous. Either way, his dreams of instant wealth made him a mark for salesmen of El Dorado. His son George would prove just as vulnerable to a glib pitchman.

Writing to Nicholson on July 10, 1798, Putnam alluded to competing offers from other "interested parties . . . saying they wanted counsel on the spot to keep a look out and proposed to pay me a large fee." Not only did Putnam decline, he wanted his principals to know that his loyalty went even further; he had tried to scare off the rival investors by telling them that their title to the land would be contested. Despite his efforts the sale went through—uncontested—before all parties to it were ruined.

Whether or not Putnam Catlin was deemed to have earned his fees, by the turn of the new century, the Asylum Company's bubble had burst, with both its high-flying masterminds in disgrace. In 1800

Nicholson joined Morris in prison. He died that same year, an apparent suicide, leaving a widow, eight children, and $4 million in debts.

It seems unlikely that Putnam Catlin's reputation could have remained untainted by his role as agent of the Asylum Company. Evidence was surely not lacking that pointed to his collusion with his employers in their shady practices, especially as these involved exploiting his own neighbors. Within a few years Catlin had closed his law office and sold his property on what is now South Main Street in Wilkes-Barre. Citing health problems, he moved with his family to Broome County, near Windsor, New York, taking title in 1804 to a farm with a large house and two hundred acres of land.

BEFORE ITS DESTRUCTION during the Revolution, Windsor had been one of the four principal Oneida communities on the continent. Its location, at the confluence of the Susquehanna and Delaware Rivers, placed the village at the crossroads "where Indians from the south and west met White traders from Albany and Schenectady," but throughout the previous century, it also sheltered refugees from other tribes of the Iroquois Confederacy—Delaware, Mohican, Nanticoke, and Tuscarora.

By the time Putnam Catlin and his growing family settled there, the area's only reminder of the once-powerful presence of Native Americans was the cleared land they wrested from the forested wilderness, and what still lay just beneath the soil these first farmers had cultivated. There eight-year-old George was first granted the freedom to roam unsupervised, and a hole dug with a child-size shovel might reveal treasures for his own early collection of Indian relics: "The plows in my father's field were daily turning up Indian skulls or Indian beads or Indian flint arrowheads," the artist recalled. A few years later he made his his most thrilling find—a tomahawk fashioned from a length of rusted iron pipe. Its blade, sharpened, polished, and pressed into a contest of skill, glanced off a tree trunk and sank into the boy's cheekbone. The wound took six months to heal, leaving a lifelong scar.

Within the year the weapon's imprint joined a deeper experience of the Indian as exile and victim. An Oneida, one of thousands who had been driven from their ancestral settlement on these same farmlands to the vicinity of Lake Cayuga, 150 miles away, had returned on foot to hunt deer in the woods near his old home. Early one morning nine-year-old George came upon the man, his first flesh-and-blood encounter with those who existed in his mind as "phantoms." Seated on the fallen trunk of a large tree, on a piece of the Catlin property nearest the river, the visitor, whose name the boy anglicized as "On-o-gong-way" was first seen "wiping his huge knife upon the moss and laying it by his side, and drawing from his pouch his flint and steel, and spunk [a fungus used for tinder], with which he lit his pipe, and from which it seemed, in a few moments, as if he was sending up thanks to the Great Spirit, in the blue clouds of smoke that were curling around him." Three decades later Catlin evoked the flashing emotions—fear, excitement, and a kind of recognition—summoned by all the stories he had heard of the "savage race," now fused into the most "exciting moments" he would ever know: "For here was before me, for the first time in my life, the living figure of a *Red Indian!*"

With these two images—of the knife wiped clean of blood, and the freshly lit pipe of thankfulness and peace—Catlin the painter and writer enshrines conflicting perceptions of the Indian. When the boy rushed home to announce his discovery, his father returned with him to greet their "guest." In yet another symmetrical pairing, the first confrontation of savage trespasser and frightened child dissolves into a social encounter of sympathetic families:

"We found my Indian warrior seated on a bear-skin spread upon the ground . . . with his wife, and his little daughter of ten years old, with blankets wrapped around them, and their necks covered with beads, reclining by the side of him; and over them all, to screen them from the sun, a blanket, suspended by the corners by four crotches fastened into the ground, and a small fire in front of the group, with a steak of venison cooking for their breakfast."

Making themselves at home once more on their ancestral land, the Indian family found their assumption of welcome confirmed by the new settlers' hospitality; Putnam ushered them back to the farmhouse, where Polly Catlin pressed additional provisions upon the little family who had walked so far. In return the young Indian father treated George like a son: He fitted a new hickory handle to the iron-pipe tomahawk, shafted and feathered his flint arrowheads, and crafted a deerskin quiver to carry his new weapons. To complete the boy's costume On-o-gong-way made him a hickory-lined bonnet fanned with woodpecker feathers. But then farewells were exchanged, and the Indian family set off on the long walk home. A few days later On-o-gong-way's body was found, not ten miles from the Catlin property. He had been killed by two rifle bullets. There was no trace of his wife and daughter. Soon thereafter the adolescent George Catlin graduated from arrows and tomahawks to white man's firearms.

IN 1838, WHEN he was forty-two and famous, George Catlin revisited the farm at Windsor where, a quarter century earlier, "I held alternately the plough, fish pole and my rifle. . . . The rifle was my passion before I was able to raise it at arms length," George remembered. Sneaking his older brothers' guns, he avoided punishment by persuading his parents that skill trumped both size—he was small for his age—and disobedience. Then, with his own rifle, "even when it was rested over a log or poked through a fence," he claimed "to have felled many a noble buck," supplying the household with fresh meat and earning his nickname: "The Hunter."

Food—anything beyond what they could raise themselves—was welcome to the land-poor family. Farming was to have made Putnam

Catlin's still-growing household self-sufficient, but it seems to have done little else to improve his fortunes. He sold the Windsor property in 1812 for six thousand dollars, moving back across the river to Hop-bottom, Pennsylvania. They left behind their first daughter, Clara, four years older than George and dead at sixteen, and another girl, Juliet, who died in infancy.

Working for the reckless Philadelphia financiers seems to have infected Putnam Catlin with land fever—that most virulent contagion. After the debacle of the Asylum Company, Putnam again served as agent, this time for the Wallace family, who had accumulated fourteen thousand acres of "beech and maple lands." His new employers seem to have paid him in kind, with transfers of property that encouraged Putnam to buy more, until by the early 1820s, he owned about 3,300 acres, including an entire valley together with the hills on both sides—that still today stretches as far as the eye can see—in the Brooklyn-Montrose area, a little over thirty miles north of Scranton. He apparently invested the whole six thousand dollars from the sale of the Windsor property, counting upon selling small parcels to ensure steady income. This misplaced confidence, especially when based upon credit and worthless paper money, was the ruin of speculators large and small in nineteenth-century America. When debts fell due, or were called in, as happened in the Panic of 1819, property sales withered. And just as often ruined investors brought their lenders, including local banks, down with them.

FOLLOWING THE CATLINS' move back to Pennsylvania, money was scarce and every penny counted. For the three boys there were now school fees; Putnam was insistent upon a classical curriculum, but the Wilkes-Barre Academy, the only such program available in the area, was too far for a daily commute; the new pupils would have boarded part-time, at additional expense. A surviving copybook, dated 1812 on the cover, offers evidence of family economies—made the more urgent by the birth of another son, John, that same year. As long as a single page remained blank, the notebook passed from Charles, the oldest, to George, to be saved for Lynde, then aged six.

As an adult George could never reconcile income and expenses. His records are meticulous: In a beautiful copperplate hand, he noted money spent—down to the last penny—along with earnings, but his accounts of financial problems are clouded by confusion—or obfuscation, or both. Still, what sense was a boy supposed to make of such disparate clues to family finances as his father's feudal landholdings that included mountains and a valley with no boundaries in sight, and a copybook that had to serve for three brothers?

Five years later George was still at loose ends. Following two years at the academy, he tried teaching at a one-room schoolhouse conveniently located on the family property in Hopbottom. But pedagogy did not suit him. His brother Charles, six years older, was reading law with a local attorney, and it was Putnam's hope, often repeated, that George would follow, in view of reestablishing together the family practice that their elder had abandoned.

Transparently, George would always be his father's favorite—a role poised between burden and gift. The boy had large ambitions—even if these were, for the present, defined by what he did not want to do. He possessed a quicksilver quality of mind and a literary eloquence that Putnam could feel, with pride, were both a paternal legacy and a promise that whatever work he chose, George would be rewarded with the success that had eluded his parent. Apprenticing with a local lawyer was good enough for Charles. George deserved a superior legal education and a chance to see life beyond their isolated valley.

2

AWAY

George Catlin had just turned twenty-one when he set out for Litchfield, Connecticut, in July 1817. It was a symbolic-coming-of-age year to enact a drama at least as old as the Bible: the son who leaves his childhood home. Unknown to George, he also acted as courier, bearing messages to his destination. For his father, who had never returned to his birthplace since leaving almost forty years earlier, George's journey was a vicarious homecoming, one that Putnam himself would never make. Since he could not reappear among his kinsmen in triumph, his son would act as surrogate. Welcomed among the Litchfield Catlins, enrolled at the most distinguished law school in the nation, George was launched as the future hero of his father's success story.

"You are now placed more favorably for study & the improvement of your mind than you could be at any other place in the United States," Putnam wrote. When George returned home—as his father expected he would—to practice law with his brother Charles, he would be treated with the deference due a lawyer who had been educated by the best in the profession. Writing to his younger brother, George, Charles himself playfully struck the same note, acknowledging the new student as the hope of the family: "Will you be a man—a Lawyer—or a poor lazy devil like me? I shall now read hard to be as good a lawyer when you return as yourself."

Shadowed by his own sense of failure, Putnam Catlin, at fifty-three, felt he had forfeited the respect he now sought for his son. He had abandoned the drudgery of the law, only to see his hopes of a fortune, or even a decent living through land speculation, end in scandal. After that he was elected to a few honorary local offices; judge of common pleas and representative to the state legislature, but his efforts to move up met with failure. Where memories were long, his name was still tarnished by association with the Asylum Company. But there was also the slippery question of Putnam's politics: He was first a Federalist, then a Whig, then a Federalist again—always at the wrong time.

Now, in 1817, the same year that George entered law school in Litchfield, Putnam sold the Hopbottom farm and took a job as cashier (an office with the duties of treasurer) at the Silver Lake Bank in newly-incorporated Montrose—a town with a population of about 200—in an attempt to reestablish himself as a "leading citizen," a phrase much favored by newspapers of the period. Neither banking nor indoor life, however, agreed with him: "My new business keeps me constantly employed here, and will be fatiguing and full of care," he wrote to George in Litchfield. Still, he was pleased to be able to enclose forty dollars, with the promise of more help to come.

As witness to his father's thwarted ambitions, George had no wish to add to his disappointments. Despite his own complete indifference to the study of law, he put a good face on accepting Putnam's plans for his future. Without feigning enthusiasm for the arcane texts that he was now obliged to parse, George conveyed to his prickly parent constant appreciation for the family's sacrifice and concern for his welfare. Putnam's letters to his son are the only ones to survive, but even this partial view reveals a singular father-and-son relationship: Love—not merely obligation or obedience—determined George to redeem his father's failures and to justify his pride. For his part Putnam paid tribute to the difference between affection and duty. "The gratitude you express and the tenderness you reciprocate evince the continuation of that filial regard and reverence that I have always seen in you," he wrote. If his son now paid for the privileges of being the favorite child, he did so with generosity and grace.

George Catlin's trip from the Susquehanna Valley, its still-virgin forests, sleepy towns, and rolling pastureland, to the large town of Litchfield, Connecticut, might not seem much of a journey—not when compared with the road taken by thousands of his young contemporaries, leading from farm to city. But there could be no greater distance between the world that now drew him in—a microcosm of New England wealth, culture, and gentility—and the raw Pennsylvania frontier:

"Wilkes-Barre is stupid," his brother Charles would complain to George in the first days of 1818, "and can never rise while the inhabitants are poor and bankrupt." But the economic slide that would soon hit bottom in the Panic of 1819, still seemed far from Litchfield.

In the preceding months, the new law student could hardly stop gaping at the harmonies of manmade and natural beauty that characterized the town. He had never before seen graceful Federal-period houses, with columned doorways and fanlights facing the broad tree-lined streets or, more discreetly, away from public view at the side of the house, where visitors were welcomed under cool shade trees and the lush gardens of a New England July. Dominating the Green, the tapered steeple of the Second Congregational Church rose, and within its sober interior, the sermons of the brilliant young preacher, Lyman Beecher, called from East Hampton, New York, provided a weekly reminder to his congregation that as a guide to good works, study and learning were as crucial to Christian salvation as faith and prayer. Decades later, when Lyman's son Henry Ward Beecher was delivering his fiery antislavery lectures in England, Catlin, the exile, wrote to him recalling how his father's sermons that had so impressed him as a law student fully prepared him now for his son's stirring words on the abolitionist credo.

LEARNING WAS LITCHFIELD'S industry—and George Catlin now found himself at its very center, the famous law school. A one-room schoolhouse next door to the home of its founder, dean, and senior professor, the school is still known by his name: the Tapping Reeve School of Law. In fact it was a two-man American hybrid; Judge Reeve and his younger associate, James Gould, a former tutor at the Yale Law School, combined the English tutorial system of "reading" law with eminent jurists, together with lectures, quizzes, discussion, along with that simulation of real-life trial and legal argument known as moot court. His whispery voice requiring keen attentiveness, Judge Reeve read from his own opinions in the mornings, leaving students to further reading, note taking, and writing in the afternoons. His early version of the case-study method provided the mix of practice and theory that assured success in the pragmatic former colonies. Judge Reeve's first student, later his brother-in-law, was Aaron Burr, followed by others of less equivocal reputation, such John Calhoun and Horace Mann.

Tapping Reeve's particular distinction rested on its tradition of public service: Before the school closed in 1833, its two legendary teachers of jurisprudence had trained two vice presidents, six cabinet members, thirty-seven federal and state supreme court judges, 129 senators and congressmen, twenty-four governors, and countless anonymous lawyers, teachers, and businessmen.

Founded two years after Putnam Catlin left for Pennsylvania in 1784, the Litchfield Law School, as it was also known, had, in three decades, established the reputation that attracted sons of Georgia planters, New York merchants, and New England divines, persuading their families to pay one hundred dollars for the first year of tuition and sixty for the second. The fourteen- to eighteen-month program included two vacations of four weeks each, one in the spring and one in the fall. To the fees were added boarding arrangements with local families and the disproportionately high costs of long-distance travel, requiring many stopovers and changes of coach; the last expense, especially, made it unlikely that George Catlin returned home for either long holiday.

Putnam Catlin's fortunes, meanwhile, had declined still further; the Silver Lake Bank had begun discounting its paper and was on the way to suspending operations briefly in 1819, the year of the panic, before resuming business—without Putnam as cashier. Seeing where matters were headed, Putnam informed George that he could not afford the law school's second-term fee of sixty dollars, along with the living expenses. "You must therefore get as much legal science as possible while there," he advised George, "and attend to other studies on your return." But with his characteristically mixed messages, Putnam exhorted his son to greater competitive efforts while reminding him of the disadvantages he brought to such an accelerated schedule: "I sometimes fear, that placed as you now are in the midst of finished scholars who have enriched their minds with all the sciences, you will feel below the point of emulation; but that must not be; let emulation be excited," Putnam exhorted, "and let your ambition & your genius bear you forward . . . remembering always, you have but a short time left to prepare for the stage of action."

His father's words were not lost upon George, but they would not be applied to his legal studies; what little enthusiasm he had mustered to please his parent was fast ebbing: During his year studying law, he was seduced by art.

BEFORE GEORGE CATLIN was received in Litchfield's well-appointed drawing rooms, he had probably never seen a painting. It's not known where he boarded, but many of the town's leading families took in students. One possible host was the Seymour family, whose elegant new Federal-style house at 124 South Street had been finished in early 1817, just in time for George's arrival. Maj. Moses Seymour was a boyhood friend of Putnam Catlin and a fellow veteran of the Litchfield unit of the Continental Army. From the owner of a small business in the manufacture and sale of hats, Seymour had become, along with Julius Deming and Oliver Wolcott, one of the three richest merchants in the region.

These grand houses reflected their owners' cosmopolitan wealth; new fortunes made in the China trade were mirrored in porcelain and painted papers, furniture and silver from London or at least Boston, along with portraits of bewigged forebears by Ralph Earle and his followers, who traveled the former colonies "taking" likenesses of the young Republic's eminent citizens.

Litchfield had its own art form: the miniature. Painted most often on ivory, these compact portraits required the most finely detailed features—every curl and whisker delineated—whose pocket size inevitably summons comparisons with the photograph. The sources of the miniature go back to the carved cameo of antiquity, along with portable altars often carried by devout travelers of the late Middle Ages and Renaissance. Its scaled-down genius came to full flower in Elizabethan England, with great artists like Hans Holbein the Younger and Nicholas Hilliard. Anson Dickinson was Litchfield's master of the form. Born in nearby Milton to a builder-carpenter father, Dickinson was apprenticed to a silversmith, but in his spare time perfected on his own the art of the miniature. In the course of an itinerant and successful career in New York, New Haven—and even Montreal—he achieved national prominence, but he returned to Litchfield often to execute well-paid commissions. George would have had many occasions to see Dickinson's vital studies of his hosts and their friends. Along with their exquisite refinement, the master's portraits belie their scale with a Romantic force and expressiveness. Before leaving his native Connecticut, ten years before George Catlin's arrival at the law school, Dickinson had launched his career painting likenesses of the well-off students of the Tapping Reeve school: Among his sitters was Judge Reeve's son, Aaron Burr Reeve, named for his famous—or infamous—uncle.

The halfhearted law student, with his meager allowance, was grateful for invitations from his many prosperous relatives scattered around Litchfield County; among these was one from his cousin Dr. Abel Catlin. Nine years earlier Dr. Catlin had married Mary Wallace, the widow of a successful wool merchant, and adopted her two little daughters. The year before George's arrival, the elder daughter, Mary Wallace Peck, four years younger than George, had graduated from Litchfield's other school of renown, Miss Pierce's Academy, famous for the education of women. Now seventeen, she was a talented artist; eight years later she joined the school faculty as drawing teacher. In the interval Mary likely honed her pedagogic skills and earned money by giving private art lessons. Whether George Catlin was her student or whether, more informally, they drew and painted together, the couple spent enough time with each other in George's year at Litchfield for him to have inscribed in Mary's album a romantic poem, signed with the initials "G.C." Its two verses are laid out over facing pages, each verse illustrated with a naked cupid. In the first image, above stanza 1, the putto struggles with an oversize globe, pierced by love's arrows:

> *Lay down the world! you little arrant thief:*
> *What! Think you thus on worlds we wish to ride?*
> *We know thou'r't sovereign, universal Chief*
> *Of power, to tyrants & to Gods denied.*

Above the second verse the cupid has dropped his burden and surveys the globe, now shattered:

But hold, Love! die not—I did not chide thee,
The world is all thy own, I know not whether
Such evil fate would e'er betide thee:
I own 'twas thee that held the world together—

Whether art or love kept George from leaving, he delayed his departure from Litchfield long enough to miss the session of the Montrose court that was to admit him to the Luzerne County bar in August 1818. In order to employ his younger brother immediately upon his return home, Charles forwarded a postdated certificate of his clerkship in his office in Montrose as bona fides for the Connecticut bar, to which George was admitted in September 1818, while waiting for the next court session in Pennsylvania dealing with "Luzerne and adjoining counties." He had already been working as his brother's clerk through the fall months when he was listed as having been admitted to the practice of law at "Wilkesbarre" in December of that year.

Lacking other alternatives, he had bowed to family expectations. But his year in Litchfield had provided more than preparation for a career in the law, social polish, or romantically engaged affections. For the first time in his life he had observed art everywhere—as part of the furnishings of everyday life—but also art in the making, as both professional possibility and private pleasure. For the first time, too, he had become aware of the impulse to record one's surroundings as a natural reaction to the observed world.

He had never before seen such ingenious variety in expression and materials—created by amateurs who were most often women: embroideries, quilts, fans, or fanciful assemblages of hair, textiles, dried flowers, or shells, combined with painted surfaces: objects at once useful and decorative. Few wives and daughters in the backcountry of Pennsylvania had the leisure for such pursuits.

George had often sketched family and friends, but the pride of place given to portraits in Litchfield's houses was a revelation. Signed works confirmed the eminence of leading families: living and dead patriarchs, soberly dressed matrons, energetic sons, and well-married daughters, the latter displaying with subdued pride their rosy-cheeked young. But there were also mourning pictures recalling the dead, most often those taken too soon—the youth destined for great things, the young wife who failed to survive childbirth—and far too many children. Within the decade George Catlin would return to Litchfield from Philadelphia, an academician and full-fledged artist, summoned to record these same likenesses for another generation. Meanwhile possibilities, once undreamed of, opened before him.

3

GEORGE CATLIN, ACADEMICIAN

Back in Montrose, George found himself enfolded in family life just as though he had never left. His younger sisters, Eliza and Mary, as well as James, the brother closest to him in age, had married and were settled in upstate New York. George had the choice of moving back to live with his parents and the younger boys, Lynde, sixteen; Julius, fourteen; John, six; and Francis, three, or boarding with his older brother and now law partner, Charles, whose office was in the front of the small house he shared with his wife Amanda, and baby, Theodore, called "Burr"—his mother's family name. In either household George would feel the constraints of domesticity and the grind of work.

His world was now bounded by the roles of son and brother, and confined by the drudgery of the apprentice lawyer. Lacking experience, he served as "back office" partner or courtroom note taker; session after session Charles Catlin's name appears in court records of Luzerne County, where he represented clients in cases dealing with the inevitable debts or land claims. The Panic of 1819 launched a seven-year depression triggered by a credit collapse. The nation was flooded with worthless paper money; businesses, especially regional banks and their lenders, were devastated, but lawyers had plenty of work—if they could get their fees paid. Apparently Charles did not delegate these bread-and-butter cases to his new partner. In George's only recorded court appearance, he defended and cleared an Irish laborer who insisted he was guilty as charged—with stealing a broadax. His client was said to have been outraged by the acquittal: He was a thief, not a liar. If such was the reward of success, George could look forward to little satisfaction in the practice of law.

By his own account he made "a sort of *Nimrodical* lawyer." An Old Testament Hebrew monarch, Nimrod is a figure associated with rebellion, often depicted as a naked hunter stalking new territories to conquer. In court, however, George's weapons of choice had to be deployed covertly, and he "covered nearly every inch of the lawyers' table (and even encroached upon the judge's bench), with penknife, pen and ink, and pencil sketches of judges, juries, and culprits."

For almost three years he labored at the law, drawing, and possibly painting, whenever he could find or steal the time. It was easy enough to pack paper and pencils along with gun or fishing rod on forays into the woods. With the exception of the odd print, there was no art to be studied in the Wyoming Valley, and no living artists to guide him. His only course was to teach himself, summoning memories of Litchfield's rich spectrum of easel paintings and miniatures, along with his own observations of nature. Besides the motley cast of characters he recorded in court, he drew friends and family at home where, alone with his mirror, he also practiced capturing his own shifting moods and expressions on paper. Physiognomic studies enjoyed a wide currency in the training of artists. A series of fifteen sheets by George Catlin, using his own face as a model, is among the artist's earliest work to survive. Highly finished charcoal and pencil drawings, these pages suggest greater skill in following the lessons of a drawing manual than any gift for individual portraiture.

Still, with little encouragement he managed to acquire a tenacious faith in his own talent. He drew or painted whatever inspired him at the moment: nature, family, fellow lawyers, himself. The results declared these efforts to be an apprenticeship—but how different this apprenticeship felt to him, lost in the joy of work, compared with the mind-numbing labor of the junior law clerk. He also knew that the belief he harbored in his untested talent would not long survive his present circumstances. If he needed proof of a misspent life, he daily witnessed his playful, witty brother sinking into a corrosive alcoholism—stupefied at work, abusive at home. Life was so grim that Charles's spunky wife, risking social ostracism, would soon leave, taking little Burr, his sister Theodosia, and new baby, James, with her; more shocking to their devout community, Amanda Burr Catlin filed for divorce. The family was devastated. The crisis saddened George, but it served to remind him of the freedom enjoyed by a bachelor with no dependents. Now was the moment: He had earned the right to try his chances at a career in art. Ever the dutiful son, he nevertheless discussed the decision with his father. By late 1820 he "very deliberately resolved to convert my law library into paint pot and brushes," and early in the new year, George Catlin set out for Philadelphia, America's new capital of commerce and art.

Disappointed as he was, the elder Catlin made clear his belief that George, his favorite, could make a go of anything—even art. Still, Putnam had his own views about the way to succeed: "I am pleased that you at length resolved to attempt portraits," he wrote to George, newly arrived in Philadelphia on March 26, 1821, "tho' you had convinced me last year that miniatures were as valuable. Most painters of eminence have worked at portraits and history, few have confined themselves to miniatures," to which the concerned father added helpfully: "To convince you that I do sometimes think of you and your art, I here set down the names of the artists in your line that I have looked up, of whose works you will read, they were chiefly of the 15th and 16th centuries," and Putnam followed with a list of Italian masters, with a few Northern European names, all ranked by worldly success—or by the vices preventing same: "Michael Angelo . . . died immensely rich; Rubens . . . died vastly rich; Raphael . . . He was remarkably handsome, died of debauch with women, which he would not discover to his physician." A cautionary tale for a young man exposed to the temptations of life in the big city.

Neither vast riches nor costly vice would have been a problem for the apprentice artist. Even innocent entertainments, like the stylish productions of Shakespeare featured at two of Philadelphia's theaters—the splendidly rebuilt playhouse on Chestnut Street and the more "fashionable" Walnut Street Theatre—were beyond his means.

DECLARED BY FOREIGN visitors to be the most beautiful city in America, Philadelphia was enjoying a building boom; new marble-clad banks and churches rose everywhere, many on the ruins of earlier structures destroyed by frequent local fires. One of Catlin's first walks took him from his modest lodgings at Walnut near 8th Street, to the Pennsylvania Academy of the Fine Arts. Housed in a Roman Revival building on Chestnut Street, the academy was crowned by a small neoclassical rotunda; its architecture was intended to suggest a temple of painting and sculpture. Here, as George knew, the acolyte's talent would be judged and blessings conferred upon—or withheld from—his new career.

He had never before set foot inside an institution devoted to the promotion of art: painting, sculpture, and architecture. Expanding his experience beyond Litchfield's masters of portraiture, miniature or full-size, he now saw for the first time in the academy's exhibition rooms, examples of history painting and mythological subjects, along with casts of antique sculpture, recently accorded a room of their own. Too poor to offer classes and instruction, as did its European and

British counterparts, the academy had recently started to provide an opportunity for young artists to copy from classical models—the basic building block of instruction in the fine arts until well into the twentieth century. Thus, from drawing on his own, George now graduated to learning, in his father's favorite phrase, by "emulation."

In 1821 the academy's fortunes stood at their lowest ebb. Bankruptcies caused by the Panic of 1819 had cut off support from the city's financial and professional establishment. New blood and new money were needed, but there were few Philadelphians in either category ready to make the academy their cause—in part due to resistance to "outsiders" (including artists) on the part of a torpid old guard. In one of those happy ironies, however, the academy's sclerotic state worked to the advantage of young artists knocking at the gate. Where their languishing annual exhibitions were concerned, even the most conservative board members recognized that new works by established masters wouldn't fill a cloakroom. Thus, only months after his arrival in July 1821, George Catlin had four miniatures accepted by the academy for its May exhibition; these included one self-portrait, a portrait of Napoleon, and a copy of *Ariadne* by Joshua Reynolds. To be sure, this wasn't the Royal Academy, England's Olympus of the visual arts, but it was a coup nonetheless.

Just as important, the academy's rooms offered a meeting place where a new arrival could meet informally with other artists—painters, sculptors, and architects—at all stages of their careers. On one of his first visits to the rotunda on Chestnut Street, George Catlin met a talented portraitist of exactly his own age.

Born in Boston in 1796, John Neagle was the son of an Irish immigrant laborer. His father abandoned his mother, and upon her remarriage to a grocer, the family returned to Philadelphia where they had first lived. Finding his stepfather abusive, the teenaged Neagle left home to apprentice himself to a carriage maker. Shortly he was put in charge of decorating the carriage doors with escutcheons and other heraldic motifs, which enjoyed great demand in a mercantile city of predominantly self-made men. Taking advantage of his employer's offer to use the workshop after hours, Neagle began making portraits of friends; his success soon enabled him to raise his price from five to nine dollars a likeness. In 1821 he had just returned to Philadelphia after an absence of three years, during which he had unsuccessfully pursued commissions in Lexington, Kentucky, and New Orleans.

The same year, 1821, that the two young artists met, both exhibited for the first time in the academy's annual exhibition, where Neagle was represented by eleven portraits. They clearly hit it off, as the following year, Catlin and Neagle decided to paint and live together. On October 21, 1822, they signed a lease with Matthew Carey, a publisher, writer, and entrepreneur, to rent a house Carey owned at 116 Chestnut Street for "three hundred dollars, payable quarterly." Then as now, artists were viewed as less than desirable tenants, and their landlord made sure to spell out their responsibility for the condition of his property: "The said Neagle and Catlin hereby pledge themselves to keep the house in good order," the contract noted.

Living and working with Neagle in the small two-story row house with two rooms to a floor, George discovered a contemporary who could not have been more different and still have been a white American of his own age and interests. Neagle himself worried that his "outsider" status—the urban poverty of his early years, Irish immigrant father, abandoned single mother, and devout Roman Catholicism—placed obstacles in the way of his advancement within an art establishment whose leading portraitists moved in the same world as their sitters. In contrast George may have been poor, but as a descendant of early New England settlers, he was never hobbled by feelings of social inferiority. He would observe, with some astonishment, Neagle's campaign of self-reinvention: He first changed the spelling of his name from "Nagle" (whose pronunciation suggested an Irish brogue) to the Anglicized "Neagle"; he became an Episcopalian—the religion of the city's professional and social elite who were not Quakers; in his day books he made careful notes on the rules of whist, and charted his progress in the manly art of pugilism; his budget included expensive lessons at one of the stylish "studios" in town. In 1827 he would court and win Mary Chester Sully, known as "Moggy," the niece and adopted daughter of Thomas Sully, the czar of Philadelphia artists.

Sully's bustling establishment, located in "grace-and-favor" apartments provided by the city in Philosophy Hall [across the square from Independence Hall] could suggest, at various times, a royal levee, a busy studio, a gallery for exhibitions, and, not least, a home for the artist and his large family. Both Catlin and Neagle were frequent visitors. Sully employed a full-time assistant to help fill in copies of English and European masterpieces. Signed by the master, these two-for-the-price-of-one hybrids were hugely popular with collectors, and easy to delegate to an apprentice, allowing the portraitist to keep up with his many new commissions while assuring him a steady income. Given the volume of labor involved, it's likely that some of the copying was delegated to others; Catlin would certainly have been grateful for the money. Whether these visits resulted in work, or merely the opportunity to observe a great portraitist in action, Catlin and Sully maintained lifelong cordial—if intermittent—relations. When the latter was in London, working on his most famous commission, a portrait of the young Queen Victoria, he asked Catlin to find an Indian-made wooden flute for his daughter, along with a detailed drawing of a Sioux cradleboard to use as a model.

FOR THE MOMENT, though, it was Neagle's career that bounded ahead, confirming, perhaps, Putnam Catlin's doubts about the miniature. Despite his father's urging to think bigger, George persisted in working within the smaller format, and for the next three years he continued to be listed in the Philadelphia directory as "Miniature

Painter." Perhaps he feared, not unreasonably, that the traditional bust-length portrait, head close to life-size, would magnify his weaknesses. Neagle's portraits, with their dazzling technique and powerful presence, would inhibit any contemporary of lesser skills and sophistication. While George's miniatures and copies huddled in their shrunken space at the academy annual, Neagle was regularly represented by a mix of finished, probably commissioned portraits, along with informal oil sketches. Among the latter were two arresting likenesses of Indians, one a double portrait of Big Kansas and Sharitarische, chief of the Grand Pawnee, and the other of Petalesbarro, Knife chief of the Pawnee Loup, done when the three men were part of delegation that passed through Philadelphia on its way to Washington. Also in 1821, Neagle completed a formal portrait of the Omaha chief Ongpatonga, or Big Elk, now lost. Painted during the first year that Neagle and Catlin lived together, the three portraits were probably the first that Catlin had seen of Native Americans. Their expressiveness—each man so immediately and unmistakably himself, not merely a dark-skinned figure on which to hang exotic costumes—would remain with George when he came to paint his first Indian portrait, five years later. He would also recall how deeply Neagle identified with his subjects: "I always thought I resembled the Indian in character," he said. There was another, larger lesson to be learned from his friend's revelation that his native subjects were also self-portraits. The artist might dine at the tables of the rich and powerful, but, like the Indian, he remained an outsider.

As it happened, George didn't need his father's reminders of the miniature's limitations; he was already bored by its constraints and aware that at least in Philadelphia, the form had fallen from favor. Still, in 1822, when Neagle's two Indian portraits were exhibited in the academy annual, Catlin was represented by four more miniatures: The subjects were his father's distinguished friend Timothy Pickering, who had served as America's third secretary of state under Presidents

Washington and John Adams; Captain Morgan, a naval officer; an unidentified "lady" and two "gentlemen." The following year both artists exhibited only one work each: Neagle's submission was a portrait (now lost) of the Seneca chief Red Jacket; Catlin was represented by a miniature copy of a mother and child, "after West." (The great Anglo-American history painter and portraitist Benjamin West, who had moved to London and become president of the Royal Academy, needed no further identification to Philadelphia's cultured classes.) At the 1824 meeting of the Pennsylvania Academy of the Fine Arts, both "G. Catlin—miniature painter" and "John Neagle—portrait painter" were elected academicians, along with Sarah and Anna Peale, the two nieces of Philadelphia's other tutelary genius, Charles Willson Peale.

Recognized as a phenomenon in his own time, Peale remains so in ours. With little formal education, his talents and brilliance bridged the "two cultures," of science and humanism: Artist, mechanic, naturalist, inventor, collector, entrepreneur, and not least a prolific progenitor of gifted children, he towered over the arts and sciences as the new Republic's renaissance man. (He may have been the only great American artist who was also famous for making false teeth that fit well and worked.)

In 1786, when Peale first opened the doors of his "cabinet of wonders" in Philadelphia, he was inviting his fellow citizens to visit the first museum in America. A business venture, designed by the artist and later expanded with the help of three of his talented sons—the well-named Rembrandt, Raphaelle, and Rubens—the Peale Museum was conceived as "a world in miniature," the New World's walk-in version of that eighteenth-century illustrated monument to human knowledge, the French *Encyclopédie*. Art, science, and entrepreneurship—there was a brew to set Catlin dreaming.

In 1822, when George was settled in Philadelphia, Charles Willson Peale exhibited his most famous painting, completed that same year. *The Artist in His Museum* is a self-portrait in the form of an invitation.

Drawing back a fringed theatrical curtain to reveal the sweep of a long gallery, Peale points to the triumph of his organizational genius: the reconstructed skeleton of a giant mastodon at his feet, excavated from boggy farmland near Newburgh, New York. Behind him to one side we see the lower portion of the partially assembled prehistoric mammal; on the other side of the gallery, museum visitors (including a young child) marvel at the mounted displays of winged creatures arranged in rows and by species. Peale, the painter, is identified by his palette and brushes on a nearby table. In his elegant frock coat, open hand extended, it's Peale the showman who invites us inside. This image of the dual role that could be played by an artist was one that George Catlin would remember.

BIRDS, BUGS, MAMMALS, minerals, the prehistoric "monster," and a portrait gallery of patriots were reasons enough to draw a curious young artist to the top floor of Independence Hall. But the attraction that would have lured Catlin—more than once—to pay the stiff ticket price of $1.25 was not included in Peale's self-portrait. Over many decades President Thomas Jefferson and Peale had corresponded regularly, and it was through Jefferson that, in 1809, the museum had received an enormous collection of Native American artifacts from the expeditions of Lewis and Clark: "Indian costumes, leggings, tobacco pouches, ornamental belts and a magnificent beaver mantle fringed with 140 ermine skins and studded with 'prismatic coloured shells' that Lewis had worn on the journey." (The image of the explorer clad in a native chieftain's robe had to give rise to fantasies of the rewards that waited in the heart of darkness.) This horde was augmented by later contributions from the U.S. Army–sponsored journeys of Maj. Stephen F. Long. Titian Peale, a naturalist as well as painter, had been the artist accompanying the Long expedition, and he returned in 1821—the same year Catlin arrived in Philadelphia—with more speci-

mens and his own sketches of Indian life. Along with the costumes and
artifacts that Catlin would then have seen for the first time, an earlier
visitor recalled that "Indian and European scalps, &c" were included.
In 1822 Peale launched a public lecture series at the museum. George
filed away the novel experience of hearing a speaker in close proximity to the "real-life" objects he was discussing. Best of all, for young
working people, including artists, in the summer of 1822, the Peale
Museum launched its first-ever evening hours. Copies could be made
and images stored as long as daylight lasted.

The Peale Museum's Indian collection expanded still more when
its owner purchased in 1826 another unidentified collection of Indian
costumes from the Missouri and Mississippi regions, making the
museum's Native American holdings "the most complete ever seen in
Philadelphia." In 1826 as well, Catlin painted his first Indian portrait,
the haunting image of the aging Seneca chief Red Jacket. He had certainly seen Neagle's portrait exhibited in the academy annual three
years before, but with the former long "unlocated" and absent a surviving copy, it's impossible to say whether Catlin's *Red Jacket* reveals
a familiarity with the work by his Chestnut Street fellow tenant and
academician.

IT HAD BEEN two years since George was elected a member of the
Pennsylvania Academy with the right to inscribe "P.A." after his name.
In June 1824 he paid a visit home, possibly his first since leaving three
years before. While there he completed a miniature "done in one hour's
time" of a cousin on his mother's side, John Wadsworth Tyler, seventeen years old. The sitter looks unhappy in his Sunday best; his formal
costume—flowing white cravat, waistcoat and jacket—underlines the
awkwardness of adolescence.

Less than a month later Putnam wrote to George, back in Philadelphia, explaining that his brother Lynde, aged sixteen, had been victim

of an accident that had fatally damaged the boy's bladder. Putnam urged George not to "in any degree, reproach yourself for not coming on Saturday"; he further discouraged him from the "inconvenience" of returning home to mourn with the family on the following Tuesday. "Neither should you or I indulge immoderate grief," his father advised.

Surviving a brother twelve years his junior inflicted its own sorrow: Lynde was the last name to be inscribed on the cover of the copybook passed along from brother to brother, George had to reflect on the irony of his earlier visit home; weeks before the sixteen-year-old's death, when he had done the likeness of a cousin only months younger. He had no portrait of Lynde.

THAT SUMMER IN Philadelphia, however, even mourning had to wait. The entire city was carried away by preparations, two months in the planning, for the festivities to welcome the marquis de Lafayette on his triumphal return tour of America. Certainly no other city drafted artists and craftsmen to anything like the degree in which Philadelphia marshaled its talented citizenry.

When the legendary hero, friend, and comrade-in-arms of George Washington arrived at the outskirts of the city from Trenton, New Jersey, Lafayette and his entourage were met by twenty thousand rank-and-file Philadelphians who marched with them under the first of thirteen triumphal arches. Constructed of wood and papier-maché, the arches themselves were an example of the collaborative efforts of the city's artists—painted to resemble marble by William Strickland, Catlin's fellow academician. A former scene painter, now the city's chief architect, Strickland had returned to his old craft for this occasion. The most imposing of his structures, the thirty-five-foot-high Civic Arch in front of Independence Hall, featured at its summit allegorical wooden figures representing Justice and Wisdom, carved by the sculptor William Rush, and a florid rendering of Philadelphia's coat of arms painted by Thomas Sully.

The Committee on Arrangements had determined that the "Cradle of Liberty" would, literally, outshine all other stops on the general's tour of the new United States. The Peales—Charles Willson, now eighty-three, his son Raphaelle, his brother James, and his niece Sarah, were commissioned to paint a series of giant "transparencies." Lit from behind by candles and covering the second-story windows of Independence Hall, American eagles and other emblems of the new Republic appeared to provide their own illumination for the cheering crowds thronging the square or seated on "bleachers" that, as Count Levasseur, Lafayette's awestruck secretary, noted, rose to the height of the building's eaves. Philadelphia had eclipsed all other cities in its welcome: "Never could it be more truly said that a whole population came out to meet Lafayette; none remained at home but those whom age and feebleness detained," Levasseur wrote.

With the city's reigning talent pressed into service, it seems inevitable that up-and-coming younger artists and fellow academicians of Sully and the Peales, such as John Neagle and George Catlin, would have worked on these elaborate effects, which extended to floats, each with their own decorative themes, banners, and costumed participants. Passing before thousands of cheering spectators, the procession of floats included painters, umbrella makers, coopers, wagoners, the "Redmen of Pennsylvania," the German-American Benevolent Society, the farmers, and the "Ship Carpenters of Southwark." Clerks were represented by a banner heralding the "Young Men of the City," while the mechanics were distinguished by their Revolutionary cockades. Most spectacular of all were the printers, riding a float upon which a real press rolled off copies of an ode dedicated to Lafayette.

Then the gracious guest of honor was off to Baltimore and Washington, D.C., where he would remain for three months, much of that time spent posing for the portrait painters who lined up to record his likeness.

Once Lafayette was gone a collective postparty blues infected the city. Philadelphia was no frivolous place, and such a celebration had been profoundly out of character. Indeed the town's normal sobriety had already begun to weigh on Count Levasseur, diary keeper of the tour, who noted that the "elegance of its houses . . . and the good taste of its public buildings, at first sight present a seductive view; but may eventually become fatiguing from their exceeding regularity." He went on to observe: "Most of the travelers who have visited Philadelphia agree on this point, that the rigid manners and grave character of the Friends, who are very numerous in the city, have produced an unfortunate effect upon general society, by impressing upon it an air of frigidity and monotony which render it insupportable to Europeans."

And to some Americans, as well. In more than three years of living in the City of Brotherly Love, George Catlin, twenty-nine, handsome, hardworking, and sociable, had put down no lasting roots—neither ones of close friendship, romance, or professional success. It was time to move on.

4

A JOURNEYMAN ARTIST

George kept his two floors of the narrow row house on Chestnut Street that he shared with John Neagle, but he was spending less and less time in Philadelphia. Like his fellow artists—including the Peales and Sully—he went wherever the offer of work took him. Unlike these established Philadelphians, their names synonymous with sitters of wealth and prominence, Catlin, the miniature painter, was never summoned to Annapolis mansions or Tidewater plantations to spend profitable weeks painting entire families.

Looking ahead, all George could see was the prospect of a stagnant career in a city with the closed mind of a small town. From his father and brothers he had absorbed the American faith that moving out was moving up. By late 1824 he was finding portrait commissions that took him away from Philadelphia and its limited opportunities. Upstate New York turned out to be particularly fertile ground. Both his married sister and brother, Eliza and Francis (the former with a prosperous husband), lived in and around Utica and Lockport, and both families helped to spread word of their talented relative. George was summoned to Owego to take likenesses of members of the Collier-

Lewis clan, who shared the Catlins' Litchfield roots. Commissions in that family included portraits of two prominent lawyers—father and son—and their wives, along with "several ladies of the village." His sitters' reactions to the finished works were mixed, but favorable word of mouth must have prevailed because Catlin's next stop was Albany and the governor's mansion.

In December 1824, when His Excellency Governor DeWitt Clinton sat to George Catlin for his portrait (a miniature on ivory), Clinton, then fifty-five, had just begun his second term in office. The graceful mansion on the corner of North Pearl and Steuben Streets, where Catlin arrived with easel and paints on a freezing winter morning, was among the grandest George had seen. Indeed, an English visitor had declared it the equal of London's finest residences.

For Clinton, who had served as senator and then mayor of New York City before running successfully for governor of New York, the year had been one of political vindication and personal tragedy: After his enemies had ousted him as chief of the Erie Canal Board several years earlier, the triumphal completion of this great public works project had led to Clinton's reinstatement, along with his reelection to the highest office in the state. But his oldest son, a promising naval officer, had died at sea of yellow fever.

A classically educated scion of upstate landowners, DeWitt Clinton saw himself as heir to the European eighteenth-century Enlightenment. As mayor of New York, a city consecrated to commerce, he proved himself a friend of science and the arts, leading the way in establishing such bastions of high culture as the New York Society Library, the New-York Historical Society, the Philosophical and Literary Society, and in 1808, the Academy of Fine Arts. In planning the new city hall, whose construction began in 1803, Clinton's special interest in portraiture was confirmed by his inclusion of a "Governor's Room." Completed in 1815–16, the portrait gallery still exists, a Valhalla of republican virtues, both military and civil, where New Yorkers can be inspired by likenesses of Washington and Lafayette, along with their worthy peers and successors.

The governor's greatest legacy, the one to which he devoted his energy with monomaniacal passion, was the Erie Canal. It was dubbed "Clinton's Ditch" by its detractors, but in 1824, after seven years and seven million dollars, his dream of constructing a waterway linking the eastern shore of Lake Erie to the upper Hudson River was about to be realized.

Despite its reduced scale, Catlin's miniature conveys the full measure of Clinton, the man and the politician. The fierce and determined intelligence and the somber inward gaze are subverted by an ugliness destined for caricature: The face punctuated by drooping jowls and bulbous chin suggests one reason for the governor's ultimate failure to claim higher office; another was the patrician's cold and, to some, arrogant manner. Still, Clinton seems to have harbored little physical vanity, commissioning at least two more equally unflattering portraits from Catlin. Just as important, he introduced George to another fervent supporter of the canal, one who would prove to be as good a friend to the artist as he was to the politician.

WILLIAM LEETE STONE was one of those nineteenth-century American demons of energy, brains, and ambition fired by entrepreneurial skill, who gravitated to journalism. Like Catlin, Stone was raised in the upper Susquehanna region, but following three years as an apprentice on an upstate New York newspaper, he began his career of buying and selling periodicals of every kind, for every reader, all of which he published, edited, and largely wrote himself. His most influential organ, however, would be the *New York Commercial Advertiser*. With the *Advertiser* as his platform, Stone became a tireless publicist for both Clinton and the canal, and when the time came to commemorate the great occasion of its opening, Stone wrote, edited, and published the official souvenir book of the blowout of all time: *Narrative of the Festivities Observed in Honour of the Completion of the Great Erie Canal.* To balance his fevered prose, Stone chose Catlin to make most of the illustrations—eight sober black-and-white lithographs recording the progress of the waterway's construction—from bucolic harbor views to detailed renderings of first cuts, complete with navvies operating the primitive rock-hauling machinery, and including the official portrait of Governor Clinton, based upon Catlin's likeness of the year before.

At dawn on the day of the celebration—October 4, 1825—the governor left Buffalo Harbor aboard the steamboat *Seneca Chief,* accompanied by a flotilla of smaller craft. Alongshore the cheers of thousands mingled with the firing of cannons, whose reports were timed to cue other big guns in towns downriver, setting off an echo effect that boomed the length of the Hudson. At journey's end in the Narrows of New York Harbor, Clinton poured a flask of water from Lake Erie into the Atlantic, symbolically "wedding" inland waterway and ocean.

As Stone's *Narrative* reported, the cabin of the *Seneca Chief* "superbly fitted up for the occasion, . . . was adorned with two mural paintings," both by Catlin; one appears to have been a conventional view of Buffalo Harbor with Lake Erie, and Buffalo Creek and its junction with the canal. The second Stone described as a "classical emblematic production of the pencil." On the extreme left of the composition was "exhibited a figure of Hercules in a sitting posture, leaning upon his favourite club & resting from the severe labor just completed." The center shows a section of the canal with a lock, and

in the foreground is a full-length portrait of Governor Clinton, in a Roman costume; he is supposed to have just flung open the lock gate, and with the right hand extended (the arm being bare), seems in the act of inviting Neptune, who appears upon the water, to pass through and take possession of the watery

regions which the Canal has attached to his former dominions.
The God of the sea is on the right of the piece and stands erect
in his chariot of shell, which is drawn by sea-horses, holding his
trident, and is in the act of recoiling with his body, as if con-
founded by the fact disclosed at the opening of the lock; Naiades
[sic] all sporting around the sea-horses in the water, who, as well
as the horses themselves seem hesitating, as if half-afraid they
were about to invade forbidden regions, not their own. The artist
is a Mr. Catlin, miniature portrait painter.

We should be grateful for Stone's detailed account of Catlin's allegorical tribute to Clinton and his legacy; as far as we know, the mural,
now lost, was the artist's only work in this genre, and it demands some
effort of the imagination to conjure the image of the forbidding lawmaker, bare arm emerging from his toga, pointing the way to frolick-
ing naiads and splashing sea horses.

As Catlin's friend, patron, and publicist, Stone made sure to give
him full credit in the text of his *Narrative*. But Stone's designation
of the artist as "miniature portrait painter" was already out of date:
Slowly George was moving beyond the miniature and its finicky
single-hair brush. What better vehicle to declare his independence
than a full-scale self-portrait? A work with this title was shown in the
1824 exhibition of the Pennsylvania Academy. Listed as "Portrait of
George Catlin, 1st attempt in oil from life painted by Himself," the
self-portrait was George's first submission as a newly elected academician and it would be his last.

A portrait of Catlin,[*] long believed to be a self-portrait, has recently
been reattributed to John Neagle. The loosely painted three-quarter
head shot, wavy hair blown forward, white cravat knotted with art-
ful carelessness, suggests that the backwoods limner, hovering on

---

[*] Now in the Gilcrease Museum, Tulsa, Oklahoma.

the margins of the Philadelphia art establishment, has disappeared, reborn in Neagle's likeness as the archetypal Romantic artist; George Catlin as Lord Byron—but a Byron starting from the East and heading westward.

For the time being, though, George still had to mine connections closer to home, scratching for commissions, large or small: One such involved a return to Litchfield, his first visit since leaving the law school, where he was now called to paint a mourning picture of a dead infant. The Sanford baby had died while the father was on a trip to Boston, but instead of being buried right away, the body remained at home for three days waiting for the stricken parent to return; during that time Mabel Seymour, a relative of the bereaved Sanfords, had engaged Catlin for a memorial likeness: "I am very glad I did, as it is a great pleasure to the afflicted father," she wrote to a cousin, Delia Seymour, adding: "Was you here, I certainly would have you paint with Mr. Catlin, it would be of great advantage to you—he is taking a likeness of your grandfather & a perfect resemblance."

He was also taking a more businesslike approach to his work. While in Litchfield, Catlin conceived an enterprising scheme: He would make lithographs based upon an earlier portrait he had done of Judge Tapping Reeve, selling each print for $1.00 by subscription and $1.50 from open stock to the jurist's former students and neighbors. He put down nine subscribers immediately, including Lyman Beecher, and all but three from Litchfield. But the plan fizzled—not the last of George's failed efforts to yoke art and commerce.

BY SPRING 1826 Catlin had finally decided to make the move from Philadelphia to New York. On arriving he seems to have written Neagle giving a provisional address, probably a boardinghouse. Six months later Neagle noted in his meticulously kept account book: "Sent to George Catlin a box containing all unsold articles by his request."

Neagle also settled an unpaid bill with a Mr. Murphy in the amount of $8.96 "for Mr. Catlin."

Despite sharing the Philadelphia house for more than three years, and frequenting the same circles, Sully's studio in particular, the two young artists never seem to have moved beyond cordial relations. Professional rivalry may have remained an obstacle to unguarded friendship. George was not among the wedding guests when Neagle married his "Moggy" in her adoptive father Thomas Sully's house on May 28, 1826. Still, the newlyweds spent time with George while on their honeymoon in New York, primarily a business trip for the bridegroom. Neagle had recently contracted with a printer and lithographer named Poole for a series of theatrical portrait busts, including one of the celebrated actor Edmund Kean, who was so popular that he regularly caused riots among his female fans.

Catlin's move appeared to be well timed. New York had recently overtaken Philadelphia as a hub of artistic activity: Commerce was the engine that drove the island port, for which the opening of the Erie Canal proved the dynamo. The city's population swelled to 250,000; propelled by the demand for goods and services, businesses flourished, bringing the arts with them. It was New York's unique role as a marketplace that drew—then as now—the young and the talented. "The distinctive quality of New York City as a cultural center," a recent historian observed, "has not been as the home of writers and artists but rather as the place where their books are published, their plays produced, their paintings sold."

Ironically it was the Philadelphian John Neagle who opened doors for Catlin to New York's vibrant mix of politics, patronage, and art. One of the centers for this interchange was the thriving Broadway shop of another printer and lithographer, Peter Maverick, which churned out bookplates, maps, banknotes, and book and magazine illustrations. Inheriting the thriving business from his father, the younger Maverick developed closer ties with artists, encouraging them to think commercially, or in terms of "multiples" as a later century would call them—translating the unique work of art, such as Neagle's portraits of Kean and Edwin Booth, into series of lithographs that would hang in thousands of American parlors. The printer had adopted Neagle as a protégé, taking charge of the couple during their stay in New York; when the newlyweds returned to Philadelphia, his paternalistic help seems to have been extended to Catlin. (He already knew George's work, as his shop had done the lithographs for Stone's Erie Canal souvenir album.) Earlier still, Maverick had formed a partnership with Asher B. Durand, once a printmaker himself but now enjoying greater success as a painter. A charter member of the Hudson River School, a loose association of landscape artists, Durand revealed, in canvases of heroic scale, a sublime wilderness—not across the far Missouri, but in upstate New York, as yet untainted by human imprint. When he wasn't fixing the majesty of Catskill waterfalls and virgin Adirondack forests, Durand played an influential role in the city's art establishment. His sponsorship alone ensured that Catlin, just before leaving Philadelphia in 1826, was elected a member of New York's National Academy of Design, a group that had recently broken away from the city's National Academy, over the upstarts' radical insistence upon exhibiting only living artists. True to form, the rebels themselves were a contentious crowd, and Catlin's first nomination was stalled in dispute. Even his subsequent election took place over the objections of some members: The minutes state that George Catlin was elected by the unanimous vote of those present, as opposed to the required tally of all members. The second favorable outcome suggests a certain arm twisting from above. But things went badly from the start, and all too soon the doubts of some of his fellow academicians would be confirmed.

New York in 1826 was a small town, confined to present-day lower Manhattan. Along with every kind of commercial activity, the rich and the poor—in sight and smell of wandering pigs and piles of garbage—

lived, worked, rooted, prospered, and festered in close proximity. By the time Catlin moved to New York, the better classes were beginning the exodus uptown. Washington Square, a former military parade ground, had become the fashionable new address, "with many handsome private dwellings." The rich left behind respectable middle-class neighborhoods to the west of Broadway, the main north–south artery, including Cortlandt Street, where Catlin settled, at number 3. To the east of Broadway sprawled the insalubrious wards, including the infamous Five Points, populated by newly arrived immigrants, eighteen thousand of whom had swelled the area in the years between 1800 and 1825 alone. They were blamed for epidemics of typhoid and cholera, along with the permanent threat of crime in every form posed by the "poor and dangerous classes."

Catlin arrived to find relatives who were well-established citizens: One, Lynde Catlin, bearing the same first name as George's late brother, had been a founding member of the distinguished but short-lived Friendly Club, which, despite its democratic name, was a social organization for cultured New Yorkers of advanced amateur interests—natural sciences and classics, or others who had distinguished themselves in the learned professions as clergymen or academics. Then there were his rich Litchfield cousins, merchants who often traveled from Connecticut to New York to oversee the flourishing family business of importing ladies' finery, sold at their grand emporium on Canal Street.

In fact George felt little need to make new friends or seek the companionship of elderly relations. As soon as he moved to New York, he was joined by his younger brother Julius, who had just resigned his officer's commission in the First Pennsylvania regiment of the U.S. Army. Eight years George's junior, Julius had earlier planned to follow his older brother in his career as a painter of miniatures. Their father had other ideas, however: One artist in the family was enough; once again, Putnam pulled strings—successfully this time—securing through Timothy Pickering a place for his son at West Point.

With his fey humor and a child's unmediated sense of the world, Julius at twenty-three, far more than his older brother, seemed to be the artist personified. Moving in a chaos of lost possessions, he could not have been expected to last three weeks at the military academy. But he surprised everyone. Sturdy, resilient, and adept at assuming protective coloration, Julius endured the plebe's harsh discipline, and after winning his commission, survived the rigors of his first posting to a remote frontier fort, then called Cantonment Gibson, in the Arkansas Territory, near present-day Tulsa, Oklahoma. Established in 1824 to discourage raids by Osage warriors against other tribes, the primitive outpost offered Julius scope for his other passion; when he wasn't painting and drawing in his scarce leisure time, he collected mineral and plant specimens. Soon, though, his distaste for army life prevailed; Julius resigned his commission but not his love of Indian country. For the year or so between 1826 and 1827 that the brothers lived together in New York, they pondered how they could earn and save enough to explore the western territories together. On short strolls from their rooms to the end of Cortlandt Street and the steamboat landing on the Hudson, or on longer walks all across Manhattan by way of the newly widened Fulton Street to the East River, where they peered up at the tangle of masts and lines soaring above the piers, Julius evoked unmapped lands and their native inhabitants that George, unlike his brother, had never seen—more distant and foreign than any of the countries where these ships would sail.

In the following year, 1827, Julius left Manhattan for the promise of work in Morristown and Moorestown, New Jersey, where his career indeed seemed to flourish. He wrote to George to send more sheets of ivory for his growing number of commissions, as "the unusual proportion of pretty girls (sweet creatures) are more than ordinarily fond of miniatures (their own)."

Even alone, George did not reach out for male companionship, and if he sought the company of women, none were mentioned in letters home. Relations with Peter Maverick and Asher B. Durand were friendly but professional; he may have seen something of Rembrandt Peale, recently removed from Philadelphia to New York, where he was charged with opening a branch of the family museum, advertising at the same time for portrait work.

At this point, however, George could afford to play the conquering outsider. In late 1826 or early in the following year, the Common Council of New York (now the City Council) commissioned Catlin to paint a full-length portrait of Governor DeWitt Clinton. In the year since the opening of the Erie Canal, the economic bounties of that waterway were just making themselves felt, and Clinton himself was bathed in glory. New York Harbor had become the destination of inland shipping, and the port through which the Republic's riches— raw and manufactured, in volumes hitherto unimaginable—were sold throughout the world; hence the timing of the council's request to the governor to sit for his official portrait "at full length" to be placed "in the Gallery of Portraits in the City Hall." A fee of six hundred dollars was allocated, with the choice of portraitist left to the governor; the only restriction was that that the artist be American.

This was Catlin's third portrait of Clinton; once more he traveled to Albany, and on May 21, 1827, the council "read and accepted" an invitation from the artist to visit the "nearly completed" portrait of Governor Clinton "at the artist's House, No. 3 Cortlandt Street." Following the viewing, a warrant was issued by the council releasing two hundred dollars to the artist. A few weeks later Catlin engaged a notary, M. D. Seixas, as his representative to secure another (probably unscheduled) payment from the council, until on June 18 he was paid the balance for the finished work.

With this official version Catlin attempted—for the first and probably the last time—a neoclassical portrait in the Grand Manner. Garbed as a Roman senator, Clinton holds the edge of a flowing garment (somewhere between a toga and a dressing gown). The lumpy features so faithfully rendered in earlier likenesses have been smoothed away: Gone are the wattles and potato-shaped chin. Like a conjuror, the governor draws back a curtain to reveal the waterway he had brought into being. Catlin was certainly thinking of Charles Willson Peale's famous self-portrait as he lifts the curtain to reveal his museum, along with his own earlier likeness of the governor as ruler of the seas. But where naiads and sea horses once frolicked (at least in Catlin's lost mural), a cargo ship rides low at anchor.

Catlin himself was riding high on Clinton's favor, and it showed; the artist was starting to assume the imperial style of his patron. When William Stone wrote to the painter proposing another plum assignment, George's reply reads almost as a parody of self-importance:

> The "Commission" named . . . is flattering to me, and though I refuse all orders, I will attend to it in the best manner that I can, though it may be somewhat inconvenient for me to do so. I have had within the last years more orders than I could have painted, but have refused all of them, as I have more of my own orders than I can attend to for some time to come.

His claim, moreover, that he had more work than he could handle seems doubtful: Only weeks before his reply to Stone's offer on January 7, 1827, Catlin tried to leverage the prestige of his official likeness of Clinton, petitioning the council to engage him to make a copy of Sully's full-length portrait of Thomas Jefferson, painted at Monticello in 1823, and now hanging at West Point. When a second petition on his part elicited no interest, Catlin offered, in March 1828, to make the copy at his own expense and to sell it to the council for three hundred dollars. George had already painted paired watercolor views of the West Point parade ground; he may already have completed the Jefferson copy when he solicited the commission from the council. At the same time he offered to sell his version of the Sully, he asked leave of the council to "alter or retouch" the Clinton portrait already hanging in City Hall, in view of exhibiting it at the National Academy of Design. The council agreed, but even with the offending features smoothed out, the governor's image inspired one critic, writing under the name "Demon," to dismiss Catlin's portraits generally as "leaden caricatures"; while a fellow academician, William B. Dunlap, a theatrical producer, playwright, painter, art critic, and a founding member of the academy's board, attacked his new associate personally and professionally. Every word under the entry for "George Catlin, Esq." in Dunlap's famous *History of the Rise and Progress of the Arts of Design in the United States*, exhales a supperating envy, starting with the title "Esq." affixed to the artist's name. Noting that Catlin was "educated for the bar," he sneered: "What induced him to prefer painting I do not know." The giveaway is provided by Dunlap himself. The two had met in Albany, where, according to the painter-turned-critic, his rival had "gained the good will of De Witt [*sic*] Clinton, and was making an attempt in small oil painting of the governor. This was certainly very poor, but it led to greater things," namely, Clinton's choice of Catlin for his full-length portrait. "His motive was undoubtedly praiseworthy," Dunlap concedes of the governor,

> as it must have been to aid the young artist, but he was wrong: The City of New York was entitled to a portrait from a man of established reputation, if not from the best painter in the State, and Catlin was utterly incompetent. He has the distinguished notoriety of having produced the worst full-length which the city of New York possesses.

The envious are not always wrong. Seen alongside the grand visionary canvases of Durand and Thomas Cole, the polished productions of Henry Inman, Samuel F. B. Morse, and the recently arrived Philadelphian Rembrandt Peale, George's weaknesses as a self-taught artist appeared glaring: He would always suffer from a shaky grasp of anatomy and perspective, and often from a hit-or-miss application of the chemistry of color required to produce effects of light and shade, and of skin tone. He had found his metier, along with a powerful patron, but he had yet to invent the technique and, more crucially, find the subject that would distinguish him from his academically trained contemporaries. In this bazaar of a city, clamorous with rival claims for attention, Catlin himself realized that one had to make a "big noise" to get noticed.

He found new quarters a few blocks west at 61 Cortlandt Street, where he was closer to the river, but the move also suggests larger space with better light. He could feel justified in anticipating more work flowing from Albany to New York, like the current that had brought the *Seneca Chief* downriver on the great celebration day. Then, suddenly, all hopes of preferment from political connections evaporated: On February 11, 1828, DeWitt Clinton, aged fifty-eight and in declining health for some years, died of a heart attack after dinner, while dictating to his son in his study.

Clinton's patronage had conferred upon the outsider Catlin prestige, connections, and not least income: The principal share of his earnings came from the governor's sittings in Albany, and indirectly from work elsewhere attributable to Clinton's influence. Following his illustrations for Stone's Erie Canal *Narrative*, Catlin did an extraordinary series of paintings depicting Niagara Falls from different perspectives. A strange blend of documentary and fantasy, the six canvases include an aerial view that could have been painted from a helicopter, a double image of both the Canadian and American falls, a composition that seems to anticipate the famed Hokusai print *The Great Wave*, as well as George's own later visionary landscapes of cliffs above the Missouri River.*

---

* Catlin seemed to have recognized the originality of the Niagara views, as he took the unusual step of patenting them.

Beyond his role as official portraitist, Catlin had come to rely upon a bracing paternalism in his relations with the governor. A powerful authority figure, himself a father of ten children, Clinton offered George—still floundering at age thirty-two—affirmation of a different order than Putnam Catlin's gassy letters of fatherly advice, his homilies on success from *McGuffey's Reader*, all accompanied by copious examples of his own failure. With Clinton's death George had lost his only reliable source of support, one all the more welcome for being distant, formal, and undemanding. And now his adoring acolyte of a brother had left him to strike out on his own.

Loss and the prospect of starting over, of playing courtier for commissions, had the effect of bringing out George's touchier side: He already felt a certain lack of regard in the way his work was treated by fellow academicians. In May 1828 he showed twelve paintings in the academy's third annual exhibition, held in the upper story of the Arcade Baths in Chambers Street. "For the first time," the academy's historian notes, "a difficulty arose in consequence of the arrangement of the works on exhibition. Mr. Catlin, N.A., was dissatisfied with the places awarded to his productions, and serious and unpleasant words passed." Following this stormy meeting, Catlin wrote requesting the immediate return of his pictures and, at the same time resigning his membership in the academy. Reporting to the board, the president, Samuel F. B. Morse, painter, inventor, and a grandee of the New York cultural establishment, noted that the pictures had been returned, and that on the question of Mr. Catlin's resignation, it was "resolved unanimously that the same be accepted."

WITH SO MANY bridges burned, George finally made a friend and one who would soon become a brother. Four years George's junior, Dudley Gregory probably met Catlin through the overlapping circles of those involved with the Erie Canal; the younger man had begun his career with the canal board; then, going off on his own, he soon prospered as a sharp businessman, investor, and go-getter in the best New York tradition. Gregory would have been impressed with Catlin's status as one of DeWitt Clinton's official portraitists—indeed, if the two young men had not already met in the capital on one of Catlin's earlier visits to the governor's mansion. The Gregorys were Albany neighbors of Clinton, and as one of the capital's richer families, they would have been on the governor's guest list for the large receptions he frequently held for friends and supporters.

Among the younger set, George found himself drawn to Dudley Gregory's sister, Clara. With her glossy dark ringlets, large light eyes, and fine cameo features, Clara, at eighteen, was the image of a Romantic heroine, one worthy of her baptismal name—Clarissa, the perilously virtuous heroine of Samuel Richardson's eponymous novel; indeed she was soon painted as such by her ardent suitor, George Catlin. When they met, Clara was only two years older than George's sister of the same name, dead at sixteen. Whatever doubts the elder Gregory might have entertained about his daughter marrying an artist were assuaged by Governor Clinton's patronage. More reassuring still was the friendship between the portraitist and his son Dudley, a hard-headed young man with his eye on the main chance, who promised to outdo his father by making millions. Clara was besotted by her glamorous painter, but she also yearned for a home of her own. Her mother had died when she was six; her first stepmother was dead four years later, and she was reportedly on poor terms with her father's third wife, who had three young daughters and no time for a lonely adolescent. So, skipping a lengthy engagement, Clara Bartlett Gregory, nineteen, and George Catlin, thirty-two, were married at Saint Peter's Episcopal Church in Albany on May 11, 1828.

The date seems to have been set hastily, with too little time for Putnam and Polly Catlin to make the arduous journey from Hopbottom to Albany. In any case, news of their son's marriage reached the older

Catlins when they had returned from a trip to Niagara Falls and a reunion with their other children in Lockport. Polly Catlin suffered an "unavoidable dread of steamboats," and her usual anxiety had turned to panic at the prospect of travel on swollen spring waterways; for this reason "she could not summon courage enough to go round by Albany & New York," Putnam wrote to George.

For once Putnam's fatherly advice took a romantic turn: He seems to be urging his son—an elderly bridegroom by the standards of the day—to let himself go, to be less cautious and more expressive of his feelings: "Take good care of Clara and love her as much as you please. It is written 'Thou shalt not worship any graven image,' but it is nowhere written thou shalt not idolize your wife." And he added a delicate reminder: To idolize his beautiful young bride was not to place her on a pedestal of purity beyond physical affection: Her sisters-in-law were so enamored of the new member of the family that the absent Mary "almost envies Eliza the privilege she has of embracing Clara." Did Putnam fear that his son needed hints on both the joys and the duties of conjugal love? If so, he hastened to evoke scenes of domestic bliss in which Clara would play both mother and muse:

> I will anticipate seeing you very happy as a husband, with a wife looking over your shoulder, encouraging and admiring the arts, rather than leading you by the heart-strings into the fashionable mazes of luxury and dissipation. You will now be more happy and composed, what is the world now to you? In your room, and in your little parlour by your own fireside you will find contentment and solace, nowhere else.

He could not have been more wrong.

5

WANDERERS

With his marriage the pace of Catlin's travels—with and without Clara—quickened. George was keenly aware that he was expected to support a wife and, in the near future, a family, and most of his moves in the next two years were linked to commissions—actual or hoped-for. But other trips involved family visits—first to introduce Clara to his parents in Hopbottom, to her sisters-in-law and their families in upstate New York, and a return visit to the Gregorys in Albany.

He had kept the rooms in Cortlandt Street, but his outburst at the academy meeting four days before his wedding on May 11, 1828, followed by his resignation from that body, fairly ended Catlin's connection to the New York art establishment. William Stone, through his *Commercial Advertiser*, remained the artist's loyal supporter, but with the end of the Clinton era, the publisher's pipeline to official patronage had run dry. A scattering of work came George's way, once again from West Point, where two officers each commissioned a portrait, a single sitter and a group, earning George forty and sixty dollars respectively. Although New York City's Common Council had turned down his repeated offers to copy Sully's portrait of Thomas Jefferson, hanging at the academy, the Franklin Institute of Rochester, New York, devoted to the encouragement of science, proved eager to own a copy of Catlin by Catlin: The institute, funded by a newly hatched Board of Manufacturers, commissioned the artist to make another version of his portrait of DeWitt Clinton, father of the Erie Canal, which had turned the village of Rochester into a boomtown. The city's bubble would burst the following year, in the recession of 1829, so Catlin's commission had come in the nick of time.

Working from the original portrait, recently returned by the National Academy of Design to the Governor's Room in City Hall, George asked Julius to bring the completed copy to Rochester. The errand also gave the brothers an excuse for a welcome reunion, as Julius had to come from New Jersey, a two-day trip, to collect the painting in Cortlandt Street before heading upstate. After discharging his errand in Rochester, Julius set off to sketch the lower falls of the Genesee River, a few miles south. Once on the banks, he was tempted by the heat of early September to undress and plunge into the water for a view from below of both the cataract and the wooded shore opposite. A fisherman reported hearing cries of "Help me, for God's Sake!" Whether the witness ever tried—or tried but failed—to rescue the slightly built swimmer was never determined. Julius's body washed up the following day. At the inquest the question of foul play arose; the drowned man was recalled as wearing an elaborate "watch establishment" (as the local obituary described the timepiece), a reference to the attached fob and possibly ornamental seal of what was certainly a family heirloom. The prized possession was nowhere to be found among the clothes and sketching materials left on the bank. It was even hinted in the lengthy newspaper account that the unnamed witness of the drowning man's cries for help may have been his assailant. Julius was buried in Rochester before the family had even learned of his death. George was the first to hear the news, and it fell to him to notify their parents.

Julius's death was a blow from which George never recovered. Clever, dreamy Julius, with his playful feline ironies, had been the ideal Other and a foil to George's bouts of earnestness. Disciple and confidant, his brother had foreclosed the need for friendships, leaving him the more bereft. George never would find in women that refuge from male rivalry sought by many of his contemporaries, for whom female attachments—romantic, sexual, platonic, but especially domestic—offered a "haven in a heartless world." If anything, the surviving brother's grief seems to have widened the distance between the newlyweds: His provincial bride's innocence and piety invited painful reminders of the ways that failures in understanding reinforce solitude. From now on Catlin would treat Clara more like a precious object than a life companion. With economy as his excuse, she would be shipped home to Albany or dispatched on long visits to George's sisters, then "redeemed" for short periods of time, before being deposited at her father's house once again. As the Gregorys were largely supporting the newlyweds wherever they happened to be, it seems an unnecessary humiliation for Clara to have been regularly returned to her family.

What time the couple did spend together was marked by continued professional discouragement for George and ill health for both of them. In late 1828 or early in the New Year, they moved to Washington, D.C., in pursuit of portrait commissions, but also to escape the harsh winters of New York, both city and upstate.

In "Washington City" one could live cheaply and eat well almost everywhere. The average cost of a boardinghouse was four dollars a week per person for room and full board. Large numbers of slaves, moreover, made the most modest lodgings feel luxurious to northerners, especially to George. Clara would have grown up with servants, but Polly Catlin had only a hired girl to help with chores and children.

Neither George's health nor his prospects of work improved: His ailments are never specified, but fears voiced by his mother that he had inherited the "weak lungs" of the family point to upper respiratory problems. Washington's climate was mild compared with winters in upstate New York and Pennsylvania, but the capital was still rebuilding fourteen years after being torched by the departing British army, and the town was deemed more unhealthful than before the fire of 1814. "Every new building increased the menace of the Tiber Creek," a contemporary guidebook warned. A sluggish tributary of the Potomac, two-thirds of a street wide, the creek was widely held to be the source of the local "plague of Miasma"—an all-purpose set of symptoms that seems to have covered everything from consumption to cholera.

Bad weather caused so much sickness that "on a single day, toward the end of 1829, every member of the cabinet save one was confined to his bed." There were clouds of mosquitoes everywhere, breeding unchecked in the low-lying marshes; George's debility could certainly have been malarial. Medicine had not yet identified the insects as carriers of disease; it is still less likely that George's physical sufferings were seen as related to his emotional devastation.

Adding to Catlin's sense of failure, he had calculated that a civilian army of job seekers would need their own camp followers: portraitists ready to transform smalltown politicians into statesmen. He had also harbored grander hopes of winning a federal commission to decorate one of the gleaming new temples of government rising from the swamps. Many artists aspired to the legendary success of John Trumbull. In 1817 a representative democracy that had long seemed to reject the European model of monarchs as patrons of the arts had commissioned Trumbull to paint four scenes illuminating events from the War for Independence, to be installed in the rotunda of the new Capitol. Only the artist's fee—a staggering $32,000—exceeded the grandiosity of the project, and inevitably produced the spiteful reviews that envy alone inspires. As Catlin and others would learn to their disappointment, the Trumbull coup was a one-off, and the handful of other, lesser federal commissions went to the same favored few: Morse and West, who, unlike Catlin, moreover, were established masters of history painting as well as of portraiture. As to the supply and demand for portraits, George wrote dejectedly to his father, there were many other artists "ahead" of him.

In the forefront of the capital's leading artists was Charles Bird King. Sitting or former presidents, vice presidents, cabinet secretaries, and distinguished foreign visitors all made their way to the studio of Washington's acknowledged master of the portrait, whose subjects would include John Quincy Adams, John Calhoun, Henry Clay, James Monroe, and Daniel Webster. The artist's splendid establishment was conveniently located only three blocks east of the White House, and Catlin lost no time in calling upon King shortly after he arrived in Washington.

WHEN CATLIN PAID his visit, King was forty-four, a little more than ten years his senior and at the height of his career. Although George had been a frequent visitor to Sully's well-appointed house, studio, and exhibition rooms in Philadelphia, King's grander style and surroundings pointed to the artist's success in his adopted city, and also to his inherited wealth; his father, descended from generations of sea captains, decided to migrate west from Rhode Island with his family, but was tomahawked and shot in the Ohio Territory, probably by local Pawnee. A strange destiny led his only son, then four years old, to become the first officially sponsored American painter of Indians.

Thanks to his inheritance, King, aged fifteen, had been sent to New York to study painting, before spending six years honing his talents in London as apprentice to Benjamin West, the American expatriate and president of the Royal Academy. It was in Washington, where he finally ended up settling, that his social and professional lives seamlessly merged.

Of special interest to Catlin would have been King's singular coup of government patronage. Eight years earlier in 1821, when a delegation of Plains Indian chiefs from the upper Missouri area arrived in Washington, the newly appointed superintendent of Indian trade, Thomas McKenney, chose King to help realize his long-cherished vision: establishing an Indian museum, to consist of objects from McKenney's own collection of Native American material culture, along with portraits of tribal chiefs and notables in their delegations. In the years following, King's steady stream of representative Indian sitters also revealed the government's purpose in inviting the delegations to Washington. They would meet the president, receive and exchange gifts, and keep translators busy as both hosts and guests delivered speeches pledging goodwill, loyalty, friendship, an end to violence, protection of rights, and other promises soon to be broken. A political motive behind these ceremonial invitations was to woo those tribes west of the Mississippi from dealings with British fur traders, but the visits also served to encourage a trust in Washington that would make it easier for historic treaties and land grants to be overridden, dishonored, or sold for token payments in thousands of dubious "cessation agreements." King's portraits, and later Catlin's, often portrayed tribal leaders whose ornaments seem chosen to set off the large silver medal bestowed by the Great White Father or his emissaries on one of these memorable visits.

McKenney's Indian museum, for which King would paint more than 143 portraits, also revealed this prescient bureaucrat's sense that Native Americans were doomed to extinction: "Their destiny as a race, is sealed. They will soon be lost to our sight and forever," he wrote. As a field agent he had witnessed the depredations of whiskey and disease, along with the unstoppable juggernaut of America's westward expansion, whose appointed instruments were white settlers, most of them operating illegally, supported by the local militia and the states' or territories' representatives in Washington.

Along with certainty about the inevitable fate of all native peoples, both King and McKenney as Washington insiders would have heard early rumors of plans for the impending removal of eastern tribes from their ancestral lands. Although President Andrew Jackson is officially credited with the passage of the Indian Removal Act, which he signed into law in 1830, his predecessor, John Quincy Adams, laid the groundwork for the legislation. The new law mandated the forced march of hundreds of thousands of men and women, including the very old and young, natives of eastern tribes to designated government reservations in territories west of the Mississippi—on lands occupied for centuries by other indigenous peoples.

There was no doubt about the memorializing impulse behind King's portraits, but by the time Catlin arrived in Washington, he could study King's images of visiting Indians only at the artist's own gallery. Seven years earlier Superintendent McKenney, who favored assimilating Native Americans through education and conversion to Christianity, had been fired for insisting that the government continue to protect the tribes' commercial interests through a system of regulated trading centers. Instead the administration of John Quincy Adams yielded to pressure from John Jacob Astor to privatize the fur trade, the main source of Indian revenue, allowing Astor to treat directly for control of the "peltries," raw skins that were made into the buffalo robes and beaver hats worn throughout the world, and the basis of his fortune. Following McKenney's dismissal, his Indian Museum, installed in the gallery of the Department of War, was banished to political limbo. For some time, however, a private group, calling itself grandly (if misleadingly) the National Institute, had cast a covetous eye on both the gallery and its permanent exhibition, which consisted of McKenney's collection of Native American artifacts and King's commissioned Indian portraits.

Founded in 1818 by an association of well-off Washington "professional gentlemen," the institute was first called the Columbian Institution for the Promotion of Art and Science. The change of name reflected the founders' hope of being the beneficiary of Englishman

James Smithson's bequest of $500,000 to their nation's capital of his projected Smithsonian Institution. They soon learned that Smithson had his own plans, but two years later, Congress made the National Institute the official curator of "all collections in the arts and sciences in the custody of the federal government," granting space for its holdings in the brand new Patent Office building at Eighth and G Streets. McKenney's old Indian Museum was readily "deaccessioned" by the War Department and moved into its new home. The institute's triumph was short-lived: In time-honored federal practice, no funds had been allocated for even minimal curatorial maintenance of the collection; Congress instead chose to bestow its official blessing and additional monies on Smithson's instititution, to which the National Institute's Indian holdings were transferred following its official demise in 1858. There, in 1865, a fire at the Smithsonian finished off what decades of neglect had begun, sparing only a few original works by King from the ashes of Washington's first museum.

Catlin later tells us that he was inspired by the very existence of the War Department's "interesting collection" of paintings to head for Indian country where, unlike King's studio portraits, he intended to paint the natives in their quotidian existence, from life. There were other political lessons to be learned from the fate of King's portraits, banished as a government collection by an administration that wanted no more sympathetic images of the "savage race." But Catlin would have had to peer too far into his own future to profit from the warning. Instead he seized upon a more immediate reality: Nothing moved in Washington without the motor of official patronage. In the capital George had no Colonel Stone to act as his go-between and publicist. It was up to him to make his own case, not only as an artist worthy of support but as a public-spirited citizen whose gifts would benefit his country.

In the equivalent of a cold call, on February 22, 1829, Catlin wrote to Peter B. Porter, secretary of war under John Quincy Adams. One of the "War Hawks" who had pressured President Madison into hostilities with Britain, Porter was an equally vehement proponent of Indian removal and subjugation. George had no mediating connections or an introduction, but he knew that as secretary of war Porter was also charged with administering the Department of Indian Affairs; those seeking permission for any project relating to his wards had no choice but to seek his approval. Catlin had two ideas that would enable the secretary to help both a poor artist and the department's Indian constituents.

At thirty-three, Catlin explained to Porter, he was overcome by the feeling that "life was short and I find that I have already traveled over half of it without stepping out of the beaten path in the unshackled pursuit of that Fame for which alone, the Art to me is valuable, and for the attainment of which I wish to devote the whole energies of my life."

If the secretary read on, he would have learned that this obscure painter—of name unknown to him—was sick of portraiture "that limited and slavish branch of the arts." Instead, Catlin confided, "the ultimate object of my ambition is Historical painting."

"I have thought of two ways in which you may possibly have it in your power . . . to place me in possession of *time* and the *best models* which our country can afford for the progress of my studies . . . ," Catlin wrote. "The first of these is the Professorship of Drawing in the W. Point Institution." (The obstacle to this piece of the proposal was the French-born incumbent, the artist Thomas Gimbrede, who had held the post for years.)

"The other would be an appointment to some little Agency among the Savage Indians up the Missouri River, which would pay my expenses for a year or two." On its face this second idea appears the more realistic—even hardheaded:

> With regards to the other proposition (supposing that you have
> the power of appointing the Indian agents &c. on the frontiers)

I have thought it possible that you might yet have some agent of that kind to appoint up the Missouri . . . and to the duties of which you would feel proud of appointing one who would forever feel thankful for the patronage you had thereby shewn him in his favorite Art.

By now it would have been apparent that the writer of the letter was seeking an appointment as Indian agent on the Missouri. As he had yet to visit a trading post, the artist may be forgiven for assuming the job to be largely honorific; he could not have known that agents represented the government in commercial and political dealings with local tribes, treated with British and French competitors, and received visiting representatives from Washington and abroad. Catlin planned to spend most of his time perfecting his art. These two years, he continued, would not only "enrich me with subjects for a lifetime of painting" but would allow him to realize grander entrepreneurial ambitions—enabling him to "open such a Gallery, first in this country & then in London as would in all probability handsomely repay me for all my labours." George Catlin may have been the first seeker of government patronage in America simultaneously to apply for subsidy as both an artist and a future businessman. He saw his proposal in the same light as do contemporary applicants for government support of their art projects: The nation invests in its talented citizens for work that cannot be expected to pay its way today but that may enable the recipient to become tomorrow's success story.

In his mind Catlin had found the subject to achieve all this and more. If the government gave him time in the West—"the finest School for an Historical painter now to be found in the world," he would create a uniquely American kind of history painting, one not based upon conventional anecdote and narrative but inspired by a native classical ideal, where "among the naked Savage, I could select and study from the finest models in Nature, unmasked, and moving in all their grace and beauty."

As far as we know, Porter never replied. In fact he may never have seen Catlin's letter. Eleven months after he had moved into his head-quarters at the War Department, and less than three weeks after Catlin had dispatched his proposal, the secretary was ousted from his post—an early victim of President Jackson's "spoils system."

AFTER MONTHS OF spending money without earning any, Catlin gave up on Washington. Sometime in the late fall of 1829, he and Clara moved to Richmond, Virginia, where a potentially important commission had come his way. He was invited to paint a group portrait of the historic Virginia Convention of 1829–30, convened for the framing of a new state constitution.

Less a portrait of living legislators than a valedictory to dying ones, the subjects—115 delegates—including venerable relics of the early Republic, seem to have depressed the artist. This would be the last official gathering of Madison, Monroe, John Marshall, and John Randolph. The preponderance of black-clad shrunken bodies reflects the physical realities of old age; the outsize heads offer the portraitist's solution to the challenge of providing recognizable likenesses of so many individuals all squeezed into a narrow space.

The opening session took place on October 8, 1829, in the Hall of the House of Delegates, and the first speaker was former president James Madison, who had helped to frame both Virginia's first constitution in 1776 and the Constitution of the United States. They worked through the fall and into a snowy winter before moving on January 14, 1830, to the old First African Church on the corner below Monument Avenue. Catlin's crowded benches suggest the latter location.

In the artist's rendering, several cartoonishly large heads, evoke political caricature: Catlin would certainly have seen examples of the great English masters of this genre—James Gillray, Thomas Rowlandson, and William Hogarth. Turning Virginia's founding fathers into freaks, however, was not the way to endear the painter to his patrons. Catlin's oil sketch was certainly intended to serve as a preliminary study for a grand rotunda-size work, probably destined for the state capitol; the results explain why the project never went further.

After cramped boardinghouse life in Washington, the newlyweds had tried to make the Richmond visit an occasion for both profit and pleasure; staying at an inn outside town was cheaper and healthier, encouraging walks in the piney woods and the rolling meadows of plantation country. Nonetheless, it was here that Clara succumbed to the dreaded "intermittent fever" of the Piedmont, probably malarial in origin; she may already have been infected in Washington: She suffered from night sweats and chills, diminished energy and little appetite, becoming more skeletal with each passing day. According to an earlier undocumented account, Dolley Madison, the former first lady, learned of the artist's gravely ill young wife languishing at the inn and she rushed from town daily to make sure that Clara took some sustaining nourishment, thereby ensuring that George could finish the painting while the convention was in session. Yet during the former president's long retirement, the Madisons left Montpélier, the plantation in Orange County, Virginia, only once—to attend the constitutional convention in Richmond. It seems highly unlikely that Dolley Madison would have made a daily trip in bad weather to minister to Clara in a country inn. With or without the former first lady's ministrations, Clara recovered sufficiently to return north—most probably back to Albany—to complete her convalescence.

GEORGE NOW FOUND himself alone in New York, in the Cortlandt Street rooms the brothers had shared. It was thirteen months since Julius's death. His stay in Washington had given him new ideas but done nothing to advance them. He had had no reply from Secretary

Porter. The Richmond commission had been a disaster. As a measure of his isolation he was persuaded to join fourteen other founding members in launching an organization of young lawyers, three of whom had been his contemporaries at Tapping Reeve Law School. "We hereby agree to associate ourselves as a Club for our mutual improvement in the discussion of legal questions and a knowledge of the law," began their statement of purpose. Loneliness may have induced Catlin to join his classmates in starting this unlikely club, but desperation about his career seems more likely: Ex-secretary Porter was also a Litchfield law graduate, and George may have harbored hopes that an old boys' network would succeed where his individual plea had apparently failed.

These last defeats only moved Catlin to pursue a more grandiose plan of patronage: He needed an all-powerful father to take on the world for him, one who could redeem the fiasco of the Virginia oil sketch, and his earlier failure to obtain subscriptions to his portrait engraving of Judge Tapping Reeve. He decided upon having engravings made of the convention group portrait abroad. To oversee the project on the spot, as well as lend his name as patron to lure subscribers, Catlin wrote a series of letters to the marquis de Lafayette, who had been retired at his country house, La Grange, outside Paris since his return from his triumphal tour of America five years earlier.

Vaguely alluding to having met the general on his visit here in 1824, Catlin's first letter, written on August 1, 1830, begins by soliciting the use of his name: The right to emblazon "'Lafayette, friend of George Washington, of Liberty and of America,'" as patron of Catlin's publication of the Virginia convention lithograph, "would render me an essential service in its success in this country." In order for this historical print to reap the profit of robust sales, time was of the essence. An aquatint of the painting would have to be ready for the press before the convention adjourned the following spring of 1831. French engravers were acknowledged to be the most skilled at their craft; they were also known to be willing to bargain. It would be up to Lafayette to act as the artist's agent. In his next letter Catlin enclosed a drawing (admittedly "deficient," as he noted) of the painting. On receipt of same, he announced, Lafayette must rush to Paris and see that his rendering be "placed in the hands of one, only who will, proceed with the work immediately, and upon the condition that the whole amount shall be paid, the moment that the plate is finished, and no part of it before that time." His representative's glittering name should allay any engraver's fears of completing the work before he saw a sou. As he had no time to correct the inadequacy of his drawing, George would leave it to Lafayette to arrange with the lithographer to make the necessary improvements to the delegates' bodies; heads must remain as indicated, he instructed. Of course the marquis must keep his eye on the work's progress and report back to him regularly.

Silence was the only response to Catlin's letter. Lafayette, well known for his exquisite manners, may have been too stunned even to instruct his secretary to decline on his behalf. The project was dropped. Over the next few years, however, hearing nothing from France, Catlin followed up with several more letters: Admitting his presumption, he requested the return of the drawing, but he also struck an aggrieved note, claiming that with a thousand dollars in subscriptions received by 1830–31, he could have published the print "to great advantage."

Catlin's own word—"presumption"—to describe his solicitations to Lafayette has been echoed by recent writers on the artist. But presumption implies an element of plausibility, of a pushiness that often carries the day. George's call upon the aged nobleman to act on his behalf—not merely by lending the luster of his name but by serving as agent and factotum—suggests something more profound: a need that verged on desperation, casting George back into the role of helpless child.

What to do now? He refused to accept a future of chasing portrait commissions, only to have his paintings ridiculed by critics and fellow artists. He needed an assured income, an undemanding sinecure whose few duties would allow him time to paint, but he also wanted adventure: Julius's tales of Indian country returned with greater clarity as he clung to memories of his brother. Now their shared vision of a new life—painting, exploring, collecting specimens in the West— gained in urgency. Neither Julius's death nor his own marriage, not even recent failure in obtaining patronage, would lead George to abandon his dream: to paint what he saw and to invent himself as a new kind of artist.

6

A FREE MAN

At thirty-three, with "half of his life over," as he told Porter, Catlin felt more than the call of adventure: He had been chosen to preserve the history and customs of the Indian for posterity. "Nothing short of the loss of my life" could prevent him from becoming the chronicler of "Natural man," he wrote in an 1841 serialized account of his travels. But, like all heroes, he would first have to struggle alone, to confront and conquer enemies on every side, the most insidious being those who would thwart his journey out of love. "I opened my views to my friends and relations, but got not one advocate or abettor." In defiance he found the strength he needed—to need no one. He had exchanged dependence for a soaring faith in his own powers. "[A]nd I broke from them all,—from my wife and my aged parents,—myself my only adviser and protector."

When he first began to think about painting native subjects, it was not in the context of the portrait at all. History painting enjoyed a prestige as the summa of art. Its place in grand neoclassical public buildings was proof of the genre's exalted status. Portraiture could be a lucrative affair, but whether the sitters were royalty or merely merchant princes, the painter remained a courtier. Still dreaming of commissions like that of the Capitol rotunda, George fantasized working on the grand scale and reaping the lavish rewards of history painting.

In April 1823, just as Neagle would have been finishing his portrait of Red Jacket, Catlin wrote to his father of his plans for a large painting depicting the 1794 council at Canandaigua, New York. The gathering had been called to redress the injustices of two previous "punitive settlements" and to "secure peace and friendship and lead the Indian to civilization." Putnam Catlin had been present at the meeting, to which he had accompanied his friend Col. Timothy Pickering, then "sole Commissioner" appointed by President Washington, and designated to treat with Red Jacket, the powerful dissident Seneca leader. Now George asked his father to plumb his own memory, and to write to Pickering, asking his friend to recall every element of the scene that might add color and drama to his planned work.

Indeed Putnam seemed to have remembered every detail about the event, beginning with Pickering's welcoming speech to the Indians as they "came marching in straggling order" across the pitch pine plain, at which point the federal emissary "captured their attention by noting that he had brought some spirits to wash the dust down their throats, etc." Then Red Jacket, "famed for his oratory[,] advanced and made a reply to Colonel Pickering in very handsome style."

Catlin senior was as acute an observer as his son would prove to be, and the moment that remained the most vivid after almost thirty years was the "position" of the legendary Seneca chief. As Red Jacket began to speak, "he stepped on a log to gain a little elevation, and perfect silence was observed, except that the infant lashed to his back, with its face outwards began to cry. At that instant, his wife standing near him advanced on the log, as he stepped to the ground, and gracefully gave her breast to the child so as to prevent the least interruption of the oration."

This extraordinary image—the feared leader, his child strapped to his back on a cradleboard as he launches into a speech of diplomatic import, his wife joining him on the improvised platform to nurse the fretful baby—suggests a missed opportunity; it may be that Catlin found it too intimate a moment for an official work—or too tender a depiction of a male of the "savage race." For his part Timothy Pickering dismissed the event as unrevealing; nothing had taken place that would be "of any interest in an historic painting; in a word, I think the entire scene of too little moment to be the subject of one." Catlin dropped the project, but not its principal figure, whose portrait he would ultimately paint three times.

THERE WERE OTHER native leaders as famous as Red Jacket, but none seized the imagination of his contemporaries—especially artists—so powerfully. Called "the perfect Indian" while he lived, Red Jacket— pursued and painted by Neagle, King, and Inman—came, inevitably, to stand for his imperfect and thus doomed race that must be "captured" in all its heroic, rebellious, and futile struggles before its fated destruction. The fact that the mythic Seneca did not allow any likeness to be taken of him until he was nearly seventy years old added to the elegiac aura of his portraits: Images of the fiery orator, and a full-length biography by Catlin's friend and publisher William Stone, all emphasized the chief's fierce intelligence and force of character. At the same time he is Emerson's Representative (Red) Man as tragic hero. Even as they recorded the visible ravages of age, drink, and despair, each artist also evoked Red Jacket's prideful defiance, which endured to flay the conscience of the white viewer.

Born about 1750 as Sagoyewatha, Red Jacket had been a runner for the British at Niagara, who rewarded him with a red military jacket, hence his English nickname. At the close of the Revolutionary War the Six Iroquois Nations, including the Seneca, found themselves again divided; those who remained below the United States–Canada border ceded vast tracts of ancestral land to the Americans, whose sovereignty

over the rest was part of the agreement. This double betrayal became
Red Jacket's lifelong cause: No warrior, he made himself admired and
feared through the power of the word alone; his speeches—against
fraudulent treaties, against gullible or greedy fellow Indians, against
missionaries and Christianity, traders, and alcohol (of which he was
a famous victim) were translated and widely published. In 1792, at
the height of his prestige, he was among forty-nine Iroquois chiefs
who traveled to Washington to negotiate with government leaders
for financial assistance and an end to land appropriations. On this
occasion President Washington presented him with an engraved silver
medal, a tomahawk, and a peace pipe. He was especially attached to
the enormous oval pendant and wore it for almost all of his portraits.
The sorrow of Red Jacket's last years was to see most of his people
convert to Christianity (including his wife) and despite his most eloquent efforts, to witness the seizure or sale of lands assigned them by
historic treaties. The fallen Seneca chief was among those reduced to
barren lives on the shrunken parcels allotted to reservations. One of
these, near Buffalo, is where Catlin painted *Red Jacket*, his first Indian
portrait, in 1826.

In Catlin's oil sketch the chief's prized decoration fastens the folds
of his robes like a Roman toga, reinforcing the image of Red Jacket in
the classically tragic role of deposed leader, transcending ethnic or
historical particularity. This portrait conforms to other artists' depiction of the Seneca's features as Caucasoid. In Catlin's full-length watercolor portrait done the following year, however, Red Jacket, shown
in profile, holding a tomahawk and long-stemmed calumet, or carved
ceremonial pipe, is shown as notably dark skinned. The third Catlin portrait of the declining Seneca chief is intriguing, first, because
it has long been lost, but also because the work seems to have been
painted at the subject's behest; as the artist recalled, on this occasion
he "indulged [Red Jacket] also in the wish he expressed, that he might
be seen standing on the Table Rock, at the Falls of Niagara, about

which place he thought his spirit would linger after he was dead." The subject may have chosen the setting, but the artist painted him with the dark hindsight of history. Catlin reminds us that "not all the eloquence of Cicero and Demosthenes would be able to avert the calamity that awaits his declining nation—to resist the despoiling hand of mercenary white man, that opens and spreads liberally, but to entrap the unwary and ignorant within its withering grasp."

During his stay in Washington in 1829–30, Catlin made several drawings of individual members of a Winnebago delegation visiting the capital. Although not as "gruesome" as a contemporary scholar has described them, the sketches have a cartoonish character, evidence of the self-taught artist's persistent struggles with human anatomy and proportion. Certainly they give no hint of the inspired revelation, as recalled by Catlin, that led him to his destined subject.

Discouragement was another potent impulse behind Catlin's redirection of his art. The sense of wasting his life, of being "stuck," that George had earlier bared to Secretary Porter reveal the artist to be among those Americans who went west in the belief that they had nothing left to lose, seekers defined by what thcy fled more than by what they sought. Adding to his recent professional setbacks, he felt burdened by the hopes of his own failed father and by his obligations as husband and provider.

Early in the new year of 1830 George made up his mind. That spring he parked Clara with his parents in Hopbottom and took off, a free man once again.

SINCE LEWIS AND CLARK had set out from the river port of St. Louis thirty years earlier, the boomtown on the Mississippi had served as the staging area for the West and for Indian country. Thanks to the explosion (sometimes all too literal) of steam-powered river craft, getting there by water was easily arranged—but expensive: If Catlin had been able to scrape up the money, he could have made the entire trip by steamship down the Ohio from Pittsburgh: Auguste-Marie Chouteau, a member of the fur-trading dynasty that had recently joined forces with John Jacob Astor, all but commuted by steamboat from St. Louis to Washington, where he lobbied lawmakers for regulations favorable to the Chouteau interests in pelts, whiskey, and land.

Approaching the water gate of St. Louis in the late spring of 1830, Catlin would have seen a river town more European than American. Below the smokestacks of double- and triple-decker steamships waiting to disgorge passengers and freight, the brown water was barely visible—its surface covered with pirogues from St. Louis's sister city of New Orleans; with flatboats and keelboats hauling lead from Wisconsin and Iowa, along with their crews—black skinned, or swarthy métis, laborers of mixed race, many of them from Canada, looking to hire out as voyageurs—skilled as both navigators and translators from French and Indian languages. On the cobblestone streets above the wharves rose a city of tall houses whose verandas alone were visible above discreet walled gardens—more like a frontier New Orleans than the port of New York familiar to Catlin.

In the high tide of dawn, Catlin would have noticed another dramatic difference between this river port and New York. Few foreign crews and passengers clambering from the oceangoing schooners moored at Manhattan's South Street piers could have been anywhere so diverse or exotic as the populace milling on the levees here, or on the streets of the upper town. St. Louis was a vast marketplace—everyone he saw seemed to be hawking goods or services: Before he would ever visit Indian country, Catlin counted more native people, silent men wrapped in blankets against the chilly morning, than he had ever observed in the delegations visiting Washington or Philadelphia; here they came to trade "birchbark sacks of maple sugar, skins of wild honey, horsehair lariats, moccasins, herbs, buffalo tongues and bear grease," the shortening of the frontier cook, but also the hair dressing of frontier men, slicked up for town. With trappers serving as interpreters, they traded these for blankets, stirrups and saddles, coffee, tobacco, knifes, tin cookware and—under the counter—whiskey, the fuel of life in the West.

Here, too, for the first time George encountered an unfamiliar population of white men. Mingling with the French and half-breed voyageurs and traders with their strange patois, he noted brawny, whiskered "mountain men," already a legend in the East; smartly uniformed young officers from Jefferson Barracks; and, eyeing the nearby crowd for marks, gamblers and the pickpockets who preyed upon travelers everywhere. There were also more black people than Catlin had noticed in New York: freedmen servicing the steamboats as stokers, firemen, and porters, but also slaves working as domestics, as household servants or coachmen and porters owned by the one grand hotel in town, Planter's House; the latter were waiting on the quay to greet plantation families and their slaves arriving on a new luxury steamer from downriver, come for the entire "Season" to enjoy city life in the most luxurious surroundings St. Louis had to offer.

Catlin could only gawk at such privileged travelers. He would be lucky to find a cheap boardinghouse and a room shared by one other male lodger—preferably not far from the levee, as he had considerable luggage. For all that he had tried to travel light, George Catlin was also weighed down by the unknown. How far from this riverfront city would he eventually find himself, navigating waterways or penetrating the interior on horseback, and how long would he be gone? His most valuable baggage, though, contained supplies for the work he planned. Wrapped in cylinders of waterproof oilskin, he carried rolls of canvas, brushes and pens, portfolios of paper, and bladders filled with pigment—including cakes of valuable vermilion, the truest red ever seen, made of cochineal, a substance harvested from tiny insects feeding on cactus and harvested in Mexico. He had also packed a few finished portraits, probably miniatures, and landscapes that he would offer as calling cards. He counted on commissions to pay his way.

Leaving all but the last at his lodgings, he made his way to a compound of buildings at North Main Street, housing the home and offices, council room, and Indian museum of Gen. William Clark, commissioner of the newly created Missouri Territory and the most powerful American west of the Mississippi. To one of Clark's house slaves Catlin presented a letter of introduction, either from Gen. Peter Porter—who in his retirement seems to have warmed to the artist— or from Porter's successor as secretary of war (and thus in charge of Indian affairs), John C. Eaton. Moments later George Catlin shook the hand of the legendary General Clark.

A six-footer from the age of fifteen, Clark stood almost a head taller than his slight visitor. But the man who now greeted George with an openhearted warmth would have been arresting under any circumstances: The sixty-year-old Clark's famous copper mane had whitened. Otherwise the vigor and force of character of the huge figure whose looks had so astounded the Indians that they named him "Red-Headed Chief" seemed unchanged by time.

AFTER HIS TRIUMPHAL return to St. Louis with the Corps of Discovery in 1805, Clark's next career, of civilian administrator, had proved that there are indeed second acts in America. His fame, shared with his fellow leader of the legendary expedition, Meriwether Lewis, had barely dimmed when Clark was appointed governor of the Missouri Territory, with Captain Lewis named to the same post in Louisiana. But depression and bad luck had continued to hound Lewis, ending with his death in 1809, almost certainly of self-inflicted gunshot wounds. In contrast Clark's professional life went from strength to strength; with his new appointment, commissioner of Indian affairs, came power—over people and territories—to a degree unknown outside Washington.

Like George Catlin, Clark grew up on horseback cradling his gun, or striding mountain streams with a fishing rod. A soldier since boyhood, what he lacked in book learning Clark possessed in knowledge of the kind that his government most needed. He knew more about Western Indians than any man alive; the new commissioner had been chosen for the post by President Andrew Jackson for his experience in dealing with Northern Plains tribes, first as military adversaries and later as administrator: Clark was familiar with tribal languages, beliefs, and customs, but also with long-standing intertribal alliances and enmities, including each tribe's history of relations with the French and British. Over decades he had also forged mutually profitable relationships with the principal agents, subagents, and fur traders of the region. A few of these men were themselves power brokers with networks of their own: The self-made, hugely rich French émigré Auguste Chouteau, Astor's chief agent for the region, became Clark's business partner, as did the Scot Kenneth McKenzie, an adventurer who rose to become a bourgeois, one of the civilian heads of military forts that also served as trading posts. With the help of these associates Clark had eyes and ears throughout a vast empire that extended from New Spain to the south, north to the Great Lakes, and reaching west to the Rockies.

Washington was stingy, however. Despite his power, Clark's salary did not begin to cover his official expenses. Thus he felt forced to earn money through various commercial ventures—from a store on his property to real estate investments. Even in an era when private enterprise often included public office—especially in the open-minded West—Clark's entrepreneurial activities, specifically his partnership with Chouteau in the Missouri Fur Trading Company, combined with constant land speculation and increased holdings around St. Louis, continued to raise questions about his ethics. Given the bargain they were getting, his principals in Washington appeared more than willing to overlook the conflicts of interest that described the commissioner's wheeling and dealing.

In the separate house on Clark's property that served as a council room, George Catlin was now invited to observe the suave negotiator in action: He had never before witnessed a demonstration of political skills, and George could only marvel at the patience and the seamless collaboration with interpreters who returned the natives' stylized rhetoric and long speeches with perorations of Clark's own, until finally—the test of all successful mediators—each tribe's leaders left the table believing that "they" had won their case. In fact they had all lost. Clark, representing his government, was the only winner. He had cultivated the art of listening, of advancing opposing interests in a measured and impartial manner, or of switching gears and hectoring one or another party. Then he would appear to find solutions that appeased competing needs and egos, thus earning the Indians' trust. In matters of their legally established rights against lawless settlers, those assembled could feel secure that the "Red-Headed Chief," acting as their protector, spoke on the side of justice and for his government's commitment to honoring historical treaties.

Clark fully supported the president's Indian removal policy, which after Jackson's tireless promotion would be signed into law in 1832. As commissioner he saw his job as enforcing the compulsory removal of tribes east of the Mississippi, persuading chiefs to sign treaties "in which they agreed to relinquish earlier claims to these lands for a pittance," accepting their peoples' relocation to territory a fraction of their original home—lands long inhabited by other tribes, among them the Osage and Shawnee. He eloquently repeated and promoted the "humane" federal argument: Removal was for their own good. He may have even believed it. Whatever it took—outright lies, promises, playing rival leaders against one another, even secret support of military intervention—Clark carried out his government's policy. From his terse late journal entries and letters, his biographers have teased out hints of guilt and conflict over his past role: playing advocate while betraying the trust of those whom he was charged to represent. But there is no reason to suppose that Clark, ever the loyal soldier, counted any authority higher than his president and commander in chief.

George observed firsthand the shifting tones of cynicism, realpolitik, and perhaps, self-delusion. Of more immediate interest to his new protégé was the fact that William Clark had acquired the first great collection of Indian artifacts in America. From the outset the Corps of Discovery had been charged by President Jefferson to collect specimens of scientific interest in the course of their exploration of unmapped lands; and from their first encounters with tribal peoples, Lewis and Clark had extended the president's desiderata: Along with samples of minerals, fossils, plants, and bones of prehistoric creatures, the expedition's leaders shipped to Monticello examples of native weaponry, baskets, beadwork, and feathered bonnets, robes, cradle-boards, calumets—even entire painted tipis. But Catlin would have already seen some of the eight hundred objects Lewis had given to the Peale Museum in Philadelphia, where he first marveled at their beauty, ingenuity, and craftsmanship. Clark did not end his collecting with his new civilian post: Through tribute, exchange of gifts, purchase or from his network of agents and subagents (no questions asked) the commissioner acquired still more. Displaying a fraction of his hoard on the walls of his council room, he surrounded tribal leaders with familiar objects. At the same time the hospitable and public-spirited administrator opened his collection to interested St. Louisans. In this informal way Clark's "Indian Museum" became the first museum in the American West.

Among the constant stream of visitors—European princes, Indian chiefs, Washington officialdom, fur traders and speculators, fellow St. Louisians and their endless relatives from far and wide—Clark had not yet played host to an artist. He had never met anyone like the young portrait painter seeking help for a stalled career, certainly not one burning with a passionate claim to a new vocation—a vocation that, as it happened, fit neatly into Clark's own interests. The commissioner, already known for a graciousness and hospitality that went back to his Virginia roots, now outdid himself. He put all the facilities of his office at George's disposal, inviting him to set up his easel in the council room and museum. This was George Catlin's first Western studio.

Clark's successful dealings with the tribes in the Missouri Territory depended upon a character defined by paternal authority: His appointment as Western emissary of the Great White Father in Washington was a role that came naturally to him: He was a concerned and engaged parent to his own five children and two stepchildren, along with two nephews of a widowed sister, all sent to him so he could supervise their education. Now, in George Catlin, he took on another floundering son, one on the brink of middle age and still looking for help and guidance, which Clark seems gladly to have offered. In this lucky encounter Catlin found the last and most crucial father figure he would ever know, and the man who enabled him to realize his art.

SAVAGE AND CIVILIZED TRIBES

Under Clark's wing Catlin flourished. In the governor George found a nurturing and powerful father, a friend, and soon an Indian guide with few equals anywhere in the Western territories. It was the first of these qualities, namely Clark's paternal role, that helped to feed a hunger George would never outgrow. Unspoken comparisons with his own father—anxious hypochondriac of failed hopes, forever harping upon his son's success—shadow George's homage to Clark. His new patron was the same age as Putnam Catlin, but—a whirlwind of energy—he seemed a decade younger. "Governor Clark, whose whitened locks are still shaken in roars of laughter, and good jests among the numerous citizens, who all love him, and continually rally around him in his hospitable mansion," George rhapsodized.

Competition for Clark's attention was keen. Other younger men also looked to the commissioner as an ideal parent, strong, loving, and protective, "a man of primitive and heroic character, made up of firmness and tenderness," one recalled. George was used to being his father's favorite, and he made a point of assuring his readers (and himself) that he was loved best. However busy he might be, Clark always found time for "daily interviews" with him, Catlin wrote. "My works and my design have been warmly approved and applauded by this excellent patriarch of the Western World; and kindly recommended by him in such ways as have been of great service to me." Indeed Clark went out of his way to help loyal young associates, including numerous relatives whom he placed in strategic positions in St. Louis's commercial and political circles. His Indian clients, too, recognized in the commissioner a natural authority that went beyond any title conferred upon him by Washington. As his flame-colored hair turned to white and his complexion paled, his tribal counterparts merely changed his title from the "Red-Headed" to the "White Chief."

As both territorial governor and commissioner of Indian affairs, Clark assumed the role of St. Louis's official host. He received the most revered foreign visitor of the century, the marquis de Lafayette, who, on his triumphal return to America in 1824, made a detour to meet the famed survivor of the Corps of Discovery, and to admire the marvels in his Indian museum. At his family farm, Marais Castor (Beaver Pond), Clark also played host to the author Washington Irving in 1832, when, after seventeen years abroad in the consular service, he decided to embark on a tour of Indian country.

Compared with Irving, Catlin was a nobody, but there was something intensely appealing about George, all brash ambition and provincial innocence. He was Candide, carrying canvases and paints. It seems likely that Clark, along with inviting George to set up his easel in the council room and brokering portrait commissions from the local gentry, extended the hospitality of his country home to the visiting artist. Catlin would feel an extra measure of gratitude at his rescue from the bachelor's boardinghouse existence; more than the feast of homegrown food, he savored the welcome of his patriarchal host. George was always eager to embrace family life—as long as he could be a guest at the party, free to leave anytime he chose.

From master of an antebellum plantation, Clark now became Catlin's guide to a vastly different scene, a fraught tribal council convened by the commissioner, under pressure from both Washington and from the Indians under his jurisdiction. On June 24, 1830, a few months after his arrival in St. Louis, Catlin boarded the steamboat *Planet* as Clark's special guest, part of an entourage that included the council's co-commissioner, Col. Willoughby Morgan, a military detachment from Jefferson Barracks commanded by Col. Stephen Kearny, a rising military star—soon to marry Clark's stepdaughter, Mary, the child of his second wife, Harriet Radford Clark (both of whom accompanied the delegation)—along with the Clarks' six-year-old son, Pompey. After almost two weeks of chugging up the low waters of the Mississippi in the sultry summer heat, the group arrived at Prairie du Chien, Wisconsin, an eight-mile-long meadow above the mouth of the Wisconsin River.

On July 7, 1830, Clark opened the council, whose declared purpose was to negotiate a treaty between the Sioux, Sauk, and Fox, on the one hand, and the Omaha, Iowa, Oto, and Missouri on the other. Unofficially, however, the agreements would help to seal the fate of millions of Native Americans, stripping them of their lands and livelihoods, their culture and sovereignty.*

In February of the previous year Clark and his family had journeyed to Washington as guests of the new president, Andrew Jackson, to celebrate his March inauguration. Jackson's inaugural address launched his Indian policy: Forcing eastern and southern tribes from their ancestral lands to territories west of the Mississippi. Enlisting the lan-

---

* Catlin could have been present at the treaty signing, but his name does not appear on the document as a witness. He may have conflated this council and its treaty with a second cessation agreement with the Sauk and Fox tribes alone, dated September 27, 1836, and signed by Catlin and his traveling companion, Robert Serrill Wood, an Anglican priest of scientific interests.

guage of paternal concern, Jackson announced his administration's intent to direct "humane and considerate attention towards native Americans, through acts consistent with the habits of our government and the feelings of our people."

It fell to his commissioners, William Clark and his counterpart in the Michigan Territory, Lewis Cass, to put into practice the president's agenda. The Indian Removal Bill, signed into law by Andrew Jackson on May 28, 1830, officially authorized the federal government to "exchange public land in the West, beyond the states of Missouri and Arkansas, for Indian land in the East." In practice the law legitimized the seizure of millions of acres of tribal lands through the forced removal of their rightful inhabitants, while protecting the interests of illegal white settlers, lead miners, and traders in fur and whiskey. The paltry sum allocated for this massive relocation—five hundred thousand dollars—all but guaranteed the sufferings called the "Trail of Tears"—from the outright slaughter of recalcitrant tribes to countless deaths from disease, exposure, and starvation.

Three hundred miles up the Mississippi from St. Louis at the mouth of the Wisconsin River, Prairie du Chien ("dog prairie") was both a military garrison, Fort Crawford, and a government-sponsored "factory," or trading center, where every year close to ten thousand Indians came to trade with one another and with British agents. On this vast flatland, baking in the July heat, George Catlin reported his first sight of Plains Indians in their own territory; he claimed to have watched the ceremonial arrival of the famed Sauk leader, Keokuk, along with 112 other chiefs and headmen. Some, like the Omaha, the Sauk's sworn enemy, already showed the ravages of hunger, symptoms that would worsen as the diminishing herds of bison upon which they depended were fought over by rival tribes.

Following a week of negotiations all native leaders present signed the treaty. It was rumored that many had no idea of what they were signing and that others had been bribed. In affixing their marks to the document, they ceded to the United States a forty-mile-wide no-man's land in present-day Iowa whose stated function was to separate the Dakota Sioux to the north from the Sauk and Fox to the south. As an observer of Clark's tactics over the past months, Catlin would have been aware of how much the Omaha's earlier stance of rejection and their present state of famine would cost them: They now signed away rights to millions of acres of their age-old hunting grounds in western Iowa for an annuity of $2,500 for "ten successive years," along with the services of a blacksmith.

In his later accounts of these events, Catlin emerges as quick to seize the implications of what he beheld. He would write that the Indians, a happy and flourishing people of sixteen million who were originally "undisputed owners of the soil," were undone by the arrival of thirty million of their supposed Christian saviors "scuffling for the goods and luxuries of life, over the bones and ashes of twelve million of red men; six millions of whom have fallen victims to the small-pox, and the remainder to the sword, the bayonet, and whiskey; all of which means of their death and destruction have been introduced and visited upon them by acquisitive white men."

The remaining two million (in Catlin's estimate) were at equal risk; in its consuming hunger for land their government viewed the tribes as obstacles in the "course of empire." Each treaty further deprived the native inhabitants of inherited legal and human rights, legitimizing every crime carried out against them as "for their own good."

It's hard to know whether Catlin saw his patron, the "excellent Patriarch of the Western World," as among those conflicted white men some of whom acted as sorrowful agents of the destruction of native tribes. First there was Clark's official role as Jackson's commissioner, entrusted with carrying out the president's policy of Indian removal. Then, in his entrepreneurial capacity, Clark was himself active in the whiskey trade, and he enjoyed profitable dealings with the American Fur Company, whose empire depended upon its success in acquiring

Indian territory along with its fur-bearing population. If Catlin was enlightened—or disillusioned—during his early months in St. Louis or later, he continued loyally to uphold Clark's reputation as a just and impartial administrator, until the latter's death in 1838, when he eulogized his host's life as "one of faithful service to his country, and, at the same time, of strictest fidelity as the guardian and friend of the red man." Among other lessons George learned from Clark was the slippery meaning of the word "friend."

IN THE LATE summer and early fall of that year, 1830, Catlin painted his first series of Indian portraits. Although the date of the trip remains conjectural, he possibly made a detour on his return from Fort Crawford and Prairie du Chien to a place near Cantonment Leavenworth* in northeastern Kansas.

From now on in fact, "conjectural" and its every synonym waft from most accounts of Catlin's comings and goings. Time, memory, and the artist's own narrative rearrangements share equal blame for the murky chronology of his visits to Indian country. Anyone assembling notes years after the recorded events took place may be forgiven for memories turned hazy, for scrambling people, places, and dates. But it is also true that Catlin was capable of inventing material out of whole cloth—because a new version made a better story or showed him as the "first," a solitary heroic figure in uncharted lands. To this end, in the published editions of his writing, he rarely supplies dates; his paintings, too, are often left to be dated by others, either on the basis of style or from external evidence—the places and people named or depicted; the records of business associates, collectors, or creditors (the last two often one and the same).

Catlin himself, for example, makes no mention of Clark as his first

---

* Renamed Fort Leavenworth in 1832.

guide to Indian country or of the seminal opportunity provided by the invitation to the Prairie du Chien Treaty Council; he will later allude to friends or traveling companions, or even (by name) the Indian-speaking French or half-breed voyageurs who paddled his canoe while he painted. In keeping with his loose form of quest narrative, the hero must be tested through overcoming obstacles (including his own fear) and meeting dangers—alone. We are left to wonder, then—not for the last time—as the council drew to a close, how and with whom did George make his way from Fort Crawford, Prairie du Chien, to Cantonment Leavenworth, the westernmost garrison in the long chain of military fortifications that traced a frontier reaching from Spanish territories in the Southwest to the Great Lakes. Whether he made this lengthy detour on his return to St. Louis or on a somewhat later visit starting out from that city, we can assume that George's travels were facilitated—if not actually planned—by Clark, down to the last letter of introduction.

ARTISTS HAVE ALWAYS led a precarious existence, but never more so than in the young Republic. With the exception of the most fashionable portraitists in East Coast cities, and a few lucky history painters who enjoyed federal commissions, patronage was scarce. Catlin had shown himself to be more entrepreneurial than most, scratching for lithography work and working influential connections, such as William Stone, for help. Journeying west to realize his life project, his existence became still more hand to mouth. In every way he now found himself in uncharted territory. His few commissions in St. Louis—portraits or small landscapes—obtained through Clark's help, were not going to see him through his ambitious travel plans to penetrate farther into Indian country.

Though Clark was cash poor himself, his power nonetheless translated into a network throughout the territory consisting of those who owed him favors or who hoped for the same: He could easily arrange for horses, both pack animals and riders known for their endurance and speed, along with canoes and flat- or keelboats. Together with navigators, this same small army of subagents, scouts, and guides was now engaged to mediate between the artist, a stranger to this country, and his chosen Indian subjects.

Its itinerary mapped (and his safety as far as possible assured), George's first stay among tribes who had been removed to the area around Cantonment Leavenworth yielded twenty-eight portraits: Delaware, Shawnee, Kickapoo, Potawatomi, Kaskaskia, Wea, Peoria, Piankshaw, and leaders of other Woodland or "Civilized Tribes," as they were known, sat for the white visitor. With this group of subjects Catlin first observed and recorded living evidence of the new administration's Indian policy; his first sitters were representatives of uprooted peoples displaced from their ancestral homelands.

In the canon of Catlin's Indian portraits this initial series, done around Cantonment Leavenworth in 1830, is taken as a prelude to the great flowering of work and assured style that would emerge in the next two years. Still, in contrast to other portraits done at this time—right up to his "gift" to Clark of that same year—a full-length likeness of his patron as the deadest white man ever painted—Catlin's first Indian portraits, conceived as a group, speak to us with a collective eloquence. Exiled to no-man's land, these refugees inhabited a swath of frontier officially forbidden to whites and Native Americans alike. The Indians who settled uneasily in the area around Leavenworth formed the vanguard of a human tidal wave of displaced tribal peoples. By the time Catlin first saw them, these sad clumps of Great Lakes "Civilized Tribes" had been further ravaged by their proximity to civilization and all its ills—disease, alcoholism, and the white man's religion.

Three of the artist's Kickapoo subjects (and others of the Potawatomi tribe) are depicted holding prayer sticks, whose invention, manufacture, and marketing is attributed to another Kickapoo leader: "Foremost Man, chief of the Tribe," also known as "the Prophet." As Catlin heard his story, this tribal chief had earlier rebuffed a Methodist missionary, but not before converting to his faith and appropriating both his pastoral message and style. He "commenced preaching and instituted a prayer, which he ingeniously carved on a maple-stick of an inch and a half in breadth, in characters somewhat resembling Chinese letters."* In the artist's ironic telling, Foremost Man is first and foremost an entrepreneur with a healthy dose of charlatanism. A forerunner of the electronic ministry, the Prophet "introduced [the sticks] into every family of the tribe, and into the hands of every individual, and as he has necessarily the manufacturing of them all, he sells them at his own price; and has thus added lucre to fame, and in two essential and effective ways, augmented his influence in his tribe."

In Catlin's *Cock Turkey, Repeating his Prayer*, the Prophet's disciple Cock Turkey is shown reading from the prayer stick in question. His Indian physiognomy is sculpted by the play of light against dark copper skin and high cheekbones; his head, shaved but for the "roach" of black hair, crowds the frame. Even the sitter's hands—always Catlin's weak point—serve to dramatize the preacher's eloquence: One grasps the prayer stick incised with his text, while he gesticulates with the other.

With Catlin's first portraits of 1830, the collision between "civilized" and "savage" mirrors the artist's ambivalence. When he comes to paint tribal leaders whose mixed birth or lofty ambitions led them to adopt European dress, he reverts to the conventional pose of the academic portrait: "a gentleman" interrupted in his study—body turned at a three-quarter angle, legs crossed. In his likeness of Little Chief, a Kaskaskia leader whom Catlin describes as "half-civilized, and, I should

---

* With its short perpendicular endpieces, the prayer stick suggests a Byzantine cross of equal branches.

think, half-breed," the sitter's elegant multicolored silk stock warrants greater painterly attention than do his face and hair: For these features unmodulated brown-and-black wash suffices. To finish off this ambiguous hybrid, Little Chief holds a hatchet, but only the handle of the weapon remains visible; the blade has been "buried" below the picture frame.

While the French actively encouraged intermarriage and cohabitation as a means of extending influence through religious conversion and economic loyalty, Anglo-Indian relations were always haunted by anxiety about "mixed blood." Catlin was prone to insist, in written descriptions of his "half-breed" subjects, upon the evidence of dominant—and thus superior—Caucasian genes. A tiny seminomadic tribe whose origins were in present-day Indiana, the Wea had merged with neighboring Piankshaw, a more settled farming people in 1830, when together they moved from their homeland to Illinois, later to Missouri, and finally to Kansas. Along the way there had been extensive sexual contact with whites. Several Catlin portraits emphasize the sitter's blue or light hazel eyes. In his portrait of a Wea warrior, *Stands by Himself, a Distinguished Brave*, Catlin pays tribute to his youthful subject—shown in full tribal regalia, hair spiked with feathers, hatchet blade exposed, a bearskin thrown over one shoulder—by noting his "intelligent European head."

Earlier a hero had towered over his debased people. "The 'Shawnee Prophet,'" Catlin wrote, "is perhaps one of the most remarkable men who has flourished on these frontiers for some time past." Younger brother of the famous warrior and rebel leader Tecumseh, his name was Ten-squat-a-way ("the Open Door"). He had earned his title of Prophet by predicting an eclipse of the sun, but his fearsome reputation came from continuing his brother's mission: to unite the tribes in the Mississippi Valley in a confederacy to battle white seizures of their territory. In fiery oratory "the Open Door" preached a policy of nonviolence whose most potent weapon would be the boycott: Earlier in the century, Catlin learned, the Prophet had traveled from Mandan to Sioux and other camps along the upper Missouri; at each stop he exhorted his growing band of followers to reject all the goods of white material culture as though infected by the plague: tools, blankets,* clothing, and of course the cancer of alcohol. He was said to have acquired magical powers through his "medicine or mystery fire" and a "string of sacred beans." His acolytes among young braves pledged never to allow the fire to be extinguished and touched the beans to mark their dedication to both brothers' cause.

Defeated in 1811 by the American troops under Gen. William Henry Harrison at the Battle of Tippecanoe, Ten-squat-a-way was pensioned off by the British and forced to flee to Canada. Reduced to the status of fugitive, his power and prestige long gone, he returned to Kansas in 1828. Two years later Catlin painted the fallen leader as both hero and martyr. Blinded in one eye as a child, the chief is shown with that side of his face in three-quarter view: It is raked with red as though clawed by a wild animal, and he stares unseeing into space. A casualty of history, Catlin called the Prophet, adding, "circumstances have destroyed him, as they have many other great men before him; and he now lives respected, but silent and melancholy in his tribe."

GEORGE RETURNED TO St. Louis a man possessed. Beyond the frontier there still lived primitive and heroic tribes untainted by civilized conquerors. So far he had only seen and recorded vestigial and degraded remnants of the real thing. Time was running out.

Money, too, was in short supply. His plans to push farther into Indian country would need a transfusion of cash. By late fall he was

---

* It was widely suspected that blankets infected with smallpox had been deliberately traded to Indian settlements along the Missouri, causing the epidemic that all but destroyed the Mandans, and decimated other tribes.

in Washington. In light of his earlier failure to obtain portrait commissions in the capital, it seems strange that Catlin would now see
the city as a likely source of work. Painting Menominee and Seneca
delegations on their official visits in January and February of the new
year, 1831, would have been work done entirely on speculation; even
if he found buyers for these pictures the sales were unlikely to generate significant income. Still, a Washington visit was always useful
for cementing old contacts, like the helpful Charles Bird King and
Thomas McKenney, or trawling for new patrons in the incoming Jackson administration, such as John C. Eaton, the president's secretary
of war and the overseer of Indian affairs. President Jackson had even
invited the noted portraitist Ralph Earle to live in the White House—a
first for any administration.

Meanwhile George worked on finishing the canvases from his first
forays in the West; the speed with which he was obliged to paint dictated his method. He took as much time as he needed in the field to
model heads and faces (including the symbolic painted stripes and
circles)—the soul of a portrait, as he well knew; later, from detailed
notes, he filled in the rest—robes, headdresses, jewelry, and weapons.

In Albany he rescued Clara from six months of extended visits to
friends and family. The Gregorys' relief at seeing husband and wife
reunited took the form of extending credit for the couple's immediate needs. Clara may have accompanied George back to Washington,
but at that point they appear to have parted ways. Neither Clara nor
George replied to letters from his family, including Eliza, Clara's favorite sister-in law. Putnam sniffed trouble: "We can hardly conceive how
you can well bear the separation for the winter, or that you can both
be contented," he wrote.

But George bore the separation for more than a year. Back in St.
Louis on December 31, 1831, he would remain there for three months,
determined to find sources of patronage that would send him farther
west.

In the course of the six years, on and off, that Catlin would spend in Indian country, he passed days and weeks alone. Yet he was the antithesis of the solitary romantic artist. Along with a gargantuan capacity for work, George was gregarious and a great talker who loved holding forth on myriad subjects (no wonder Putnam Catlin thought his second son would be the successful lawyer in the family). But he was an acute listener, too. He fed his boundless curiosity through questions and their answers: from people more than from books. He knew whom to ask about what he needed or wanted to know: Indians, agents, fur traders, trappers, surveyors, engineers, ethnologists.

In St. Louis his circle of intimates soon included one of the foremost students of the Indian in America, along with the most important patron after Clark that Catlin would ever have. John Dougherty would become Catlin's companion and guide in his explorations on the upper Missouri. They had met at Cantonment Leavenworth, where Dougherty had been appointed Indian agent for the surrounding frontier tribes. Four years older than Catlin, Dougherty was a published ethnologist before becoming a tribal administrator. He had accompanied Stephen H. Long's expedition to the Rockies in 1819–20 as an interpreter joining that legendary band of scientists, engineers, and naturalists (including an artist), in observing the Pawnee, Oto, Iowa, Missouri, and Omaha. In a collaborative report with the naturalist and explorer Thomas Say, Dougherty provided "detailed descriptions of Indian dress, hunting methods, habitations, dances and ceremonials, standards of behavior, and religious beliefs." From his new friend John Dougherty, Catlin obtained an entire education in Northern Plains Indian life.

Dougherty himself had learned the commercial side of his new profession—Indian agent—by working for the legendary Spanish fur trader Manuel Lisa. The responsibilities of his earlier position at Cantonment Leavenworth, where he was charged with administering the "stateless" tribes of the frontier, had brought him face-to-face with the worst sufferings of Indian removal; he had often begged Clark for food and clothing for his freezing, sick, and starving wards. His sympathies notwithstanding, Dougherty also contrived to become a rich man, retiring to a plantation called Multnomah in Missouri, where he became famous for his lavish hospitality.

Maj. Benjamin O'Fallon, Commissioner Clark's nephew, served as the U.S. Indian agent for the Missouri River tribes. Before Catlin arrived in St. Louis, O'Fallon, like his uncle, collected native artifacts, and by the time the artist first visited Missouri, O'Fallon's home, Indian Retreat Plantation, "was a veritable museum of Native American material culture." Encouraged by Clark, O'Fallon promptly purchased or commissioned from the artist a substantial group of pictures, landscapes as well as Indian portraits.[*]

Dougherty and O'Fallon, both prominent in Indian affairs, mirrored the conflict personified by Clark himself: They agonized over the victimization of the Indian, while making fortunes through his sufferings. As Catlin's mentors, patrons, and guides, they provided lessons in denial and doublethink that were their legacy and curse.

[*] In 1894, one of O'Fallon's daughters sold the entire collection—numbering about forty-two pictures, to the Field Museum in Chicago for $1,250. The museum deaccessioned most of them in the 1970s. Of four remaining paintings auctioned on December 1, 2011, one, *Interior of a Mandan Lodge*, sold for $1.3 million, setting a record for a work by George Catlin.

8

BORDER CROSSINGS

Shortly after he arrived in St. Louis, George became attached to a much younger man whose shadowy presence—deliberately obscured, perhaps—would keep emerging in Catlin's new life. Joe Chadwick had just turned nineteen when he and thirty-five-year-old George Catlin, first met. In his published letters from the West, Catlin mentions Joe by name more than fifteen times. With his first appearance, the boy is already "my old friend." Coincidence seemed to connect them in so many ways before they met that George felt he had known the younger man forever.

Their family narratives were so similar, they might have been brothers. Both were the sons of lawyers who struggled to feed large families. Catlins and Chadwicks numbered among the earliest settlers of New England. The Chadwicks, however, had remained in New Hampshire; a road, Chadwick Lane, is now on land belonging to Phillips Exeter Academy, from which Joseph March Chadwick graduated in 1827, aged fifteen, with special mention in English. With no money for further schooling, the family used its political connections to enable Joe, like Julius Catlin, to win a place at West Point.

From the day Joe Chadwick was delivered to the academy on July 1,

1829, it was clear that the decision had been a mistake. In letters to his older sister, Elizabeth, a schoolteacher, the plebe confided his misery: He suffered from paralyzing anxiety over his studies, and homesickness; he found the company of his fellow students so "barren that I fear I will forget how to communicate. . . . My only pleasure is in drawing," he said.

Early in 1831 Chadwick seems to have suffered a breakdown. He took off without permission for New York City, returning only to tell his instructor that he found himself "totally unable to go on." With the formal consent of his father, Joseph Chadwick was allowed to resign his commission, effective April 30, 1831. By November, Joe was settled in St. Louis.

The boy's ecstatic "disbelief" at finding himself "on the West Side of the Mississippi" was tempered by the drudgery of spending long days "confined" as a clerk in his uncle Enoch's new wholesale grocery business, including "five Saturdays," he wrote to his sister. Still, the handsome, artistic youth found time to "dissipate myself at a few parties," and "liked St. Louis better than any place under the sun."

Yet adventure was in the air, and Joe Chadwick was hungry for his share. He longed to visit Santa Fe and hoped to cross the Rocky Mountains in the spring, he told his family. Every man he spoke to was either setting out for—or had just returned from—the territories, including George Catlin.

When he met George, the older man appeared to be a seasoned explorer: He had riveting tales to tell of the tribal council at Prairie du Chien the year before, and of the hundreds of Indians encamped in tipis surrounding Cantonment Leavenworth. Catlin dazzled the young clerk with his stories, illustrated with a private viewing of his first Indian portraits.

The sixteen-year difference in their ages fell away as they discovered all that they had in common: large families and failed fathers burdened with debt and burdening their sons with expectations. In his flight from a military career, his passion for drawing, his air of romantic melancholy, Joe burst into George's life as a reincarnation of Julius, brother and twin soul, dead three years earlier, before they could realize their dream of striking deep into the West together.

During the early months of his friendship with Joe, in 1832, George remained in St. Louis to plan what would be the historic journey of his career. He was to sail with the steamer *Yellow Stone* on the new boat's second attempt to accomplish what it had tried and failed to achieve on its maiden voyage. This time the renovated steamboat would set a record, forging beyond Council Bluffs as far as Fort Union, the northernmost military post on the Missouri River.

Two thousand miles above St. Louis, sited at the confluence of the Yellowstone and Missouri Rivers, Fort Union had been reached by Lewis and Clark traveling by canoe, flatboat, and overland portage thirty years before. The power of steam, however, created as many problems as it solved. No one could say how long the ship and its passengers and crew would be gone. With Clark's patronage, and waving several official letters from Washington, George Catlin was traveling as a guest of the boat's owners, Pierre Chouteau, Jr.—called "cadet," or second son—nephew of Auguste, the dynasty's patriarch, and more distantly of the Chouteaus' principal, John Jacob Astor, founding head of the American Fur Company. There was no possibility that Joe Chadwick, the twenty-year-old clerk paid a pittance by his uncle, could command the time or money required for a trip with no date of return. He and George would not see each other for two years, while the feelings that bound them grew stronger.

ALL ST. LOUIS was on holiday—or so it appeared from the crowds lining the quays at midday on March 26, 1832. Even clerks were given time off to wave "bon voyage" to the *Yellow Stone* and its crew and passengers. Improvements made since its last trip did nothing to solve the major challenge of river navigation on the upper Missouri: It needed a lighter hull for greater mobility in skimming sandbars and snags—branches rising from trees submerged invisibly under the mud-colored water. But a fresh coat of blazing white paint with yellow trim covered the entire boat, including a new deck, added to accommodate comfortable cabins for ladies and well-appointed public rooms.

Both mechanical fine-tuning and new amenities had been rushed to be ready for the most important passenger on board: On this sailing the *Yellow Stone* carried *le patron*, Pierre Chouteau, Jr., himself, along with several of his most important agents and traders, first among them Maj. John F. A. Sanford, subagent to the Mandan, and fiancé of Chouteau's daughter Emilie, also on board. Now all passengers, distinguished and anonymous, massed on the starboard deck to watch the boat cast off; to the tooting of horns, shiny black smokestacks (called "pipes" on the river) belched clouds of white steam, while an oversize American flag billowed above the company's proud pennant.

George Catlin's name does not appear on the ship's manifest, but neither do the names of fellow passengers also known to have made this particular voyage. The crew, on the other hand, along with a complement of Chouteau's more powerful agents, all seem to have been inscribed—sometimes only by first name: We know the master (or captain), mate, engineers, pilot, steersmen, carpenter, deckhands, steward, cooks, and cabin boy. Firemen (by tradition, black, whether slaves or freedmen), are listed by name and job description; other crew members' names are noted but with no mention of what kind of work they performed.

Several of Chouteau's chieftains, however, are listed by name when they were well-documented as being elsewhere: Kenneth McKenzie, the tough high-living Scot who ruled Fort Union, appears on the manifest when in fact he was onshore midway between his home base and St. Louis to welcome his boss upriver. But this was no slip of the pen.

A chorus of pleading, directed to the federal government, had long demanded an end to the scourge of the unlawful sale of alcohol to tribes, especially to "frontier Indians" whose settlements were near military trading posts, where alcoholism was rife. The voices of the reformers—both religious and political—had finally been heard. A new law limited the amount of whiskey, as measured in numbers of barrels that could be carried aboard riverboats, to a daily allotment for each crew member; any quantity above that would be confiscated as destined for illegal sale to Indians. For this trip the *Yellow Stone*'s hold carried fifteen hundred gallons of whiskey; word was out that government inspectors now meant business. Ingenuity was needed to get around the new regulations, which is said to explain the inflated ship's manifest, naming both crew and the company's upper Missouri agents in contrast to carelessly listed passengers, some of whose names didn't appear at all.*

It would take the *Yellow Stone* three months after leaving its St. Louis berth to travel two thousand miles to Fort Union. Their days on the water, numbering nearly one hundred, Catlin recalled, were filled with "almost insurmountable difficulties which continually oppose the *voyageur* on this turbid stream." No obstacle, however, was so great that "by degrees [it was not] overcome by the indefatigable zeal of Mr. Chouteau, a gentleman of great perseverance, and part proprietor of the boat. To the politeness of this gentleman I am indebted for my passage from St. Louis to this place, and I had also the pleasure of his *company*, with that of Major Sanford, the government agent for the Missouri Indians."

With these sentences, Catlin paid homage to his host and made full disclosure—or, as "full" as he was able to make at the time. What he could not see were the pitfalls of co-option, the insidious ways in

---

* Disguising whiskey sales destined for Indians soon became more sophisticated. Distilling equipment was shipped in parts that were easy to hide amid all the other boiler room machinery, allowing whiskey to be manufactured and sold on the spot, using local ingredients.

which favors rendered Catlin the artist by his hosts, the Chouteaus, would be called in, pressuring him to put their activities in the best light and muting any exposure of whiskey trading to Indians: There were no free rides on the *Yellow Stone*. The fortunes of the American Fur Company and its owners and agents depended upon providing the tribes with drink and slaughtering their basic food, buffalo.

Among George's fellow passengers on the *Yellow Stone* was the young Assiniboin warrior Wi-jún-jon ("Pigeon's Egg Head"), called "the Light." Catlin had first painted him in 1831 on the latter's departure from St. Louis to Washington, where he was part of a delegation that was an official guest of the secretary of war.

"Sullen as death" was the artist's first impression of his sitter: "In his nature's uncowering pride, he stood a perfect model; but superstition had hung a lingering curve upon his lip, and pride had stiffened it into contempt." So much for the native's religious belief, which elsewhere Catlin professed to find morally superior to any "civilized" creed. At that point the Light's appearance, confirming both his glamour and heroism, still set him above his white contemporaries: "Dressed in his native costume, which was classic and exceedingly beautiful," Catlin notes, "his leggings and shirt were of the mountain-goat skin, richly garnished with quills of the porcupine, and fringed with locks of scalps, taken from his enemies' heads. Over these floated his long hair in plaits, that fell nearly to the ground."

Now, one year later, the Light was returning from Washington via St. Louis to Fort Union, where several thousand of his tribesmen had pitched their tipis, ready to greet him as he disembarked from the steamship. To Catlin's amazement he had exchanged native dress for "a complete suit *en militaire*, a colonel's uniform of blue, presented to him by the President of the United States, with a beaver hat and feather, with epaulettes of gold—with sash and belt, and broad sword, with high-heeled boots—with a keg of whiskey under his arm and a blue umbrella in his hand."

Catlin's judgment is graphically expressed in the double portrait *Pigeon's Egg Head (The Light) Going to and Returning from Washington* (1837–39), painted (or completed) five to seven years after this shipboard encounter. Compared with the impassive tribal leader, rendered sketchily in profile, the Anglicized Indian, seen almost from the back, is depicted in meticulous detail: With his stovepipe hat, tightly rolled umbrella, deployed fan, and a cigarette dangling from his lips, the Light has become a living caricature, similar to the cartoons to be published during Reconstruction, which portrayed former slaves as apes sporting loud checkered suits, complete with watch fobs and bowler hats.

Dressed in his increasingly tattered uniform, Pigeon's Egg Head told—and retold—his hour of glory in the nation's capital, but skepticism soon replaced wonder on the part of his fellow tribesmen. Within a few years he was killed as an impostor by a young warrior. His murder points an accusing finger—but not one directed at Wi-jún-jon's aspirations; his finery, along with the status it conferred, had been provided by his hosts in Washington. The "double" in this famous double portrait was not confined to the subject. Catlin's own uneasy mix of censure and sympathy reflects a conflict that would follow him to the end of his life. His writing often indulges a patronizing—even mocking—view of the Indian, doubtless because this played well with many readers of a popular newspaper such as the *New York Commercial Advertiser*, where his writings from the West first appeared in the form of "Letters." In his art, though, Catlin's double portrait of Pigeon's Egg Head remains an anomaly among his images of the Indian. Individually and collectively they bear witness to the ties that bound painter and subject.

ONE OF THE *Yellow Stone's* first stops was at a Ponca village some three hundred miles southeast of Fort Pierre or midway between St. Louis and their final destination of Fort Union. The Ponca settlement

was among those whose proximity to the frontier made the inhabitants vulnerable to the ravages of whiskey and smallpox, conveyed
by traders who traveled from one Indian village to the next. A more
stealthy destroyer of their way of life was the skin trade. As Catlin
noted, the tribe numbered "not more than four or five hundred, of
which at least two-thirds were women," the disparity explained by
"the continual losses which their men suffer." The depletion of the
buffalo, their main source of food and clothing, "killed or driven out
by the approach of white men, who wanted their skins," forced the
tribal males to travel ever greater distances, thus "exposing their lives
to their more numerous enemies" far from home.

George invited the Ponca chief, Shoo-de-ga-cha ("Smoke"), to be
his guest on the docked steamboat. Sitting with Catlin on the *Yellow
Stone's* deck, the Indian leader described his people's still-unfolding
downward spiral to oblivion. Catlin was impressed by his guest's
objectivity: "The poverty and distress of his nation, related to me with
great coolness and distinction . . . with the method of a philosopher,
[he] predicted the certain and rapid extinction of his tribe . . . which
he had not then power to avert."

Though moved by the stoical nobility of the Ponca leader, Catlin
seems to miss the point of his powerlessness: In the face of the white
man's planned disposal of his people, Shoo-de-ga-cha had no choice
but to accept its collective fate. George, however, saw his tragedy
as territorial: "Poor, noble chief; who was equal to, and worthy of a
greater empire!" And Catlin likened him to "Caius Marius, weeping
over the ruins of Carthage."*

---

* Catlin almost certainly plucked this comparison from a well-known painting by John Vanderlyn, *Marius Amid the Ruins of Carthage* (1808). Made popular
through engravings, it depicts the Roman consul Caius Marius weeping over the
destruction of an outpost of his empire but not, significantly, over its inhabitants,
who remain invisible.

It was too soon into his journey for George to grasp the irony of their situation: Indian chief and white artist, surveying the sad "little cluster of wigwams" from the *Yellow Stone* deck, were both guests of its owner Pierre Chouteau, Jr., who had filled the ship's hold with as much contraband spirits as could be slipped past inspectors; all the while Catlin's hurried notes recorded the blows that had reduced Shoo-de-ga-cha's tribe, which "had once been powerful and happy. . . . [H]is people had foolishly become fond of *fire-water* (whiskey) and had given away everything in their country for it—that it had destroyed many of his warriors, and soon would destroy the rest."

The Ponca's reduced numbers made them easy prey for the tribes around them; they were now

> met and killed by the Sioux on the North, by the Pawnees on the West; and by the Osages and Konzas on the South; and still more alarmed from the constant advance of the pale faces—their enemies from the East, with whiskey and small-pox, which had already destroyed four-fifths of his tribe, and soon would impoverish, and at last destroy the remainder of them.

For the length of his long life, Catlin would shift moral gears; like the lawyer he had once been, he could be sharply prosecutorial, assigning blame for the destruction of the Indians to white greed, but just as often he reverted to airy platitudes about the inexorable march of history, to which he was a mere bystander who "contemplated the noble races of red men . . . melting away at the approach of civilization." His Christianity, too, was a source of ambivalence about the "savage race." If George never experienced the evangelical conversion that his mother and two of his brothers professed at this time, his basic faith never seems to have wavered. Even as he vaunted the ways in which Indians must be seen as morally and spiritually superior to civilized Christians, pointing to their shared property and sense of communal responsibility of each for all, he continued to harbor the belief that, without accepting Jesus Christ, they would be doomed as much by their failure to be saved as by the white man's iniquity.

IT WAS TOO late to save the Indian, but his lands, emptied of all but token tribal remnants, could redeem their appropriation through preservation. Catlin became the first to urge that large tracts of wilderness be set aside in perpetuity by government decree,

> where the world could see for ages to come, the native Indian in his classic attire, galloping his wild horse, with sinewy bow, and shield and lance, amid the fleeting herds of elks and buffaloes. What a beautiful and thrilling specimen for America to preserve and hold up to the view of her refined citizens and the world, in future ages! A *nation's Park*, containing man and beast, in all the wild and freshness of their nature's beauty!

Enlightened as Catlin was about the need to protect the wilderness, the role of the Indian in his scheme has more in common with that of wild animals in an "environmentally correct" zoo: Their captivity disguised by skillful landscaping, lions, free of cages, roam an illusory veldt. The artist's proposal for "a *nation's Park*" seems closer to America's first theme park.

CATLIN'S STOP AT the Ponca village became the model for a lifelong process involving art and science, observation and invention, painting and written notes—thousands of pages of description, often used to fill in the detail of a broadly outlined portrait, or a sketchy visual record of games and ceremonies, buffalo hunts and horseraces.

His words tumble breathlessly as he tries to pack in every detail of all that he experienced in those few days. Everything amazed him, especially what he observed from close contact with Indian women and girls—starting with their tattoos. The neck and arms of Hee-la 'h-dee ("the Pure Fountain"), the chief's wife, were covered with these dense patterns of colors, "done by pricking into the skin, gunpowder and vermilion."

Even to members of his own family, George could appear puritanical. He neither drank nor smoked, and more than many young bachelors, he seemed constrained by the sexual taboos of his time and class. Predictably he now found himself fascinated—obsessed, even—by the freedom from inhibition of the "savage race," in particular the Indian's exaltation of male sexuality; in a culture that took phallocentrism for granted, "the more, the better" operated as both belief and practice.

The Ponca chief's son, aged eighteen, whose portrait, along with that of his father, George painted, had "distinguished himself in a singular manner the day before our steamer reached their village, by taking to him *four wives in one day!*" the artist reported. His proud father had provided him with horses and other gifts as presents to his future fathers-in-law. Catlin found especially fascinating that most brides were between twelve and fifteen years old, but he added that girls as young as eleven became wives and that "the juvenile mother has been blest with her first offspring at the age of twelve!" A certain envy threads through George's writing about these barely pubescent brides. Seeking to allay the "surprise and almost incredulity" of his readers, he contrasts Indian couples favorably with their Christian counterparts, especially "the facility in dissolving the marriage contract in this country, which does away with one of the most serious difficulties which lies in the way in the civilized world, and calculated greatly to retard its consummation." So, too, did he admire that these child brides were allowed to "flourish" unspoiled by "education and accomplishments"—all of which suggests that painful contrasts were on his mind.

———

SHORTLY AFTER THE expedition's visit to the Ponca village, the *Yellow Stone* ran aground on a sandbar. A day's work of sounding convinced the pilots of the impossibility of progress until there should be a rise in the river, and they remained there—as becalmed as the Ancient Mariner—for an entire week.

For Pierre Chouteau time was money. He now set off on foot with twenty men to cross two hundred miles of plains to Fort Pierre, at the foot of Teton River, in present-day Idaho. "To this expedition I immediately attached myself," Catlin recalled, sounding as exuberant as he did on the day they left. Knowing there would be a great Sioux encampment waiting to see the legendary steamship, "I packed on the backs, and in the hands of several of the men, such articles for painting, as I might want; canvases, paints, and brushes, with my sketch-book slung on my back, and my rifle in my hand, I started off with them."

More than the river journey, the arduous portage plunged Catlin into a little-known danger of the West: the psychological assault upon the traveler faced with the vast distances and emptiness of the Great Plains; the "level prairie, without a tree or a bush in sight to relieve the painful monotony." He walked for six or seven days, "testing the muscles of my legs," and trusting to the experience of their half-breed and French Canadian guides, "whose lives are mostly spent in this way, leading a novice, a cruel, and almost killing journey." He reached the point where he "felt like giving up . . . and throwing myself on the ground in hopeless despair"; other fellow travelers had collapsed entirely, bringing their leaders to do an abrupt about-face and convene a "war council" about the inexperienced explorers' tortured feet, but as soon as one of their guides showed Catlin how to "*turn my toes in*" as the Indians did when walking, progress resumed, with George "taking the lead of the whole party, which I constantly led until our journey was completed."

This was the testing experience he had sought. By the time their little group arrived at Fort Pierre Catlin had turned defeat into triumph; both his senses and his feet had survived.

Fort Pierre, at the mouth of the Teton River, had been named for the steamboat's owner and most prominent passenger—an exceptional honor for a civilian and a Frenchman at that (Catlin still referred to him as M[onsieur]). To welcome Chouteau, Major Sanford, and their guest, George Catlin, the Sioux had prepared a feast of dog meat, "the most honourable food that can be presented to a stranger, and glutted with the more delicious food of beavers' tails, and buffalo tongues." Suffering from cabin fever after weeks on the river, with only short breaks on land, Catlin was much enraptured by the tranquil rituals of Sioux hospitality as they unfolded; their reception was "luxurious," he emphasized, "for this is truly the land of Epicures."

Other visitors found Fort Pierre a dismal place. Steadily stripped of native trees, the timberless bluffs and dome-shaped hills protruding from endless prairie resembled pinkly bald pates with patches of verdant hair. George, however, could imagine "no sight more pleasing," he wrote of his new Eden. He found its situation idyllic, "in the center of one of the Missouri's most beautiful plains, and hemmed in by a series of gracefully undulating grass-covered hills on all sides; rising like a series of terraces, to the summit level of the prairies, some three or four hundred feet in elevation, which then stretches off in an apparently boundless ocean of . . . swelling waves and fields of green."

IN THE NEXT year Catlin would paint dozens of small landscapes, magical works that seem to have been composed with a camera eye. Zooming from long shot to close-up, he establishes his narrative with a panorama of tipis, painted from the ramparts of Fort Pierre. (Six hundred Sioux families were encamped below, he reported precisely.) Observed from his favorite heights, the scene recalls the tents of a medieval army, the more so when the artist added figures of horses and their riders streaking across the canvas. Occasionally the single microscopic figure of the artist himself appears, to give a sense of scale, but also to express a feeling of oneness with nature he now experienced for the first time. He is no longer the unmoored tourist from the East overcome with dread at being "out of sight of land." He loves this country with such abandon that seeing himself as a speck in the boundlessness of sky and prairie feels like a natural state.

Tension between the closely observed phenomena of nature—what one writer has called Catlin's "eye of the geologist"—and the state of transcendence made visible that characterizes the Romantic landscape, confirms these small-scale scenes along the upper Missouri as among the most original visionary works of the century. But Catlin is no Hudson River School romantic let loose on the Missouri. In some works an eerie shadowless light illuminates the striated colors of his cliffs, rising above grass of an almost radioactive green. There are landscapes that seem held in an airless state of suspended animation, waiting for a coming apocalypse: an explosion, a blinding light, and a mushroom cloud.

Whether he felt intimations of Armageddon, as proclaimed by the fiery preachers of his backwoods youth, or the post–Ice Age calm of a landscape from which glaciers seem to have just retreated, this was Catlin's country. Unlike the cities where he had felt lost, ignored, or dismissed, in this emptiness he found himself reborn. Exploring alone what lay beyond the river: "I often landed my skiff and mounted the green carpeted bluffs, whose soft grassy tops invited me to recline, where I was at once lost in contemplation," he recalled. ". . . A place where the mind could think volumes; but the tongue must be silent that would *speak* and the hand palsied that would *write*."

In everything he now saw, in the "enameled plains" and "velvet-covered hills" of the prairie, he found the "redeeming beauty" he had only glimpsed earlier, when the *Yellow Stone* first escaped the river's shallows. He felt a bliss he had never imagined.

9

THE FUR FORTRESS

"I arrived at this place yesterday in the steamer 'Yellow Stone,' after a voyage of nearly three months from St. Louis, a distance of two thousand miles."

Catlin's spare lead sentence introduced his first report, headed "Letter—No. 2, Mouth of Yellow Stone, *Upper Missouri*, 1832," which appeared in the *New York Commercial Advertiser*. A few lines later, though, he succumbed to the high drama of the approach to Fort Union "under the continued roar of cannon for half an hour, and the shrill yells of the half-affrighted savages who lined the shores," and promising his readers, in the new tradition of "you-are-there" reporting, "sketches of scenes that I have witnessed, and *am witnessing.*"

To the terrified natives the *Yellow Stone* "belching steam" appeared not as a vessel to move passengers and goods but as a deadly weapon. As Catlin's vivid account makes plain, their perception was attributable neither to naïveté nor to ignorance of modern technology, but to an accurate reading of the ship's message to the Indian population.

"We had on board one twelve-pound cannon* and three or four

---

* Catlin appears to have been unaware that the weight, as given, refers to the ball and not the cannon.

eight-pound swivels, which we were taking up to arm the Fur Company's Fort at the mouth of the Yellow Stone," he explained, "and at the approach to every village they were all discharged several times in rapid succession." As word of the ship's arrival spread, the Indians streamed toward the river; in their "utter confusion . . . some of them laid their faces to the ground, and cried to the Great Spirit—some shot their horses and dogs, and sacrificed them to appease [Him] whom they conceived was offended—some deserted their villages and ran to the tops of the bluffs some miles distant." From this vantage point they tried to see what fate had befallen their chiefs who, like Smoke, Catlin's Ponca guest downriver, had ventured aboard to treat with the vessel's masters. The crowding at the cliff's edge precipitated its own catastrophe, when the onlookers "were instantly thrown neck and heels over each other's heads and shoulders—men, women and children, and dogs—sage, sachem, old and young—all in a mass, at the frightful discharge of the steam from the escape-pipe, which the captain of the boat let loose upon them for his own fun and amusement."

CONFUSION, POSSIBLY INTENTIONAL, surrounds the term "fort" used to describe the chain of well-defended civilian outposts strung the length of the Mississippi and Missouri Rivers. Military in plan and structure, they were fortresses of fur, the "soft gold" of the upper Missouri. Tribes camped beneath the walls while their leaders traded in designated rooms within. Here, items of Western manufacture; gunpowder, calico, cookware, ornaments of tin and glass, were exchanged for peltries.

On his way upriver Catlin had visited Fort Pierre, but that makeshift trading post hardly prepared him for the commanding presence and civilized life of Fort Union, their final destination. Manned by forty or fifty men, the fort stabled 150 horses; cannons pointed visibly from the porthole-shaped windows in the bastions. Every aspect declared that in the "principal head-quarters and depôt of the Fur Company's business in this region," America's commercial, military, and national interests were one. It was there that Kenneth McKenzie, commandant of Fort Union, ruled as "King of the Upper Missouri."

To special guests who could be useful to his enterprises, such as George Catlin, artist and journalist, McKenzie extended his famous hospitality that enhanced the fort's reputation as an oasis of civilization, starting with their host's residence, whose eight glazed windows were the talk of all visitors. Indeed, Catlin's first "Letter" from Fort Union to appear in the *New York Commercial Advertiser* paid tribute to the post's reigning monarch. "He has, with the same spirit of liberality and politeness with which Mons. Pierre Chouteau treated me on my passage up the river, pronounced me welcome at his table which groans under the luxuries of the country," Catlin wrote, "with buffalo meat and tongues, with beavers' tails and marrow-fat." These delicacies were washed down by free-flowing spirits. "Good cheer and good living . . . and good wine . . . for a bottle of Madeira and one of excellent Port are set in a pail of ice every day, and exhausted at dinner."

One of the traders attached to the fort, Charles Larpenteur, was a notable teetotaler, who "instead of getting drunk in his leisure time, kept a diary." He recorded his awe on first entering the dining room, where the "extremely well-dressed" McKenzie, dazzling in a top hat and swallowtail, presided over the head table, "splendidly set" with snowy linen and "served by two waiters, one a Negro." Everyone at this privileged seating, which included the clerks and the manager's guests, was also obliged to wear a coat—even at breakfast, served as late as 9:00 a.m., as McKenzie was not an early riser.

OPENHEARTED AND STRAIGHTFORWARD, Catlin was inclined to take people as they came. Where others might have been wary, he was always eager to believe the best of men in positions of power who, recognizing ambition and talent, took him under their wing.

"Mr. McKenzie is a kind-hearted and high-minded Scotchman," George declared to his readers. But most of those who knew the all-powerful ruler of Fort Union would have recognized in George's description only the man's country of origin. Born in Scotland, Kenneth McKenzie had come with his family to Canada as a teenager and learned the business of fur as a clerk for the Northwest Company. In 1822 McKenzie moved to St. Louis and within a few years had become head of the Columbia Fur Company. By 1827 he parlayed his unmatched knowledge of the finances of the fur trade to persuade John Jacob Astor's American Fur Company to buy him out—at his asking price—and appoint him head of the newly formed "Upper Missouri Outfit," one of the company's divisions. McKenzie now commanded a territory larger than many European countries. His financial empire was still more imposing: He presided over a trade worth millions of dollars annually in peltries.

The diplomatic skills McKenzie displayed in dealing with Indians were bolstered by an immovable confidence which had led him to establish Fort Union in the heart of Assinboin country. There he had converted a hostile tribe to allies. Toward any signs of white competition, McKenzie was infamous for a ruthless competitive rage that refused to quit until the adversary was destroyed. (He reputedly never forgave Astor for buying out a rival Scot, Robert Campbell, when, in his view, they could have ruined him at no cost at all.)

This was the frontier, however, and McKenzie's absolute control of the upper Missouri was owed as much to his physical endurance and skills with horses and guns. There was nothing that any trapper, mountain man, or Indian agent could do that Kenneth McKenzie couldn't do better. Small and wiry, Catlin's host was famous as a tireless rider who would take on any horse, and a crack shot whose feats as a buffalo hunter were legendary.

Shortly after George's arrival, the fort's depleted larder required a group to "go for meat." "Rallying some five or six of his best hunters, [McKenzie] leads the party," George reported, "mounted on his favourite buffalo horse . . . trailing a light and short gun in his hand, such a one as he can most easily reload whilst his horse is at full speed."

Catlin had hunted since he was a boy, and he was used to spending days on horseback. Still, the buffalo hunt was new to him, a collective effort with its own traditions and even language. In the stylized choreography of a bullfight, the riders stripped themselves and their horses of any extraneous encumbrances, then approached the buffalo "all of us abreast, upon a slow walk, and in a straight line towards the herd, until they discover us and run." At this point McKenzie's men mounted their horses. When they discovered the hunters, the herd "wheeled and laid their course in a mass. At this instant we started! (and all must start, for no one could check the fury of those steeds at that moment of excitement,) and away all sailed, and over the prairie flew, in a cloud of dust which was raised by their trampling hoofs."

George was after other game: With brush and paint he would bring this great creature, the bull buffalo, as near to extinction as the Indian—back alive.

Under his massive dark coat the great beast's eyes, whites gleaming through the encompassing blackness of the mane, deliver, in Catlin's great bison portraits, extremes of emotion that the artist rarely plumbs in his stoical Indian subjects. Captured in primal roars of rage, terror, or pain, his dumb beasts express the essence of tragedy: an awareness of their fate.

Led by the intrepid McKenzie, Catlin "discovered a huge bull whose shoulders towered above the whole band, and I picked my way through the crowd to get alongside of him." Galloping neck and neck with the buffalo, Catlin shot him in the shoulder and breast. The two adversaries then faced each other, George recognizing that his wounded prey had strength for one last and fatal spasm of wrath. Yet despite the "fury" in the buffalo's eyes, "I found the sagacity of my horse alone enough to keep me out of reach of danger; and I drew from my pocket my sketch-book, laid my gun across my lap, and commenced taking his likeness."

Like the matador who goads the wounded bull with the flaring movements of his cape driving him toward the "moment of truth" when he will deliver the final dagger thrust, Catlin prolonged the beast's agony for the sake of his art. "I rode around him and sketched him in various attitudes, sometimes he would lie down, and I would then sketch him; then throw my cap at him, and rousing him on his legs, rally a new expression, and sketch him again."

This was art as blood sport, and Catlin the writer liked to remind his readers of what Catlin the painter had risked. From these encounters, fraught with danger, he had captured "some invaluable sketches of this grim-visaged monster, who knew not that he was standing for his likeness." He felt no need to enlighten his fellow hunters about his own ends: fixing his prey on canvas.

Instead he savored the theatrical dimension of the party's triumphal return: After the six hunters' "parched throats were . . . moistened" by several bottles of wine, "the gate of the Fort was thrown open, and the procession of carts and packhorses laden with buffalo meat made its entrée; gladdening the hearts of a hundred women and children, and tickling the noses of as many hungry dogs and puppies, who were stealing in and smelling at the tail" of the convoy, watching as "the door of the ice-house was thrown open, the meat was discharged into it."

What Catlin brought back alive from the hunt remain among the great animal portraits of all time: The bloodied glare of the huge doomed bison spares us nothing of his agony. In contrast the subjects of his Indian Gallery, a portrait of collective tragedy, derive their power from reticence: what they refuse to reveal of suffering and loss. "Every artist paints himself," Leonardo declared. The bison and their native hunters stand as Catlin's self-portraits.

10

"WHITE MEDICINE MAN"

George had proved himself a hunter of heart and courage in pursuit of the buffalo. His host, however, was aware that the artist was after bigger game. Before Catlin arrived McKenzie had already designated one of the fort's two-story white stone bastions as George's field studio. Its elevation and the openings pierced on four sides of the blocky structure ensured more light than could be found in any building inside the fort. As he set up his easel the artist could see a sweeping stretch of land and water that led from the tribal encampment below the walls to the blurry confluence of the Yellowstone and Missouri Rivers and, thanks to the latter's low-lying banks, to a lake faintly visible beyond. As though waking to a dream, George now found himself "with my paint pots and canvas, snugly ensconced, in one of the bastions of the Fort, which I occupy as a painting room."

Then, according to Catlin, word went out to a "host of wild, incongruous spirits—chiefs and sachems—warriors, braves, and women and children of different tribes—of Crows and Blackfeet— Assineboins [sic]—and Crees or Knisteneaux [sic] encamped about the Fort" that a white man, one possessed of great "medicine," or power, invited them to enter the gated enclosure of the fort, to climb the stairs of the bastion to the room where the white shaman sat on his cannon, fixing an empty square of fabric tightly to the top of a three-legged wooden stand. There they could observe how—as the artist moved a brush and colors around the cloth—the familiar features and expression of one of their number, including all his trophies of battle and rank, would miraculously appear.

To the supernatural powers of a medicine man Catlin now added the attributes of a peacemaker. Mornings and evenings, he reported, "these wild and jealous spirits who all meet here to be amused, and to pay me signal honours; but [also] gaze upon each other, sending their sidelong looks of deep-rooted hatred and revenge around the group." And he predicted that dark thoughts would soon erupt into acts of violence, when "death and grim destruction will visit back those looks upon each other, when these wild spirits again are loose and free to breathe and act upon the plains." Anticipating just such an outbreak, McKenzie had decreed that upon entering the gates of the enclosure, all weapons must be deposited in the fort's arsenal.

Thanks to Catlin an armistice of art was in effect. Leaders of warring tribes now crowded into the room where the artist was at work on what would be his most famous portrait: *Buffalo Fat Back.* Stu-Mick-Sucks, first chief of the Blackfoot nation, was one of Catlin's first portraits as artist in residence at Fort Union. For the tribal leader the taking of his likeness was also an opportunity to remind any adversaries present of his superiority: "Whilst sitting for his picture," the artist observed, "he has been surrounded by his own braves and warriors, and also gazed at by his enemies, the Crows and the Knisteneaux [Cree], Assineboins and Ojibbeways," whose representatives "have laid all day around the sides of my room, reciting to each other the battles they have fought, and pointing to the scalp-locks, worn as proof of their victories."

Catlin was alert to the exceptional—even historic—nature of this particular cessation of tribal hostilities; chiefs and warriors had gathered in his room for a common purpose. "This is a curious scene to witness," he reported of the eerie truce that obtained in the name of art,

> when one sits in the midst of such inflammable and combustible materials, brought together, unarmed, for the first time in their lives; peaceably and calmly recounting over the deeds of their lives; and smoking their pipes upon it, when a few weeks or days will bring them on the plains again, where the war-cry will be raised, and their deadly bows will again be drawn on each other.

His sitters, tribal chiefs and their entourages, were no less aware of the artist's extraordinary role. Above the murmur of voices a sense of the sacred pervaded the improvised studio where the foremost men of their tribes waited their turn to be captured by the medicine man's brush. The artist's rituals, as he faced his easel, adding strange-smelling water to the colors on his palette, invited comparison with the well-known priest Father de Smet. The Jesuit traveled the forts and settlements of the upper Missouri, performing marriages and baptizing babies before his portable altar. In the painter's potions, brushes, and palette, the assembled chiefs and sachems saw an animistic power closer to their own apprehension of the priest, whose sacred medicine bags contained the holiest of herbs, animal remains, powders, and oils. The artist too might be the mediator between this world and the next: "The operations of my brush," Catlin observed, "are mysteries of the highest order to these red sons of the prairie, and my room [their] earliest and latest place of concentration."

George would later claim that lingering suspicions about him, the "White Medicine Man" conjuring likenesses from the "operations" of his "*mysterious* brush," were fomented by envious tribal practitioners of healing and exorcism. Thus Catlin's portrait of a Blackfoot medicine man may have been a political offering to placate an adversary.

Half human, half animal, it is among Catlin's most dynamic—and terrifying—likenesses. Caught in motion, the figure, one leg raised, head and neck completely covered by a wolf mask, conjures the sound of rattles and of chanting, of screams and cries.

Among the tribes neighboring the fort, the status conferred by sitting to Catlin for a portrait trumped any dark messages about evil spells, fatal illnesses, or (as was feared from later photographers) stolen souls. Catlin's account of his sitters, lounging and telling stories while lying about the painting room, evokes members of an elite men's club. Primal vanity dispelled fear. Buoyed by pride in this marvelous tribute to their power and prestige, the tribal leaders saw their distinction confirmed by finely detailed symbols of bravery and prowess in battle: the black scalp locks that trim the seams of a white buffalo-skin shirt; horns mounted upon a fur headdress; the exquisite workmanship lavished upon wives' "rich and costly dresses," as the artist described them—each Catlin portrait fed the demand for others.

The month Catlin spent in Fort Union proved the fulfillment of his dreams, his prodigious talent and productivity facilitated by help and hospitality on every side. His best portraits from this period have the sheen of authority that comes when an artist, closing the gap between vision and achievement, fully inhabits his subject. In these images, the familiar and the strange, the intimate and the formal, achieve a balance rare in portraiture of any period or subject. Artist and sitters seem to share a secret: They were outsiders who came to trust one another. The images, with their oddly neutral settings, claim a privileged space where the white painter and his Indian subjects have stepped out of history.

IN ONE MONTH Catlin painted—either in his studio or exploring outside the fort—an incredible sixty-six portraits; when scenes of buffalo, of Indian life in the settlements, together with uninhabited landscapes are added, the total number climbs to 135. He left some works, usually portraits, unfinished, with details of costume or even faces to be completed during the coming winter, which he planned—reluctantly—to spend back east.

Speed was his muse. He was running out of money and painting supplies. Aware that his time on the upper Missouri was drawing to a close, George now pushed himself to frenzied efforts. His output alone suggests that not a single tribal emissary who appeared at the door of the painting room, arrayed in gorgeous ceremonial or battle attire, was turned away. Although he reported that women and children were among those who crowded into the space, they were more likely to have been present in the painting room as spectators, their likenesses taken by Catlin closer to their homes in the settlements below.

Gazing from their portraits with the gravity of children, the Indian girls painted by Catlin look barely pubescent. Baby fat together with large breasts (the latter heavily outlined by the artist) seem to have been paired attractions of these child brides. Literally trophy wives, the youngest and most alluring would have brought the highest price in horses and other valuables to their fathers. (They could also be resold if their husbands tired of them.)

Catlin did not limit himself to brushes and pigments to record what he saw. His portraits derive much of their force from a simplified facture, with large thinly brushed areas or blocks of unmodulated color: As a writer and privileged witness to history, however, he would not omit a single fact or observation. It's his words that evoke in sensuous detail the luxury of the young wives' exquisite attire: The Mandan chief's favorite, Mink, as befits her name, is robed in a "mountain sheep skin dress, ornamented with porcupine quills, beads and elks' teeth." She wears a wide cuff bracelet, dangling earrings, and a finely worked necklace of chains and multicolored stones.

Highlights from his field notes became the popular "Letters" for readers of the *New York Commercial Advertiser;* these in turn were expanded for the two volumes of *Letters and Notes*, and they remain a crucial source for detailed descriptions of the tribes' material culture; tipis and lodges, clothing and ornaments; but also skin color, hair style, sacred rituals, sports, and games.

No reader of his exhaustive written observations will be surprised to learn that, through the first half of the twentieth century, Catlin was listed as an "artist and ethnologist." He qualified as an early "participant-observer," before the professional transformation of anthropology from an "amateur" interest into a branch of the social sciences. He was intrigued by the terra-cotta shade of the pipestone from which the prized calumets were carved, and he became obsessed with their source, a sacred quarry in present-day Minnesota. A century before Claude Lévi-Strauss examined tribal cultures in terms of the cooked and raw foods they ate, Catlin reported from the front lines of feasts of stewed dog and the delicacy of steaming organ meat straight from the disemboweled animal.

He was honest, too, about his own agenda of acquisition: To furnish his future Indian Gallery, George purchased or bartered for the best examples of native craft, such as the white buffalo-skin robe worn by the Mandan chief Mah-to-toh-pa, or Four Bears, when Catlin painted him. Already he planned to exhibit the robe alongside his portrait of the great chief wrapped in its flowing whiteness. The artist's written account would thus provide his own objective evidence as scientific "proof" of what he had recorded on canvas. Then, in an early example of "appropriation art," Catlin added his own colored drawings to the robe. Rendered in a pastiche of native pictographic style, his contributions followed the stylistic lead of Chief Four Bears—himself a noted tribal artist—in tracing a linear narrative to evoke the great warrior's major victories.

Once Catlin fixed upon a coveted object of desire, he would not let go. He had purchased another chief's "beautiful costume," the same worn in his full-length portrait. George could not initially induce him

to part with his headdress of "war eagles' quills and ermine, extending quite down to his feet." Daily Catlin importuned his sitter, until
the chief, seizing the chance to drive a hard bargain, told the artist that "if [he] must have it, [I] must have two horses for it," which
Catlin immediately "procured of the Traders at twenty-five dollars
each, and the head-dress," he announced in triumph, "secured for my
Collection."

With his frantic schedule, George had no time to learn Indian
languages; inevitably his reliance upon translators led to errors and
misapprehension. Still, he now counted these same interpreters as his
friends whom he could pursue with questions as these occurred to
him: McKenzie himself spoke four or five Indian languages. Other
agents, such as his friend John Dougherty, were known to have mastered seven or eight. The *engagés* (day laborers) and *navigueurs* (river
pilots) employed by the fort all spoke the languages of the tribes whose
country was their home for most of each year, along with their own
"franglais" patois. These men had become fluent first because their
livelihood depended upon daily interchange with the tribes who
came to trade at the fort, requiring them to act as constant mediators
between their Indian clients and white employers.

THERE WAS ANOTHER reason for the multilingual fluency of the
white men who worked along the upper Missouri. Almost all cohabited with Indian women, either in common-law unions or ones consecrated by Christian and/or Indian marriage. Single young men attached
to the river forts, like the majority of their contemporaries who settled
in the West, found themselves more than a thousand miles from the
nearest white woman. The first Anglo-European female to approach
Fort Union was noted momentously by the Swiss artist Rudolph Kurz
in 1851, and it remains unclear whether the unidentified lady (probably the captain's wife) even disembarked from the steamboat.

Catlin chose to see these unions as driven by economic interest alone. "Almost every Trader and every clerk who commences in the business of this country, speedily enters into such an arrangement, which is done with as little ceremony as he would bargain for a horse," he wrote. In noting the "enslaved and degraded" condition of the many wives of tribal leaders, toiling at agriculture, domestic labor, and child rearing along with the finishing of furs for trade—all without servants—George presumed the desirability of being sold to a white suitor of status: "The young women of the best families only can aspire to such elevation; and the most of them are exceedingly ambitious for such a connection," which would allow them to enjoy "exemption from the slavish duties that would devolve upon them" if married to men in their tribe. Once chosen by the white trader, they are "allowed to lead a life of ease and idleness, covered with mantles of blue and scarlet cloth—with beads and trinkets, and ribbons, in which they flounce and flirt about, the envied and tinseled belles of every tribe."

He was forthright about the fathers' role in the prostituting of their daughters, arrangements "conducted purely as a mercenary or business transaction . . . practiced with a deal of shrewdness in exacting an adequate price" from whatever "purchaser" could best afford "so delightful a commodity."

More than other Anglo-European writers, Catlin seems uncomfortable with the possibility of love, or even enduring sexual attachments, uniting white and Indian. And he avoids exploring the social status of the "tinseled belles" within the community, along with any mention of the large numbers of half-breed children noted by all other visitors. Mixed-race sexual connections were a commonplace on the frontier: Although Catlin was charmed by Mandan child brides, his silence about the role played by native women in his hosts' lives suggests that his fear of the Other—sexual and racial—threatened his own peace in Indian country.

———

AFTER A MONTH at Fort Union as honored guest and artist in residence, Catlin felt ready to head downriver and then east. The small
world of the fort had finally begun to pall: Gossip fueled all conversation; everyone—from the lowliest clerk to Kenneth McKenzie
himself—knew everything about his neighbor, down to the last glass
of whiskey drunk or Indian lady entertained late into the night. George
had shipped off the most complete record of tribal life ever painted—
and all in four weeks. He didn't need his father's letters, waiting for
him in St. Louis and postmarked months ago, to remind him that it
was time to think of making a real home with Clara, who, like an
unwanted maiden aunt, was forced to pay long visits to sympathetic
relations. It was time to make specific plans to amaze the world, to
show his paintings and prize war bonnets, to give his talks with anecdotes of feasts and fearful ceremonies. But not just yet.

11

A STRANGER IN
PARADISE

For George leaving Fort Union for the trip downriver did not
mean a return to St. Louis, nor to Clara, nor to the work of
making his way in the world. He had unfinished business.
He had just found his subjects and only begun to paint them. He
was barely beginning to know Indian life—how they lived, played,
hunted, and made war; how they saw the natural world, and what
they believed. In these fleeting encounters he caught sight of himself
as he wanted to be.

McKenzie had had a canoe "made of green timber" constructed
especially for Catlin's new journey. Accompanying the artist in the
"snug little craft" were two *navigueurs*, the Yankee Abraham Bogard,
"an old hunter" as George described him, and "Ba'tiste," a French
Canadian whose yeasty dialect Catlin tried, with mixed success, to
reproduce phonetically. Paddles in hand, his companions occupied,
respectively, the middle and bow, while George, assigned the steering
oar, was seated in the stern.

Catlin shapes his narrative of their trip downriver as a voyage backward in time. No obstacle impedes their way; the canoe rides the
current like a paper boat. On the "enchanting shores" he finds the

landscape and its native settlers suspended in a state of nature before the Fall, before the white course of empire had seized and despoiled the land, corrupted and uprooted its indigenous peoples. The tribes onshore who now welcomed them did so with an openness and trust that suggested to George that Lewis and Clark's expedition, which had traced this exact route more than thirty years before, might never have taken place.

Descending the Missouri, they seemed to be entering a primitive paradise. Sleeping under buffalo robes "in these realms of pure air and dead silence," his reward at the end of the day was to stumble upon a vision of nature's perfection—without man: "At the base of some huge clay bluffs . . . the river expands itself into the appearance . . . of a beautiful lake; and in the midst of it, and on and about its sand-bars, floated and stood, hundreds and thousands of white swans and pelicans."

In this "land of enchantment" he marveled at every changing prospect, seeking answers to the region's geological phenomena in the earth's history. Looking for clues to the dome-shaped protrusions that suggested the ruins of some displaced Byzantine empire, he took mineral samples from the dazzling striated cliffs rising from the waters in bands of yellow, green, and coral. And he painted.

By now he had attained the technical proficiency to render the likeness of his Indian sitters in a style recognizably his own. No longer defined by their clothing and ornaments, his native men and women emerge in all their humanity, expressive of themselves, not merely as representatives of a tribe. The problems that had defeated him in Philadelphia—line, volume, modeling, light—were largely resolved on the upper Missouri. His subjects completed Catlin's education as an artist.

ON A MONDAY, "the seventh day from the mouth of the Yellow Stone River," Catlin reached a Mandan village near Fort Clark and, thanks to the American Fur Company agent James Kipp, George was welcomed into the lives of the mysterious people who had crowded the shore to greet him. Everything about the Mandan delighted him, starting with the place where they had settled centuries before, when the small tribe had migrated from the Ohio Valley. Their surroundings suggested to Catlin yet another paradise preserved, persuading him of the Mandan claim to have been "the *first* people created on earth." To him the Mandan had in fact preserved a collective innocence, uncorrupted by knowledge of evil or sin. To his artist's eye the tribe's physical beauty gave further proof of nature's favor: He noted that they were possessed of such natural grace and elegance that even their cleanliness (in stark contrast to other tribes) shone forth, signifying an inner purity.

Jacques D'Eglise, the first trader from St. Louis to venture as far up the Missouri as their tribal villages, had reported in 1790 that the Mandan "are white like Europeans, and much more civilized than any other Indians."* Other visitors were more specific, noting the prevalence of blue or gray eyes, and hair of a distinctive silvery color.

In England and on the Continent, the Romantics embraced the theory of "lost tribes" to explain the otherwise inexplicable. Thus, three years later, in 1793, John Thomas Evans, son of a Welsh minister, made a pilgrimage to the upper Missouri to try to prove that the Mandan were actually a lost Welsh tribe who, led by their chief, Prince Madoc, had settled in the New World. Despite Catlin's acknowledgement that neither linguistically, nor by any other measure, was there evidence linking the Native American tribe with any early Welsh forebears, he himself succumbed—at least briefly—to a related theory that named the Mandan as the lost tribe of Israel.

---

* A more recent theory, also discredited, attributed Mandan "mixed" blood to pre-Columbian contact with Vikings. A large stone found in present-day Minnesota and incised with what could be early Scandinavian inscriptions, was offered as evidence that Viking exploration had reached the interior, possibly through the Great Lakes.

It was more puzzling to Europeans that the Mandan seemed to reject the violence that characterized most intertribal relations. Their lives seemed dedicated to pleasure. Observing their day-to-day existence, Catlin noted that "small-talk, gossip, garrulity, and storytelling are the leading passions with them, who have little else to do in this world, but to while away their lives in . . . innocent and endless amusement." George's first impressions, however, of a people at perpetual leisure were soon dispelled by evidence of their elaborate organization and disciplined work habits. As George would learn, the Mandan's prosperity was based upon a seasonal alternation of agriculture and buffalo hunting, including the move to summer and winter villages; further, they were known throughout the region as shrewd and experienced traders.

Initially Catlin's eagerness to paint these handsome men and women and to record their games and ceremonies appeared likely to be as easily arranged as had been his sittings at Fort Union. Just as Kenneth McKenzie had reassured tribal leaders upriver that they could safely trust the artist's "magic" brush in recording their likenesses, McKenzie's longtime friend and associate James Kipp was primed to play the same mediating role for Catlin in the Mandan settlements.

George's new friend, interpreter, and guide had worked his way up through American Fur Company ranks alongside McKenzie, whom he had known since they were both young clerks in the Canadian fur trade. From clerk-trader, Kipp took on the vital role of master builder; having planned and completed the building of Fort Union about five years before Catlin's arrival, he was now supervising the construction of other outposts of McKenzie's expanding empire: Fort Pierre, Fort Clark, Fort McKenzie (inevitably), and the latest, Fort Piegan, on the Marias River. Acting as surveyor, architect, engineer, and chief contractor, Kipp chose sites and, assembling workers and supplies, either built from virgin land or transformed crumbling

ruins of abandoned trading posts into imposing and secure fortresses of commerce, designed to serve the needs of the American
Fur Company.

Fort Clark, close to the Mandan settlements, was Kipp's base of
operations. There he served as the tribe's agent, but he had other, more
personal reasons for spending much of his time in the Mandan villages. Early in his career Kipp had married a daughter of Four Bears,
second chief of the Mandan.*

In the 1830s Four Bears was "the most publicized Indian of the
Upper Missouri." Beyond his fame, however, he enjoyed the singular
affection and admiration of both his own people and the white trading
community. McKenzie had bestowed upon the Mandan chief the title
"Soldier of the Fort," a somewhat equivocal honor that suggested the
bearer would defend Fort Union against Indian attack.

As both resident agent and Four Bears' son-in-law, Kipp benefited
from special status, a position reinforced by his everyday outfit of top
hat and swallow-tailed coat, identical to that of his counterpart, Kenneth McKenzie at Fort Union. He promptly introduced Catlin to the
revered chief, and relation by marriage, acting as liaison and interpreter.

Kipp's role as go-between was complicated. Sometime after his marriage to Four Bears' daughter, he acquired a white wife and children in
Liberty (later Independence), Missouri. It was a delicate situation—or
not, depending upon whom one asked. Among prominent Plains Indians, polygamy was taken for granted. Native chiefs and warriors might
have four or five wives. Thus Kipp's separate families would not have
strained relations with his Mandan father-in-law. Neither would Kipp's
decision to end the union with his Mandan wife—had he chosen to do
so—have been a cause of social opprobrium in the Indian community.

---

* This lesser title gives no real notion of the prestige of this leader. "First chief"
was the honorific bestowed upon the most valiant veteran warrior, which, for a
peace-loving tribe like the Mandan, counted for less than it might suggest.

In the absence of religious ceremonies joining couples, the dissolution of marriages among Plains Indians carried no moral stigma; divorce was easy to obtain. Kipp's double life, however, brought him censure as a bigamist from his Anglo-European Christian associates at the fort, and he felt obliged to defend his domestic arrangements (which included long visits to his white Missouri family) with the excuse that he did not want to abandon his older, chronically ill Mandan wife. Still, his reluctance to leave the earlier marriage may have owed more to the status of his revered father-in-law, and the larger influence with the tribe that his ties to Four Bears conferred upon him.

Catlin could hardly have been unaware of the relationship between Kipp and the Mandan chief, lively evidence of the union being the "many papooses" who were always identified as Four Bears' grandchildren. Yet, alone among visitors to Fort Clark, George never mentions the tie that bound his host, the powerful agent, to his tribal counterpart—a bond that would also be key to Catlin's access to the most sacred of Mandan rituals.

AS SOON AS George met the famed chief, he joined the ranks of Four Bears' ardent admirers: "There is no man among the Mandans so generally loved," he said. "Free, generous, elegant, and gentlemanly in his deportment—handsome, brave and valiant; wearing a robe on his back, with the history of his battles emblazoned on it; which would fill a book of themselves, if properly translated."

Politically astute and a great host, Four Bears lost no time in establishing warm relations with the honored guest, inviting Catlin to a feast "in his hospitable wigwam," where following a rib roast of buffalo and other delicacies, he presented his guest with a "beautifully garnished robe." Before his own death in the smallpox epidemic of 1837, Four Bears watched his people hurl themselves over the cliffs to cool their fevered agony in the river below. He raged against the white man for deliberately infecting his tribe and cursed his own trust in visitors—whom he had treated as his friends.

NOW FOUR BEARS gladly sat for Catlin on several occasions, even selling him the entire costume in which he had posed for his full-length portrait. Describing his painting of the chief, Catlin revealed that he had "simplified" the outfit, eliminating distracting accessories. He saw his subject as a hero in the antique tradition: "No tragedian ever trod the stage, nor gladiator ever entered the Roman Forum, with more grace and manly dignity than did Mah-to-toh-pa. He took his attitude before me, and with the sternness of a Brutus . . . he stood until the darkness of night broke upon the solitary stillness."

In pursuit of Indian subjects it had been easy for George, aided by McKenzie, to win the trust of the tribal leaders encamped below Fort Union. The Mandan, however, were proving resistant to his call for sitters. Despite the diplomacy of Kipp and the friendship of Four Bears, George now encountered an entrenched and powerful opposition, one altogether new to him: women.

Rumblings of hostility orchestrated by the Mandan women began with Catlin's portraits of the two chiefs, the veteran warrior and medicine man Old Bear and Four Bears, painted in the very robe mentioned earlier, which the beloved leader, himself an artist, had decorated with scenes of his greatest victories. The campaign gained ground after these portraits were so fervently admired within the tribe as to approach objects of veneration.[*] The artist was now proudly "recognized . . . as a 'great *medicine white man*,'" one who could tell

---

* When he began to lecture about his travels on the upper Missouri, Catlin showed the portraits alongside the native artifacts, which together he began calling his Indian Gallery.

his readers: "I now hold a place amongst the most eminent and envied personages, the doctors and conjurati of this titled community."

To satisfy the eager throngs of potential male sitters, women and children were denied admittance to Catlin's painting room. The portraits of the two leaders had been fixed together over the door, "so that the whole village had a chance to see and recognize their chiefs." The effect was akin to a revival meeting—or a riot:

> The likenesses were instantly recognized, and many of the gaping multitudes commenced yelping; some were stamping off in the jarring dance—others were singing, and others again were crying—hundreds covered their mouths with their hands and were mute; others, indignant, drove their spears frightfully into the ground, and some threw a reddened arrow at the sun, and went home to their wigwams.

They next demanded to see the "strange and unaccountable being" who created such likenesses. Adults touched, poked, and prodded at the painter as he emerged into the plaza, later recalling that his "legs were assailed (not unlike the nibbling of little fish, when I have been standing in deep water)" by dozens of little girls and boys.

Catlin continued:

> They pronounced me the greatest *medicine-man* in the world; for they said I had made *living beings*; they said they could see their chiefs alive . . . they could see their eyes move—could see them smile and laugh, and that if they could laugh they could certainly speak, if they should try, and they must therefore have *some life* in them.

Too much life, it now appeared. Dissenting from the general euphoria, "the squaws generally agreed that they had discovered life enough in them to render my *medicine* too great for the Mandans," arguing that the making of a living man's likeness "could not be performed without taking away from the original something of his existence." The angry squaws did not make their views known discreetly. In what was clearly a well-planned and organized demonstration, they "commenced a mournful and doleful chaunt against me," George reported, "crying and weeping bitterly through the village, proclaiming me a most 'dangerous man; one who could make living persons by looking at them; and at the same time, could, as a matter of course, destroy life in the same way, if I chose.'" Their conclusion: "That my medicine was dangerous to their lives, and that I must leave the village immediately."

George lost no time in fighting back. Playing to male solidarity, and to the humiliation that he assumed Mandan women's infamous sexual freedom inflicted upon their men, he (according to his own account) gained admittance to the leaders' sacred conclave, where he assured those present that "I was but a man like themselves—that my art had no *medicine* or mystery about it, but could be learned by any of them if they would practice it as long as I had and that in the country where I lived, brave men never allowed their squaws to frighten them with their foolish whims and stories." Following George's remarks, the tribal leaders "all immediately arose, shook me by the hand, and dressed themselves for their pictures."

"After this, there was no further difficulty about sitting," he added in a triumphant postscript, "all were ready to be painted,—the squaws were silent, and my painting room a continual resort for the chiefs, and braves, and medicine men, where they waited with impatience for the completion of each one's picture."

There were still whispers of opposition, however, this time from a powerful medicine man himself. But Catlin had honed his diplomatic skills, along with his painterly ones, in his time on the upper Missouri. It took only a flattering portrait of the troublemaker to convert the last adversary into an ardent supporter. George was now within days of his greatest coup.

From the visits of the first French traders, the Mandan had haunted the imagination of all who encountered them. But their allure—of "beauty touched by strangeness"—their seductive grace and gaiety and charm, the mystery of their "whiteness" held a dark opposite: the hidden side that George Catlin had to see.

12

O-KEE-PA

"Oh! '*horribile visu—et mirabile dictu!*' Thank God, it is over, that I have seen it, and am able to tell it to the world."

Cloaked in Latin, too terrible to be named, the "it" that opens Catlin's twelfth letter, headed "Mandan Village, Upper Missouri," refers to O-kee-pa, the tribe's annual ceremony of renewal. His reluctance to utter the word, his repetition—three times—of "it," the pronoun of dread, foreshadows what we are about to hear: O-kee-pa's fearful secrets revealed in rituals of agony and election.

From the moment Catlin had heard about the ceremony, either from conversations with William Clark or later at Fort Union, he became obsessed with seeing for himself this darkest of tribal mysteries. His visit had been well timed. A few weeks after his arrival at Fort Clark, he could report that the four-day celebration "I have for so long been wishing to see, has at last been enacted in this village, and I have fortunately been able to see and to understand it in most of its bearings, which was more than I had reason to expect, for no white man, in all probability, has ever been before admitted to the *medicine-lodge* during these most remarkable and appalling scenes." Catlin's disclaimer—"in all probability"—elides the evidence that Kipp, son-in-law of Four

Bears and George's interpreter and host, would surely have preceded him as the first white man to witness O-kee-pa. He undoubtedly rationalized that Kipp, having married into the Mandan, was no longer an outsider.

Among the mysteries of the sacred ceremony was its timing. Traditionally O-kee-pa began "when the willow leaf is in full bloom below the river bank." As it happened, though, George had no need to wait for cues from nature. He was staying with James Kipp when, at sunrise one day, "sitting at breakfast . . . we were suddenly startled by the shrieking and screaming of the women, and barking and howling of dogs, as if an enemy were actually storming their village."

"Drop your knife and fork, Monsr.," Kipp told George as he sprang from the table, and "get your sketch-book as soon as possible, that you may lose nothing."

"I seized my sketch-book," Catlin recalled, "and all hands of us were in an instant in front of the *medicine-lodge*." Looking up, they saw that "groups of men and women were gathered on the tops of their earth-covered wigwams . . . and all eyes directed to the prairies in the West where was beheld at a mile distant, a solitary individual descending the prairie bluff and making his way in a direct line towards the village!"

Sighting the herald, Nu-mohk-much-a-nah (First [or Only] Man), signaled the start of O-kee-pa, the Mandan Creation narrative, whose opening ceremony reenacts the tribe's origin. As the runner approached, "the entire community joined in the general expression of great alarm, as if they were in danger of imminent destruction: bowstrings are tuned, horses are run back from the prairie into the village; dogs were muzzled." While the warriors blackened their faces—the traditional preparation for combat—they could see that "First Man's body, chiefly naked, was painted with white clay, as to resemble at a little distance, a white man," Catlin recalled, and "as he ran, a long robe of four white wolf skins billowed behind him."

Once the strange figure emerged into the central plaza, he was symbolically acknowledged as a benign emissary from the Great Spirit, and embraced by chiefs, warriors, and their families. The only living creature saved from the Flood, he had survived, First Man explained, by landing his big canoe high on a mountaintop to the west, where he then lived. Now, with the help of four acolytes, he was charged with opening the great round medicine lodge. Sweeping away the debris of earlier O-kee-pa, they decorated the walls and scattered the dirt floor with a "profusion of green willow boughs, wild sage and other aromatic herbs, over which they arrange a curious group of buffalo and human skulls."

At sunrise the next day First Man reappeared, followed by about fifty young men in single file, "candidates for the self-tortures which were to be inflicted, and for the honours that were to be bestowed by the chiefs on those who could most manfully endure them." Their bodies, all but naked, were painted with clay of different colors; some red, others yellow, while still others, like First Man himself, were covered in white clay, giving them, too, the appearance of white men. Each carried in his right hand his medicine bag, the prized reward of a boy's coming-of-age; on the same arm he bore a shield of bull buffalo hide; in his left hand he held his bow and arrows, a quiver slung over his back.

Once they entered the lodge the candidates became prisoners. Under constant surveillance, the naked boys were placed, at equal intervals, around the walls. Each was obliged to remain in precisely the same place, in a reclining position, medicine bag and weapons suspended above his head. Before he disappeared First Man urged the chosen youths to show pride in their election and courage for the ordeal to come.

In Catlin's account neither his friendship with Four Bears nor his ties to the latter's son-in-law and George's host, James Kipp, was key in gaining him admission to the "*sanctum sanctorum*"—the great round ceremonial lodge and its bloody rites. Rather, George attributed his welcome to his timely portrait of another, still more influential figure in the tribe.

Before First Man disappeared over the bluffs, he delegated his authority and passed his power to Old Bear, an elderly medicine man. Painted bright yellow and invested with the medicine pipe, Old Bear was the new master of ceremonies. Catlin's good luck was to have painted a full-length portrait of this "great magician or high priest" only the day before, in which he was depicted in the "performance of some of his mysteries."

Old Bear as Catlin painted him looks flatteringly young. In a frontal pose the nakedness of the priest's bare chest contrasts dramatically with the clothed parts of his lower body: The head and paws of a brown bear cover his genitals, hanging to the tops of the fringed and beaded leggings that reach to his moccasins.

The portrait was a great success. "Old Bear," Catlin wrote, had been "exceedingly pleased as well as astonished" by his likeness because "he could see its eyes move." Conferring with his fellow "doctors," Catlin reported, "they agreed that the artist should be welcomed into the ranks of the "*white medicine man* (or Spirit) *painter.*"

Thus anointed, George, accompanied by Kipp and the latter's two clerks, was escorted to a place of honor "comfortably placed on elevated seats . . . in full view of everything that transpired in the lodge." The deference shown the artist and his entourage, however, encouraged Catlin to press for further access to the forbidden: The most sacred objects used in the ceremonies were four ancient leather sacs sewn to resemble giant tortoises, said to hold water from each of the four corners of the earth. George made an offer to purchase these ritual "medicine bags," a proposition rejected in disbelief and whose effrontery, Catlin admitted, placed at risk "the *medicine* operation of my pencil, which was applied to everything, and even upon that they looked with decided distrust and apprehension, as a sort of theft or

sacrilege." Nonetheless he was forgiven and allowed to sketch the proceedings freely.

LEAVING THE CROWDS of villagers in the public square, Catlin had
"entered the *medicine-house* of these scenes as I would have entered a
church," he recalled, "and expected to see something extraordinary
and strange; but alas! Little did I expect to see the interior of their
holy temple turned into a *slaughter-house* and its floor strewn with the
blood of its fanatic devotees."

For the chosen young men who had been lying around the periph-
ery of the great chamber, deprived of food or drink for four days, the
psychological torment of waiting had ended and the physical agony of
torture began.

While they lay on the ground watching, an elaborate system of scaffolding had been erected that reached from the floor to the ceiling of
the lodge. At the appointed moment priestly acolytes appeared whose
function was to insert a pair of thin wooden skewers, some six inches
apart, into the breasts of each of the supplicants: The skewers were
then attached to rawhide cords flung over the top post of the scaffolding. Like the strings of puppets, these were controlled by a priest
positioned on the roof, who manipulated the bodies to be hoisted and
hung from their skewered wounds.

To the sound of constant drumming, each of the youths submitted to variations of this procedure; some were skewered from the
back, with buffalo skulls attached to the ends of the sticks, or were
pierced through the arms and knees. A later observer was amazed to
see how far the hanging men's skin would stretch, "pulling out a distance of 12 or fifteen inches." They became "appalling and frightful
to look at," Catlin noted, even as he marveled at their "unflinching
fortitude . . . each one as the knife passed through his flesh sustained
an unchangeable countenance." Several of the victims seemed to have

moved beyond pain, approaching an ecstatic state. When they saw him sketching, Catlin said, they "beamed the pleasantest smiles as they looked me in the eye and beckoned me to look at their faces." George could not enter their transcendent state. Still, the artist's drive to record triumphed over the horror of what he saw, and even while he "could hear the knife rip through the flesh and feel enough of it myself, to start involuntary and uncontrollable tears over my cheeks," he kept on drawing.

For his subjects, hanging senseless from rawhide cords or tearing at their flesh to free themselves, their martyrdom had just begun. Dozens of designated torturers, costumed as "imps or demons" and holding long poles, prodded each suspended body to turn, ever faster, his screams unabating, Catlin wrote, "until, by fainting his voice falters, and his struggling ceases."

Only then was the victim's form, to all appearances lifeless, gently lowered to the ground. There he was left unattended until, mustering the strength to drag himself, "he crawls, with the weights still hanging to his body to another part of the lodge where there is another Indian sitting with a hatchet in his hand; after commending the little finger of his left hand to the Great Spirit, he places it upon a dried buffalo skull, where the other chops it off . . . with a blow of the hatchet!"

In the four scenes he painted from O-kee-pa, Catlin does not depict this last rite of mutilation; the canvases were too small for the scale of the ritual, which would lack the drama of bodies held fast by their skewered wounds. The artist's curiosity continued to be piqued by other observed phenomena, such as the tiny quantity of blood that flowed from each amputated finger. Following a "close inspection of their wounds from day to day" George learned that the slight bleeding "soon ceases, probably from the fact of their [the victims'] extreme exhaustion and debility, caused by want of sustenance and sleep, which checks the natural circulation." But Catlin the scientist, whose observations are worthy of any medical researcher of his day, also pays homage to the mystical source of the ceremony and its role in the survival of the sufferers. Their faith, he notes, "admirably prepares them to meet the severity of these tortures without the same degree of sensibility and pain which, under other circumstances, might result in inflammation and death."

Their torments end finally with the ceremony called "the Last Race." While "the whole nation was assembled as spectators," the survivors, divided into small groups—splints still piercing their flesh—were forced to race the others until they dropped to the ground. Then, face-down in the dirt, each boy was dragged "with all possible speed" over stony terrain until the weights attached to his wrist were pulled out. If he managed to rise, the crowd, who "all raised the most piercing and violent yells and screams they could possibly produce, to drown the cries of the suffering ones," parted to make way for the martyr, when, "reeling and staggering like a drunken man," he disappeared into his wigwam, where at last family and friends were allowed to minister to his wounds.

Among its other purposes this pitiless trial assured survival of the fittest, and the continuity of an elite leadership through the next generation. Young men from the most prominent families and clans had proved themselves morally and physically to be without equal in self-mastery: faithful, fearless, and all but indestructible.

His Mandan hosts had invited him with the understanding that he would draw and paint all that he witnessed. For the purpose of translating his on-the-spot sketches of the grisly proceedings, Catlin was provided with his own "earth-covered wigwam with a fine sky-light over my head." He set up his easel, arranging paints and palette, but instead of working face-to-face with his sitters, he transformed the pages of the quick sketches he had made in a small notebook into four of his most famous paintings, the only ones ever made depicting rituals so "barbarous and cruel . . . I am almost ready to shrink from the task of reciting them."

In *The Cutting Scene*, the most brilliant of the four, scaffolding trans-
forms the medicine lodge into a starkly modern stage set. In this room
without walls the danse macabre unfolds with the viewer as audience
and voyeur. Two hanging bodies rotate, prodded by naked torturers
wielding poles. To increase their torment, the victims' extremities
are shown weighted by buffalo skulls attached to the skewers piercing their ankles. Both young men appear to be unconscious: the head
of one lolls backward; the other's is hidden from our gaze, having
dropped to his chest. Waiting their turn, the next group of candidates
to be strung up no longer reclines on the lodge floor; they sit rigidly
upright, arms clasped around their knees as though for support, their
shields ranked behind them with military precision.

CATLIN PUBLISHED THREE different versions of *O-kee-pa*, an account
of the ceremony. The earliest, dated 1832, and closest to the events
described, remains the most vivid. In all three, however, the artist
felt compelled to express feelings of shock bordering on disbelief—not
only in face of the barbarous cruelty he witnessed but also at what he
found to be an irreconcilable paradox: How could a gentle and civilized people inflict acts of open savagery on their own young? At the
same time the artist maintained the modern ethnologist's distance
from, but also respect for, the values and beliefs of a culture foreign
to his own, along with an effort to find common ground between the
two. While Catlin deplored the horrors he witnessed as "shocking and
disgusting," he paid tribute to their proof of the "Indian's superior
stoicism."

In the America of the young Republic the ability unflinchingly to bear
pain and suffering embraced a spectrum of values and beliefs from life-
and-death survival, especially on the frontier, to the symbolic: For Catlin
and his contemporaries, stoicism remained the measure of manliness.

"I am ready to accord them in this particular, the palm," he wrote, "the credit of outdoing anything and everybody, and of enduring more than civilized man ever aspired to or ever thought of." While his own heart

> has sickened also with disgust for so abominable and ignorant a custom, . . . still I stand ready with all my heart, to excuse and forgive them for adhering so strictly to an ancient celebration, founded in superstitions and mysteries, of which they know not the origin, and constituting a material part and feature in the code and forms of their religion.

George proved wise in the ways that prurience, envy, and rivalry—even sincere doubt—would arise to challenge his account. Anticipating charges of exploitation, of sensationalizing or outright lying, he obtained "Certificates" from James Kipp, from L. Crawford, one of Kipp's clerks, and from Bogard, his own voyageur (not coincidentally one of the few Yankees who plied this trade), all attesting to the accuracy of Catlin's four paintings depicting O-kee-pa. These bona fides required a trade-off. Like all explorers, the artist was eager to win the title of "First"—and to let the world know it. In this case the crown, he insisted, belonged to him: the first white man to witness the closed rituals of O-kee-pa. Then, however, challenges to his accuracy forced him to adjust his account to reflect the presence of Kipp and others.

UNSPARING AS HE was in portraying graphic eyewitness depictions of O-kee-pa's rites of torture, Catlin shrank from revealing, in word or image, the opening and closing ceremonies that played an equally crucial role in the rites. Earlier travelers had recorded the frenzy of sexual activity that, to their amazement, all took place in public, with visitors invited to participate.

In 1804–5 Meriwether Lewis and Catlin's friend William Clark, along with the Corps of Discovery, had camped for several months near the Mandan villages. Dependent themselves upon buffalo meat for survival, they quickly grasped the most urgent purpose of the four-day ritual, which took place out of doors, at the same time as O-kee-pa unfolded within the lodge. The Buffalo Calling Ceremony paid tribute to the primacy of sexual power in obtaining divine favor and in assuring a successful hunt. To this end homage was paid to the role of women in transmitting sexual authority from the elders of the tribe to young males.

Several members of the Corps of Discovery had participated in the ceremony, in which the braves offered their wives, the girls' naked bodies displayed under an open robe, to the old men waiting outside the lodge. While the young women and their older sexual partners writhed on the ground, the husbands disappeared tactfully, to return bearing gifts for the aged recipients of their wives' favors. Nicholas Biddle, the brilliant banker who served as the editor of Lewis and Clark's account of their expedition, explained the visitors' warm welcome, noting: "White men are always considered as o.m. [old men] and are generally preferred by the Squaws because they will give probably some present and," he added, "for other obvious reasons"—the "obvious" no doubt alluding to his own view of the white male's superior sexual attributes, at least in relation to the Indian.

Within the complex cycle of O-kee-pa, sexual activity was not confined to the ritual transfer of sexual potency through women: From the last flickers of the weak and elderly to the young and vigorous men of the tribe; the sexual act played a continuous role throughout the ceremonies. Like the beating of drums or the chanting that punctuated all the interlocking rites, erotic games took place publicly, with changing combinations and partners throughout the four days, but they were a central attraction of the opening and closing ceremonies.

One year after Lewis and Clark had returned east, in July 1806, Alexander Henry, a Northwest Fur Company trader, spent about ten

The Cutting Scene, Mandan O-kee-pa Ceremony, 1832. Catlin was the only artist allowed to witness and to record O-kee-pa, the Mandan coming-of-age ceremony. He painted four episodes, of which *The Cutting Scene* functions as the high point of the drama, when the victims were hung, skewed, and flayed. As in Renaissance panels, the artist shows several stages of the ritual torture taking place simultaneously.

Medicine Man, Performing His Mysteries over a Dying Man, 1832, Blackfoot/Siksika. While painting this Blackfoot medicine man, Catlin became obsessed with owning his costume, cajoling, begging, even threatening, until the owner gave in and sold it to the artist for an unrecorded sum. Catlin took the outfit abroad with him, donning it to great effect when he introduced "live" Iowa and Ojibwa performers in London and Paris.

Osceola, the Black Drink, a Warrior of Great Distinction, 1838, Seminole. Catlin's likeness of the Seminole leader is the most controversial portrait he would ever paint. In 1838, the artist rushed to the chief's prison cell at Fort Moultrie, South Carolina, in order to be the first and, as he hoped, the last, to portray the captive leader hours before his death. Catlin's exploitation of his subject's condition was seen as adding another betrayal to that of the U.S. Army, who had lured Osceola and his followers out of hiding and into chains.

Interior View of the Medicine Lodge, Mandan O-kee-pa Ceremony, 1832. The scene is set and the ceremony prepared; the young men about to be tested through torture are seated around the walls, hung with their shields and flowering green branches. Pairs of skulls, both animal and human, have been placed at their feet. Raising his head and left arm, a medicine man invokes the blessing of the Great Spirit.

The Last Race, Mandan O-kee-pa Ceremony, 1832. One of two exterior scenes of Catlin's cycle, *The Last Race* depicts the final test for the survivors. Cut down from their cords, skewers removed from their wounds, the boys' bodies were dragged over stony soil by two tribesmen, costumed as demons, before the victims were left—dead or alive—to be collected by their families.

Ru-ton-ye-wee-ma, Strutting Pigeon, Wife of White Cloud, 1844, Iowa. Catlin painted every member of the Iowa and Ojibwa tribes that he showed in Paris—thirty-five portraits, including wives and young children. The tender intimacy of the Iowa mother, the wife of White Cloud the Younger, and her child has allusions to the Madonna with the baby Jesus. Strutting Pigeon's somber, faraway gaze, like that of the Virgin, seems to foresee a dark future.

Sha-kó-ka, Mint, a Pretty Girl, 1832, Mandan/ Numakiki. A fresh-faced adolescent, Mint may have been chosen by Catlin as a sitter because the silvery streaks in her long, unbound hair highlighted the Mandan feature all visitors found unforgettable. The destruction of the Mandan in a smallpox epidemic five years later lends Mint's portrait—a young girl on the cusp of womanhood—unintended poignance.

Kee-o-kuk, the Watchful Fox, Chief of the Tribe, on Horseback, 1835, Sauk and Fox. In 1835, the Black Hawk Wars pitted rival leaders of the Sauk and Fox tribes—Black Hawk and the established chief Keokuk—against one another. Both chiefs ended up as prisoners in Jefferson Barracks, near St. Louis, where Catlin painted the two men and their followers. For the artist, the rebel Black Hawk was a hero, and Keokuk, the government puppet, a vain impostor.

Dying Buffalo, Shot with an Arrow, 1832–33. A skilled rider and expert marksman since boyhood, Catlin joined in bison hunts with enthusiasm and daring. His portrait of a bull in his death agony becomes a tribute to the creature's tragic nobility worthy of Goya. The artist seems to prophesy the sacrifice of millions of bison for sport, leading to the virtual extinction of the herds that once covered the Great Plains.

Niagara Falls, View of Table Rock and Horseshoe Falls, from Below, 1828. Niagara Falls became an early favorite of painters in search of the sublime, but in Catlin's sequence of small, square pictures, the artist's musings fall somewhere between science and science fiction, imagining, for example, aerial views of the falls. In this mysterious scene, the rushing waters appear suspended, as if anticipating Hokusai's famous woodblock print *The Great Wave* (ca. 1831). At the same time, Catlin the inventor applied for a patent on his series.

Prairie Meadows Burning, 1832. Catlin loved speed—in fire, horses, or men—and to catch its course, he learned to use oil like watercolor, rendering a vortex of clouds, hurtling flames, fleeing horses, and Indians with fast impressionist strokes of near transparency or heavy impasto.

Shon-ta-yi-ga, Little Wolf, a Famous Warrior, 1844, Iowa. Of the troupe of thirteen Iowa that Catlin toured throughout Britain, Little Wolf, he declared, was the handsomest as well as the best dancer. When the star's little son, Corsair, died in his father's arms in Scotland, Little Wolf was too grieved to perform. Shortly after the troupe arrived in Paris, Corsair's mother, O-kee-wee-me, succumbed to tuberculosis. Catlin seemed more distressed by Little Wolf's absence from the show than by the loss of his wife and son—tragedies that would soon be mirrored in the artist's own family.

William Fisk (1796–1872), *George Catlin,* 1849. A week before the Revolution of 1848 toppled the French monarchy, Catlin fled from Paris, where, a few years earlier, his wife and only son had died. He arrived in London, greeted by debts, forgotten as a man and artist. In the midst of these years of defeat, William Fisk painted this portrait as a study in nostalgia. Looking ten years younger than his fifty-three years, dressed in the buckskin of his glory days on the frontier, this is the George Catlin who had been famous a decade earlier. Painted as he wanted the British to remember him, he is shown here, palette and brush in hand, working in a studio "tipi" in a Blackfoot village on the upper Missouri. In homage to his art, he is watched by a couple, themselves adopted from portraits in Catlin's Indian Gallery.

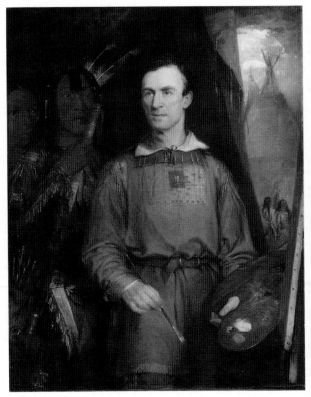

days with the Mandan. His arrival seems to have coincided with the final day of O-kee-pa, when Henry described a classically Dionysian celebration. Wakened around midnight by "extraordinary noise" coming from the settlement, Henry observed "about 25 persons of both sexes, entirely naked, going about the village singing and dancing. They appeared to take turns withdrawing in couples, before rejoining the group in its musical progress." In his written account Henry reveals himself as a keen observer with near-X-ray vision: "During this short separation from the rest," he noted of the happy pairs, "they appeared to be very closely engaged, and notwithstanding the night was dark I could perceive them occupied in enjoying each other with as little ceremony as if it had been only the common calls of nature."

"In the course of two hours, the group danced and sang their way around the village several more times," following the same pattern of men and women separating in pairs for the "lascivious performance" that Henry described earlier, before rejoining the other celebrants. He was never able, however, to learn the "meaning of the ceremony," he confessed.

At the very end of O-kee-pa the meaning of this parallel sexual play was revealed as a symbolic narrative about the power of women. On this last day a figure called O-ke-hee-de, "The Owl" or "Evil Spirit," rushed through the village. His arrival from the prairie confirmed his role as that of First Man's double, and the emissary of him whose welcomed first run through the village had launched the ceremony four days earlier. Now his malign opposite thrust himself into the area of the buffalo dancers, "to the terror of the women and children."

As soon as O-ke-hee-de appears, Catlin draws a circumspect veil over the proceedings. Like all veils, however, this one was intended to draw attention to what lay beneath. In his account of the ceremony that appeared in his *Letters and Notes*, the artist describes both the costume and behavior of the Evil Spirit in a kind of "pig Mandan," an invented Indian language used to suggest what could not be said in civilized society.

The first two published versions of *O-kee-pa* retained this "tease" of transparent opacity. A third edition, however, appeared in London in 1845, published as a *folium reservatum*, or privately printed limited edition, intended for "gentlemen only"—or collectors of erotica. Initially Catlin denied authorship or even knowledge of this "pirated" edition, but eventually it became known that the disputed text had been a moneymaking effort by the artist to raise badly needed cash.

Titled simply *O-kee-pa*, Catlin's privately printed edition reveals O-kee-he-de as terrifying the villagers, first by his appearance: Naked, he had "attached, by a small thong encircling his waist, a buffalo tail, behind; and from under the buffalo hair covering the pelvis, an artificial penis, ingeniously (and naturally) carved in wood, of colossal dimensions, pendulous as he ran, and extending somewhat below his knees. Like his body, the artificial organ was painted jet-black, with the exception of the glans, which was of as glaring a red as vermilion could make it." The huge extension, swinging as he ran toward groups of women, set them "tumbling over each other and screaming for help as he advanced upon them." But he had also contrived a primitive hydraulic action of his organ; as he approached, he "elevated with both hands his delicate wand, and as he raised it over their heads, there was a corresponding rising of the penis, probably caused by some small, invisible thong connecting the two together."

O-kee-he-de makes several further attempts, more likely mimed and symbolic rather than actual, to force himself upon the women; each time their leader rebuffs him with her magic medicine pipe. The Evil Spirit then returns to the buffalo dance where, playing the role of the rutting bull, he mounts another performer; then, elevating his wand, inserts his erect penis under the skin of the prone figure who, in Catlin's description, "continues to dance with his body in a horizontal position."

Their fears dispelled, the women and children now dance and shout their approval of this enactment of buffalo procreation; the ritual will be auspicious for the fruitful multiplying of the herd and success in the hunt. In a final burst of energy, O-kee-he-de leaps over four of the eight dancers until he drops, exhausted from his efforts. Visibly spent and harmless, the Evil Spirit is now the butt of the women's mocking sexual overtures: Catlin himself gets into the spirit of the Mandan women, bent upon humiliating their former predator: "They danced up to him and back, in lascivious attitudes, tempting him with challenges which, with all his gallantry, he was now (apparently) unable to accept." Emboldened still further by his impotence, the women smash his wand, and drive the useless creature back to the prairie, where "the frightful appendage is wrested from his body, and brought by its captor [the leader of the Furies] triumphantly into the village, wrapped in a bunch of wild sage, and carried in her arms as she would have carried an infant." As if this image—the giant wooden penis, herb wrapped and cradled by the woman warrior as she marches with her followers back to the settlement—weren't drama enough, the final act of O-kee-pa offers an Amazonian apocalypse of female power. Then the goddess of war, or "Mandan Bellona," as Catlin calls her, "escorted by two matrons, [was] lifted by them onto the front of the Medicine Lodge, directly over its door, from whence she harangued the multitude for some time, claiming that she held the power of creation, and of life and death over them; that she was the father of all the buffaloes, and that she could make them come or stay away as she pleased."

From her position above the door, like the central relief in the Parthenon frieze, the regnant divinity (never named by Catlin) "orders the buffalo-dance to be stopped and the Pohkhong or torturing scenes to commence within the Medicine Lodge." She then demands, in exchange for the trophy male organ, "the handsomest dress in the Mandan tribe, which the Master of Ceremonies had in readiness, and presented to her." When she is thus gorgeously arrayed, he cedes to her his powers, appointing her "to the envied position of conductress of the *feast of the Buffaloes* to be given that night."

We may wonder which Catlin found more disturbing: the public sex—actual and symbolic—or the female takeover of the primal ceremonies of Creation and of the life-giving buffalo hunt? He had fled the needs and dependency of women in his journey to the upper Missouri; now among the Mandan, he confronted the full force of their implacable fury and revenge.

13

"PROBLEMS OF SHADE, SHADOW AND PERSPECTIVE"

Catlin's reluctance to leave the upper Missouri, with the male fellowship of its forts and his privileged access to tribal life, was reflected in the meanders of his return downriver. He felt with certainty that he would never return to this Eden: the Mandan girls' laughter as they dived and splashed in the early-morning sun; the buffalo herds blackening the prairie from the horizon to where the hunters stood, rifles cocked in readiness. There's even a valedictory tone to his notes on O-kee-pa; George denounces its pagan cruelties, but he knows these will be matched by Christian barbarisms inflicted in the name of westward expansion.

After spending some time at Fort Leavenworth doing more sketches—portraits to be filled in later or scenes of daily life that would be re-created from memory into "studio productions"—Catlin arrived back in St. Louis around October 20, 1832, just ahead of the ice and freezing cold that would seal off the upper Missouri for the next nine months. He planned to remain in the city for the winter, finishing uncompleted works, with a view to exhibiting them the following year. He did not ask Clara to join him.

While he was away St. Louis had been steadily expanding; there were new buildings, shops, and even streets that George had never seen, thronged with newcomers to the city whose population had swollen to 10,755.* Still, it seemed as though the bigger the town had become, the more confined he felt. Reworking material done on his travels evoked days of limitless freedom, confirming his present sense of shrunken space. His mentor William Clark was busier than ever, having been named by President Jackson co-commissioner charged with "providing for the extinguishment of Indian [land] titles remaining in the states of Illinois and Missouri." However, Ben O'Fallon, Clark's nephew and George's friend and patron, would certainly have welcomed the traveler back, and better still, added a number of new portraits and landscapes to his collection of Catlin's work.

WHAT CONSOLED GEORGE most, though, was his reunion with Joe Chadwick. When Catlin had left St. Louis, Joe had been an overworked clerk in his uncle Enoch's wholesale grocery business, whose best customer, it turned out, was the U.S. Army. At the start of the Black Hawk War—Illinois territorial governor John Reynolds's name for sporadic attacks on white settlements by followers of that Sauk chief—he called for a volunteer militia. Joe Chadwick rushed to enlist but thanks to his uncle's connections as chief food supplier, Chadwick was soon commissioned special aide to Reynolds, with the rank of colonel. In all likelihood encouraged by Catlin, he planned to record in pencil and paint his battlefield adventures, and he asked his sister Elizabeth to send him his old manual, *Problems of Shade, Shadow and Perspective.*

He had little time to draw; shortly after enlisting, Chadwick fought in the Battle of Yellow Creek, one of the bloodiest events of the Black Hawk War. After serving as paymaster to his fellow militiamen, Joe was demobilized and back in St. Louis with Uncle Enoch's ledgers.

---

* St. Louis Township had increased by 140 percent since 1824.

He had missed by one month the historic Battle of Bad Axe, on July 21, 1832, where, after two days of fighting, Black Hawk and the other rebel leaders among the Sauk and Fox were captured.

With Joe Chadwick's connection to Governor Reynolds, Catlin would have had no trouble obtaining permission to paint Black Hawk along with his eleven fellow captives, now imprisoned at Jefferson Barracks, ten miles south of St. Louis. In a year Black Hawk and his lieutenants—warriors and counselors, including two of his sons— would be paraded in chains through Washington and other "Atlantic capitals," George noted, where "thousands lined the way to see the feared Indians, now manacled in irons, weighted by musket balls, like slaves on the way to market." The parade of prisoners conveyed a double message: The captives served the function of assuring potential settlers in the West that they had nothing to fear, but also that, should there be violence, the government was there to subjugate the savage and offer protection to its white citizens. Their tour ended at Fortress Monroe, Virginia, where the portraitists Charles Bird King and Robert Sully (son of Thomas Sully, the Philadelphia master) would have a chance to satisfy the curiosity of those who did not get to gawk at the native prisoners, chains clanking as they slowly walked or stood atop wagons pulled along the main avenues of Eastern Seaboard cities.

At Jefferson Barracks, through the good offices of Joe Chadwick and his uncle, Catlin was treated as a distinguished guest: He was given rooms at the fort hospital to use as a studio and perhaps temporary residence, with his sitters made available as long as the artist might need them to pose.

In the last weeks of October, Catlin painted nine known portraits of the imprisoned Indians: Among them were two recent adversaries, chiefs Black Hawk and Keokuk, both of the Sauk and Fox tribes. After the War of 1812, Black Hawk had led his followers, including his eldest and youngest sons, Whirling Thunder and Roaring Thunder, his brother Nah-Pope ("the Soup"), and White Cloud, called "the

Prophet," to defect, forming the British Band of Fox and Sauk. In the Black Hawk Wars, this group had challenged the leadership of Black Hawk's fellow prisoner, incumbent Sauk chief Keokuk, the ally—some would say "puppet"—of the U.S. government.

Unanswered questions still hover over Catlin's portraits of the prisoners at Jefferson Barracks—just as they would cling to his best-selling portrait of another captive, the Seminole chief Osceola, painted in his prison cell at Fort Moultrie, South Carolina, five years later.

In both instances his sitters' circumstances inject the word "capture" with double meaning. For Catlin the artist (as for any portraitist) to capture is to "fix" the likeness of the painted object on paper or canvas, wood or stone. At Jefferson Barracks, however, his subjects, Black Hawk and his followers, were available precisely because they had been "captured" as prisoners of war and as enemies of the state. Moral issues, then, arise in taking his sitters' likenesses when they were deprived of the right to refuse. Further, Catlin would be dogged by accusations of having exploited the captives' subjugated condition for gain. (This would be especially true of the artist's later portrait of the imprisoned Osceola.)

Black Hawk's portrait by Catlin manages to suggest these conflicts, starting with the artist's declaration that the sitter and nominal leader of the war party—"this man whose name has carried a sort of terror through the country where it has been sounded," and who gave his name to the hostilities—was in fact "distinguished as a speaker or councellor rather than as a warrior; and I believe it has been pretty generally admitted that 'Nah-pope' and the 'Prophet' were, in fact, the instigators of the war; and either of them with much higher claims for the name of Warrior than Black Hawk ever had." Between Governor Reynolds and Joe Chadwick, Catlin was privy to insider intelligence—or hearsay.

Closing in on his subject, Catlin subverts his own classical ideal. In his famous bust-length portrait of Black Hawk, the bony structure of the chief's skull seems to poke through his skin, the impression of a death mask emphasized by the modeling of the prominent cheekbones and plucked forehead, hair pulled severely back under a spray of feathers. Most of all the asymmetry of the features undermines the image of an idealized Roman statesman: One of Black Hawk's eyes is noticeably smaller than the other; his nose, bulbous at the end and slightly askew, suggests a battered gladiator, while a slight droop of his mouth hints at a stroke or evidence of other trauma.

Black Hawk was clothed for his sitting, Catlin recalled, in a style that underscored the great chief's simplicity as the source of his power: "He was dressed in a plain suit of buckskin . . . and held in his hand his medicine bag, which was the skin of a black hawk from which he had taken his name . . . and the tail of which made him a fan which he was almost constantly using." But in late October or early November, his sitter's constant fanning of himself suggests, along with unseasonably warm weather, discomfort caused by nerves or even a fevered state.

Clearly the artist felt the need to idealize the captives, transforming wretched native prisoners into stoical Roman statesmen. While Catlin was at work on his portrait of the Soup, Black Hawk's brother and second in command, another anonymous observer caught the tug-of-war between the painter and his subject:

> When Mr. Catlin, the artist, was about taking the portrait of . . . Soup, he (the sitter) seized the ball and chain that were fastened to his leg, and raising them on high, exclaimed, with a look of scorn, "Make me so, and show me to the Great Father." On Mr. Catlin's refusing to paint him as he wished, he kept varying his countenance with grimaces to prevent him from catching a likeness.

A familiar political dimension emerges from this standoff over captives' treatment at the hands of the U.S. Army. Was Catlin trying to protect his military patrons by "brushing out" the prisoners' chains as evidence of their captors' inhumanity? Or was he insistent upon conveying the Indians' transcendent dignity—to the point of removing their "irons" of humiliation and pain? Who "owned" the images of the captives? Who got to decide how they should be seen by the world? Soup saw the sanitizing of his likeness as a denial of his affliction, and he would have none of it.

Washington Irving, last heard exclaiming over Superintendent Clark's famous hospitality at Marais Castor, followed his visit there with a stop the following day, September 14, 1832, at Jefferson Barracks. A month before Catlin arrived to paint Black Hawk and his followers, Irving reported on finding the imprisoned leader no fearsome warrior or Roman senator but an old man in chains, "emaciated and enfeebled by the sufferings he has experienced . . . fanning himself with the tail feathers of a black hawk."

AT THE END of December, Catlin rolled up dozens of canvases, packed as many sketchbooks filled with drawings, along with notebooks covered in writing, and left St. Louis. He took with him more than a hundred works he planned to exhibit in the East; the remainder he entrusted to his friend and patron Ben O'Fallon. He arrived in Pittsburgh suffering from exhaustion and a bronchial infection. After a separation of more than a year, Clara joined him. As George was still convalescent, they celebrated the new year quietly in their boardinghouse.

With George gone, his friend Joe Chadwick sank into his old depression, blacker now than ever. *"Let no one see this letter—burn it!"* he begged his sister—twice. With his Puritan upbringing, he was shamed by his despair, and perhaps by other feelings as well.

"I have almost everything in St. Louis to make me happy," he wrote to Elizabeth at the end of February, two months after Catlin had left. "Good society—kind friends, etc. But there is something—I know not what—that makes me discontented—I cannot divine what it is—But

still it is there & it defies my endeavors to cast it out—I feel as sometime a melancholy which I cannot account for. . . . It wears on me. I
know not where it will end." He will never marry, he tells Elizabeth.
Besides his sister there was only one other who had breached his isolation, and without him he was more alone than ever.

Whether George suffered from their separation is something we
cannot know with certainty. But hardly had he arrived in Pittsburgh,
still weak and coughing, to join Clara, than he left again for St. Louis.

The ostensible reason for his return, in the freezing January weather,
was to pay a call on Pierre Chouteau, Jr., in his offices at the American
Fur Company. George had heard rumblings of displeasure from the
chieftain of the upper Missouri trade, to the effect that Catlin's letters
about his travels among the tribes in the region, published irregularly
in the *New York Commercial Advertiser*, had caused "unwanted attention" to focus upon the company's activities, especially the cargo of
their two steamboats, the *Yellow Stone* and its sister ship, the *Assini-
boine*; implicitly Chouteau and his principals appeared to link George's
reports to a sudden government zeal in enforcing new laws against
selling whiskey to Indians, resulting in a recent confiscation of surplus
barrels of spirits in the ships' holds, along with parts of distilleries to
be assembled where needed onshore.

According to Catlin himself, he now read aloud to Chouteau a draft
of his latest as-yet unpublished letter to the newspaper. What Chouteau heard convinced him that the artist was no whistle-blower: Catlin's text as it appeared in the *New York Commercial Advertiser*, June
20, 1833, dated "4th ——— 1833,[*] sounds a hymn to the heroic role
played by the American Fur Company in securing the friendship of
the tribes on the upper Missouri and, more crucially, their allegiance
to the United States. The company supplied the Indians with "plenty

---

[*] As the newspaper noted, "By accident, the month is obliterated in the copy,
and we therefore leave it blank."

of food, arms, ammunition, and other necessities of life"; but more important from a military standpoint were the bonds the company forged with the Indians which served "to prevent them from going to the British Company, who stand ready to supply them and to monopolize the fur trade in our own country, and cultivate an influence over them extremely dangerous to our frontiers."

Catlin had once shared the accepted view that John Jacob Astor had further enriched himself and his representatives from his fur-trading enterprise on the upper Missouri—just as the great tycoon had first done in the Northwest trade in beaver skins. Now he wrote: "Having witnessed the extreme difficulties of transporting their goods to that country—of extending their trade to the mountains—the enormous expenses of the establishment, and the continued liability to heavy losses, I should very much doubt whether the profits, at this time, could be considerable." Once he had established the American Fur Company's heroic role in securing the "friendship and trade of the Indians," at great risk and with a razor-thin profit margin, Catlin moved to his most startling argument:

> To add to the very great many difficulties which this company has had to encounter, Congress has added another by prohibiting the further introduction of *spirituous liquors* into this country, which act (if continued in force) will undoubtedly destroy all prospects of trade in that section of the country, and greatly endanger the lives of persons employed in it.

In defense of maintaining a steady flow of whiskey to the tribes upriver, Catlin explains that the high price charged to these Indians with whom the company does business functions as a deterrent since "they can afford to drink but little; it is sipped in small but precious draughts," as opposed to the "pernicious effect that it produces amongst the bordering tribes, where whiskey is so easily obtained that they fall miserable victims to its baneful influence." Thus even the company's pricing system, based upon scarcity, must be seen in an altruistic light.

In its published form this letter suggests that Catlin had performed a complete about-face, abandoning his earlier convictions that whiskey had been the primary agent in corrupting and degrading the Native American. Now we learn from George that providing the Indian with alcohol was an act of pure patriotism: Maintaining their dependence upon whiskey and its steady flow into the region assured the tribes' loyalty to the American Fur Company and, by extension, to the Republic itself.

It seems likely that Catlin's summary to Chouteau of the letter's contents represented a revised version of an earlier, less flattering one. Possibly Chouteau himself had a hand in the final draft before it was posted to New York.

By the time the letter was published in late June 1833, Catlin was launched on a new and uncertain phase of his career, and he could ill afford to lose powerful friends.

14

A MAN WHO MAKES
PICTURES FOR A
TRAVELING SHOW

George and Clara were reunited at Great Bend, Pennsylvania, yet another new property of the elder Catlins. The visit was as brief as George could make it: Bad news always seemed to lie in wait for him at home. On arriving, he learned that his older brother Charles had died in September, apparently by his own hand. Alone and drinking heavily after his divorce, Charles had tried and failed to make a new life in Buffalo, New York. Eighteen months later he was followed by twenty-two-year-old John, next youngest after Francis and another casualty of alcohol; he had left a suicide note. Within five years four of George's brothers would be dead; none had reached the age of forty-five.

George's answer to any shivers of mortality was to keep moving. Now that he had almost 150 new works, he needed a place to show them. By mid-March he and Clara were in Washington. His plans to exhibit a representative group of his paintings, together with Indian ceremonial clothing such as war bonnets and weapons, accompanied by the artist's commentary, to audiences throughout the East would be expensive. He could not count on ticket sales or a scattering of commissions to finance travel and living expenses for himself and Clara.

Nor could he depend upon indefinite help from the Gregorys. He had to think of selling his Indian portraits and scenes of tribal life—but to whom?

During their brief stay in Washington, George called upon Maj. Thomas H. Hook in the Commissary General's Office. Hook, partially paralyzed from a duel with a fellow officer in the War of 1812, had flourished in the capital's military bureaucracy. On his death at the age of fifty, in 1841, his obituary would emphasize his helpfulness— to civilians as well as fellow military, including artists. His eulogist did not mention that Hook was a collector with a particular inter- est in Native American life and art. That far-from-common pursuit had led him to a heralded self-taught young painter of Indians, Peter Rindisbacher, who had settled in St. Louis in 1829. Arriving a year later, Catlin would have probably seen examples of the younger man's much-praised painting, and in the small town that the riverport still was, it would have been surprising if the two artists never met. A letter printed in the *St. Louis Beacon* at the end of 1829 drew readers' attention to Rindisbacher's originality, exalting the youthful Swiss émigré as having "marked out a new track, and almost invented a new style of painting. . . . His sketches of groups or single Indians are deserving of the highest admiration." At this point Catlin, ten years Rindisbacher's senior, had yet to see his own work praised in print. The young artist's growing renown may have been a factor in George's decision to leave St. Louis; in the tradition of movie West- erns, the town wasn't big enough for both of them. George might have remained in St. Louis, however, had he known that Rindisbach- er's dazzling career would be cut short by his sudden death in 1834, aged twenty-eight.

Meanwhile, mutual interest in Indian culture drew Catlin and Major Hook together. The Hooks' house in Washington, where the couple entertained frequently, was known for its intriguing display of native artifacts, attracting among others that sharp-eyed literary guest Washington Irving, who inventoried the contents as "fancifully decorated with Indian arms, and trophies, and war dresses, and the skins of various wild animals, and hung round with pictures of Indian games and ceremonies, and scenes of war and hunting." Since Irving wrote several years after Catlin's visit to Washington in March 1833, we can hope that along with scenes of tribal life by Rindisbacher, Hook's collection now included works by George Catlin, fresh from his upper Missouri travels.

In his characteristically direct way Catlin stated plainly what he hoped Hook would do for him: He wanted, first, to extend his travels, and he prodded Hook to intercede on his behalf with the latter's powerful friend, Lewis Cass, who had recently been promoted from territorial governor of Michigan to Jackson's secretary of war. Cass was the man to grant what Catlin now sought—an appointment as official artist attached to a military expedition to the West: "Such facilities as Government might think proper to afford me in this way would be of great service to me in my difficult, laborious & expensive undertaking," George wrote.

More problematic for Catlin, he yearned to be included in a new "National Collection," a revived version of the moribund Indian Museum, where—locked away unseen—Charles Bird King's portraits, along with part of the artist's collection of native costumes and artifacts, still hung in the War Department, next door to the office of the ex-superintendent of Indian affairs, Thomas McKenney. As soon as President Jackson was inaugurated, he had fired McKenney and promptly replaced him with Lewis Cass, precisely because of the latter's fervent support for the Jacksonian policy of Indian removal, and the zeal with which, as governor of Michigan, he had implemented the new law. Although Cass was known to have scholarly interests in tribal history, culture, and art, he was first and foremost a Jackson loyalist, unlikely to offer government space for any revived Indian Museum, especially one that displayed images of "hostile natives" such as Catlin's portraits of Black Hawk and his followers, portrayed as figures of tragic nobility.

George had done all he could to galvanize his Washington connections. By April 4, 1833, he was back in Pittsburgh to launch the first exhibition of his work—more than one hundred paintings from his recent travels on the upper Missouri, with a running commentary by the artist.

WHY DID CATLIN pick Pittsburgh to try out his exhibition-and-lecture road show? Belching smoke and soot from its new industrial prosperity, the city might have seemed an odd-enough choice three months earlier when George, holed up in a local boardinghouse, spent almost all of January breathing the town's insalubrious air while he recovered from his bronchial infection. In 1833 Pittsburgh was as unlikely a venue for the promotion of art as it was for the improvement of health.

He had "done" St. Louis. That feeling, along with his lingering illness, accounted for George's feverish impatience to leave. Returning from the upper Missouri, he faced the thriving reputation of the wunderkind Peter Rindisbacher, and the still-troubling intensity of his friendship with Joe Chadwick. Then, too, in St. Louis, Catlin's native subjects were part of the cityscape; along the riverside quays Indians were a familiar sight. His friend William Clark could be counted upon to help George in his new venture, just as he had opened doors to him in the past. But Clark's own Indian Museum, long open to St. Louisians and visitors alike, would dull the excitement George hoped to create with his pictures and commentary. Catlin would always proclaim the all-American belief in novelty as the key to success.

As to his reasons for choosing Pittsburgh, it may simply have been that he was invited. In this case energetic local boosters, in a city not known for its cultural offerings, whom George encountered during his convalescence there in early January 1833, must have urged him to come and arranged the details of his engagement, including expenses. He had survived his pulmonary infection in Pittsburgh. Now, returning in health, he was ready to conquer.

In 1833 Pittsburgh was a major hub of glass, iron, tin, and brass production; there was new money everywhere, along with the suffocating black particles. It was also a city in a hurry. No wonder Catlin felt at home there. Michel Chevalier, a French traveler and student of social conditions in his own country and abroad, declared: "Nowhere in the world is everybody so regularly and continually busy . . . there is no interruption of business for six days in the week, except during the three meals, the longest of which occupies ten minutes."

Still, the men whose industry had created these new fortunes had yet to provide their wives and daughters with the "cultural advantages" offered by more established cities; places to hear music, see paintings, be improved by visiting lecturers; gatherings where they could forget the dirt and smoke outside. Catlin's subject—Indians and his dangerous and thrilling adventures among them, visiting their villages, riding their horses and hunting bison alongside them—assured the men in his audience that George Catlin (another Pennsylvanian) was no effete artist from a snooty Eastern city or worse, a European one: Sporting his well-worn fringed buckskin tunic bristling with native quillwork, George embodied the bold and fearless explorer whose pictures brought back alive all that he had seen and done among the savages. Pittsburgh was the perfect town to launch George's new enterprise and make other places take notice of a new phenomenon: the artist as action hero.

On April 19 an advertisement in the *Pittsburgh Gazette* invited the local citizens to come that evening or the following one to a room next door to the Exchange Hotel, when "Mr. Catlin will endeavor to entertain them . . . with the Exhibition of 100 Indian Portraits, explaining at the same time, their peculiar manners, customs &c."

The second header of the text announced in boldface that portraits of Black Hawk and nine of his followers (noting—inaccurately—that that they were still prisoners at Jefferson Barracks) "are amongst the number" to be shown, while the rest consisted of "the wildest tribes in North America, and entirely in their native costume." At fifty cents, admission was expensive, and the cost, together with the hour, 7:00 p.m. on a weeknight, suggested an outing for the city's elite manufacturing class.

Appearing in the same issue of the *Gazette*, next to Catlin's own advertisement for the exhibition, the review was favorable, even indulgent. Of the more than one hundred paintings "most of them are yet in an unfinished state," the critic noted. He attributed what others might have found slapdash, if not insulting, to Catlin's strenuous travels, hard work, and productivity (Pittsburgh's wealth, after all, was based upon quantity and speed—the goals of mass production—not finicky handwork), "the artist only having had sufficient leisure to secure correct likenesses of the various living subjects of his pencil and the general features of the scenery which he had selected, the backgrounds and details being reserved for the labors of a future time."

George's manner—simple and open—won over the local gentry, and word of mouth helped sell tickets for two additional performances, extending his stay in Pittsburgh to a full week. The *Gazette's* anonymous critic had been further impressed, and not a little amused, by the "precaution" George had taken "to secure the certificates of different persons, to prove that the portraits were actually taken from the individuals whom they professed to represent, and that the costumes were really as represented," and that "there was no deception practiced." This "expedient," the reviewer agreed, made sense, but for another reason altogether: "His collection of portraits is destined to become more and more valuable, as the various tribes of Indians which they represent disappear from the face of the earth." According to Catlin's admiring critic, the artist's own rationale for his "certificates"—the need to establish his credibility—was rendered superfluous by his very presence: the "modest and unassuming deportment, the simple and unostentatious manner of his explanations and narrations, were perfectly satisfactory guarantees of the truth of every assertion which he made."

Following the fourth and final performance, George and Clara left Pittsburgh in triumph, heading for Cincinnati. With a tailwind of admiring reviews (reprinted in local newspapers wherever Catlin appeared with his paintings) and word of packed exhibition rooms, expectations among their new hosts ran high.

THE CATLINS HAD many connections in Cincinnati; among them was James Hall, founding publisher, editor, and star writer of the region's most distinguished publication, The *Western Monthly Magazine and Literary Journal*. A social lion and sparkling if opinionated conversationalist, Hall, known as "the Pontiff," would himself soon be reknowned as the author of the classic and successful work on Plains Indians, the three-volume *History of the Indian Tribes of North America: With Biographical Sketches and Anecdotes of the Principal Chiefs* (coauthored with Thomas McKenney).* Hall and Catlin had met during the artist's earlier stay in Washington, through their mutual friend, then-superintendent of Indian affairs Thomas McKenney. Returning to his home base in Ohio, Hall played an influential role in Cincinnati's cultural life, pointing to him as one likely source of George's invitation to show his Indian Gallery in a city avid for art and conscious of the importance of Catlin's project.

Another Catlin booster was Walter Gregory, Clara's younger

---

* Among its other contributions, this great work, published between 1836 and 1844, preserved, in the form of beautiful colored lithographs, most of Charles Bird King's Indian portraits when the original paintings were destroyed by fire. The authors would later try—unsuccessfully—to persuade Catlin to contribute a selection of his tribal portraits to the project.

brother. Like his older sibling, Dudley, Walter had inherited their father's Midas touch and was well on his way to spectacular success in Cincinnati. Within the next few years he would become an established pillar of the community and a promoter of its cultural and scientific advancement; among his other philanthropic activities, Walter was a founding board member of the Cincinnati Observatory. His connections helped assure that the Catlins' stay was both a social and professional success. The couple settled into the Pearl Street House, the newest and most luxurious hotel in town. In all likelihood Walter Gregory footed the bill—a huge one for a stay of almost six months. He is also reported to have paid for reframing the more than one hundred paintings that George would exhibit and discuss, along with underwriting newspaper advertisements and handbills: Even when he was broke and dependent upon credit, Catlin never stinted on publicity; luckily, the free-spending young entrepreneur, was glad to act as banker. It wouldn't do to have his brother-in-law appear before the cream of Cincinnati society looking like a shabby salesman of patent medicines. So at a cost of fifty-one dollars, Gregory treated George to a brand-new suit from the best tailor in town.

Advertisements kept Cincinnatians tantalized by the coming attraction, now officially baptized "Mr. Catlin's Indian Gallery"; George, meanwhile, kept working to finish the paintings that had remained uncompleted in Pittsburgh—now numbering 140.

As James Hall discreetly revealed in the review that appeared in his *Western Monthly Magazine*, he had been privileged with an early private viewing of the works. He had the advantage of familiarity with both the artist and his subject—the endangered Indian—and his review still stands as the most knowledgeable and authoritative of any contemporary appreciation of the artist. Hall grasped the full scope of Catlin's mission, along with its incalculable importance as a record:

"There is now in this city a collection of paintings, which we consider the most extraordinary and interesting that we have ever witnessed; and one which constitutes a most valuable addition to the history of our continent, as well as to the arts of our country." Published toward the end of Catlin's stay, the article makes it clear that Hall had come to know the artist, his travels, and his paintings well, being acquainted with "an equal number" to those on view, which only the invited could see "in an unfinished state, which have not yet been submitted to public inspection."

Although Hall and McKinney's first volume was several years from publication, his expertise was well established, and he could be relied upon to evaluate the fresh contribution of Catlin's art: "These are not the portraits of the depraved savages who linger upon the skirts of our advanced settlements, debased and emasculated by an intercourse with the whites. They are those of the manly Indian, as he exists in his own wide plains, joint tenant with the buffalo, the elk and the grisly [sic] bear." He did not fail to note the four paintings (probably on view here for the first time) depicting the "successive stages" of the Mandan religious ceremony, or the "variety of ingenious and excruciating torture" to which the young initiates were obliged to submit.

After praising Catlin's patriotism in being, like John James Audubon, a "native artist" focusing on his own country, Hall echoed Catlin's sense of urgency in insisting upon the essential mission: to record in word and image his firsthand witness to a vanishing race:

> We lingered in this gallery of portraits with a melancholy pleasure. . . . The race is melting away as the winter snow before the vernal breeze. In a few years more we shall know them only in tradition and song, in painting and history. . . . For they recede as we approach. We shall occupy their hunting grounds, and tread upon their graves; but we shall never mingle with them in council or sit by their firesides. There is a curse in our touch that withers them. Wherever we come in contact, they perish, or are contaminated— they are swept from the face of the earth or live in degradation.

———

KNOWING THAT CLARA was looked after by her brother Walter allowed George to take off—alone—when he felt so inclined, which seems to have been often. He brought the Indian Gallery across the river to Louisville, going on to New Orleans, where he gathered more admiring notices. Later George would claim he had ascended the Platte River to Fort Laramie at this period, visiting (and painting) Pawnee, Omaha, Oto, Arapaho, and Cheyenne, traveling as far as the shore of the Great Salt Lake. The requisite time required, there and back, makes this journey a near-impossibility—as does the fact that in 1833 Fort Laramie did not yet exist.

For George, plans—even hopes—had a way of turning from hazy future into present reality. Arrivals always felt coercive; they hardly figure in Catlin's letters. In contrast the exultant "I am leaving" appears often, rising like a shout from the page.

15

"WE ARE INVADERS OF A SACRED SOIL"

From Cincinnati, in the fall of 1833, Catlin stepped up his campaign to garner War Department support for his next adventure. He wanted to join the new dragoon regiment, mustered at Jefferson Barracks, for its first assignment to Fort Gibson, in Arkansas Territory.

The plan, as Catlin learned, probably from Major Hook, was to deploy the regiment on a series of expeditions deep into Indian country. Officially these forays were a gesture of friendship and peace. Implicitly they would constitute a show of military force directed at the Pawnee Pict (Wichita), Kiowa, and a warning to the feared Comanche. Catlin, however, saw the campaign as an irresistible opportunity: Embedded with the dragoons, he would return with an "exclusive" visual and written record of the regiment's activities at the farthest boundaries of the Republic. He was not asking for money, he wrote to Maj. Thomas L. Smith, his conduit to Lewis Cass, and to Maj. Gen. Alexander Macomb, commander of the army; he was confident that both these farsighted military leaders would "feel willing to aid me in the way I ask. I wish to go at my own expense and on my own account, asking for nothing but their countenance and protection." But Catlin the lawyer wanted every *i* dotted: He asked for a permit or orders specifying his duties as a civilian member of the regiment, while making it plain that he would also remain free to come and go as he pleased. As always, when George wanted a favor, he adroitly turned his benefactors into beneficiaries: Together, he assured the commanders, they would "astonish the *Civil* ones in a little time."

According to the artist's grandniece, Marjorie Catlin Roehm, the editor of the only published collection of Catlin family letters, George's request to Cass stipulated that his friend Joseph Chadwick receive permission to accompany him to Fort Gibson. Chadwick's earlier service in the volunteer militia, and his present job as draftsman in the St. Louis federal land office, lent credibility to his role in the expedition, but Cass had other reasons to see Chadwick's presence as a valuable addition to the first dragoon deployment in the West. Like Chadwick, Lewis Cass was descended on his mother's side from one of Exeter, New Hampshire's, founding families; both men had spent their early years in the New England town, but dearest to the secretary's heart, both were graduates of Phillips Exeter Academy: The name of Lewis Cass stood at the pinnacle of the school's roster of distinguished graduates, and there was no more devoted "old boy" than the secretary of war. On the basis of Catlin's request that Chadwick, a recent honors graduate of the academy, accompany him, his application would have been sure to receive special attention.

Major Smith's support may not have been crucial, but he nonetheless proved an ideal intermediary; he promptly forwarded Catlin's request, attaching his own recommendation for an immediate affirmative response. Shrewdly Smith cast the artist's mission in technical terms: Along with a German botanist and his young assistant, Catlin and Chadwick would be accompanying the expedition "for *scientific purposes*." On October 23, a week after receiving Catlin and Smith's communiqués, Cass replied with his official permit, followed the next day by confirmation from Major General Macomb.

BY SPRING, CATLIN would be leaving—that magic word—on his way to Arkansas Territory and its barely mapped boundaries. Most of all George was eager to engage with the elusive Comanche. A tribe as mysterious as it was powerful, their presence was felt and feared as horsemen, traders, and not least, warriors who spread terror through both Indian and white settlements, covering a vast swath of the southwestern United States and Spanish territories. The "Comanche Empire," as it has recently been called, was everywhere and nowhere.

No sooner did his commission come through than George began to have dark presentiments about the expedition—feelings that the voyage out from Natchez only served to confirm: The Arkansas River ran to extremes, from its infamous "boils," when the high waters rose from their sandy bottom "like a pot of boiling water"; at other times powerful freshets chewed off acres of riverbank at a time, which crashed into the river with the sound of an earthquake. Like most Western waters, observed another young officer assigned to the same dragoon regiment and headed to Fort Gibson that same spring, the Arkansas was very crooked: "Sometimes you may travel ten or twenty miles and come back within 20 or 30 yds. of the same place."

When the steamship *Arkansas* pulled away from its berth "under the Hill," the riverfront of Natchez, George Catlin and Joe Chadwick were both on board. With Joe coming from St. Louis and George arriving from New Orleans, they would have had to plan well in advance in order to meet and set off together. Then, within two hundred miles of their destination, the ship ran aground; the "water falling fast, left the steamer nearly on dry ground." For more than two weeks George, Joe and another young army officer, Lieutenant Seaton, made the best of the boat's immobility by nonstop pursuit of diversion, rowdy "hunting and fishing, and whist, and sleeping and eating." George enjoyed playing older brother to the two younger men—both in their early twenties. In a rush to join his regiment, Seaton had forgotten the trunk with all his clothes, and he therefore had to borrow George's shirts to pursue their sporting adventures "catering for our table, in getting fish and wild fowl." Catlin's reunion with Joe, and now the sight of their new friend wearing George's clothes, felt like a physical bond uniting them: "We became yoked in amusements," Catlin wrote.

They arrived at Fort Gibson in mid-April, to discover that only three platoons of the eight recruited and trained at Jefferson Barracks were assembled; the other units, raised in states as far away as New Hampshire, had been held up by the vagaries of travel and failed supplies, including uniforms. Another reason for the understaffing of the expedition: There had been so many desertions from Jefferson Barracks it had been thought futile to try and bring them to justice.

For the next two months they waited. Temperatures rose. The balmy spring of the Southwest, which had been a critical element in planning the expedition, turned into the stifling heat of high summer on the southern plains. Catlin's spirits remained undampened. He had the constant presence of Joe Chadwick, and the company of other young officers, many so freshly commissioned they resembled schoolboys more than leaders.

Catlin casts this unexpected idyll in a haze of nostalgia. With Joe Chadwick as his "inseparable companion," he thrilled to the beauty of their surroundings—unappreciated by most visitors. There were also new tribes to paint. Fort Gibson had been planned as a strategic center to implement President Jackson's Indian removal policy. In the immediate vicinity of its ramshackle buildings lived "an immense number of Indians, most of whom have been removed to the present locations by the Government, from their Eastern original positions, within a few years past," Catlin noted. But it was soon apparent that their tragedy offered a welcome opportunity for his encyclopedic ambitions: "I had two months at my leisure in this section of the country, which I used in travelling about with my canvass, and note-book, visiting all of them in their villages." And he happily ticked off additions to his burgeoning Indian Gallery: "Cherokees, Chocktaws, Creeks, Seminoles, Chickasaws, Quapaws, Senecas, Delawares, and several others."

Among the "others" was the tribe most associated with the region around Fort Gibson (near Tulsa, in present-day Oklahoma) and the largest native presence in the vicinity. The Osage, according to George's calculation, numbered about 5,200 persons inhabiting three villages within an eighty-mile area of surrounding country. Catlin was enthralled by their appearance: "the tallest race of men in North America, either of red or white skins." (Of below-average height himself, George never failed to comment admiringly on men who towered physically above others.) Far from appearing ungainly, they were "well-proportioned in their limbs, and good-looking. . . . Their movement is graceful and quick." In George's view the Osage retained their godlike appearance by having "studiously rejected everything of civilized customs . . . starting with whiskey and . . . strictly maintaining their primitive looks and manners."

In keeping with his idealized sense of the tribe, he portrayed their chief, Clermont, in the relaxed seated three-quarter pose, with legs crossed, of neoclassical portraits of statesmen and savants: The Osage leader was painted with the presidential peace medal prominently displayed upon his bare chest. A paired portrait of his young wife is an exceptionally intimate image of mother and child; she, too, is shown seated, holding their naked baby; standing unsteadily on his mother's lap, he caresses her neck and hair.

Thanks to this period of enforced inactivity, Catlin was able to observe and record, in both word and image, an extraordinary document of another local tribe—the Choctaw at play: With elements of soccer and lacrosse, their signature game fielded several teams at the same time, each of which consisted of hundreds of players, requiring squads of referees and accompanied by a brisk business in betting. Bodies leaping, tackling, running, passing, and reaching for the ball, playing offense and defense—Catlin manages to seize the controlled chaos of today's football, imagined in greater depth on a vastly wider screen, a supersize Super Bowl, teeming with hundreds of players.*

George was chafing restlessly, impatient to set out on the expeditions for which he had traveled all this way: the quest to encounter the Pawnee Pict and Comanche. Already he envisioned the drama of the moment when eight hundred mounted dragoons would approach the *"gaping and astounded multitude* of Comanchees and Pawnees." Not for the first time Catlin saw the encounter from the native perspective. Torn by familiar questions of identity, he had to confront other fissures within himself: the conflict between the artist and conqueror deepened by his role in the expedition and, finally, by the nature of his attachment to Joe Chadwick, as dangerous as it was crucial to his survival.

"I have become so much Indian of late," he confessed, "that my pencil has lost all appetite for subjects that savor of tameness." Impatient to goad "these red knights of the lance" to violence—like the tarantulas and scorpions that he and Joe caught and incited to kill one another, "for it is then that they shew their brightest hues—and I care not how badly we frighten them, provided we hurt them not, nor frighten them out of sketching distance."

A recurring theme during this, one of Catlin's last Indian adventures, was liberation: "I take an indescribable pleasure in roaming through Nature's trackless wilds and selecting my models, where I am free and unshackled by the killing restraints of society."

Because this male and military world afforded him "perfect protection"—not only against danger from Indian attacks, but from the laws

---

* The Mandan had their own favored sport, a more challenging form of shuffleboard in which the players, wielding a pole stuck with stiff leather flanges, try to hook an iron bagel-shaped object as it slides past on a smoothed track.

of "the *Civil*," George once again felt qualms about the real purpose of the expedition. He wanted to believe the official version, but two months of hanging around with nothing to do but observe and paint the Indians in the vicinity of the fort, had raised doubts about the provocative nature of their forthcoming deployment across the ancestral lands of unknown and hostile tribes:

"The object of this summer's campaign seems to be to cultivate an acquaintance with the Pawnees and Comanchees," he noted cautiously. Only these roaming tribes' "extreme ignorance of us," he hazarded, could explain the fact that [they] "have not yet recognized the United States in treaty; and have struck frequent blows on our frontiers and plundered our traders who are traversing their country." As he reminded his readers, these nomadic tribes were caught in a pincer action between the Spaniards, "advancing upon them on one side, and the Americans on the other," both "fast destroying the furs and game of their country, which God gave them as their only wealth and means of subsistence."

He wanted to believe that the U.S. military expedition harbored a loftier purpose:

> This movement of the dragoons *seems* to be one of the most humane in its views, and I heartily hope that it may prove so in the event, as well as for our own sakes as for that of the Indian. I can see no reason why we should march upon them with an invading army carrying with it the spirit of chastisement.

Already he sensed a different agenda, one fraught with danger, and whose dubious purpose must surely affect the outcome.

HARD RIDING WOULD be the order of the day, and a reliable horse the best protection. To this end George invested the staggering sum of $250 in a superb, even legendary horse. "Charley," a cream-colored mustang, with a sweeping black mane and tail, had been broken and trained by the Comanche before his purchase by an officer of the garrison. Feeling the debility of age, Colonel Birbank now found the spirited creature too hard to control. He was happy to sell him to Catlin, an experienced rider and lover of fine horses. Joe Chadwick, delighted with his purchase from an Indian hunter of a "nimble slender-legged little buffalo chaser . . . was now," George recalled, "everywhere my companion."

They set off under blazing skies on June 19. Instead of the eight hundred mounted dragoons who were to have formed the expeditionary force, 455 men marched from Fort Gibson, to the traditional bugle fanfares and cheers of the flag-waving crowd, consisting of officers' families together with local ranchers and homesteaders. Because of the officially diplomatic nature of the expedition, General Leavenworth was to accompany the troops for the first two hundred miles, or as far as the False Washita River, by which point he hoped for an encounter with the unknown tribes; once this meeting had taken place, he planned to return to home base, after being relieved by Colonel Dodge,[*] who was to lead the troops for the remainder of the seven-hundred-mile trek across the southern plains to the base of the Rockies[†] and back.

Once on the march Catlin was quickly alerted to the tactics that would be employed. His earlier enthusiasm for a strategy of provocation became troubling when he saw it in action:

---

[*] The change in command represented a humiliating demotion for the more experienced Leavenworth. Its reasons remain murky, but may be assumed to have been political.

[†] Catlin and his contemporaries believed this high and rugged range to be a spur of the Rockies, but in fact the Washita Mountains, geologically far older, are unrelated.

The prevailing policy amongst the officers seems to be, that of flogging [Indians] first, and then establishing a treaty of peace. If this plan were *morally right*, I don't think it *practicable;* for, as *enemies*, I do not believe they will stand to meet us; but as *friends*, I think we *may* bring them to a *talk*. . . . We are over the Washita—the "Rubicon is passed." We are invaders of a sacred soil. We are carrying war in our front.

His zest soon returned. He and Joe now had the best of both worlds. They enjoyed the protection of the dragoon regiment, while doing as they pleased—alone. "During the march, we were subject to no military subordination," George recalled. "We galloped about wherever we were disposed . . . and running our noses into every wild nook and crevice . . . we travelled happily, until our coffee was gone and our bread; and even then we were happy upon meat alone."

Then the scourge descended. A "bilious fever," almost certainly malarial, swept through the troops, "until at last each one in his turn . . . both man and beast, were vomiting and fainting, under the poisonous influence of some latent enemy, that was floating in the air, and threatening our destruction." Once struck, the victim had little chance of recovery; in day after day of scorching heat when the temperature never dropped below 105 degrees in the shade, fevers continued to rise. Food supplies diminished, and a relentless sun burned away every source of fresh water; what remained were brackish pools, the bigger ones used as buffalo wallows.

No respecter of rank, the sickness swept through the regiment; officers and men, along with horses, were "daily dying," George reported, with nearly half of the command "on their backs with the prevailing epidemic," starting with General Leavenworth under whose tent, Catlin noted, he was writing the present letter. The commander himself "lies pallid and emaciated before me, on his couch, with a dragoon fanning him, whilst he breathes forty or fifty breaths a minute, and writhes under a burning fever, although he is yet unwilling to even admit that he is sick."

Desperate to salvage the expedition, Leavenworth ordered Colonel Dodge to "select all the men, and all the horses able to proceed, and be off tomorrow at 9 o'clock upon the march towards the Comanche, in hopes thereby to preserve the health of the men, and make the most rapid advance towards the extreme point of destination." Of the four hundred or so men who had set out from Fort Gibson, there were left "but 250 men who were able to proceed . . . and that again reduced some sixty or seventy by sickness."

Catlin and Chadwick were among those presumed spared by the disease—but not for long. George, along with others who daily fell out from the ranks, had been harboring the fever before symptoms appeared. Dated July 18, Colonel Dodge's official report to the Adjutant General's Office noted: "Six litters [of sick] including Mr. Catlin."

Joe Chadwick remained untouched by sickness, and his immunity, along with his care, proved crucial to Catlin's survival. "During my illness," George remembered, in an eternal present tense, "my friend Joe has been almost constantly by my bedside; evincing (as he did when we were creeping over the vast prairies) the most sincere and intense anxiety for my recovery . . . he has administered, like a brother, every aid and every comfort that lay in his power to bring." Crucial to George's morale, Joe also served as his friend's hands and eyes; when Catlin was too sick to move, Chadwick became his surrogate. He made the drawings that record the historic moments of the expedition—notably, the visit to the Wichita village.

Some four days of marching westward brought the dragoons into the heart of Comanche country, which also happened to be the territory of New Spain. For the first time the scouts found signs of fresh horse tracks, and plumes of smoke were visible atop far-off bluffs.

At noon on the fourth day they saw several miles in the distance a large party on horseback watching their approach, and mistook them—owing to the gleaming blades of their lances—for Mexican cavalry. Soon the massed riders were revealed to be a "war-party of Comanchees, on the look out for their enemies." Men and horses now disappeared behind one bluff, only to reappear on the ridge of another, causing the dragoons to change directions several times. This produced the intended effect of disorienting the Americans. At this point Colonel Dodge ordered the command to halt "while he rode forward with a few of his staff, and an ensign carrying a white flag."

"I joined this advance," Catlin tells us, as it moved forward slowly. The Indians, meanwhile, "stood their ground" until they saw the white flag, now fully visible a half mile away, waving as a signal for them to approach, "at which one of their party galloped out in advance of the war-party, on a milk white horse, carrying a piece of white buffalo skin on the point of his long lance in reply to our flag." There followed "one of the most thrilling and beautiful scenes I ever witnessed," he wrote.

HOW WAS CATLIN, last described as a litter case, able to continue marching with those troops healthy enough to pursue the expedition to its most difficult—and dangerous—stage into enemy territory? He recalled "shaking with fever and chills," his old cotton umbrella shielding him at all times from the tormenting sun. If George was in fact present at the scene, it could only have been because Joe Chadwick, gauging the sun's angles, held the umbrella aloft as they rode together on one horse, the sick man secured in the saddle. But we'll never know whether Catlin was there as witness or only in his mind's imaginings.

He was now too weak and feverish to be moved. The regiment's makeshift "sick camp," was four days' ride behind them, so Chadwick

would have had to improvise a rest stop where he could safely leave his
friend alone, while he became his hands and eyes: "Joe took my sketch
and note-books in his pocket," Catlin recalled, and went off with the
rest of the "healthy" regiment to visit the Pawnee Pict village, where
the dragoons managed to retrieve a young boy captured—his parents
killed—in an Indian raid. The officers may have been anticipating a
battle, but instead, as with the Comanche, were met by more than
two thousand Pawnee with embraces and offers of peace. Unable to
rise from his stretcher, Catlin delegated Joe to act as his surrogate and
record the scene, but Chadwick's drawing of the riverbank bristling
with tipis declares him a draftsman, not an artist.

After an absence of fifteen days, Chadwick found Catlin—in worse
condition than when Joe had left—still in the sick bay together with
fellow sufferers, lying in an improvised hut covered with such leafy
branches as could be found to provide some shade. Along with generous provisions from their hosts, their comrades arrived back from the
Pawnee camp with crucial advice: They should return to Fort Gibson
by a northerly route, even though this would involve a detour of more
than one hundred miles. The region between their present camp and
the headwaters of the Canadian River, as the Pawnee pointed out,
was home to "immense herds of buffaloes; a place where we could get
enough to eat and where, being appreciably cooler, by lying by awhile,
could restore the sick, who are now occupying a great number of litters," among whom Catlin included himself. During their rest stop on
the north bank of the Canadian River, the healthy young dragoons—
both officers and enlisted men—"indulged in a general licence to grat-
ify their sporting propensities," Catlin noted sourly, "and a scene of
bustle and cruel slaughter it has been, to be sure!" Daily the camp lay
almost deserted as the able-bodied went hunting buffalo "dispersed in
little squads in all directions, . . . dealing death to these poor creatures
to a most cruel and wanton extent, merely for the pleasure of *destroying*, generally without stopping to cut out the meat." In the process

several hundreds had been killed, with "not so much as the flesh of half a dozen used."

This was the same George Catlin who, two years earlier at Fort Union, had eagerly embarked on similar daily killing sprees led by Kenneth McKenzie, during which George had been keen to show off his riding and hunting skills with little thought for the carnage left by their sporting slaughter. But there is also envy in his disapproval, sharpened by fear of mortality. He lay helpless among those left behind at the "deserted" camp, the sick and the dying, while the robust roared off to hunt.

THE ARTIST HAD also changed—and been changed by his experience of the West, most of all by his time spent among its native peoples. He had learned from the Mandan, who hunted for food but who otherwise felt at one with the animals with whom they shared the land. In their ceremonies and rituals, their masks and dances, life—animal and human—was held as a sacred continuum: Dogs, horses, and buffalo all figured in the tribe's daily existence as in their cosmology. From their animist culture Catlin had absorbed more than he knew. He would never again feel joy in slaughter for sport, or in the bloodlust that urged the killing of "savages." Now that he had seen the dreaded Comanche and Pawnee Pict come in peace, embracing the dragoon commanders, showing only compassion for his sick and starving comrades, he could no longer accept them as enemies.

Their return march proved more of a nightmare than any of the miseries they had yet endured. The regiment's numbers continued to dwindle, starting with the death of General Leavenworth and his aide; too ill to travel, they had been left behind to die. Almost every tent belonging to the officers had been converted to a hospital: "Sighs and groans were heard in all directions," Catlin recalled. Many more fell sick and had to be carried between two horses. Those who died were hastily buried by the wayside, still on their litters. Catlin's own fever worsened. Not for the last time, he began to see this plague as retribution. They had come under false pretenses, and their presence had proved a curse. If proof were needed that they had no business in this country, they had only to count the dead they left behind, along with the sick and the dying they carried with them.

16

"CATLIN ENCAMPED, WOLVES IN THE DISTANCE"

George was among the few who returned alive from the "slaughtering ground," as he called the country they had crossed, and he saw his survival as something of a miracle. It had taken fifteen days for the empty supply wagon that served as an ambulance to reach Fort Gibson. Lying on the bare boards, racked with fever, he was jolted with such force that the exposed skin on his emaciated body was scraped bloody.

When they finally arrived he was rushed into the post hospital—or what passed for one at the most primitive military installation in the army. There he joined other skeletal figures hovering between life and death. The presiding physician, Dr. Wright, turned out to have been an old Wilkes-Barre schoolmate of George's, and a comforting presence for that. Before sulfur drugs or antibiotics, with scant knowledge of diseases and how they spread, there was little any doctor could do for the stricken soldiers who continued to arrive on makeshift stretchers, other than providing clean water, linen, and such food as his desperately ill patients could swallow.

Some managed to reach the infirmary only to die there: "Of those that have been brought in and quartered at the hospital," Catlin reported,

four or five are buried daily; and as an equal number from the
9th regiment are falling by the same disease. I have the mournful sound of "Roslin Castle"* with muffled drums passing six
or eight times a-day under my window, to the burying ground;
which is but a little distance in front of my room, where I can lay
in my bed and see every poor fellow lowered down into his silent
and peaceful habitation.

The day before Catlin wrote this letter he counted "no less than eight
solemn processions visited that insatiable ground."

Despite the numbers of dead and dying that George saw daily from
his hospital window, he continued to share with the dragoons' chief
officers the belief that, overall, this first expedition had been a success. Confronting the human cost that had hit so close to home, the
mistakes in judgment—from decisions about the weather to the stubbornness in pressing on in the face of the troops' decimation—George,
like his military hosts, struggled to believe in their mission as worth
the sacrifice. But here was the proof:

In the course of two councils that he or Joe Chadwick had wit-
nessed, the first in Comanche territory, the second in the Pawnee
Pict settlement, the tribal chiefs had been so impressed with Colonel
Dodge and his mounted troops that "overcoming their hesitation, a
deputation of chiefs agreed to return with the colonel to Fort Gibson."
From September 1 to September 4, 1834, Choctaw, Cherokee,
Osage, and Seneca met with the Pawnee, Comanche, and Kiowa.
In light of this historically unprecedented encounter between war-
ring tribes, one engineered by their common enemy, the U.S. gov-
ernment, all those involved, from Colonel Dodge to George Catlin,

---

* Originally a romantic Scottish ballad, "Roslin Castle," on crossing to America,
became, first, a militia marching tune, before being adopted to accompany military
burials.

had reason to believe that the "foundations had been laid for lasting peace among frontier tribes," a peace brokered by their Great White Father.

Along with his faith that the sacrifice of lives was redeemed by the historic "summit meeting," Catlin was buoyed by the eighteenth-century rationalist view that he had witnessed progress and civilization at work: "For several days in succession, free vent was given to the feelings of men *civilized, half-civilized* and *wild*; where the three stages of man were fearlessly asserting their rights, their happiness, and friendship for each other." His only regret: None of the assembled tribes was willing to make the trip to Washington; not only would the journey, he opined, have been in their own future interests, but "it would have been exceedingly gratifying to the people of the East to have seen so wild a group." Before the dragoons escorted the tribes back to their settlements, Catlin seized the opportunity to paint their portraits, promoting his likenesses of the Comanche chiefs in his "Letter No. 45" to the *Commercial Advertiser.*

So, too, did he denounce the exploitation of these same tribes, openly practiced under his gaze. Joining the military escort accompanying them on the trip home was a company of eighty men, hoping to corner trade with the Comanche and Pawnee. As the first to have lived, painted, and written about the tribes inhabiting the southwestern plains, Catlin used his expertise to seize a bully pulpit: He would not stand by and see the same crimes committed against these peoples as had victimized their counterparts on the upper Missouri:

> I have travelled too much among Indian tribes, and seen too much, not to know the evil consequences of such a system. Goods are sold at such exorbitant prices, that the Indian gets a mere shadow for his peltries, &c. The Indians see no white people but traders and sellers of whiskey; and of course, judge us all

by them—they consequently hold us, and always will, in contempt; as inferior to themselves, as they have reason to do—and
they neither fear nor respect us.

Catlin's proposed remedy, however, was only a more benign form
of social control. In exchange for sharing in the profits of a market
economy—cash instead of alcohol—the Indian would give up sepa-
ratism for assimilation, the savage state for "civilization." The government would take over and regulate commerce with the Indian,
driving out the "trader in the village." By inviting "these Indians to
our trading posts," modeled on the regulated "factories" eliminated by
Astor, the tribes would "bring in their furs, their robes, horses, mules
&c . . . where there is a good market for them all . . . where they
would get four or five times as much for their articles of trade" as they
would receive from an independent agent, operating "out of the reach
of competition, and out of sight of the civilized world."

Promising a fair deal, government trading posts would also provide the higher benefits of assimilation to the uncivilized, "as they
would be continually coming where they would see good and polished society, they would be gradually adopting our modes of living
. . . our arts and manufactures," and not least, "they would see and
estimate our military strength, and advantages, and would be led
to fear and respect us." His repetition of those two words was significant. In these lines all of Catlin's own conflicts about white and
Indian do battle with one another: fairness and force, friendship
and control, carrot and stick; but always and unyieldingly—"them"
and "us."

IT WAS PAST time for Catlin's own return to civilization. He had
received from Clara the news that she was pregnant with their first
child. As it often did, George's mind played time in reverse: Almost

as if the anticipated birth had become fact, he fretted about the two thousand miles that separated him from his "dear wife and little one . . . whom I was despairing of ever embracing again." (It would seem that Clara miscarried, as there is no surviving mention of this pregnancy or of the infant.)

IN EARLY SEPTEMBER, just days after the Indian council had ended, George persuaded himself, as he tells us, that he was well enough to make the 540-mile trip—the shortest route between Fort Gibson and St. Louis—alone. He allowed that the timing of his departure "was against the advice of my surgeon and all the officers of the garrison," but he saw this journey—with all its risks—as life against death. He remained convinced that "if I could get out upon the prairies, and moving continually toward the Northward, I should daily gain strength, and save myself . . . from the jaws of that voracious burial-ground that laid in front of my room [sic]."

The camp surgeon and Catlin were both right. George gained in strength daily as his spirits soared—"rising and escaping from the gloom and horrors of a sick bed, . . . [his horse] carrying him fast and safely over green fields spotted and tinted with waving wild flowers; and through the fresh and cool breezes that are rushing about him." Still, his recovery remained far from complete. Day after day he "pranced and galloped along," but just as often he was forced to dismount, "lying in the grass an hour or so, until the grim shaking and chattering of an ague chill had passed off."

His journey, in George's telling, lasted for twenty-five days, more than three weeks. Still weak and prey to intermittent chills and fever, Catlin managed to survive on the hardtack he had brought with him, a diet supplemented by shooting prairie hens and occasionally catching fish and ducks. Crossing the Missouri Territory before arriving at the river of the same name, a distance of some five hundred miles, George had to chart his way through a "wild and uncultivated state without roads and without bridges," with only his pocket compass to steer his course, "fording and swimming the streams in the best manner I could." All these feats, he repeatedly assures us, "I performed entirely alone." In a famous oil sketch, titled by the artist "Catlin Encamped, Wolves in the Distance," George is seen from the back seated next to a small fire, a homely coffee pot at his side. Tethered nearby, Charley paws the ground anxiously. Engulfed by the "vast and . . . boundless prairie," man and horse have turned to stare at indistinct predators, massed between them and the horizon.

Catlin as Ulysses, riding his mustang Charley across corners of present-day Oklahoma and Arkansas before covering the breadth of Missouri, makes a great story. Horse and rider recapture a moment in a Homeric narrative of a return home beset with dangers, a final test of George's courage and endurance on the frontier.

The year before, Catlin and Chadwick had received permission to join the dragoon expedition together and they had arranged to meet in Natchez, where they boarded the steamship that would take them to Fort Gibson. Now, after seeing his friend off—George still weak and emaciated; Joe Chadwick, too—headed back alone to St. Louis. In the intervening months, they had been inseparable. Why now, in Catlin's version, did they go their separate ways, to the same destination—if, in fact, they did?

The survivor owns the tale. Like George's mythic solitary journey, its tracks as lost to time as footprints through a tall grass prairie, the story of Catlin and Joe Chadwick becomes what the artist has chosen to retrace, leaving blank spaces or gaps, evoking absence as much as presence. Like most accounts marked by guilt or pain or fear, what seeps around the edges is the crucial part, and memory staves off loss.

Protégé, friend, brother, caretaker, and, probably, lover, Joe Chadwick claimed Catlin's deepest feelings—feelings that had stayed locked away until they met. Engaging him in childish games, nursing him from death, Joe brought the older man back to life. Even in George's cautious telling, their time together in Arkansas Territory describes an idyll. Whether Joe was his unacknowledged companion on the twenty-five-day trek back to St. Louis, or, in fact, traveled separately, their return to the rest of their lives begins with an erasure.

FOR WHAT WOULD be the last time, Catlin crossed the Missouri, joining Clara in St. Louis "under the roof of kind and hospitable friends" with whom she had stayed for a year while waiting for him to return— "a wreck, as I now am."

By October the stinging cold of the Plains winter shivered St. Louis. Clara and George, still bony and frail, boarded a steamboat headed for New Orleans. When they disembarked on the levee, even the humid air of the Delta, "thick stagnant stuff from the Mississippi," felt like an embrace.

CATLIN MADE TWO—or possibly three—visits to the multiracial city of more than forty thousand that then consisted almost entirely of the modern-day French Quarter. He was fascinated by the sway of voodoo, its similarities to the magic of tribal medicine men, their rattles, incantations, and dances, their power over life and death: Voodoo pharmacies stocked an array of potions for all needs. He became obsessed with making a portrait from life of Marie Laveau, the legendary and feared "Voodoo Queen," and it's said that he pursued Madame Laveau across Congo Square with his request. When she refused, he rushed back to his rooms to paint her from memory: Attributed to Catlin, a copy of the portrait—the original was stolen—still hangs in the Louisiana State Museum. During a shorter stay the following year—1835—Catlin exhibited works, lectured, and gave interviews about his Indian Gallery.

After Christmas and the New Year celebrated in a city devoted to celebration, Clara and George steamed off once more, this time to Pensacola, Florida, to stay with Catlin's brother James and his wife, Abigail. They arrived on February 5, 1835, George "taken with the ague and fever on account of the fatigue of the Journey."

Pensacola itself had just gotten over an epidemic of yellow fever, but those who had fled were returning in large numbers, due to a business boom following the end of the First Seminole War. It had just been selected as the site for a federal navy yard, "the great Naval depôt for all the southern coast," Catlin announced proudly. His brother James, meanwhile, cashier of the Bank of Pensacola decided to make use of insider information, purchasing shares, along with the bank, in a proposed Alabama, Florida, and Georgia Railroad. George (backed by Dudley Gregory, his brother-in-law) invested individually as well. To help launch the offering George's "Letter—No. 36," destined like the others for the *New York Commercial Advertiser*, reads like copy for a prospectus, one that shrewdly combined the lure of profit with civic-minded boosterism: "A plan of railroad has been projected from Pensacola to Columbus, Georgia, which needs only to be completed to place Pensacola at once before any town on the southern coast, except New Orleans," he began. And he went on, knowledgeably citing losses recently incurred throughout the region, for lack of just such a transportation advantage. Despite George's persuasive marketing, however, the railroad went under after an expensive grading swallowed investors' money. It was the first but far from the last, of George's investments to evaporate.

DECADES LATER, ON the eve of the Civil War, George would recall his Pensacola visit with nostalgia, by reason of another "first": political activism. Although he had written eloquently against the Indian removal policies as implemented by the Jackson administration, it was in Pensacola that Catlin met an unlikely mentor in advocacy— John Howard Payne. Now remembered—if at all—as the composer of "Home, Sweet Home," Payne had come to Florida as a collector of Cherokee documents, and as a friend and supporter of their dissident leader John Ross. Breaking with the majority of his tribe, Ross was urging his holdout followers to stand firm against the forced relocation that would lead to the infamous "Trail of Tears," where thousands died from exposure or starvation on the march from the Southeast to present-day Oklahoma. The 1831 Supreme Court decision *Georgia v. the Cherokee Nation*, declaring the legality of the expulsion, made Ross, along with his defenders, a criminal, guilty of sedition. Now, according to Catlin's account, he and Payne rushed to Rossville, Georgia, where they both found themselves briefly sharing a jail cell with the dissenting Cherokee leader.

Once he was well, George reverted to his chronic restlessness. By the end of March, he was headed back to New Orleans to show a part of his Indian Gallery there—again. Local reviews were all that any artist could have hoped, but they did not pay the bills. He had to find a way to turn the gallery into a business proposition, one that could provide him with working capital, not just hand-to-mouth living expenses.

Worrying over these hard realities, Catlin felt stirred by a double dose of yearning. He was determined to see what he had missed of Indian country, but he also wanted to relive the adventures of the past three years. As Clara had seen almost nothing of the West, he decided that any return must include her, with all the comforts that travel on the frontier could now provide. Dutifully he booked passage on one of the newest, best-upholstered steamboats on the Mississippi for what he ironically called "a fashionable tour" of a West that was getting less wild with every passing year.

17

FLIGHT PATHS

By 1835 well-appointed steamboats, like the one that now carried George and Clara up the Mississippi, ran on a weekly schedule—a sure sign of encroaching civilization. Pier glass mirrors and white napery at meals provided George with further evidence that the days of the adventuring *Yellow Stone*, like the brave ship itself, were over.

As they left St. Louis, the dull flat vistas that unspooled for miles along the Mississippi made the restless traveler recall fondly the snags and sandbars of the Missouri. Then, above Rock Island, monotony gave way to wonder; their course meandered in and out of alternating bends until, between Prairie du Chien and Lake Pepin: "The eye is riveted . . . upon the thousand bluffs which tower in majesty above the river on either side . . . rising in the form of immense cones, domes and ramparts." As the primeval shapes thrust from the banks on both sides, "every reach and turn" breathed a sense of discovery, and George was reminded of why he felt compelled to return before he had even left.

For Clara the mystery of George's obsession with the West only deepened. They arrived at Fort Snelling on June 24, welcomed by "dashing rain," gusting winds, and numbing cold, conditions that prevailed without letup for the three weeks of their stay. Still, for Mrs. Catlin, separated from her husband for most of their seven-year marriage, the unaccustomed pleasures of being visibly a wife, even a shivering and still-homeless one, made up for the relentlessly foul weather. If she experienced the discomforts of a new pregnancy, Clara did not claim these symptoms as an excuse to keep close to the fires that were kept blazing at the fort against the unseasonable temperatures. Deciding (or possibly hoping) that she would never have to visit these parts again, she ventured forth in raincoat and stout boots, carrying an umbrella to collect specimens of local pebbles and plants.

Oblivious to the weather, George went about painting with his usual demonic energy. He made certain to secure likenesses of the leaders of the local Sioux clans, each festooned with a stylish tangle of medals awarded by the white chiefs in Washington, worn along with their own feathered, quilled, and painted attributes of prowess in battle and in the hunt. Like American men of all times and classes, Catlin was an ardent sports fan, and his homage to Indian star athletes is breathless with the kind of hero worship that warriors and medicine men rarely inspired. For his portraits of the two "most distinguished ball players in the Sioux tribe," he had them come "from the ball-play ground to my painting-room, in the dress in which they had just struggled in the play," and the artist poses them grasping their sticks, which resemble those used in present-day lacrosse.

Catlin's letter, published in the *New York Commercial Advertiser*, describes a "wild and grotesque" Fourth of July celebration at Fort Snelling which included a solo performance by a *berdache*, or cross-dressing dandy, and notes Clara's presence but makes no direct mention of her pregnancy, then in its first months; in any case, it was too indelicate a subject to appear in a newspaper. Hints of her condition, however, emerge in George's account of her welcome at the Sioux encampment. As the Catlins strolled through the village of birchbark tipis, the women gathered around Clara, "anxious to . . . shew her their children, of which she took especial notice"; then, indulging the expectant mother's sweet tooth, they "literally filled her hands and her arms with *muh-kuks* of maple sugar of their own manufacture"— the Sioux women's butter-and-egg money—which they had brought to trade at the fort.

George and Clara had been guests at Fort Snelling for more than three weeks, and despite the weather they had seen all the local sights. After Niagara, Catlin found nearby St. Peter's Falls (close to present-day St. Paul) dull. The same could be said of his first experience of fort life in mixed company: A short time before, he had complained about the heroic Narcissa Whitman, the first white woman to make the transcontinental crossing to Oregon territory, in 1836, as merely illustrating that women were unfit for travel in the West. What Catlin was really saying was that he felt more at home in the all-male society of Fort Union, where squaws and their mixed-blood children were banished to separate quarters. For Clara, however, Fort Snelling had been a gentle introduction to life on a frontier garrison, warmed by the hospitality of officers' wives whose backgrounds would have been similar to her own. Still, she was ready to leave. After seeing her off on a steamboat "with a party of ladies" bound for Prairie du Chien, where George planned to join her, he remained at the fort for another nine days, leaving only on July 27.

In less than a week he sat through tribal councils, listened to speeches by Chippewa, Sioux, and their white mediators, and interviewed leaders of both tribes. And he painted, sometimes as many as three portraits a day, according to his host, Maj. Laurence Taliaferro, Indian agent and fur trader on the upper Mississippi. Catlin called Taliaferro "the only public servant on these frontiers." The agent, in turn, noted of the artist: "The great world know [sic] nothing as yet of these things, and it seems to have been left to Mr. Catlin to open the

Sluices of information & by the magic of his pencil to hold the Mirror up to public view."

Chiefs on both sides were sufficiently acculturated to haggle with George over the price of sitting for their portraits, along with fees for enacting dances and games, including an all-women's soccer match. Catlin agreed to this early version of checkbook journalism, along with the tainted authenticity of staged events and costumes chosen by the artist—questions that would come back to haunt later white painters and especially photographers, notably Edward Curtis. There is no evidence that Catlin saw anything wrong with his own pay-to-play transactions; his openness in writing about them suggests he viewed these arrangements as a fair exchange.

Traveling separately—Clara by steamboat, George in a birchbark canoe made especially for him by the Chippewa at Fort Snelling— he and Clara convened at Prairie du Chien, Camp des Moines, Rock Island, and Dubuque; his little craft was so swift that George was always the first to arrive.

Catlin alone in his birchbark canoe—as iconic an attribute of the Indian as a feathered war bonnet—feverishly retracing his route—up, down, then up the Mississippi again—evokes the legend of the Flying Dutchman, doomed never to touch shore. In George's mind, however, doom lay in wait on the banks—in the very act of landing, of becoming grounded, settled, trapped. He needed "to revert back again to the wild and romantic life," he said, and he felt pain in knowing that the river flowed on unseen behind him.

From Camp des Moines, Catlin, accompanied by Gen. Joseph Street, the Indian agent, to the Sauk and Fox tribes along with eight dragoons supplied by Colonel Kearney, paid his last visit of the summer of 1835 to Keokuk's village, some sixty miles up the Des Moines River from its junction with the Mississippi. Black Hawk's victorious rival, Keokuk ("Watchful Fox"), now chief of the Sauk and Fox tribes, had emerged as chief through the "right" friendship in Washington, in the person of Governor Reynolds of Illinois, the territorial administrator of President Jackson's Indian removal policy. Keokuk had been designated the "good" Indian, amenable to removal for himself and his followers, but seen by most members of the two tribes for the puppet he was, with no rights, hereditary or earned, to his title. Keokuk's reward was a peaceful and, above all, prosperous retirement in his native village, two days' ride from Camp des Moines, where Catlin now came to complete his portraits of leaders, legitimate or not.

They were received with all the hospitality due a diplomatic summit. While Keokuk, his entourage, and their guests listened to General Street read aloud from documents sent from Washington, concerning his Indian host and the tribes under his sway, Keokuk placed before them "good brandy and good wine," George noted appreciatively "and invited us to drink and to lodge with him."

Their reception, however, failed to sway Catlin in favor of his sitter. He portrayed Keokuk—in prose and on canvas—as an impostor. In contrast to the artist's somber images of deposed Indian leaders—the noble Black Hawk, the ruined and heroic Red Jacket, and shortly, the tragic close-up that would be the last portrait of the captive Seminole chief Osceola—Keokuk is depicted as a preening voluptuary. This gentleman of "fine and portly figure" demanded that the artist paint him on horseback, so, as Catlin tells us with a swipe of malice, "I rendered him in that plight."

Depicted in the classic pose of the equestrian portrait, Keokuk is portrayed astride his famous black stallion. But the top-heavy rider, with his huge hams and spreading thighs, threatens to crush the delicate high-stepping legs of his thoroughbred. So vain was the chief, Catlin reported, that he brought twenty costumes to the sitting, from which he wanted the painter to choose. In the end the sitter himself chose the one that was most "purely Indian."

Horse lover that he was, George was unforgiving of Keokuk's mistreatment of his champion mount. Once in the saddle he "rode and nettled his prancing steed in front of my door until its sides were in a gore of blood." In the end the chief professed himself delighted with his heroic likeness, and "his vanity is increased no doubt, by seeing himself immortalized in that way." To reward the artist Keokuk seized a beautiful string of wampum from the neck of his favorite wife (one of seven), pressing it upon Catlin with great fanfare, before he and his entourage set off on the fall hunt.

Such was the bounty of betrayal, Catlin concluded. There's a sour and ironic tone to his account that we haven't heard before. Keokuk, the preening pawn, outdid himself as the perfect host. But to get his portrait the artist, too, had a role to play: the perfect guest.

WHEN GEORGE RETURNED to St. Louis only months later to join Clara before their planned return east together on November 5, 1835, one of his first stops on disembarking from the steamship *Warrior* was the Chouteau warehouse on the quay. Within the stone fortress were hundreds of paintings he had been allowed to ship there for storage, enabling the artist to continue working furiously while traveling light. It may have been on this visit to collect his pictures and Indian artifacts and to ask the company to send them on to their next destination, that Catlin first felt a distinct chill in the air. From the company's unofficial goodwill ambassador he sensed he had become persona non grata, who must be discredited and repudiated. The precise cause and agents of Catlin's fall from grace still remain murky: John James Audubon, racked by the kind of killer rivalry that has to shoot down every other sail on the horizon, is mentioned as a possible source for slander; certainly the great avian painter took every opportunity to diminish Catlin's talent and achievement— dismissing the veracity of his reporting as "humbug." But the itinerant French-born artist, even more dependent than Catlin on the kindness of the Chouteaus and others, hardly seems a powerful-enough enemy to have so effectively demonized Catlin as an exploitative charlatan.

Whatever the identity of his enemies, Catlin's days of Chouteau patronage were over. If he was aware of who was behind the smear campaign, he might also have cynically concluded that he no longer needed free passage on American Fur Company boats: From the *Yellow Stone*'s first successful voyage to Fort Union, to his last sight of the Missouri, he had profited from the Chouteaus' favor to see and paint more than he could have hoped or dreamed—more portraits of individual Indians, representing more tribes, rituals, games, and more landscapes and bison hunts than any other artist of the West painted or ever would. Though the Chouteau ukase tried to discredit Catlin the man, his achievement remained untouchable.

IN THE FIRST weeks of George's return to St. Louis, any intimation of trouble to come was forgotten in the happiness of his reunion with Joe Chadwick: "We had been separated for nearly two years," he later wrote.

They both knew that their reunion in St. Louis would be their last. George was full of plans: Catlin the explorer and artist would soon also play the roles of entrepreneur and new father. There was no place in his friend's future for Chadwick, so he did what young men with nothing better to do have always done: He joined the army. Governor Sam Houston was raising a new regiment to reinforce the beleaguered territorial Texas troops, worn down by a bloody two-year border war with the savage Mexican general Santa Anna. Joseph March Chadwick, West Point dropout, now received a commission with the rank of captain.

Catlin painted Chadwick's portrait, for which the sitter wore his new regimental dress uniform. During the sittings George unpacked his adventures of the past months, many of which "he had told no one," saving them for his friend alone:

> "How I should like to have been with you!" Joe said.
> "Sit still," said I, "or I shall lose your likeness."

When he looked at the finished portrait, he "rejoiced to find I had given it all the fire and *game look* that had become so pleasing to me." The constraint in Catlin's words was transmitted to his friend's likeness—a conventional portrait of a self-consciously posed young man. As fleeting as their time together, the charm of Joe's "game look" could not be fixed. Only the artist's mournful tenderness survives.

When the picture went off to Chadwick's mother in New Hampshire, her son was already on his way to Goliad, Texas. Together the Catlins left St. Louis for the last time in late November 1835. On this trip they traveled by land much of the time, crossing the Alleghenies "to my own native state," George recalled, with a rare note of homesickness.

WITH EXHIBITIONS OF the Indian Gallery already booked—the first to take place in Buffalo—George was more restless in Great Bend than ever. This time it was his work that was stuck—held in storage in Pittsburgh while nothing traveled on the icebound canals; hundreds of portraits; painted, feathered, and quilled ceremonial garments; pipes and tomahawks. While he had been seeing to these very cases, stored in the Chouteau warehouse in St. Louis, almost one-third again of his canvases and Indian works had been stolen from his cabin on the steamship *Warrior*. He wasn't superstitious, but he was beginning to fear that an evil eye had been cast on his labors.

Finally, by the end of February 1836, passengers and freight had begun to circulate. After leaving Clara with the Gregorys in Albany, George proceeded to Buffalo, where his sisters and brothers-in-law, Anson Dart and Asa Hartshorn, had both settled with their families in nearby Delta, near Lockport, New York. The entire clan, with the help of their parents, had rented and readied a deconsecrated Baptist church for the first eastern exhibition of George Catlin's Indian Gallery.

Though no effort was spared to make their launch of George's new career a success, if preparations appeared to flag, they received a steady barrage of directives from the artist, still on the road. Both Henry and Francis had been summoned to meet him in Pittsburgh for help in packing and shipping the works there to Buffalo. He chivvied those already in upstate New York about seeing to the printing of labels, handbills, tickets, and local advertising of the show, not scheduled to open until July 1.

Their father's constant reminders that they must all look after one another, including wives and children, had borne fruit. The loss of four brothers, two of them suicides, had brought the survivors closer together. They were counting on George to redeem family failures and tragedies; his success would be theirs. Now that he was back among them, the prodigal would try, in some measure, to reciprocate, to share the responsibilities for aging parents and those of guardian to his fatherless niece and nephew.

Shipped from Pittsburgh in February, Catlin's paintings and Indian collection arrived in Buffalo only in late spring 1836. George had barely begun to unpack crates and unroll canvases from their oilcloth covers when he was called urgently to Albany. Just before going into labor, Clara had taken ill. Despite appearing healthy at birth, the baby failed to thrive, "The little child got to bleeding at the navel on the 5th day after it was born," George wrote to Francis "and it not being possible to stop it, died the next morning." He does not say whether the newborn was a boy or girl. "Clara has suffered very much in her sickness," he added. The mother's illness, suggesting an infection before delivery, could also explain the baby's death.

Clara remained dangerously ill for several more weeks, her recovery slowed by grief. Her easy pregnancy and excellent health during the months of travel on land and water had seemed to promise that both mother and child would flourish. She was devastated by the death of this beloved baby whom she had held and tried to nurse for almost a week.

George had no choice but to remain in Albany, where his sister Eliza now joined them to help care for Clara. It was mid-June, two weeks before the exhibition was scheduled to open in Buffalo. He chafed at his "imprisonment," explaining to his brother that "It has been impossible for me to move from here before this. . . . Clara's sickness and the misfortune with her little babe have been the means of prolonging my delay . . . much longer than I expected." As Clara was now "doing pretty well," he was confident that the three of them (including Eliza) could leave Albany the following week; he would escort his wife and sister to the Hartshorn home in Delta, returning alone to Buffalo during the last week in June.

The death of his first child was far from Catlin's only source of grief, or even the most painful. On March 27, horror stories began trickling from Texas of a mass execution of American troops at the Presidio La Bahia, at the mouth of the Brazos River, on the Texas coast, to be known as the Goliad Massacre. In a surprise attack the Presidio was surrounded by Mexican troops; the fort's commander, Col. James Fannin, had surrendered and signed an agreement granting his men freedom in an exchange of prisoners. Instead the bloodthirsty Santa Anna ordered the unsuspecting captives to assemble in parade formation in the Presidio courtyard, where they were all slaughtered at close range. It took months for the names of the dead and missing to be published, but it was soon known that Joe Chadwick had been killed, along with Colonel Fannin and the 342 men under his command.

In his hometown of Exeter, Joe Chadwick's death in battle was exalted as an act of sacrifice. On the orders of his commanding officer, Chadwick had been on business outside the walls of the Presidio itself, his obituary reported; on his return he could have joined the few who managed to escape the mass slaughter taking place within. Instead he was said to have returned to the scene of carnage to try and bring out the wounded. Whether or not Catlin knew this account of Chadwick's death, he could only have viewed his friend's request for a portrait as prophesy or the wish to die.

For George the loss of Joe Chadwick marked the loss of intimacy itself. Overshadowed by the Alamo, the "Goliad Massacre" was quickly forgotten. But Walt Whitman remembered. In "Song of Myself" he eulogized the slain, capturing the many, who, like Joe, had found themselves surprised by death in the flush of life.

They were the glory of the race of rangers,
Matchless with horse, rifle, song, supper, courtship,
Large, turbulent, generous, handsome, proud, and
    affectionate

WHILE GEORGE REMAINED in Albany with Clara, his brothers Francis and Henry, together with their father, had been hard at work. Whatever they could do in the artist's absence to prepare for the opening of the Indian Gallery on July 1 had been done: Most of the paintings had been hung on the whitewashed walls of the former church; labels, in neat copperplate script, were affixed; stacks of handbills stood waiting to be distributed.

As soon as George appeared, it was clear to the family that more was wrong than could be explained by the death of the baby. He acted, his mother declared, "as though he was crazy." He announced that he was leaving immediately. The last boat of the summer, he explained, was about to depart for Sault Sainte Marie on Lake Superior, the first lap in the journey to the Pipestone Quarry in Minnesota. The site was sacred to the Santee Sioux (along with other tribes), and a place he had to visit. Now. The others should take down the pictures, store them carefully in Lockport (making sure to avoid heat as some of the pigment was not yet dry), settle the rent and other expenses. They would hear from him when he was on his way home.

18

THE PIPESTONE QUARRY

For George there was nothing irrational about his sudden decision to drop everything and set out for the Pipestone Quarry. Faced with his grieving wife and the hidden wounds inflicted by the death of Joe Chadwick, he had to get away. The departure of the last boat until fall headed for Sault Sainte Marie had been a sign, confirming what he knew in his heart. Another chapter of his life was about to end. This would be his final voyage to Indian country. Sacred, forbidden to the white man, the quarry would be his farewell to the shrinking lands beyond the frontier.

Like a fever, his frenzy to leave and fear of being stopped subsided as soon as the steamship slipped its moorings. With the humid July air of Buffalo behind him, the breezes of Lake Erie cooled his face and calmed his thoughts. Later George would recall his meandering voyage in an almost hypnotic recitation of rivers and riding. He forgot the urgency with which he fled the Buffalo exhibition just as it was about to open, leaving his family to deal with the chores of its unexplained closing. Neither did he mention his now-or-never rationale for the unplanned journey. Instead he recalled in detail, heightened by nostalgia, the familiar pleasures of the wandering life.

What he saw among the "semi-civilized" tribes recharged his indignation, honed on earlier observations of the illegal whiskey trade on the upper Missouri and his education at the feet of Cherokee chief John Ross in the policy of Indian removal in Georgia. Now he reported from the area around Green Bay, Wisconsin, that two companies of dragoons and three companies of infantry had been moved to the region "in anticipation of difficulties" with the Winnebago tribe. On being asked by the military commanding officer if they wanted to fight, their chief had replied " 'that they *could* not, had they been so disposed; for,' said he, 'we have no guns, no ammunition, nor anything to eat; and, what is worst of all, one half of our men are dying with the small-pox.' " "Amidst their poverty and wretchedness," Catlin concluded, "the only war that suggests itself to the eye of the traveler through their country, is the *war of sympathy and pity*, which wages in the breast of a feeling, thinking man."

Such an observer would notice that the white man's economic depredations extended beyond the buffalo, whose mass killings had reduced the Native American food supply. During their stop at Sault Sainte Marie, George realized that Chippewa, along with the local French, English, and Americans living in the region, subsisted almost entirely on the bountiful "*white fish* (young salmon) netted in the falls of Lake Superior . . . where it gains strength and flavour not to be found in the same fish in any other place." Now discovered by whites, the fishery was "filled up with adventurers," and the Indian was deemed an "intruder" forced to "dodge about in the coves for a scanty subsistence, whilst he scans and envies insatiable white man filling his barrels and boats, and sending them to market to be converted into money."

At Green Bay, Catlin found a place in a large bark canoe—his favorite mode of travel—with five wiry French voyageurs at the oars, bound for Port Winnebago and the Mississippi. With his preternatural gift for attracting kindred spirits, Catlin wasted no time in befriending his fellow passenger the Reverend Robert Serrill Wood, an English divine, intrepid voyager, and amateur scientist. Wood had brought his guitar, whose "thrilling notes," combined with the boatmen's comic songs (lyrics duly recorded by their appreciative passengers) made for much hilarity on the water.

On August 17, after almost three weeks of traveling by boat and on horseback from Prairie du Chien, Catlin and Wood reached the site of the sacred quarry itself. As the lunar landscape of walls rose suddenly before him, Catlin felt an excitement bordering on disbelief: He was finally, actually, here. The year before—1835—he claimed to have laid plans for the trip, only to have them go awry. Now he was in sight of "*classic ground*"; unlike any other the site was sacred to many tribes as "their greatest medicine (mystery) place." He felt inspired by the extraordinary meaning of the quarry as the source of legends and myths of a shared tribal memory, where dwelled "the Indian *Muse*."

Located on a wedge-shaped rise of land separating the Mississippi and the St. Peter's River, stretching across southwestern Minnesota into South Dakota, the Coteau, or "slope," so named by earlier French explorers, had been formed by successive periods of glaciations—the same forces that had shaped the region's countless lakes. Here, the earth, carpeted with a loose cover of loess, seemed to unfold, revealing a landscape of soft red stone, as though stained by perpetual sunrise. Surrounded by gently undulating prairie, the space was punctuated by jagged, sculptural forms, carved from the same mineral deposit and from the same Canadian ice mass millennia before.

Since the beginnings of recorded time, Native Americans from many tribes had made a pilgrimage to the source of the pipestone, traveling hundreds of miles to quarry for the famous mineral to be carved into calumets, or peace pipes. Their well-trodden paths became as sacred as the material pried from the strata of Sioux quartzite—harder than the pipestone itself. Thus the place, along with its unique outcroppings of soft blush-colored clay, became famous throughout the Great Plains, each tribe adding its own layers of myth and mystery to both the raw material and its final form, signifying a faith in peace among all native peoples.

If Catlin and Wood had entertained any doubts about the forbidden nature of the ground they were about to violate, they soon received unambiguous proof that they were trespassers. At a trading hut on the St. Peter's River at Traverse des Sioux, about 150 miles from the quarry itself, they were arrested by a "rascally band" of that same tribe of Santee Sioux, keepers of the site, "and held in durance vile,* for having dared to approach the sacred fountain of the pipe!" The hut was soon surrounded by a "murky cloud of dark-visaged warriors and braves." Closing off all avenues of escape, one of their number announced that the two interlopers were prisoners. While "compelled to keep our seats like culprits," twenty more warriors warned and threatened them for the entire afternoon, brandishing fists in their faces, all "grounded on the presumption that we had come to trespass on their dearest privilege,—their religion."

"No white man has been to the red pipe and none shall go," was the final warning issued by one of their Sioux guards.

FOR CATLIN THAT was a boundary he had to cross. Abandoning his usual posture of deference to all that was held sacred by the Indian— object, ritual, or place—Catlin the explorer rose to the challenge. Whatever he might say—or even believe—he would not be opposed in his plan to see the quarry, and he now decried the Sioux's *"unpardonable stubbornness"* that "excited us almost to desperation." It was not possible that he, George Catlin—the first white traveler, honored guest, and honorary medicine man, invited by the Mandan chief to observe and to paint that most secret of ceremonies, O-Kee-pa—should now be treated as a common trespasser, and worse, one whose very presence violated sacred soil.

When he learned of their reasons, however, George felt compelled to make "some allowance . . . for the rashness of these poor fellows.

---

* Archaic phrase for long prison sentence. Catlin used this obsolete legal term playfully, to mock the gravity of the Sioux's judgment of their crime.

. . . They took us to be 'officers sent by Government to see what this place was worth &c'. As 'this red stone was a part of their flesh,'" Catlin was told, "'it would be sacrilegious for white man to touch or take it away'—'a hole would be made in their flesh, and the blood could never be made to stop running.'"

Far from feeling "astounded at such a rebuff," Catlin and Wood stiffened their resistance: "We mutually agreed to go forward, even if it should be at the hazard of our lives." Catlin declared. Cowed by such a display of fearlessness, their Sioux interrogators yielded. Apparently they were also mollified by Wood's presence: Allied with the British during the Revolutionary War, many of the older warriors now displayed their royal medals ("We shook hands with our brother"). The horses were returned, "which we mounted and rode off without further molestation."

Nothing could stop Catlin from seeing the quarry. Then, in the name of science and knowledge, he further violated the sacred space. Smashing sections of rock wall with his hammer, he loaded his saddlebags with pieces of pipestone to take east with him.

A trespasser, Catlin was nonetheless rewarded with more than the ethnologist's loot bag of myths and stories, or even his stolen specimens of rock. As though the red pipestone had not been carved and traded and smoked for centuries, he found himself crowned with that familiar Eurocentric distinction, that of "discoverer" of the mineral, now named catlinite in his honor.[*]

George didn't need to smoke a pipestone calumet to leave the quarry on a high of discovery. The journey to the site had been a quest

---

[*] Catlin sent a sample of the red pipestone to Professor C. T. Jackson in Boston, who rejected the artist's theory that the stone was a new variety of steatite, relating the mineral instead, to a type of agalmatolite, a stone used by the Chinese in carving. It was Jackson who named the stone catlinite. Contemporary geologists lean toward a composite conclusion, with catlinite yielding elements of pyrophyllite, diaspore, and quartz.

fraught with obstacles and risks, and resistance from the Santee Sioux, its designated guardians, had only intensified his triumph. He had returned unscathed, his grail the shimmering red specimens pried from the rocks.

Overriding all other considerations—the call of family, professional obligations, and not least the sanctions surrounding the place itself—Catlin's compulsion to make the trip at just this moment may reflect his awareness of another reality: This would be the last act of his wilderness adventure. His fortieth birthday on July 26 had come and gone, uncelebrated, on his way to the quarries. Among strangers he may well have felt relieved of any need to acknowledge the date. By the measure of the period and its average life expectancy, he had entered late middle age, "most too *poor* to do *anything*," he wrote to his youngest brother at the end of the year. At the same time he urged Francis to keep the faith. Once he, George, (literally) got the show on the road, he was bound to make money; then he would consolidate small and scattered pockets of recognition into a firmly established national reputation. He had larger ambitions than sales of individual works.

GEORGE WAS ON his way home. Neither Clara nor his family had heard a word from him since a "public letter" that appeared in the *Commercial Advertiser* on August 3. As much as they feared that he was injured or ill, and physically unable to write, they worried as much about Clara's "distressed" state, trying, as Putnam enjoined them all, to keep up her spirits with mail from the others. At the very outset of her husband's abrupt departure, their father had written to Francis that "she could not bear the thought of his going so far as the Pipestone quarry & told your mother she should never see George again." Finally, in mid-November, Henry had a letter from Tecumseh, a town forty miles south of Detroit. George had been in a serious stagecoach accident, which left one shoulder so bruised that he was unable to travel for the pain; he would have to remain there for the next few days (the accident fails to explain the long preceding silence). On December 3 George was still in Tecumseh, writing to Putnam that he was only just able to walk around his room and venture out of doors for the first time. He expected to ride to Detroit in the next six or eight days; from there he would take a steamship to Buffalo. This time he managed to keep to his schedule. After collecting Clara from his sister in Delta, New York, the couple arrived in Utica on December 28 en route to New York City, where he knew that his Indian Gallery would draw the crowds his collection deserved.

But any immediate plans were thwarted. Ice still choked the North River and, adding to George's irritation, he now learned that the new "Great Rail Road (which was to remove and carry mountains with perfect ease) could not carry a pound of *freight* for anybody!"* Out of pocket, and with no firm prospects of an exhibition elsewhere in the vicinity, George resigned himself to a stay with his in-laws in nearby Albany. The Gregorys could be counted upon to provide the comforts of a well-run household, with ample working space. Word of his Buffalo fugue had undoubtedly circulated upstate, and he would need their help in showing his work locally—and with the discreet payment of bills. The visit offered a peaceful hiatus and time for George to regroup after his last frontier adventure and before his assault on New York.

* As it happened, the railroad's charter didn't allow for carrying freight.

19

A "GO-A-HEAD" ARTIST

The summer of 1837 brought shows for every conceivable audience to Albany and Troy, New York. Catlin's Indians didn't lack for competition: Those ubiquitous travelers, the Siamese twins Chang and Eng, last encountered by Clara and George in New Orleans, seemed to be following him: They were now appearing at the Albany Museum along with a Herr Schmidt's "Dissolving Tableaux," or panorama, this one including the artist's celebrated "Pyric [sic] Fires." Still, even as the halls filled with burghers and their families, happy to pay fifty cents a ticket to see and hear anecdotes, images, and artifacts evoking the native "savages" who had once been familiar sights to their rural forebears, Catlin ended his performances in the red. The lesson was clear: He would need bigger houses and the sale of thousands of tickets to make touring the gallery a paying proposition. His mind circled back to an earlier dream: A national museum where his work, purchased from the artist in its totality by the government, would be on view for all Americans, a vast memento mori, preserving the images and traditions of native men, women, and children, all doomed to disappear.

In mid-September, George arrived in New York City—a single man

again. Clara's baby was due at the end of December. After one mis-
carriage, followed by the death of her "sweet little bud" at five days
old, they both agreed that spending the last months of pregnancy at
home with her family would be the best assurance that this time both
mother and child would thrive.

TEN YEARS HAD passed since George had last lived in New York City,
but it might have been a century since he and Julius had shared rooms
in Cortlandt Street. Not just the look, but the sounds, the pace, and
the pulse of the city, had changed so dizzyingly that Catlin now felt
like Washington Irving's Rip Van Winkle—as if he had been asleep in
the wilderness while a metropolis mushroomed two thousand miles
away.

Arriving on the stagecoach from Albany, he found New Yorkers
suffering the worst of the Panic of 1837. As witness to the rampant
land speculation in the West that had driven so many Indians from
their ancestral lands, George was familiar with the ominous pileup
of events that was now causing financial ruin for so many. President
Jackson's Specie Circular (Coinage Act) of the previous summer of
1836 had decreed that all payments on public lands be made in hard
money, causing a run on the banks that were financing Western land
investments; most of these loans were transacted on "paper" so thinly
backed by capital as to be close to counterfeit bills. A "domino effect"
followed: England had succumbed to its own financial crisis, leading
British creditors to call in their American loans; crop failures weak-
ened the purchasing power of many farmers (including their ability
to repay debts); widespread panic exposed small banks in the South
and West as the houses of cards they were. In weeks the value of merchandise nationwide had fallen 30 percent; the stock market slide was
still steeper. On May 10 all New York banks suspended operations,
with other financial houses in the East following suit. The Pennsylva-

nia coal mines shut down, and New Yorkers dreaded the cold winter ahead. Within a few months of the bank collapse in May, about one-third of the city's laborers had lost their jobs, while the wages of those still employed fell by another third. More than ten thousand people appeared at almshouses, begging for food, most having to be turned away. Talk of "rebellions and revolutions" was in the air.

Then as now, New York housed the financial heart of the nation: One bank after another closed. Fearing "disturbances," the military were called to police Wall Street.

Still, most of New York's ruling elite remained unaffected. In September, the same month that Catlin arrived in the city, Tiffany and Company opened its doors, advertising chinese porcelain, bric-a-brac, stationery, and "fancy goods," or ornamental novelties. Five years earlier a new restaurant, Delmonico's, had opened and quickly became famous for conspicuous consumption—in every sense. Under glittering chandeliers, rich New Yorkers indulged themselves with oysters,[*] a procession of fowl and meat courses, ending with spun-sugar confections—all washed down with champagne.

The masses had to settle for the flare of gas footlights illuminating the earliest vaudeville shows. Imported from Paris theaters in working-class neighborhoods, the fast-paced lighthearted sequence of acts was heavy on slapstick humor or feats of skill and daring. Like the "madcap" Hollywood comedies of the Great Depression a century later, they helped audiences to forget lost jobs or savings, despairing fathers and husbands who, unable to support families, abandoned them or desperate sons who turned to crime.

Frenzied as he was with preparations for the opening of his Indian Gallery at Clinton Hall, at Nassau and Beekman Streets, on Septem-

---

[*] Although oysters were a working-class food for most of the nineteenth century, New Yorkers' passion for the bivalves helped launch the popularity of restaurants where they were served.

ber 25, George must have been tempted by a novel attraction like vaudeville, along with other available spectacles, such as the rowdier happenings on stage and off at the Old Bowery, where audience participation included obscene catcalls and rotten tomatoes, some tossed from the third balcony (reserved for prostitutes). He wasn't in Albany anymore. As carefree young bachelors he and Julius had taken advantage of some of the city amusements, but in the intervening decade, New Yorkers—approximately one hundred thousand more of them— had become spoiled for choice, and the artist was alert to the need to capture this new audience. Always curious and a quick study, Catlin had an innate theatrical streak; whatever he could learn from New York's popular entertainments, he would absorb and apply to his own production. To be sure, his Indian Gallery could not offer the dizzying alternations of one-act comedies, with heart-stopping acts like the Ravels, a family of eight French "[tight]rope walkers." (As such visitors also revealed, featured performers had to be "foreign.") Even on canvas, "his" Indians, went farther: They were "exotic," savage, and almost extinct. Few members of his urban audience had ever been west, or even known anyone who had. At the same time Catlin himself was absorbing a new rhythm from the denizens of Manhattan and their expectations: restless, hurried "show-me," and their taste for the quick-change artistry that shuffled performers, scenery, talents, and music in a kaleidoscope of color and sound.

On September 23 Colonel Stone's *Commercial Advertiser* announced, under its "Amusements" notices:

CATLIN'S INDIAN GALLERY. Opens for Exhibition on Monday Evening, the 25th instant and will be continued each evening. . . . In the lecture room of Clinton Hall. There will be several hundred Portraits exhibited, as well as Spendid Costumes— Paintings of their villages—Dances—Buffalo Hunts—Religious Ceremonies, etc. Collected by himself, among the wildest tribes of America, during an absence from this city of seven years [*sic*]. Mr. Catlin will be present at all of his exhibitions, giving illustrations and explanations in the form of a Lecture. . . . Each admission 50 cents.

On the day of the opening another notice in the same newspaper smartly reminded readers that this "intensely interesting" event featured no "set lectures" such as Clinton Hall audiences might expect to hear, but "spontaneous oral explanations" of these intriguing pictures and objects, which they would at the same time be privileged to see.

An artist by vocation, Catlin now revealed himself to be a born showman as well. Preceding his arrival in the city, George had dispatched his new factotum, Daniel Kavanagh, as "advance man," with instructions to blanket the town with handbills—forty thousand in all. From opening night on, Catlin's democratic vistas embraced all classes of New Yorkers wherever their resorts of recreation: He urged Daniel not to forget "the Publick Houses" in his tireless rounds. The lecturer himself took charge of inviting his more distinguished fellow citizens. The response from William H. Seward, the first Whig governor of New York State, was especially gratifying: Seward's brief visit to the city, he replied to Catlin, ruled out accepting the invitation to the Indian Gallery at Clinton Hall, but he had already seen the exhibition when it was on view in Albany; the experience had left him an ardent fan, with "the highest respect for your talents and acquirements."

Staid Clinton Hall had never seen such an opening-night crush— all the more astonishing as the event was no one-night stand but a program expected to enjoy a lengthy run. Now word of mouth did the rest. So many had been turned away on that first Monday that Catlin quickly booked larger quarters—news of the move itself generating more excitement. On October 6 he closed the Indian Gallery at Clinton Hall and reopened three days later at Stuyvesant Institute, on Broadway at Bond Street.

Delighted as George was with the runaway success of the Indian Gallery, he remained unaware of the revolutionary role of his exhibition. He had merely launched the most powerful and long-running crowd pleaser in entertainment history: The American *Wild West Show*. Although his early version remained (but only for the time being) without live Indians, bucking broncos, or staged buffalo hunts, the standing-room-only mob scene at the capacious Stuyvesant Institute was a herald of things to come. Within weeks even the grand new lecture hall proved too small to accommodate the throngs bent on hearing Mr. Catlin's talk and seeing the lifelike pictures he painted and Indian-made objects he collected in his Western travels. With only his paintings and tribal mementos as props, Catlin wove a spellbinding narrative: As Daniel placed a portrait, such as the likeness of Four Bears, on the floodlit easel, George evoked their conversations—just as though they had taken place that very morning. While he recalled his role as honored guest at a banquet in the great chief's tent, he held up the pale buffalo-skin shirt covered with Four Bear's own depictions of conquests and hunts. Quickly this was followed by his own four paintings of the shocking O-kee-pa, canvases whose small size seemed to expand as George enlarged upon the sequence of rituals, holding his audience spellbound with a harrowing play-by-play recreation of torture endured and manhood conferred.

Some present-day writers contend that Catlin's lectures included denunciations of the fur traders and of their lucrative sideline: debauching the Indian through the illegal distilling and selling of whiskey. The artist is said to have excoriated President Jackson's Indian removal policy and the thousands of treaties that persuaded trusting—or well-rewarded—tribal leaders to sell millions of acres for a pittance; in these same talks the artist was supposed to have detailed how the treaties themselves were flouted by the administration. It's been said that in his comments at Stuyvesant Institute, Catlin "spoke entirely too vehemently about the practices of the powerful fur companies" and voiced intemperate attacks on Pierre Chouteau and his boss, John Jacob Astor; he was also, according to one writer, entirely too frank about the "sins of our Government."

Although in time Catlin *would* denounce all these abuses, public and private, in print, his crusading words were actually published later, when he was safely abroad. It may be recalled that several years earlier he had "revised," at Chouteau's behest, the draft of one of his "Letters" before its publication in the *Commercial Advertiser*, presenting the American Fur Company as a paternalistic and patriotic force for good on the upper Missouri, whose occasional moistening of Indian trade with a few drops of fire water constituted the only bulwark against British co-option of native populations.

Poised to launch his own campaign for government purchase of his pictures, the artist appears the least likely candidate to use the stage of his Indian Gallery as a bully pulpit for reform. His hopes were pinned on the exhibition's New York run to be the hit that it proved to be, to showcase the paintings and to lead to new triumphs—hardly the time or place to make enemies. In any case, what Catlin actually said in Stuyvesant Hall during these show-and-tell performances remains in the realm of speculation: The first catalog of the Indian Gallery, published in New York that same year, was actually a checklist of the works on view; the lecturer's commentary is lost to time.

On November 1 a group of mystery guests made a dramatic appearance at Stuyvesant Hall. Before an audience of fifteen hundred, Keokuk, accompanied by his favorite wife and one son, together with more than twenty chiefs and warriors of the Sauk and Fox tribes, became unannounced participants in that evening's performance. The group had stopped in New York on their way back from Washington, before heading for Boston. Keokuk and his followers were on a tight schedule, so Catlin had clearly booked the travelers well in advance.

Only a month into his New York run, Catlin displayed all the skills of a seasoned impresario. He announced Keokuk's appearance—just in time to double the price of tickets from fifty cents to one dollar: They were sold out within the hour they went on sale. He had arranged to have an elevated platform constructed in the middle of the hall to accommodate all the native visitors and to ensure not only their maximum visibility but also that the guests would have a clear view of the speaker and of the paintings as those appeared on the easel. At the designated "special performance," the crush pressing to get into the institute's main entrance on Broadway was so impenetrable that the reporter from Stone's *Commercial Advertiser* had to slip into the single file of Indians headed backstage to touch up their war paint, which had started to run in the heat.

As soon as the likeness of Keokuk appeared on the easel, in the equestrian pose he had chosen for his portrait, his followers went wild. As one body they leaped to their feet, shouting and cheering their excitement at seeing their chief astride his famous warhorse. Embarrassed by such "uncivilized" behavior, the aged Keokuk, after quieting his troops, apologized to the audience. Modestly he explained that his fellow tribesmen were shouting with joy at having recognized such a famous horse, not the rider. Catlin now seized the opportunity to publicize the accuracy of his equine portrait, declaring, according to one report, that "many persons had questioned the correctness of the picture," saying that "no Indian on the frontier rode so good a horse." When George's remarks were translated by Mr. Le Clair, thoughtfully invited as an interpreter, Keokuk rose, and in a state of righteous wrath, demanded to know "why Keokuk could not ride as good a horse as any white man." At this the audience burst into applause. Upon the showing of Catlin's next painting of a buffalo hunt, one of the braves, to the delight of the audience, leaped upon a bench and "took a [drawn] bow from under his robe," explaining to his rapt listeners that this was the very weapon from which his arrow had flown through the bison's huge mass, felling the creature."

Catlin was taking no chances; he kept piling it on. Hardly had the audience recovered from the excitement of hearing an Indian hunter in their midst describe killing a buffalo, than a band of forty Sioux who just happened to be present, confirmed in unison that their tribe, too, boasted such legendary archers. If Catlin the novice showman may be accused of packing the house with Native American visitors and staging these "spontaneous" outbursts, he needed make no apologies: His success was the only defense required. The audience had gotten more than their money's worth. A still more gratifying encore was to come. As the exhausted speaker retired to the wings, applause still ringing in his ears, his publisher and tireless promoter, Colonel Stone, strode to the podium to offer the following: "*Resolved:* 'That the thanks of this meeting be presented to George Catlin, Esq. for the great labors undertaken him . . . and also for the zeal, energy, perseverance and success, with which these labors have been prosecuted. . . . That this meeting entertains the fullest confidence in the veracity of Mr. Catlin, and in the truth of his delineations, both by his lips and his pencil.'" With Stone's resolution seconded by the cheering audience, his *Commercial Advertiser* gave the imprimatur to the Indian Gallery, the printed word a bastion against skeptics' whispers to come.

A month later, excitement generated by the Indians, painted and real, had subsided. Catlin needed another event to attract new publicity. December 6 was designated a gala to which George invited the city's elite, including a distinguished visitor, the senator from Massachusetts, Daniel Webster; Mayor Aaron Clark, the first Whig to be elected and whose vast wealth came from running private lotteries; select members of the Common Council; and prominent newspaper editors. Among other leading citizens who attended the exhibition at the artist's invitation was Philip Hone, a former mayor of New York and the most exhaustive diarist of his day: Hone never seems to have left a single fire—and certainly no theatrical performance—unrecorded. An avid reader and book collector, he had a special interest in Native American culture and history. Before attending the gala, Hone had not only visited the exhibit, he had also attended an outdoor gathering of Keokuk accompanied by his Sauk and Fox followers.

Hone found himself enthralled by "Mr. Catlin's great collection of paintings," which along with the "implements of husbandry, and the chase, weapons of war, costume etc." evoked a dynamic picture of Indian life. But he especially admired the "enthusiasm, zeal and perseverance with which [Catlin] has followed up this pursuit." Hone recalled that he "had seldom witnessed so interesting an exhibition." The only feature of the gala that elicited more excitement from the diarist was the refreshments, presented by their host in the style of a tribal feast: "We had a collation of buffaloes' tongues, and venison and the waters of the great spring," Hone noted lyrically, "and smoked the calumet of peace under an Indian tent formed of buffalo skins."

AT THE END of December, Clara gave birth to a healthy baby girl, Elizabeth Wing, called Libby. Her father, however, did not head for Albany to greet his new daughter. He closed the exhibit in New York and set off in the opposite direction, to the garrison prison at Fort Moultrie on Sullivan Island, just off Charleston, South Carolina, to paint the portrait of its newest inmate, the Seminole leader, Osceola.

Since George's convalescence in Pensacola three years before, and his introduction there to chief John Ross and the Cherokee cause, he had been aware of the looming figure of Osceola, local hero of the Second Seminole War. Like many native leaders, Osceola, the "Black Drink," was of mixed blood, having been born Billy Powell in Tallassee, Alabama, in 1804. His father is said to have been a third-generation trader of Scots descent named William Powell, and his mother, Polly Copinger Powell, of English and Tuscogee parentage. When the boy was ten, mother and son joined a Creek community that migrated to Seminole country in Florida. As the Seminole forbade intermarriage with whites, Billy Powell, now their ascendant young warrior chief, reinvented himself as a full-blooded Muscogee. His new name, Osceola, combined the word for the tribe's ceremonial drink made of local black holly berries and the one for "shouter," or troublemaker.

Soon Osceola was making trouble with a vengeance. In the depths of the Everglades, he trained and led the tribes of the Florida and Georgia Territories—Euchee, Seminole, and Creek—in guerrilla-style wars of attrition against white settlers and the military garrisons that protected them. The Second Seminole War could just as well have been called the Third or Fourth. Now, thanks to the U.S. government, Osceola was transformed, even in the eyes of white Americans, from public enemy to populist martyr.

On October 21, 1837, about a month after Catlin's Indian Gallery opened at Clinton Hall in New York, Osceola and his chiefs emerged from the Everglades, white flags raised. They had accepted the government's invitation to convene at Fort Payton, a mile south of St. Augustine, with federal representatives and their military counterparts for truce negotiations. Instead, on the orders of Gen. Thomas Sidney Jesup, Osceola and his men were seized on arrival, thrown in chains, and imprisoned at Fort Marion, another of the string of military installations in the area.

Unexpectedly the entrapment of the Seminole leaders set off a firestorm of popular outrage and outpourings of sympathy for the prisoners throughout the country. Finding itself at the center of a public relations disaster, the outgoing Jackson administration made matters worse. In December, hoping that angry anti-Washington feelings had died down, the Department of War ordered the captives transferred to the more publicly accessible prison at Fort Moultrie. There the press now joined sympathetic or merely curious citizens, many bringing food and gifts, who lined up to board the boats taking them to visit the celebrated Seminole "patriot heroes."

Almost as soon as the first news of the shameful act was published,

Catlin applied to Secretary of War Benjamin Butler for permission to paint the famous prisoner. Rumors were already circulating of Osceola's failing health: Catlin now determined to get there before any other artist, returning with the last likeness of Osceola alive. Finally, on January 10, he received both official permission from the secretary and, still better, what amounted to a formal commission from Carey A. Harris, commissioner of Indian affairs, to paint Osceola and five of his nine imprisoned fellow leaders for their official portraits.

It took Catlin two weeks of daily visits to Osceola's cell, during which time he deployed his most stirring rhetoric to persuade the ailing chief and his Seminole followers to sit for their likenesses: As the artist reported to Commissioner Harris, the captives had found it "very strange" that the Great Father would want their portraits. George appears to have been surprised by their distrust; he was used to natives assimilating the white man's vanity. Given how Osceola and his men had been treated—coming in peace to Fort Payton, to be betrayed, thrown into chains and behind bars—why should they not suspect that the latest request from Washington for an "official portrait" would turn out to be yet another trap, or at least, an occasion for further humiliation? There was also Osceola's worsening illness, variously described as malaria or "quinsy throat."

Ultimately the prisoners' suspicions yielded to the artist's eloquence. Although Catlin is characteristically vague about his mediating role in the Seminole's change of heart, he admitted that, following his presentation of the government's request, Osceola now "construed it into a compliment, or rather an indication that . . . [they] were to be called to Washington soon (an event which they are anxiously looking for), and they readily consented to sit." Can we doubt that the artist dangled this message of hope among his flattering words to the prisoners?

Instead of being summoned to Washington and pardoned, Osceola died in his cell on January 30, just hours after sitting to Catlin for his portrait. Although the warrior chief is often spoken of—even today—

as an old man, he was thirty-four at his death—eight years younger than George Catlin.

It's not clear whether George, already steaming up the Atlantic coast toward New York, his barely dry canvases rolled in his bags, had already learned of Osceola's death before sending his report to Commissioner Harris on January 31, 1838, which was received by that official on February 13. In the briefest of notes he refers to the overcrowding at Castle Pinckney, where hundreds of lesser Seminole were crammed together in facilities so wretched "that their modes of life and [filthiness (?)] would eminently endanger the health of all." He then reports that Osceola's "great distress of mind" and physical state led him and Dr. Weedon, the attending physician at the prison, to agree that the chief "will not live long in his present condition." But this may be an instance of Catlin's delaying tactics: As Putnam Catlin wrote matter-of-factly to his son, Osceola was "worth much more dead than alive."

When George did learn of the extraordinary timing of his last portrait from life, he at once knew that his stock was rising by the hour. Why should he hand copies of the Osceola portrait, along with those of his trusted seconds, to the government for the pittance that such commissions normally received? (The standard payment for Indian portraits painted "in the field" seems to have been $369.)

Taking a leaf from the War Department's treatment of Osceola, the artist now ignored requests to hand over the commissioned works; nine months later the Bureau of Indian Affairs had yet to see any of the Seminole portraits. Finally, on November 15, Commissioner Thomas Hartley Crawford, Carey A. Harris's successor, pointed out the time that had elapsed between Catlin's meager report and the still undelivered pictures, stating sharply, "as I presume you have since had ample time to complete them, I have to request their early transmission and that at the same time, you will forward your accounts."

No evidence suggests that the copies ever arrived in the commissioner's office. Instead George rushed to Stuyvesant Institute, where he added the two original portraits of Osceola, one standing and the other a bust-length pose, together with images of the five other Seminole chiefs, to the works in the Indian Gallery still on exhibit. The new—and newsworthy—portraits were accompanied by fresh commentary from George's recent impressions of the dying "hero," as the newspapers now described Osceola, formed days before his death. Indeed, the full-length study of the Seminole chief as warrior, leaning lightly on his rifle, reveals, in its classical formula, an Osceola whom Catlin had clearly never seen. The justly famous frontal bust, however, skin stretched tightly over the skull, face punctured by the dark, unseeing gaze, suggests a living death mask.

Prophecy, accusation, or defense—Catlin's portrait of Osceola occupies the space between realism and symbol. But the artist's commentary, written a week before his subject's death, goes to the heart of the deadly conflicts personified by the Indian leader himself—three-quarters white yet who spoke no English—conflicts that palpably shook the artist to the core of his conscience:

> He has a mind of a wonderful construction, calculated to fortify and yet destroy itself—a lurking cunning, capable of gilding with the warmth and pleasantness of sunshine, the whirling tempest that's raging in his soul, and even in his mirth and childishness destroying him. He smiles and fawns and languishes before a gazing world; but in his solitude, or when he tells in confidence his tales of grief, though mild and smiling dew drops moisten his eyes at one moment, yet the burning hero rushes through their sockets at the next—his black brows jet over their balls of fire . . . and his clenched teeth are set in silent oaths of irreatractable [sic] revenge.

Losing no time, George incised a lithograph of the portraits, "hand colored" to resemble the originals, prints to be sold for four dollars each. As he hoped, the timely additions to the exhibition, together with his anguished report of the dying warrior, created a market for the brightly hued prints.

Osceola's well-timed death had, finally, given George a shot at the all-American "go-a-head"—in showman P. T. Barnum's favorite phrase—the chance to make real money. He had seen the opportunity and he had seized it. Catlin the entrepreneur was on his way.

20

"WITHOUT FORTUNE AND WITHOUT PATRONAGE"

Putnam Catlin was in the audience of the Indian Gallery on the night of the "gala" and could see for himself: His son had arrived. Instead of spending Christmas at home in Great Bend, buried in snow, Putnam claimed business in Philadelphia and New York, where he now stood proudly in the wings of the Stuyvesant Institute's lecture hall counting the house and reflecting on the events that, at least on this occasion, had conspired to bring about his favorite child's triumph.

As someone whose own political ambitions had been thwarted by a pompous manner and high-flown speech (along with a tendency to change parties), Putnam was amazed that, in a brief time, George had made himself a known presence in a big and impersonal city. Months of living on the frontier among plainspoken men of little education had pushed him to say more with fewer words. Even allowing a shade of exaggeration from a father, the elder Catlin took note, in a letter to Francis, of the way everyone seemed to respond to George: "I have never been acquainted with a man more popular than he is among all classes. . . . Think of the pride I have as a Parent."

In early April 1838 George packed up his Indian Gallery and set off for Washington. There was nothing random about his timing or the place he chose for the next stop on his tour. The booking appears to have been part of a phased campaign to capitalize, first, on the recent publicity garnered from two sold-out New York runs, and then to coordinate a showing in the capital with his first attempt to arrange a sale of his collection to the government—asking price negotiable. Looking ahead, he had also begun to ponder alternative plans: If he failed to sell his collection to the nation, he would take the entire Indian Gallery abroad, where royal patronage and great collectors were woven into history.

Meanwhile George felt guardedly optimistic when he opened on April 9 in the space most recently occupied by the American Theatre. While the rental was cheap at thirty dollars a week, the venue's dilapidated state required him to have the lights reglazed and considerable construction done to create display cases—all at his own expense.

The Indian Gallery was well received, but the live star of the spectacle was showing signs of strain. Two weeks into the run, George wrote to his father that he was tired of both exhibiting and lecturing, to the point that, in Putnam's words, "it becomes painful & slavish & keeps him in constant agitation, & takes up every moment of his time, and deprives him the use of his pen and brush" As to the expected profits (based also upon earnings he hoped to realize from sales of the Osceola lithographs) these were proving less robust than first promised: He was no longer certain, he wrote to his father, that "receipts will much more than meet the necessary expenses"—a worry also confirmed by weak sales of his Osceola prints: A notice from a Washington shop owner reminded George that of five hundred mezzotints left with him, from whose sale the owner was to receive a commission, only a few had been sold.

Regardless of the cost—in money and to his health—George had to keep the exhibition before the public. He had been assured by influential friends that, before Congress adjourned for the summer, a resolution would be offered to debate the purchase of his collection for the nation. As audiences and receipts dwindled, Catlin the showman rallied: He renamed the exhibition "The Wigwam," calling public attention to its most popular feature, the large white Crow tipi, holding eighty visitors, that he had erected just outside the entrance on Pennsylvania Avenue. The new structure welcomed the curious and drew fresh coverage from the press.

Finally, on May 28, nearly two months after the exhibition had opened in Washington and the Twenty-Sixth Congress neared its recess, Rep. George Nixon Briggs, a Whig of Massachusetts and chairman of the Committee on Public Expenditures, introduced the long-awaited resolution: He ordered the Committee on the Library to look into acquiring Catlin's Indian Gallery and "to ascertain from Mr. Catlin upon what terms they may be possessed by the Government."

Three influential fans of the Indian Gallery emerged as candidates for lobbying their fellow lawmakers on the artist's behalf. Daniel Webster, hero of the Catlin family and dean of Bay State politicians, had seen the exhibition in New York as Catlin's special guest; the governor of New York, William H. Seward, had visited and admired the exhibition on his own in Albany, unfortunately while George was ill at home. Henry Clay, the "Great Compromiser," seems most remote from the Catlin orbit; but it's worth noting that Clay's running mate in that year's four-way presidential race was Theodore Frelinghuysen of New Jersey, the most eloquent opponent of Jackson's Indian removal policy. Thus the political stances of Clay, Webster, and Seward (another anti-Jacksonian) would have argued for their support of the government purchase of Catlin's collection as advocates for the Indian as well as of the artist.

Despite the help of three powerful political figures, and before any action or even discussion took place, the resolution was tabled. Congress was sensitive to lingering aftershocks from the previous year's financial panic: This was not the moment to campaign for federal patronage of the arts. Then, Washington being a company town (or more accurately, a village), Catlin's continuing refusal to honor the War Department's commission of the Osceola portraits would have been known to many in the halls of Congress. Did a deadbeat artist deserve the honor of forming the core collection of a national museum?

There were other forces arrayed against this particular act of government patronage. For all that it was the nation's capital, Washington remained a Southern city. Known for his sympathy for Indians, and for his criticism of tribes' expulsion from ancestral lands, Catlin was unlikely to garner favor in the eyes of those concerned with establishing those same territories as slave states. In the end, though, the heat trumped all else: By the last steaming days of May every legislator wanted to go home. Nevertheless, his friends assured Catlin, they hadn't given up. They would regroup; a resolution tabled did not mean one voted down.

Catlin remained in Washington through the climbing temperatures and sodden air of June. He felt discouraged enough to ask Henry Clay to write a letter of introduction on his behalf to his English friend Lord Selkirk.*

George's plan of taking his collection abroad was shifting from halfhearted threat to fallback position. England, with its tradition of adventurous private collectors—royalty, nobility, commoners—as well as passionate audiences for art, was emerging as a realistic alternative. And the British travelers he had encountered in the remotest corners

---

* Dunbar James Douglas, sixth earl of Selkirk, was the son and heir to the title of the fifth Lord, as well as an agronomist and founder of the ill-fated Red River colony in western Canada. Riven by conflict among the settlers, many of the original colonists, including the Swiss-born painter, Peter Rindisbacher, and his family, had fled. It may be that Clay knew that the younger Douglas shared his father's interest in New World exploration, and thus could be helpful to Catlin in London.

of the American West convinced him that interest in the Indian Gallery would be keen in England, and also that he had friends waiting to welcome him.

Clay's letter of July 7 to Lord Selkirk paid tribute to Catlin the ethnographer but gave no hint that his work had any value as art—or even that the collection's portraits and landscapes existed at all. The Indian Gallery, Clay wrote to the Scots peer, stood as proof that "Mr. George Catlin . . . has been engaged many years among the various Indian tribes who inhabit this continent, and collected a mass of valuable information . . . surpassing that which was probably ever possessed by any man, or what is to be found in any books."

There was no reason now for George to remain in the capital. Audiences had dwindled along with receipts, as the government shut down and ordinary residents, together with transient lawmakers, fled the sweltering midsummer city.

More worrying than ever before, expenses outstripped income. Along with refurbishing the former theater for the Washington exhibition, Catlin had printed 2,500 copies of an expanded edition of the 1837 catalog that had been produced for the New York showing; then, there were 10,500 showbills and advertisements that ran for weeks in every issue of the Washington Globe and the National Intelligencer.

Where finances were concerned, George always remained exempt from the scolding and hectoring his father inflicted upon his other sons. If George lost money in mysterious ways, or counted upon profits that failed to materialize, or simply spent more than he earned, Putnam voiced only sympathy, doing everything in his power to help. For that matter, bailing one another out in times of trouble was an article of faith for the Catlin family. In their elaborate system of bookkeeping, George, along with his father and more prosperous brothers, Pensacola-based Richard and James, pooled their resources to rescue the improvident Henry, whose Lockport investments had failed spectacularly, leaving him with no means of supporting his wife and their six children. Unquestioningly George reached into his meager savings for eight hundred dollars—the first half of a promised sixteen hundred. In return Putnam Catlin, knowing that George could expect little or no earnings in the coming months, offered him an anticipated windfall that he expected from the Commonwealth of Pennsylvania as soon as it should be received. The news that George, with the expenses of a growing family, had just purchased two grizzly bears from the American Fur Company, at a cost of five hundred dollars (followed by a bill for one hundred more to cover their maintenance) seemed only to amuse his father.

There was nothing to keep Catlin in Washington any longer. On July 2, after seeing to the loading of "one car load of Merchandise for G. Catlin" on the Baltimore and Ohio Railroad, George set off on what may have been the first tour by an artist to show his own art. His first two stops were discouraging. In Baltimore he tried an educational pitch, announcing that two visits would be needed to absorb the Indian Gallery as a "course" of Indian objects, pictures, and information; tickets to be sold in bookshops. Receipts barely covered the artist's three-week stay in a shabby hotel. Philadelphia tested his ability to rejoice in the success of his former housemate and fellow academician: John Neagle had inherited the mantle of his father-in-law, Thomas Sully, as the premier portraitist of the city, and was welcome in the clubs and homes of its leading citizens. Catlin's illustrated lectures took place in a run-down indoor mall called the Arcade, where he shared space with Hungarian minstrels and a ventriloquist.

Still, for the first time, a local reviewer seized the full significance of Catlin's achievement:

"There is not in our land, nor in any part of Europe . . . anything of the kind more extraordinary," the anonymous writer declared in the *Philadelphia Sunday Courier.* "The galleries illustrative of national character and antiquities which are to be found in London, Paris, Florence, and other cities, have been collected by the power of great kings; and the outlay of immense treasure, and the apparatus of negotiations, and special ministers, and resident consuls, and agents innumerable." In contrast, as befitted a true American artist, "This is the work of a single individual, a man without fortune and without patronage, who created it with his own mind and hand, without aid and even against countenance. . . . He may point to his magnificent collection which now receives the admiration of every eye, and say with honest pride, 'Alone I did it!'"

IN MID-AUGUST, GEORGE returned to New York, where he had arranged to meet Clara and Libby. Now for the first time they would travel as a family; George, his wife, and little daughter, accompanied by a nursemaid, headed for Boston and the first New England showing of the Indian Gallery. Boston was the last stop on Catlin's East Coast tour, and his first real triumph: He could not have unveiled his Indian Gallery at a more receptive place or more opportune moment.

Two months earlier Ralph Waldo Emerson had addressed an open letter to President Martin Van Buren. Published in *The Liberator*, Boston's preeminent abolitionist newspaper, the Sage of Concord cited "sinister rumors . . . concerning the Cherokee people," specifically the "sham" Indian Removal Treaty (so called) of December 1835, "contracting to put this active nation into carts and boats and to drag them over mountains and rivers to a wilderness at a vast distance beyond the Mississippi. And a paper purporting to be an army order fixes a month from this day, for this doleful removal."

Assuming a rhetorical stance of disbelief that such evil could be perpetrated by his own government, Emerson declared:

A crime is projected that confounds our understandings by its magnitude. . . . Such a dereliction of all faith and virtue, such a denial of justice, and such deafness to screams for mercy, were

never heard of in times of peace, and in the dealing of a nation
with its own allies and wards, since the earth was made.

There was still time for the president to reject the dire legacy of his
predecessor: But the Emerson of this letter, sounding more Calvinist
than Unitarian, does not loft hope so much as he warns of retribution:
"If your seal is set to this instrument of perfidy . . . the name of this
nation, hitherto the sweet omen of religion and liberty, will stink to
the world."

Emerson's savage letter seemed timed to assure George Catlin a
hero's welcome in Boston. The cradle of antislavery and of the abolitionist movement was ready to embrace the Indian Gallery as a
reminder that the same evils, at this very moment, were being visited upon Native Americans, and by the same slaveholding politicians,
conspiring to seize Indian lands in order to multiply the number and
influence of proslavery states.

Rapturous reviews greeted the exhibition and its impresario, but
that was only one piece of Catlin's conquest of the city that was also a
state of mind: Educated Bostonians saw themselves as the moral and
spiritual conscience of America, and they embraced Catlin as one of
their own.

Clara had never before shared in her husband's triumph as she did in
the course of their two months in Boston. Writing to George's family,
she savored with them all the high points of the exhibition: Installed
in Faneuil Hall, "his collection makes a fine show on the walls, and
it elicits praise from all." Invitations proliferated from all the neighboring towns—Concord, Lexington, and Waltham were each as eager
for word of the West and its native inhabitants as the city itself. They
could easily have spent three months there, Clara noted wistfully. And
echoing her father-in-law, she pointed out that, due to the extinction
of tribes like the Mandan and the gradual disappearance of others,
George's "portraits are becoming more valuable every day."

Before the social and cultural whirl swallowed them, the Catlins managed moments of family intimacy that Clara had never yet experienced: George, happy to escape his fans, found time to get acquainted with his little daughter: "I wish you could see George acting the parental part," Clara wrote to her sister-in-law, adding that their firstborn, Libby, was "the image of her father."

Boston also offered Clara a taste of the education that, as the only girl in her family, she had earlier been denied, along with her first encounter with the fearsome New England bluestocking: To her amazement there were opportunities for self-improvement provided by women for women *only*. "The ladies here I find attend much to intellectual pursuits. There are lectures every day and night, upon something interesting. I have been attending lectures on Anatomy and Physiology given by a lady. She admits no gentlemen, and her manner is pleasing, and her lectures are very instructive." She had never enjoyed such independent diversion, or the kindness and hospitality of women who were not relations. These overtures were more than welcome since George was besieged by high-minded Bostonians of both sexes, to the point that, as Clara lamented, "his time . . . is so continually taken up, that I see him only at meals and late at night."

When they left Boston in mid-October the bubble burst. In every city where he had appeared with the Indian Gallery, the press had pointed out the irredeemable loss to the nation should the artist be forced to take his collection abroad. Influential friends in government argued his cause. And still, there was no word from Washington. Now another possibility was raised—or planted—by Catlin himself. John Ross, the Cherokee chief whom George had met during his Pensacola stay, reportedly expressed interest in taking up the artist's offer. With no hint of where the money would come from, Ross spoke of establishing a museum of Indian art—for Indians—west of the Rockies.

Uncertainty created its own limbo. Catlin returned to New York, but with no immediate plans to revive the Indian Gallery there. Most of the collection, from paintings to tipi poles, remained crated and warehoused. The exception was a group of pictures that George decided needed work, and he spent most of the winter touching up or finishing these uncompleted canvases, along with editing what would be published as *Letters and Notes*. With finances tight, he rented only one room in the Fulton Street building that had to serve as both studio and living space, while Clara, now pregnant with their second child, repaired with little Libby to the comforts of Albany: They made plans to meet at Great Bend for a visit with the elder Catlins, who had never seen their granddaughter, now a year old. George managed a visit of a few days, alone; the "extremity of the season," as Putnam said, made travel for a pregnant woman and young child inadvisable.

Other plans, too, had gone awry. While in New York, George had made two brief trips to Philadelphia in view of finding space to exhibit there again. But all "suitable rooms" had been engaged, his father reported. Now even the determinedly optimistic Putnam sounded bleak. George badly needed this period of "leisure," free of lectures and the physical labor of installing the collection, in order to "write what he has long promised the public." But the break also meant that "he will be fast spending money, instead of laying up," his father fretted. At the same time Putnam found it "very doubtful as to his selling his works to the Government."

It seems likely that George confided to his father other reasons for his soured hopes. In early February 1839 he had returned to Washington, anxiously determined to be nearby when Representative Briggs, true to his earlier word, introduced another, more strongly worded resolution. This time Briggs had, in effect, ordered the commissioner of Indian affairs to set a price for the purchase of Catlin's collection. Commissioner Crawford was one of the administrators earlier charged with pursuing Catlin—to no avail—for the portraits of Osceola and his followers that the artist owed the War Department: George could hardly have expected to find an advocate in Crawford, so he decided to risk going above the commissioner's head. Leaving Washington on February 26, 1839, a few days before the congressional session ended, Catlin wrote the very next morning to the secretary of war, Joel R. Poinsett. George must have hoped that, unlike Crawford, the secretary would not have troubled himself with such minor matters as portraits commissioned by a subagency that never materialized.

Completely demoralized, George uncharacteristically bared his feelings: He had left Washington "pretty full convinced," he wrote to Poinsett, that the commissioner wouldn't act despite the Indian affairs committee chairman's insistence that

> from day to day . . . they had resolved to make a Report in favor. . . . So the thing rests, and I shall have the mortification of having made, at their request, an offer of them at a very low price,[*] and still unable to see them perpetuated in my own country when I was in hopes to have spent the remainder of my life in adding to and completing the collection.

No written acknowledgement from Poinsett survives and neither he nor Crawford seems to have responded to Representative Briggs's order. The second resolution, like the first, expired.

Catlin seems never to have considered that writing to Poinsett would all but guarantee "inaction," since the secretary would only have turned the matter back to Crawford, his subordinate officially charged with the matter and whose requests for the Osceola portraits

---

[*] The offer seems to have hovered around $60,000, sometimes given as $65,000.

George had ignored before insulting him a second time by going over his head to his superior.

Back in New York, George went through the motions—wearily familiar by now—of getting the collection out of storage and reinstalled in Stuyvesant Institute. Predictably the "return engagement" failed to catch fire: Most of those who had wanted to see the exhibition had already done so, while its run that past winter was too recent to spark the excitement of a revival.

With no other bookings, he seized the chance for a return run in Philadelphia: This time he would not go head-to-head with Hungarian minstrels and ventriloquists; instead he decided to split the animate and inanimate elements of the Indian Gallery. While the collection was once again installed in the Arcade, the artist held forth at the sober home of useful knowledge, the Franklin Institute, where Catlin injected a brand-new element of show business into his talk. Borrowing from the popular tableaux vivants, George "dressed himself each evening in the full costume of different nations," one newspaper reported, "and presented living illustrations of the 'sons of the forest' in native grandeur."

By June he had exhausted his wardrobe of the thirty-eight tribes he was said to have evoked in Philadelphia, returning with the collection to New York and the familiar surroundings of Stuyvesant Hall. He invited his most ardent fan, his father, for a visit, the bill for Putnam's stay at the Western Hotel paid by his son. At this point both were resigned to the unspoken reality: This would be the final engagement in America before George would accompany his Indian Gallery—rejected by the government—abroad.

WHILE IN PHILADELPHIA, Catlin had spent time with his nephew Theodore. At eighteen his late brother Charles's son, called "Burr," had left Great Bend to find work in the city—without success. Everyone in the family, but especially the grandparents who had raised him, worried about the boy, whose only interests seemed to be pretty girls, parties, and, when he could afford it, the theater. These might seem normal-enough pleasures for any young man, but the family remained haunted by the frailties of his father. Burr's easygoing ways seemed to bode badly for his future; like his sister, Theodosia, a schoolteacher, the orphan Burr would have to make his own way in the world, and he appeared to be in no hurry to do so.

Where his fun-loving nephew was concerned, George proved to be an astute judge of adolescence. After all, even at forty-three, he still felt tremors of youth's conflicting needs: freedom and adventure, along with trembling dependency. He foresaw that work on the Indian Gallery would appeal to the stagestruck Burr while filling his need for a substitute family. He paid the boy's fare on the new railroad from Philadelphia to New York (cheaper at night), directing him to his uncle's rooms on Fulton Street, where his new job would combine the work of studio assistant and eventually stage manager. Almost at once the towering red-haired Burr became a hardworking—even indispensable—member of the Catlin road show, and right at home in the heart of New York's theater district.

Exhausted as he was, the prospect of leaving America indefinitely impelled George, the oldest of the surviving children, to visit his sisters and younger brothers, clustered conveniently in upstate New York. From Utica he wrote to assure Burr that he had no doubts that he and his own experienced assistant, Daniel Kavanagh, could manage until he returned to New York City. He should be sure, however, to order four thousand more handbills, making certain that "the public houses be continuously supplied."

Meanwhile Burr himself was showing a talent for painting and drawing: Artist friends in Philadelphia had found his work remarkable. In a gentler voice, tinged with pride, George insisted that, his nephew's other chores notwithstanding, Burr must not neglect his gift: "Keep your brush and crayon going at some things all the time," he urged, "and resolve to keep a steady forward course to improvement in the Art, in spite of everything else."

A wistful tone pervades George's welcome of his nephew to the fellowship of art, just as he himself was moving from this "steady forward course," destination unknown.

THE GREAT AND
THE GOOD

arly in October 1839 George received an eminent visitor in his modest Fulton Street room. Like Catlin, Benjamin Silliman had planned on a legal career. While a tutor in law at Yale College, his alma mater, Silliman's amateur interests in chemistry and geology had brought him such renown as a precocious scientific polymath that the president of Yale persuaded him to give up the law, creating for him the university's first chair of natural history in 1802. He was twenty-three years old. Experimenting with an oxyhydric blowpipe, Silliman demoted many minerals once thought to be elements. He had been greatly impressed by Catlin's "discovery" of the soft red pipestone in the quarry of the same name that George had visited in 1836. Since then the artist and the savant had maintained cordial professional relations. The purpose of Silliman's call on Catlin, weeks before George's planned departure for England, was to commission drawings to accompany the artist's notes on the striated pipestone cliffs, which Silliman could use for his geological research; Catlin needed the money badly, and he agreed to complete the studies before he left America.

But there was only silence from Fulton Street in the ensuing weeks.

Then, on November 24, the day before he was to sail for England, Catlin wrote to Silliman to explain why he had heard nothing from him. A few days after the scientist's visit, George wrote, "I was suddenly thrown upon my back, upon a cot in the Room where you saw me at my work." For almost a month he had been unable to move: He could not rise—or even be lifted—from the folding bed where he had fallen. During this period of immobility, "an abcess [sic] formed at the hip at the joint which gave me a great deal of excruciating pain and a high fever."

As a consequence of the accident, Catlin explained, he was forced to "entirely defer the promise I made you, as I have not yet been able to do anything with my brush." His original departure date had had to be delayed as well: He was to sail on the very next day. As soon as his health was "regulated," he assured Silliman, "I shall give you my theory of the Great Valley of the Mississippi, with some curious deductions and the sketches of which we spoke."

Catlin's emotional state in the weeks before he sailed left him vulnerable on all fronts: The stress and anxiety of awaiting news from Congress, guilt at leaving his aged parents and pregnant wife, due to give birth in the next weeks, added to the strain of moving heavy framed pictures around a small space. The fall, then, was a "perfect accident" waiting to happen. Now his inability to complete a lucrative commission dealt him a further blow, this one to his finances. George was always prone to project—and spend—profits before any income flowed his way. Silliman's fee would have paid most of his travel expenses: Two hundred dollars for two first-class passages, for George and his nephew, Burr; a steerage ticket for Daniel, plus eight tons of freight containing his collection, along with the maintenance of the two grizzlies over an eighteen-day voyage.

On the eve of sailing George wrote another letter, a final plea to the secretary of war, Joel Poinsett. Should the Congress act in his favor, he would return at a week's notice, he said. He hoped he would not be forced to accept a foreign offer for his collection. In closing, he expressed concern for Poinsett's recent health problems and for the worries the secretary would inevitably face in dealing with hostilities on the southwestern frontier.

Catlin's trust in Poinsett's friendship proved misplaced. While serving as congressman from his home state of South Carolina in 1832–33, Poinsett had secretly acted as President Jackson's "confidential agent," reporting on antiadministration activity in the region. Then, when Martin Van Buren succeeded Jackson, the new president appointed Poinsett secretary of war, the department with oversight over the Bureau of Indian Affairs. In this capacity the former legislator and diplomat was charged with implementing the Indian removal laws, along with prosecuting the Seminole Wars. Poinsett was a political animal. Neither his own sympathies nor those of the presidents he served suggest that he would ever do anything to advance the sale of Catlin's Indian portraits to the nation.

Finally George's last-minute letters had been written and posted; the eight tons of crates and boxes stowed, and the grizzlies, safely locked in their iron cage, delivered on deck. At dawn on November 25 George and Burr Catlin arrived at Orleans Wharf at the foot of Wall Street, where they were shown to their passenger cabins aboard the *Roscius*; Daniel disappeared into steerage. There was no one to see them off.

FOR CATLIN THE steamship itself glittered with the promise of his new vocation. The *Roscius* was the pride of "the Dramatic Line," the aptly named company owned by E. K. Collins, a flamboyant entrepreneur with a genius for publicity. All his ships were named after theatrical figures—the *Roscius*, for the famed Roman actor, followed the *Siddons* and *Garrick*—and Collins often entered them in racing competitions with ships of other lines. Skippered by Capt. John Collins, the owner's uncle, the new *Roscius*, launched only the year before, and built for both speed and comfort, had already proved itself the fastest packet boat on the high seas. One of its owner's most-talked-about innovations was to move the cabins—three times larger than those of the rival Black Ball Line—from below to above deck, affording the passengers ample fresh air and light. The Dramatic Line's food, wine, and décor, moreover, were said to set new oceangoing standards of elegance.

One week out the *Roscius* proved its mettle, heading straight into an Atlantic winter storm. For three days, while the steamship pitched and rolled, tossed by waves of terrifying height, the grizzlies, George reported, suffered most. Their "hideous howlings" could be heard everywhere, rising above the gale-force winds and lashing rains. The beasts rattled the bars of their cage, terrifying those passengers who braved the elements to have a look at the exotic creatures on deck nearby. Then one of the crew, playing clown—or hero—passed too close to the cage; a gigantic paw shot out between the bars and swiped the sailor's face, leaving his nose hanging by a thread of skin. A doctor aboard was able to reattach the organ, provisionally, until they landed in Liverpool, where, as he warned the victim, he would be submitted to further torture at the hands of surgeons.

George acknowledged that the grizzlies—each weighing eight hundred to one thousand pounds—were not merely "the most awkward part of my freight . . . but altogether the most troublesome." Expensive, destructive of property, they now proved dangerous to humans as well. Yet the central question about the bears has never been addressed: Why did Catlin take them?

As with all animals, the grizzlies provided a revealing image of their owner. At this turning point in his life, Catlin's bears, together with their master, seemed to look both backward and forward. Natives of the Rocky Mountains (where in fact George had never set foot), the grizzlies were displayed as living proof of the artist's explorations of uncharted wilderness. They shared a past, too, serving as surrogate children of an indulgent father who, at the time of purchase, was still childless. When he first acquired the cubs "they were not much larger than my foot," George recalled, and over the next four years he had raised and fed them. During that time they had "clawed and chewed their way through half a dozen cages, and the price of as many dogs used up" in wrangling them home.

Historically, bears embody a long performative tradition. In poor countries they add greater pathos to the pleas of street beggars. In the circus they mime every human role: clowns and acrobats, riders, skaters—even masters of ceremonies. Catlin's grizzlies, rattling their cages on the deck of the *Roscius*, also point ahead to the future, and a new role for their owner: ringmaster and showman.

Now in the worst of the gale George couldn't be found anywhere, leading Captain Collins to fear that he had been eaten by his own mammoth charges. In fact he had taken refuge belowdecks in steerage.

Despite years of "roughing it" in the West, living closely with trappers, traders, boatmen—men of scant literacy and few standards of hygiene or privacy—Catlin remained, in terms of class, a sheltered patrician. With no experience of urban poverty, he was appalled by what he saw in shipboard tenement life: "The circumstance of sixty passengers, men, women, and children, being stowed into so small a compass, and to so familiar an acquaintance" clearly shocked him.

As soon as the *Roscius* docked in Liverpool on December 18, George was assaulted by the worst of English poverty: "Ragamuffin children," he wrote, beset him on all sides,—"begging to carry [my] baggage to earn a few coppers." Like many other visitors to Victorian Britain, Catlin was struck by the stark and public extremes of wealth and poverty, the shaming contrasts between the pinched faces and shrunken, half-naked bodies of the poor and the well-upholstered rich, insulated even from the weather.

With the other cabin passengers, George spent the night at the Grecian Hotel; Daniel, meanwhile, had earlier arranged to shift the bears into the yard of "an unsuspecting old lady," while he moved nearby to cope with the disaster that was not long in coming. Before dawn the grizzlies had escaped their cage and destroyed everything in sight— instigating threats of the first legal action brought against Catlin in his new life.

Shortly afer arriving in London, he would be summoned back to Liverpool, first to help Daniel quell the outrage caused by the griz- zlies, then to assist the bemused customs inspectors in making a list of the strange objects and images entering Britain. The task of transcrib- ing Indian names into English proved so daunting that, with relief, both parties agreed on a simple system of numbering, in which Chief Ten-squat-a-way, for example, became "Portrait No. 9."

A DECEMBER DAWN in the City of London, banks and commercial houses still shut, is no cheering sight. From the cab that took him from the terminus of the Liverpool coach that morning, Catlin could see almost nothing: A sinister oozing fog cloaked the great capital. Despite the bleak prospect, however, as soon as Ibbotson's Hotel pro- vided him with "breakfast and a clean face," he braved the yellow- brown miasma outside to find for himself the places whose charmed names had "rung in my ears since early boyhood, Fleet Street, the Strand, the Haymarket and Cheapside."

Rich in history, London was worse than Liverpool when it came to the poor, visible everywhere but invisible to well-off neighbors. Soon to be a father again, Catlin found himself especially shaken by the sight of young children whose rags left their nakedness exposed. One girl thrust a sickly baby up to the close view of passersby. George felt sure that the infant would not long survive in the bone-chilling cold.

WELL BEFORE HE boarded the *Roscius* in New York, Catlin's friends and acquaintances had paved the way for the Indian Gallery's launch in London. Letters of introduction from America and the efforts of English connections on his behalf had opened more doors than George even knew existed. His spontaneity and charm (and perhaps a somewhat manic intensity) made a lasting impression on all those he met.

The Hon. Charles Augustus Murray claimed title to the role of angel on George Catlin's shoulder. Scion of an ancient Scots family, Murray, despite being the second son of the fifth Earl of Dunmore, nonetheless inherited a substantial fortune along with fewer responsibilities than his older brother and heir to the title. Equally favored with other attributes, Murray was tall and handsome with a splendid physique; he excelled at riding and cricket and shone as a prize winning classical scholar while at Eton and Oxford.

Murray's independent interests included the study of North American Indian tribes. His grandfather, John Murray, the fourth Earl of Dunmore, had been the last royal governor of Virginia, serving between 1771 and 1776 and waging "Lord Dunmore's War" against the Shawnee on the borders of the Commonwealth. When Charles Augustus was twenty-two, and a passionate fan of James Fenimore Cooper's Leatherstocking novels, he was introduced to the American best-selling author in London and later saw him in America.

Catlin and Murray had met on a downriver voyage on the Mississippi in early June 1835, when the young Scot was at the end of a year spent wandering the United States. For this last chapter of his adventures he debarked at Fort Leavenworth, where he had arranged to meet a visiting party of Pawnee, and to ride back with them to their settlement—a journey of several hundred miles on horseback; there he would remain with the tribe for three months or the entire summer.

Murray had little interest in the Indian as either vanishing noble savage or fearsome adversary. In the first of his many scholarly publications, *Travels in North America*, published in 1839, the same year as Catlin's arrival in London, Murray assumes the detached "scientific" perspective of the ethnologist, a point of view that, well into the twentieth century, was believed to be untainted by bias. He reported on the vermin that covered his hosts' food and bedding, their "swinish" addiction to whiskey and sex, the relegation of their women to the level of "brutes"—apparently unaware that similar observations could have applied to many of his fellow Britons.

In the course of his action-packed year in the New World, Murray fell in love with Elise Wadsworth of Geneseo, New York. Her father, a wealthy merchant, disapproved of the match and forbade all communication between Murray and his daughter. It's thought that Catlin acted as go-between for the separated sweethearts, enabling Murray to write to his beloved by way of covered mailings. This would explain his tireless efforts to return the favor as soon as he learned of George's plans to show his collection in London.[*]

Catlin's first official call in the capital was to Buckingham Palace, where Murray, now Master of the Queen's Household, had a corner office. George arrived in style, alighting from a borrowed horse-drawn carriage, accompanied by a liveried footman. For his part Murray reverted to the free and expansive traveler in the company of his American friend. He had already written to George that subject to his approval, he, Murray, had taken the liberty of booking the largest room in Egyptian Hall, the most fashionable place in London to see and be seen while viewing the latest spectacle—and at the palace he enthusiastically described to George the advantages of showing the Indian Gallery there.

Built in 1811–12, the new exhibition space in Piccadilly had an exuberant facade that led to its instant naming as Egyptian Hall. Indeed its appearance seemed awaiting a future premiere of *Aida*, featuring towering oblong portals and twisted pillars flanking an entrance guarded by nude caryatids. From the outset, exhibitions there lured Londoners

---

[*] The faithful lovers waited eleven years to marry (in 1850, a year after the death of the bride's father). Sadly Elise, Lady Murray, died in childbirth one year later. Their son, however, survived, eventually serving as MP for Coventry.

with a dizzying mix of high and low. Over the years the hall's offerings tilted toward the New World or those cultures that appeared to
have remained impervious to civilization. These included "Ancient
and Modern Mexico"; a family of Lapplanders "complete with house
and reindeer"; a rippling panorama of the Mississippi unfolding on
three miles of painted canvas, along with an earlier live appearance of
a Brazilian tribe of Botocudo Indians.

Chief among Murray's arguments in favor of showing at Egyptian
Hall was the singular size of its main gallery—106 feet long with ample
space for three hundred portraits, more than two hundred landscapes,
spears and tomahawks, and the startling white Crow tipi, twenty-five
feet high with a capacity of eighty visitors. Catlin couldn't help but
agree. With the addition of two smaller rooms, he readily signed the
lease for 550 pounds* annual rent, to begin that very day, December
30, 1839: entrance fee, one shilling.

Murray's excitement was contagious—not that George needed help
from others to get carried away by auspicious beginnings and the shimmering mirage of success. In the next days, however, an inspection
tour disclosed the sobering reality: The interior of Egyptian Hall was
revealed to be as gloomy as any pharaoh's tomb. Its peeling walls, filthy
broken windows, and dim, out-of-date kerosene lights cried out for swift
and costly repairs; needless to say no one had thought to negotiate these
with the owner; all improvements would be at the tenant's expense.

Now, beside the first quarter of the rent, due on signing, Catlin noted

---

* Estimates for historical conversion of currencies, as well as those involving
pounds sterling into dollars, vary. The most widely accepted for this period, around
1840, notes that one pound would be worth about one hundred dollars. Another
useful indicator is the weekly wage of a skilled laborer: A carpenter at this time
earned between eight and twenty shillings a week (twenty shillings to the pound).
The rent of Egyptian Hall—550 pounds in 1840 has been calculated at between
$61,782 and $69,768. (The Victorian Web, www.victorianweb.org.)

in his meticulously kept account book outlays of two hundred pounds for repainting the facade and whitewashing the interior; there were also bills for glazing, lighting, heating, cleaning, along with the shockingly high costs for carpentry, construction of shelves and cases and furniture for the smaller rooms, in which hospitality must be offered to distinguished visitors—especially ladies. According to Burr's calculations, London labor cost twice as much as the equivalent services in America.

Once the repairs had been completed, Murray took on new roles—those of publicist and impresario—with characteristic zest, orchestrating what he hoped—no, fully expected—would be the most successful launch of an exhibition that London had ever seen. To say that the Hon. C. A. Murray was well connected gives only the merest hint of the breadth of his social reach. He discreetly announced three days of private viewings for the end of January, by invitation only, before the exhibition opened to the public. Starting with his own friends, Murray began wrangling the rich, titled, and fashionable before spreading the word to related circles of tastemakers and cultural luminaries, fanning interest and excitement among prominent editors, religious leaders, and even sober scientific institutions.

With the help of carpenters, Catlin, Burr, and Daniel whirled through a frenzy of preparations: Climbing ladders, they hung five hundred paintings three deep as well as robes on the barely dry whitewashed walls. From the floor they arranged bonnets, calumets, and cradleboards, spears and tomahawks, on shelves or in glass cases, all of them placed to make the most of London's weak January daylight, followed by the new gaslights essential to illuminate the darkness that fell by afternoon.

At ten o'clock on January 29 George and the two others, together with ushers, stood ready to receive the first distinguished guests, leading them through the blackness of an anteroom, into the light of the main gallery and its centerpiece, the white Crow tipi. In the course of the next three days the great and the good streamed, blinking, into the vast and dazzling room.

Along with leavenings of Rothschilds, royal-watchers counted ten dukes with their duchesses, five earls and their countesses, two bishops, and unnamed lords, baronesses, and knights; those whom Catlin called the "most conspicuous" included HRH the Duke of Cambridge, the Duke and Duchess of Sutherland, the Duke of Wellington, the Bishop of London, with most of the press, as well as "private literary and scientific gentlemen."

At the end of each day Catlin delivered his prepared talk, modified for British listeners. But his guests had come to meet and chat informally with the celebrated artist, explorer, and adventurer. Each had specific questions, anecdotes of his own travels to relate, all of them requiring personal attention. Happily, George had another authority close at hand: C. A. Murray, in morning coat and dazzling linen, a duchess on each arm, gracefully assumed the duties of "docent"; his own recently published *Travels*, known to most of those present, conferred on him an expertise almost equal to that of his friend Catlin. Now, surrounded by knots of rapt nobles, he gladly filled in with recollections of dances, buffalo hunts and his personal impressions of some of the very chieftains staring somberly from the walls.

Publicity, especially in the popular press, was one area where Catlin needed no prodding. As soon as the exhibition opened officially on February 1, George placed a long notice, sometimes running daily, in London's fifty-one newspapers and periodicals, noting that Mr. Catlin has returned

from the "Great Far West" after an absence of seven years, with an immense collection, consisting of "300 PORTRAITS OF DISTINGUISHED CHIEFS AND 200 OTHER PAINTINGS." The 200 OTHER PAINTINGS consist of landscapes, together with Indians Villages, Indian Dances, Buffalo Hunts, Ball Plays, &c, &c.

In a separate category, the only one to merit an individual description, was the group of "Four Paintings . . . descriptive of the MANDAN RELIGIOUS CEREMONIES, In which the Mandan Youths are doing Penance by passing Knives and Splints through their Flesh, and suspending their Bodies by their Wounds, &c."

The press campaign—both Catlin and Murray doing their share of "briefing" in print and in person at the exhibition—reaped rewards that neither man—in his moments of wildest optimism—could have anticipated: Popular newspapers and learned periodicals alike devoted unheard-of space and ink to the new sensation.

Noting the extraordinary range of native objects on display, "from a wigwam to a child's rattle," the *Literary Gazette* observed smartly that "no book of travels can approach these realities" and marveled further: "We saw more distinctly the links of resemblance between them [the 'Red men'] and other early and distant people." Then, lest this tribute to the exhibition as a lesson in comparative ethnology scare off the general public, the reviewer added an irresistible selling point to families: It was not the "philosophical enquirer" alone who would delight in the exhibition: "The curious child of seven years of age will enjoy it with present amusement and lasting instruction."

Critics and reviewers, including the most ecstatic, united in praising Catlin's brilliant mind, his energy and courage, the extraordinary historical value of the collection—all the while ignoring him as an artist. The originality of the portraits and their painterly qualities were never discussed; even the staggering number of images was mentioned only in passing: The *Art-Union*, while paying tribute to the entire collection as a "work of deep and permanent interest," seemed indifferent to Catlin's art: "It was not a common mind that could have conceived so bold a project, nor is he a common man who has so thoroughly accomplished it."

In an ironic twist the critic from the *Quarterly Review*, the periodical of the educated elite, took it for granted that "Mr. Catlin's avowed object in visiting England is to sell his collection to our Government," and the writer concluded with the hope that his fellow Britons would not fail to seize this opportunity. But George clung to the belief that his own country would take action in his favor—soon. He issued a gracious denial: The collection was not for sale.

WHEN CATLIN WASN'T lecturing or talking informally with the crowds that, following the private viewings, now flocked to Egyptian Hall, he was singing for his supper after closing hours. But more often than not he had to forgo supper. Beginning with a Rothschild dinner in his honor, the courtiers who had come to the exhibition at Murray's behest followed suit. Every morning George found invitations to the grandest houses delivered to the gallery, often with the scribbled assurance from the hostess that at *her* home, he could count on an evening of rest and refreshment. Predictably, however, what was wanted was more—more of the lionized guest who was expected to continue talking, answering questions, recalling anecdotes—in a more intimate setting. Admittedly, once George got going it was hard for him to stop. Often supper was "held off" until, his fellow guests having enjoyed full access to the celebrity, were ready to dine, and Catlin too exhausted to think of anything but getting home to bed. At that late hour there were no cabs or omnibuses, and George found himself walking three miles across a deserted London, from his hosts' mansions to his lodgings in Piccadilly.

Success was quite literally killing him, "As I was daily growing richer," he recalled, "I was daily growing poorer.—i.e. I was day by day losing my flesh, not from the usual cause, the want of enough to eat, but from derangement of the lungs and the stomach, both often overworked, with a constant excitement and anxiety of the mind."

Only the looming disaster of a serious illness just now could have brought Catlin, the stoical Yankee, to a physician's examining room.

There he was categorically forbidden to lecture more than three times a week and probably advised to cut down his late-night informal "conversations" as well.

For George, though, this respite was merely an opportunity to take up unfinished work. He used the time away from the exhibition to complete a final draft of his *Letters and Notes*, too often laid aside for more pressing business. Now his friend Murray took on yet another essential role. He became Catlin's literary agent, determined to find a publisher for his first book.

Murray's first choice was London's preeminent imprint, John Murray. Charles Augustus was no relation to John Murray II, but he moved in the same circles as that down-to-earth Scot, publisher of Sir Walter Scott and Mrs. Rundell's *A New System of Domestic Cookery*, the best-selling British cookbook of all time; and the two men were great friends.

Murray was not a man to take avoidable risks, but the ebullient publisher seemed delighted by his visit to the Indian Gallery, probably with both C. A. Murray and Catlin as guides. Before calling on the publisher in Albemarle Street, George left his letter of introduction from another of Murray's best-selling authors, Washington Irving.

From then on, according to Catlin, his friendship with the publisher had flourished: Murray dropped in on George's rooms "almost daily" to hear more tales of Indian life, while once a week he included Catlin at his legendary dinner table, where fellow guests such as Thomas Moore, the Irish poet and first biographer of Byron, broadened the American visitor's acquaintance among London's literary world.

Perhaps Catlin should have been alerted when Murray demurred from reading the manuscript of *Letters and Notes*. It's clear that when the publisher heard that the work was "to be illustrated with more than 300 steel plate illustrations" he suffered an attack of frugality. Not wishing to appear stingy or pessimistic about the book's prospects, however, Murray offered a brilliant reason for turning the book down—quite possibly the most original rejection in the history of publishing. "He loved me too much," George recalled Murray telling him, "to share with me the profits of a work which he said should all belong to me for my hard labour and the risks of my life I had run in procuring it."

"I would advise you," Murray had said, "as one of your best friends, to publish your own book; and I am sure you will make a handsome profit by it." By way of further advice John Murray suggested that the exhibition itself would be a likely place for Catlin to gather subscribers in person for his self-publishing venture. And of course the artist would save money by making the engravings himself.

George tried to put a good face on this unexpected blow, but in fact he was devastated. He had counted on Murray to publish the work, but also, as a practical matter, to reimburse him for the enormous investment he had already made, contracting with printers and engravers who were well into their labors and expected periodic payment for their work. In order to break even, he would need to sell one thousand copies of a book whose price was a staggering two and a half guineas.* And where would he find time to make the engravings himself? Finally, one could not count on subscriptions even to cover expenses, not to speak of profits.

Repairing for consolation to the other Murray's office in Buckingham Palace, George found his friend to be no less surprised by the bad news. Almost as practical as the publisher, however, Charles Murray immediately began drawing up a subscription list of glittering names—the sort who would attract others, less glittering perhaps but more solvent. On his own Murray promptly signed up crowns and coronets: starting with "Her Most Gracious MAJESTY the QUEEN,"

---

* A gold coin worth about twenty-one shillings; a price quoted in guineas denoted luxury goods—real estate, art, wine, horses. It was phased out with decimalization in 1971, but lives on as a "concept."

followed by HRH Prince Albert, the queen dowager (William IV's widowed consort, Princess Adelaide of Saxe-Meiningen), the Duchess of Kent; the Duke of Sussex, and extending the glitter to the continent included the king and queen of the Belgians, and Leopold, Duc de Brabant. Murray did not stop with royals; librarians of the major learned institutions, primed by visiting the exhibition, also put their names down for the book.

Published by the author at Egyptian Hall, *Letters and Notes* did not appear until October 1841. Critical reception proved even more rapturous than the response to the exhibition itself. Reprinting a selection of the reviews twelve years later, during one of his life's bleakest periods, Catlin poignantly noted the number of pages each notice was allowed. The *Literary Gazette* led the pack with "*Three Notices, Twenty-five Columns. 'Catlin's Book on the North American Indians.—An unique* work! A work of extraordinary interest and value. Mr. Catlin is *the* Historian of the Red Races of mankind; of a past world, or at least of a world fast passing away. . . . We need not recommend it to the world, for it recommends itself, beyond our praise.'"

"This is a remarkable book, written by an extraordinary man," was the lead in the *Westminster Review*: "'*Twelve pages*'" Catlin noted, ending with the thoughtful hope that "'its extensive sale will amply repay Mr. Catlin for the great outlay he must have incurred.'"

Addressing the general reader, London's *Morning Chronicle* declared that the author's "free and easy conversational style, plentifully sprinkled with Americanisms, gives a peculiar charm to his descriptions, which are not merely animated or life-like, but *life* itself."

Meanwhile speaking engagements added scholarly prestige to Catlin's celebrity. The exhibition had been open for only two weeks when he delivered an invitational lecture at the Royal Institution, to the "loud & repeated cheers" of an audience numbering more than one thousand, he reported to his parents. Newspapers covering the event praised the speaker for his "clearness—for self-possession," giving George all the more confidence as he began a second course of lectures at Egyptian Hall.

IF HE DID not wake up one day, like Lord Byron, to find himself famous, Catlin had for the moment become the social and cultural lion of London. Invitations, engraved on heavy cream-colored cards embossed with gold coronets, piled up on his mantelpiece. He wrote home proudly that he had attended the young queen's opening of Parliament as Lord Monteagle's guest.

None of this paid the bills, however. Money would always remain the problem that Catlin could never solve. By the end of February 1840, he had already spent two thousand dollars on rent, renovations, advertising, and personal expenditures. A later mention of "re-paying Mr. Gregory" suggests that, besides accepting his brother-in-law's support for Clara and the children—the new baby, named for her mother, had arrived at the end of December 1839—George also borrowed money from Dudley Gregory for his London expenses. The crush of visitors to the exhibition, each paying one shilling, and many buying the catalog for another shilling, barely covered Catlin's costs. The next year, 1841, George's installment payments for self-publishing *Letters and Notes* added a further burden of debt to his income. On the back of a letter home, Burr Catlin's scrawled lines said it all: "32,500 visitors to the exhibition[.] About 9433 dollars taken in Year ending Jan. 31st. 1841. Spent *all*."

22

HIGH SOCIETY

In the six months that George Catlin spent alone in London, he was celebrated in every sense of the word, welcomed as a peer by scientists and cultural luminaries. His homespun Yankee style and inexhaustible supply of stories and jokes proved a distinct social asset: Even when George was dressed by London's best tailors, he seemed to be wearing buckskin.

His first invitation to lecture came from the most distinguished association in London. Established in 1799, the officially named Royal Institution of Great Britain was founded by two leading scientists of the day, Henry Cavendish and the aristocratic amateur, George Finch the ninth Earl of Winchelsea. From the beginning the RI—as it soon came to be called—took for its mission the scientific education of the public through its famous lecture series, while also providing a professional affiliation for such Olympians of research and discovery as Michael Faraday and Humphry Davy. It was no small distinction for an American artist who wrote on ethnology—disputed as scientific terrain—to be invited to speak, and George's pride in this signal honor shines from the pages of his letters home.

Without fanfare, Catlin's talk at the Royal Institution on February

14, 1840, quietly introduced another first: Before its "venerable" members and guests, the speaker illustrated his remarks with "several living figures [Londoners hired for the occasion], dressed in Indian costumes with weapons in hand," along with his usual accompaniment of paintings displayed on easels.

Seizing the moment, Catlin used the occasion to introduce to British audiences and to the press his "grand scheme" for a "Museum of Mankind," an idea he claimed had been "for many years my favourite theme." In Catlin's vision the museum would "contain and perpetuate the looks and manners and history of all the declining and vanishing races of man." Implicitly the new museum would work for George Catlin as Charles Willson Peale's museum had functioned for its artist-founder—an "advertisement for myself"—since, as George noted, "my collection would ultimately form the basis of such an institution."

Unveiling his grandiose plan to this influential London audience, George shrewdly framed the idea in terms of its relevance to the expanding British Empire. First, his museum would be housed in a ship: Whether in port or waterborne, the experience of visiting the collections and exhibits onboard would serve as a reminder of the ebb and flow of populations and progress. Like its American counterpart of westward expansion, the inevitable course of Her Majesty's spreading dominion over indigenous peoples would claim victims. The object of the Museum of Mankind was to make certain that the distinctive art and artifacts created by these races, soon to be crushed by the juggernaut of their civilized conquerors, did not perish with them. As Catlin reminded his listeners, "Great Britain has more than thirty colonies in different quarters of the globe, in which the numbers of civilized men are increasing, and the native tribes are wasting away—that the march of civilization is everywhere, as it is in America, a war of extermination, and that of our own species."

Thus, speaking in 1840, George Catlin stands among the first to have equated colonialism with "extermination." Lest anyone misunderstand his meaning, he hammered it home:

> For the occupation of a new country, the first enemy that must
> fall is *man*. . . . Our war is not with beasts or with birds; the griz-
> zly bear, the lion, and the tiger are allowed to live. Our weapons
> are not employed against them: we do not give them whiskey,
> and rum, and the smallpox, nor the bayonet; they are allowed to
> live and thrive upon our soil . . . but to complete a title, man, our
> fellow-man, the noblest work of God, with thoughts, with senti-
> ments, with sympathies like our own, must be extinguished; and
> he dies on his own soil, unchronicled and unknown (save to the
> ruthless hands that have slain him, and would bury his history
> with his body in oblivion).

Like his enthusiastic audiences, Catlin was fixed in many of the attitudes of his time and place. He never saw his floating museum as theft on a global scale, akin to grave robbers descending just before the "extermination" of subject peoples to rescue their material culture.

The excitement that greeted the proposal of the Museum of Mankind (helped by the surprise appearance of costumed "Indians") buoyed George with pride, but also confirmed his belief in a shared mission and a call to action. Following his triumph at the Royal Institution, he found himself overwhelmed with invitations to give the same talk at the Royal Geographical, Geological, and Historical Societies. His welcome into the company of "literary and scientific men" opened other doors. Thanks to his new associates he was about to enjoy a privileged course in continuing education, with free access to the "noble collections and libraries under their superintendence."

But there's a poignant note to his gratitude. Self-educated as an artist, writer, and reader, Catlin was never comfortable with the discourse of high culture. At law school in Litchfield he had felt disadvantaged in the company of young men who brought to their legal studies a university or college education in the liberal arts. Now he was expected to hold his own with classically educated scientists who would soon be acknowledged by history as groundbreaking researchers in their respective fields. His new friends, however, admired Catlin precisely because he had done it all himself. His explorations and fieldwork, his brilliantly written and painted record of unknown tribes made him, in their eyes, more than worthy to be treated as a peer, and their generosity proved as large as their erudition: "I was here at once . . . ushered into a new world," he exulted,

> a new atmosphere—and in it was met and welcomed every where with the utmost cordiality and kindness; libraries, museums, laboratories, and lectures were free to me, and not only the private tables of the advocates of science, but their public tables in their banqueting halls, prepared a seat for me.

Among those banqueting halls—but hardly a public table—was the annual dinner of the Royal Highland Society, where George now found himself an honored guest. Catlin the student of comparative ethnology noted how closely his hosts and fellow guests, all wearing "their kilts, and with the badges and plaids of their peculiar clans," resembled the Plains tribes he knew well, especially the Scottish chiefs, who "wore the eagle's quills for the same purpose and in the same manner that the Indians do."

The evening's most singular moment, where George was concerned, should have been the least remarkable. For the first time since he had arrived in England; after months of exhibiting more than six hundred of his portraits and landscapes, scenes of buffalo hunts and of battle, Catlin finally received homage as an artist, and from a fellow painter.

At fifty-five Sir David Wilkie was at the height of his fame and popularity as a painter of affecting genre scenes; his best-known work,

Chelsea Pensioners Reading the Gazette of the Battle of Waterloo, had assured his reputation. In 1830 he had been appointed Painter in Ordinary, or official court painter, to George IV; knighted by his successor, William IV, the artist had been retained in the post by Queen Victoria.

On the occasion of the Royal Highland Society dinner, Wilkie followed the toasts raised to him by thanking his hosts for the honor of being seated next to a fellow artist whom he admired as much as he did George Catlin. He then quoted from the many ecstatic reviews Catlin had received, affirming the importance and value of the entire collection. Unique to Wilkie's public praise, however, was his personal tribute to the artist: "He took especial pains to compliment me for the execution of my paintings, many of which, he said, as works of art, justly entitled me to the hands of artists in this country, and he was proud to begin by offering me his, in good fellowship, which he did, and raised me from my seat as he said it."

SOON CATLIN'S PLEASURE in his warm reception at the dinner was overshadowed by Charles Murray's invitation to George (and Burr) to the Caledonian Ball, held annually at Almack's Assembly Rooms on King Street, off Piccadilly. Since 1765, membership in Almack's, an invitational club (the first to admit both men and women), had been the imprimatur of admission to society—as defined by its governing body of "lady Patronesses," six or seven women of rank who were the "fair arbiters" of social standing. Titles alone did not qualify aspirants for the coveted "vouchers," which could also be withdrawn at any time. Founded to exclude the Regency's* nouveaux riches from its

---

* So called for George IV's period as prince regent—between roughly 1811 and 1820, and synonymous with an exhuberant flowering of the arts and extravagant expressions of wealth and sexual license—during the "madness" of his father, King George III.

Wednesday-evening assemblies, Almack's still carefully vetted members' guests, which must have made George and Burr feel all the more honored to be attending an event in a venue famed for "the most brilliant and splendid affairs that can be seen in London, presenting the most gorgeous display of costumes and diamonds that the world can exhibit, short of royalty itself." The blinding show of gems, however, also confirms that by the 1840s, Almack's strict standards of birth, breeding, and behavior had loosened somewhat, to admit new money and—according to some—explicitly sexual encounters.

Though the invitation was the high point of Catin's London "Season," his host, Charles Murray, still enamored of his American heiress, could think of nothing duller than waltzing with the same marriageable young women or bored young wives to whom he bowed every year. Then Murray had an inspired idea: He, George, and Burr would "make a *sensation*" by attending the Caledonian Ball disguised as Indians.

Gleefully Catlin raided the walls and cupboards of his private rooms in Egyptian Hall, choosing the "finest costumes . . . along with weapons, head-dresses, scalping knives &c." At 3 p.m. on the day of the ball, the three assembled to "fit us with our respective dresses and go through a sort of rehearsal in our songs, dances, &c., which we might be called upon to enact during the evening, and in which it would be a great pity for us Indian knowing ones to make any mistake."

Burr Catlin, standing six feet two inches tall in his stocking feet, "with a bold and Indian outline of face," as his uncle described him, was arrayed as "the Big Sioux—the Great Chief Wan-ne-ton" and crowned with the headdress of that tribal elder made of war-eagle's quills and ermine skins. It was agreed, George recalled, that to give nothing away of his real identity, he was to "hold himself entirely mute upon his dignity, according to the customs of the country."

George's portrait of Burr in Indian dress (1840–41) is one of the few full-sized works he painted in England and the only known one of a white man that he made in those years. The face, with its uniform "Coppertone" makeup, and especially its features, are rendered with high finish and attention to detail. So, too, are the shaved head and roach, both painted a bright orange, while the dark intelligent eyes and serious set mouth suggest that the twenty-one-year-old had matured since his party-loving ways had so worried his grandparents. In contrast Burr's costume is indicated perfunctorily, as Catlin more often did with smaller oil sketches. The quick "filler" brushstrokes, with their flat color, make little effort to suggest texture—feathers, fur, skin—and there is only the vaguest indication of a tomahawk thrust into the belt.

For the ball George chose to appear dressed as a Sauk warrior, his ornaments of red and white quills, he explained, "denoting his readiness for war or peace." As producer and director of their act, Murray cast himself in the role of a mixed-race Bois Brûlé, a tribe that often functioned as interpreter/translators on the frontier, making him the perfect mediator between the impostors and other guests. Dressed for action in a lighter, less richly adorned robe, Murray wore a headdress consisting of a wig of long black hair spreading over his shoulders and falling to his calves, the cascade surmounted by a single eagle's feather.

At 9 p.m., six hours after they had convened for their dress rehearsal, the three were ready: To the copper-tinted faces were added

> bold daubs of vermilion and green or black paint, so that, with our heavy and richly garnished robes of the buffalo, thrown over our shoulders and trailing on the floor as we walked, with tomahawks and scalping knives in our belts, our shields of buffalo hides on our arms, with our quivers slung and our bows and arrows clenched in our hands, we were prepared for the sensation we were in a few minutes to make.

Reactions to the trio's sudden entrance, accompanied by their tremendous yells, exceeded their wildest hopes. Several ladies screamed in terror, and the little group was instantly surrounded by such a densely packed crowd that only Burr was visible above the crush—"flourishing his enormous headdress of eagle's quills . . . and quietly rolling his eagle eyes around over the multitude."

Prodigious linguist that he was, Murray invented a mumbo-jumbo consisting of French, German, and English (pronounced with a broad "American" accent), spiced with a smattering of the two or three Indian languages that he had picked up in his Western travels. As a precaution against his voice being recognized by his many friends and relations present, he rolled a rifle bullet in his mouth while he was talking. According to Catlin, Murray's own brother Lord Dunmore failed to recognize him.

Comical Indian names added to the joke that the performers shared with one another, and whose authenticity went unquestioned by their fellow guests. As George related:

> The introductions I had on that night, to lords and ladies, and to dukes and duchesses, as *Na-see-us-kuk* [Now-See-Us-Cook] a famous warrior of the Sacs, and my nephew, as *Wan-ne-ton* [Wanton], that great Sioux Chief, were honours certainly that he or I could never have aspired to under any other names; and our misfortune was, that their duration was necessarily as brief as the names and titles we had assumed.

One of the beauties in attendance took a shine to George, and seductively tried to clasp on his wrist a "magnificent bracelet" she had detached from her own arm, asking, in exchange, "a small scalplock from the seams of [Catlin's] leggings." This he tore off and gallantly pressed upon his lovely admirer, promising to return her valuable jewel at the ball's close. As the evening wore on, however, the heat of the crowd, the "Indians'" heavy costumes and their "violent exertions" from a staged Sioux war dance, produced a literal identity crisis. As their makeup melted, "a flow of perspiration . . . carried away the paint in streaks from our foreheads to our chins," George recalled.

The game was up. The "whiteness" of the trio revealed the familiar features of at least one of the savage guests. Shrieks of laughter and jokes greeted the reappearance of their old friend, kinsman to many present, the Hon. Charles Augustus Murray. At this point party favors in the form of scalplocks and feathers plucked from the warriors' headdresses were distributed to all the ladies, whose own jewels were duly restored.

In the rush for carriages at the door, none of the grand guests thought to offer a ride to the "whitewashed" Indians who had been the stars of the evening. After waiting half an hour in vain for an available cab, the three set off on foot for Egyptian Hall. "It was now past sunrise and raining in torrents, as it had been during the whole night." The rain, mud, and sharp paving stones made quick work of the once "white and beautiful moccasins," the trailing robes, and drooping headdresses (or what remained of them after they had been ravaged for souvenirs). With their smeared war paint, spattered buffalo skins, and scraggly bonnets, the three Indian chiefs soon acquired followers—a "gang of boys and ragamuffins," who shouted "'Indians! Indians!'" to astonished early-morning passersby.

Thanks to the night porter who had waited up for them, the bedraggled trio eluded their hangers-on and were quickly admitted to the hall. There, divesting themselves of the damaged ceremonial garments, they were able to "gaze and grin at each other, and deliberately and leisurely to scour ourselves back again to our original characters."

IT'S HARD TO know how to read Catlin's feelings about the ball at Almack's: All that we learn of the event comes from the artist himself, and his account, written more than ten years later, fairly bubbles with gleeful and guileless nostalgia. He seems to have harbored no second thoughts about their little group's travesty of the Indians: their racial features, ceremonies, language, even their names—all held up to ridicule. Nor did he appear to question the damage or complete ruin of some of the most splendid examples of native crafts in his personal collection. He seemed to value them no more than if they had been disposable crêpe-paper costumes fashioned for a children's party.

Distance—in time and space—played into Catlin's growing sense of estrangement from his Indian subjects. A decade had passed since he had lived on the upper Missouri and painted many of the portraits on view in Egyptian Hall; the same number of years had gone by since he had acquired the precious robes, headdresses, and moccasins. In the interim the men and women who had made them, who had been his hosts, inviting him to observe and record their most secret and sacred ceremonies, seem to have faded from both his memory and his affections. Now that his vivid recollections of life among the Plains Indians, as he relived them in *Letters and Notes*, were about to be published (at the author's expense), the people themselves had been reduced to caricatures, copper-faced versions of London's popular "coon shows," also imported from America.

Around this time, yet another resolution for the U.S. government to buy Catlin's collection was tabled in Congress, and on some level George seems to have blamed his Indian subjects for this crucial defeat. By portraying the Native American with unmistakable sympathy, respect, and love in both painting and writing, he had taken on—implicitly and sometimes frontally—the most powerful forces in America. He had confronted the worst abuses—those pursued, condoned, or ignored by government as the inevitable consequence of westward expansion. Now in London, Catlin could not fail to suspect that he was paying a price for having stood with the Indian—even if waveringly—and against the interests of the fur trade, the military, Western settlement, and the abrogation of treaties. The third rejection foreclosed any immediate reason to return home. George Catlin's long, slow exile had begun.

WHAT HAD STARTED as a short stay abroad, whose purpose would be the defiant sale of his collection in England or on the Continent, followed by a triumphant return home, was now extended—indefinitely. Once again optimism turned to impatience. There had been no offers to buy his collection, or so far to publish his illustrated letters. Despite the accolades, the audiences, the patrons in high places, he could not seem to translate his triumphs into the wealth he sought: "I wish really that I was making more *money* than I as yet am," he told Putnam, explaining that he wanted the means to "do more to gild your latter days, with comforts & luxuries."

In fact George had put his finger on a seismic shift that went far beyond his own ambitions, one that would come to characterize his entire generation of single-minded men who had come of age with the new Republic. "We who are younger, are more eager & impatient for the goods of this world, and more uneasy if we do not acquire them," he wrote his father.

Success measured solely by the visible accumulation of wealth—the faster the better—was something new in America, and Catlin was in the vanguard of a new breed: the artist-turned-entrepreneur. To be sure, the Peale museums had been a family business, but the idea had been that the Peale collections should support the Peale artists, who otherwise could never have pursued their vocation while raising large families.

A decade earlier, when George abandoned conventional portraiture to paint a record of vanishing tribal life, he never dreamed of becoming a rich man through his art. Now, led on by the prospect of wealth glittering just out of reach, he was suffering the multiple strains of acting as front man as well as financial backer of his Indian

Gallery, while at the same time he was running up debts to become a self-published author: These investments required a large return—and soon. Receipts from the exhibition, "well-attended & fashionable" as it was, hadn't a prayer of paying off the debts—close to ten thousand dollars—incurred in the publication of the magnificent illustrated portfolio, which also swallowed many hours of supervision of both text and plates. As he soon concluded, "I see no great chance of making a fortune in London unless I sell my collection."

While George poured out his frustrations to his father, Clara, Libby, and little Clara, accompanied by Bridget, the nursemaid, were three days out of New York on their way to joining Catlin in England. And lest Putnam worry that his son now cared only for making money, he assured his father that when the family arrived, "Oh what feelings of joy and thankfulness I shall have! It will be the happiest moment of my life, certainly—!"

Worries about mounting bills and debts coming due were pushed aside by the high spirits of the reunited family. Their arrival in London, coming at the height of the "Season," when the Court Calendar, Parliament, and social and professional life, were in full swing, meant that Clara could be included in the whirl of balls and parties, dinners, and receptions. Watching her husband in easy exchange with his scholarly peers, and mingling with the general audiences at his public lectures, Clara observed George in his glory, honored as an artist, ethnologist, author, and more exalted still, in this capital of talent, as the best of America: "I felt now as if I had a sort of citizenship in London," he recalled, noting that "it was an opportune moment, also, for the arrival of my dear wife and her two infant children . . . to share the kind attention and compliments that were being paid to me."

All thoughts of economy were brushed aside. He rented expensive rooms at 3 Old Cavendish Street, close to Egyptian Hall and as fashionable an address as a transient family could find in town, the right location being as important to London life as the right clothes. Now that Mrs. Catlin had arrived, they would be expected to receive guests in style. In the twelve years of their marriage Clara had never had a home of her own. Now, within weeks, she had to assume the role of hostess as well as consort to a celebrated guest, and to be seen as appropriately dressed for both. Hardly surprising to read George writing to his parents, "Clara has seen but little of London as yet, she has been so busy preparing her clothes & her apartments where we are commencing to live."

A month later, on the evening of July 27 a Catlin reception included George's old friend, the painter Asher B. Durand, along with another American artist, George P. A. Healy of Boston, now enjoying great success as a portraitist in Paris. Still feeling pangs of homesickness, Durand felt happy to encounter "more familiar faces than at any other time during my sojourn in London." In the course of several visits to Egyptian Hall, he even felt grateful to the wooden mannequins draped in Indian robes and the painted "multitude of the representative faces of the Red men of my native country who surrounded and welcomed me as I entered." The generous-spirited Durand was "glad to learn that Mr. Catlin is, in common parlance, 'doing well' here with his Indian Exhibition, for well he deserves to do."

CLARA'S BLOSSOMING GIFTS as a hostess encouraged George to make Cavendish Street a regular gathering place for Americans, especially those who could be helpful to him professionally. At twenty-six George Palmer Putnam was already an established publisher, a partner in the New York–based firm Wiley & Putnam. In September 1840, determined to make London a base for acquiring Anglo-European work and selling his American authors, he arrived in England on the *Roscius*, the same packet that had brought Catlin the year before. This was his third stay in the English capital, and he was now doing well enough to move the firm to larger offices and to hire more help.

Putnam was engaged to a beautiful sixteen-year-old orphan, the romantically named Victorine Haven of New York. Concerned about the youth of their ward, Miss Haven's guardians (her older sister and brother-in-law), insisted that the couple be separated for a year before any official betrothal, thus explaining Putnam's long working stay abroad.

Soon after his arrival, Putnam made several visits to Egyptian Hall, where he was much impressed by the collection and by Mr. Catlin. That same month—September—Putnam's London office had announced that it was publishing another Catlin venture, the artist's two-volume edition, in expensive portfolio format, of *Manners, Customs and Condition of the North American Indians.*

Then, on October 18, Putnam, together with a shipboard acquaintance, a Colonel Johnson from Missouri, called on the Catlins again. What impressed the Harvard-educated publisher was not his host's knowledge or even the fluency with which he related anecdotes of his travels among the Plains Indians; his new friend, Putnam wrote to Victorine, "is an extremely interesting man & unassuming & he tells his adventures with so much *naivete* and simplicity that you cannot help believing even his most marvellous stories, which is more than can be said of all travelers." The Catlins made it clear that they were always "at home" to George Putnam, who noted happily to his wife-to-be, "I think I shall go to see them often—for they are the *nicest* people I have met with here."

But despite his affection for Catlin and admiration for his work, Putnam, like John Murray, ended up declining to publish the lavish portfolio. Although he apparently helped with its distribution, once again the new and still more costly publication—along with its debts— was left to the author.

Putnam did his best, however, to compensate for changing his mind about publishing Catlin's work. On his annual visits to Washington, where he would soon serve as unofficial lobbyist for the American publishing industry in general and for copyright laws in particular, Putnam supposedly tried to persuade his many lawmaker connections to make further efforts to secure the purchase of Catlin's Indian Gallery. He was no more successful than the artist's influential political friends had been.

Meanwhile, expenses kept mounting while income lagged. George was obliged to defer his commitment to send his father a second installment of help, a promised five hundred dollars; any disposable cash had to go instead to repay money borrowed from his brother-in-law Dudley Gregory. More painful still was to declare himself unable to come to the aid of his sister Eliza and her husband, Anson Dart, whose disastrous investments had forced them to sell everything they had in Utica, New York and relocate with their children to land Dart already owned in the Wisconsin Territory; there, with no nearby housing, the family had to build a log cabin in the freezing wilderness near Green Bay. It was discomfiting for George to admit that, despite the sinking shares of the Pensacola Bank, Richard and James were pitching in to help the others, but that he, George, could afford to send nothing: "Would to God that it were in my power to aid him now," he lamented of his brother-in-law, "at the time when aid would be more kind to him than it ever can be again, but alas, I *cannot*." Defensively Catlin invoked

> a family of seven, whom I have shipped across the ocean, and for whose daily food, and return also, I am responsible, with other enormous expenses continually accruing, and the liquidation of those that I incurred at the time of leaving, I find it difficult to lay bye anything as yet, to help a friend in time of need, or even in time of absolute distress.[*]

---

[*] Catlin seems to have inflated family members by including earlier passengers, including Burr and Daniel Kavanagh.

He enclosed one hundred dollars for his parents in lieu of the amount they had expected. It would not have been tactful to mention that the "enormous expenses" included bills from upholsterers, caterers, dress-makers, and tailors.

Not for nothing was Clara Gregory Catlin an accountant's daughter. She kept track of every pound earned, spent, or owed—unless her husband decided to "spare" her certain personal debts. She was pleased to write to her in-laws that, in reward for George's prompt quarterly payment for Egyptian Hall and renewal of the lease for the coming year, the rent had been reduced by fifty pounds; he was also allowed to sublet the lecture room, which, as Clara explained, he no longer used, thereby reducing the rent further to a total of 250 pounds. The British Museum was rumored to be on the verge of making an offer for the collection, but she doubted that it was prepared to give "full value" for the works.

But she also fretted. Reading newspaper accounts of George's success, everyone at home assumed he was making a fortune: "But they little know of the heavy expenses, of rent, advertising and expense of living, which keep a man poor, if he is successful." She was thankful that the grizzlies, along with their maintenance, were now the burden of the London Zoo. (The bears, however, failed to thrive in foreign captivity and died within the year.)

Clara was not only practical, noting income and expenses; she quickly grasped one of the most brutal features of British law: the criminal sanctions applied to debtors. She, too, grieved that they could do nothing to help George's family. "But we are here in a strange land struggling for a living, and if a man is unfortunate here, there is a set of harpies ready to pounce upon him and take all he has."

"TABLEAUX VIVANS"

However precarious his finances, Catlin refused to sacrifice appearances. Quite the reverse: With money fast disappearing, it became all the more crucial, George believed, to maintain an appearance of prosperity. London society always had a weather eye for reversals of fortune, however subtle the signs. Economies had to be invisible, or disguised as advantages,

With the flow of visitors thinning at Egyptian Hall, Burr had become another mouth to feed, and unlike the indispensable Daniel, his nephew had to be respectably lodged, dressed, and given pocket money. So when Asher Durand invited Burr to accompany him, the landscape painter John Kensett, and other artists to Paris and the Lowlands, both uncle and nephew jumped at the offer—for different reasons. If anyone asked, Burr was doing a short version of the Grand Tour, one during which he could also work on his painting in the company of masters.

Burr had made a singular contribution to the success of the exhibition, one not lost upon his uncle George. He had brought off a memorable impersonation of a young warrior chief. With his towering frame, head shaved and painted orange to match his roach, Burr seemed to have stepped from the pages of Cooper's Leatherstocking novels. "That big chief, egad, he is six feet and a half. I'll be bound that fellow has taken many a scalp," was George's spoof on the impression Burr made upon the local gentry. Taken together, the success of George, Burr, and their friends at playing Indian gave new life to the exhibition at Egyptian Hall, where Catlin, too, now always appeared in native costume.

One evening George and Clara attended the Polish Ball at Mansion House, a benefit for Poles in exile from czarist repression. Here it would be more accurate to describe the Catlins and their entourage of five or six men disguised as Sioux warriors as being among the principal sights, far outdoing the Polish patriots as exotic attractions. This time the burden of the event fell upon "My dear little *Christian* Clara," George recalled, "whose sphere it was not, and who never wore an Indian dress or painted her fair face before," but who now surmounted her fatigue and, "inspired with a wish to see the splendour of the scene, proposed to assume the dress of an Indian woman and follow me through the mazes of that night as an Indian squaw follows her lord on such occasions."

Outfitting his five or six "masqueraders" in native attire required "heavy contributions," Catlin tells us, from his own Indian wardrobe, George devoted special care to Clara's costume. He chose for her

> one of the prettiest and most beautifully ornamented women's dresses . . . made of the fine white skin of the mountain sheep; and with her hair spread over her back, and her face and her arms painted to the colour of a squaw, and her neck and ears loaded with the usual profusion of beads and other ornaments, and her fan of the eagle's tail in her hand, she sidled along with us amidst the glare and splendour and buzz and din of the happy throng.

Their group avoided any strenuous war dances, lest, as at Almack's, their paint should run, instead simulating Indian movement by keeping in single file. No one had foreseen the strain this attempt at authenticity would place upon Clara. Tiny and heavily pregnant, she had difficulty following "in the wake of all the party of men when we were in motion" More exhausting still, "the place assigned to Indian women on the march, rather than by the side or on the arms of their husbands," inevitably separated her from George and their friends, while "wending our tedious way through the bewildering mazes of this endless throng." The staring, thrusting crowd, the stress of being forced to stand through the entire evening—all this, George admitted, "was growing too much for her delicate frame to bear." Even the stoical and uncomplaining Clara confessed, "This, in the street or in the wilderness or anywhere else would have been tolerable," but in her present condition was "insupportable."

George reported and published Clara's reproaches, admitting them to be deserved: She had been the victim of his indifference. "The idea was so ridiculous to her, to be the last of a party of Indians (who always walk in single file) so far behind her husband, and then the crowd closing in upon her and the danger of crushing her to death." Her state of panic finally persuaded him to find a closed room upstairs, which mercifully turned out to be a private box, providing them with comfortable seats along with a good view of the festivities below, until "our curiosity was all gratified, and we were ready to return home."

BY LATE FALL 1840, when the gentry trickled back to town, Catlin decided to introduce "live" performing Indians at the exhibition. His new friend, George Palmer Putnam, was not merely privy to the innovation about to take place but had become a collaborator. As the publisher reported to his fiancée, there were now, accompanying the lecture at the gallery,

> about 20 American gentlemen [who] dressed themselves up in
> his Indian robes and painted their faces to show off the costumes

and the particular dresses which Mr. Catlin has collected. . . .
Each of the imitation Indians stood on the platform successively
while Mr. Catlin explained the dresses and then they had a war
dance with all the whoops and yelps and scalps etc.

Colonel Johnson, the gentleman from Missouri, whom Putnam had
brought to meet the Catlins, now played one of the mock Indians.[*]

Primed by George's indefatigable publicist, Charles Murray, audiences came back to enjoy the new "live" additions to the Indian
Gallery. White American "Indians" such as Colonel Johnson, were
probably well-off tourists, friends of friends, in transit to the Continent or on their way home. But their success persuaded George that
a pickup troupe inducted as players in an amateur theatrical needed
reliable paid replacements. Hardly had the word gone out than an
eager crowd of out-of-work Cockneys assembled to audition for parts
as Plains Indians. Soon the suspiciously familiar *ee-ow* diphthongs
and dropped "aitches" of Limehouse and Stepney, doing their best to
evoke the sounds of Sioux war cries, echoed through Egyptian Hall.
Whether or not new audiences at the exhibition saw through the disguise of their fellow Londoners, they recognized in these living illustrations of Catlin's talk and his paintings a popular art form then at
the height of fashion.

An arrangement of living figures costumed as allegorical or mythological characters, the "*tableaux vivans*"—as Catlin misspelled it—had
its roots in medieval mystery plays and crèches with congregants playing the Holy Family. By the end of the eighteenth century the living
statues enjoyed a secular transformation as stylized elements in operas

---

* Recent studies of "playing Indian"—from children's games to Wild West
shows and movie Westerns—point to a demonizing and destructive hostility at the
heart of these imitations, in which, it's also acknowledged, Indians themselves
often collaborated.

and ballets performed at court. From there it was a short distance to their role in private theatricals in the grand houses of the rich.

Since the seventeenth century Londoners had glimpsed from afar stately delegations of Indians, or "aborigines" from North and South America. So when Catlin drafted, first, American and English friends, followed by paid working-class Londoners, to dress up and play Indian, he was feeding a curiosity for closer encounters with the savage creatures of legend and foreign travel, now safely domesticated. Played by Catlin and Charles Murray, with their firsthand experiences of the American West, make-believe Indians acquired the stamp of authenticity.

Meanwhile George offered his audiences a new experience. He galvanized the static images of the tableau into dynamic motion; silent pictures became "talkies." Chants and war whoops animated the traditional posed and mute bodies. George now renamed his tableaux vivants "performances," deciding that, together with his lectures, they would only take place at night, thus elevating the Indians' appearance to a stylish evening outing. Whether this change of scheduling rekindled Londoners' interest in the exhibition or Murray undertook to attract those in his wide circle who had earlier escaped his promotional zeal, Clara was able to report to her in-laws in late October 1840 that, with the opening of the new "Season," ticket sales had started to revive.

Aristocratic visitors reappeared. Clara noted that their royal highnesses, the Duke of Coburg and Prince Ernest, the father and brother of Prince Albert, at that time on a visit to the Queen and the Prince, toured the exhibition, making it easy to sympathize with George's disappointment that the queen herself, but especially the prince consort, with his passion for discovery, including the ethnographical, had inscribed their names as subscribers for the book but had yet to visit the exhibition. Murray, however, arrived one day with HRH the ten-year-old duc de Brabant, son of the king of the Belgians. Then, early in

1841, George met HRH the duke of Sussex, who invited him to break-fast at Kensington Palace, followed by invitations to the "noble mansions," as George recalled, of the dukes of Devonshire and Sutherland.

That summer, in July or August, Clara gave birth to their third daughter. The first to be born on English soil, she was named Victoria Louise, for the young monarch, but called Luty. In October, Catlin's great work, his *Letters and Notes on the Manners, Customs and Conditions of the North American Indian* was finally published—at the author's expense. At the end of that same month, which ought to have been a period of relief and pleasure at seeing the work, with all its engravings, actually in print, his eldest daughter Libby "narrowly escaped with her life, from a violent fever," the distraught father wrote home to Great Bend. In an era before sulfur drugs or antibiotics, such narrow escapes for the very young or old verged on the miraculous.

AT THE END of 1841 the most famous English novelist and best-selling author on both sides of the Atlantic declared himself Catlin's ardent fan. Charles Dickens met the artist when he visited the Indian Gallery at Egyptian Hall. His first visit seems to have been followed by a second, when he also bought a copy of the recently published *Letters and Notes*. Creator of the most vivid characters in all of English fiction, the novelist paid tribute to Catlin's own presence in his writings about Plains Indians: "He is an honest, hearty, famous fellow; and I shake hands with him at every page," he wrote to a friend.

Dickens's enthusiastic response to Catlin—the man, the collection, and the book—was singular, as, with notable exceptions, his remarks about most of the Americans he encountered on his tours of the United States tended toward the derisive, while his response to the Indian expressed a racially motivated loathing so intense as to verge on hysteria: a "howling, whistling, clucking, stamping, jumping, tearing savage," in manner and in character "cruel, false, thievish, murderous."

For George, the year's end promised to redeem earlier failures and financial worries, with a happy portent of things to come. Queen Victoria and the royal technology fan, Prince Albert, invited Catlin to present to the monarchs at Windsor Castle his "elaborate" scale model of *The Falls of Niagara*.

Currently on view at the exhibition, the model, constructed of wood, boasted pulleys, gears, levers, winches—all assuring that the cataract gushed from its heights to splash in a pool below. It had been built some thirteen years earlier, from "an accurate survey of the grand scene," when Catlin had painted and obtained a patent for a series of views of the falls. These included a horizontal diorama-like perspective of the several cataracts, a minutely detailed "bird's-eye view" of the falls that seemed to anticipate aerial photography, and a conventional "framing" of Horseshoe Falls from the perspective of the artist, who appears to be working on a ledge beneath an arched stone cover. All these were painted with a finish unusual for Catlin. Like certain of his Western landscapes, the Niagara series, predominantly square in format, have a strange quality of being suspended in time. The rushing waters seem frozen, giving the sequence an unsettling aura of magic realism.

George claimed that the "accuracy and execution" of the wooden model, shown at one of the annual exhibitions of the American Institute in New York,* had led that body to award him "a handsome silver medal," in 1839, struck for the occasion. He avoided, however, declaring that he made the model himself. Once again behind-the-scenes efforts by Charles Murray seem to have won the day. And Murray wasn't the least bit bashful about claiming credit for the royal invitation. He declared that his own firsthand familiarity with the falls, together with his many visits to study the scale model on view at Egyp-

---

* A museum and library dedicated to science, it was established in 1828.

tian Hall, gave him special authority to argue the case for Catlin's presentation at Windsor, together with his marvelous replica of America's
most famous natural wonder. With only a day's notice from Murray,
Catlin, bearing his intricately constructed model, appeared in one of
the castle's drawing rooms. There he found himself upstaged by his
sponsor, as Murray explained and demonstrated the model's features
to the monarchs, while relating his own vivid recollections of navigating Horseshoe Falls. Instead the queen and her consort, George
recalled, plied him with questions about Indians, "for whose rights
they said they well knew I was the advocate."

IN APRIL 1842, George wrote to Putnam Catlin with the "afflicting
intelligence" of his father-in-law's death. Clara was "broken-hearted
and disconsolate in the extreme," her grief made worse by her absence
from her father's bedside. During his final weeks of excruciating pain,
he was constantly attended by her brothers and their uncle Matthew.
"The thought that she is to return to America and yet never again see
his face is heart-rending to her," George wrote.

Relaying the sad news to his parents in Great Bend, George's buried
feelings of guilt toward his own father emerged. Not with the greatest tact, perhaps, he repeated to Putnam recent word from his niece,
Burr's sister, Theodosia, that her great-uncle Putnam was failing,
assuring his father:

> No one, my *dear, dear* parent, can tell what is my anxiety for your
> health and the prolongation of your life for a few years at least—
> that I can battle through the struggle I have undertaken amidst
> strangers and critics, and amidst the enormous expenses attend-
> ing my exertions. I *will* work my way through in a little time, and
> I hope be along side of you.

But in fact George's letter, dated April 3, 1842, had been written three weeks after Putnam Catlin's death, on March 12, at age seventy-eight.

His father hadn't lived to read his son's happier news: The family had moved from central London, with its fog- and coal-clogged air, to the then-suburb of Walham Green (now Fulham Broadway). Three miles from the sprawling sooty metropolis, George had found "beautiful little 'Rose Cottage,'" surrounded by an acre of ground, "elegantly furnished," and for less money than they were paying in the city. Bridget, the Irish nursemaid brought from America, was replaced by a proper English nurse, and they added a cook and parlormaid to the help. At the same time that their calendar was crammed with invitations, Rose Cottage was close enough to town for the Catlins to continue to be at home to visiting Americans as well as English friends, such as Sir Thomas Phillipps.

Phillipps was among the notables to whom the Hon. Charles Murray had addressed a letter of introduction he gave to Catlin immediately upon his friend's arrival in London in 1839. Within a year the baronet and artist had become friends; when Clara arrived, bachelor dinners in town expanded to include family visits between Cavendish Street and Thirlestaine, Gloucestershire, where Phillipps lived with his long-suffering second wife and three daughters, his family increasingly crowded, neglected, and impoverished by an exploding collection of books.

The illegitimate son and heir of a textile manufacturer, Thomas Phillipps is still ranked as one of the greatest bibliophiles and collectors who ever lived. "I wish to have one copy of every book in the world," he declared, and in 1840, when he and Catlin, four years his junior, met, Phillipps was close to halfway into his "frenzied quest." His self-described "vello-mania" was aided by history: When he launched his hunt for early manuscripts, the French Revolution's seizure of the monasteries had thrown thousands of their illuminated treasures on the market, and Phillipps or his agents were there to snap them up for his library for shillings. He spent all his income—and more—on books; indebtedness became a way of life for a man who had to have what he coveted. Like many of his betters, especially among the aristocracy, Phillipps's answer to bills was never to pay those he could get away with ignoring. Thus he is said to have forced many booksellers and tradesmen into bankruptcy.

Phillipps also had his own press, Middle Hill, named after his estate, and largely dedicated to printing selected manuscripts from his own collection. It was this facility that drew Phillipps and Catlin into their long and fraught relationship.

In the fall of 1840, at just the time when Catlin committed to self-publishing the two-volume *Letters and Notes*, with its some four hundred engravings, Phillipps approached Catlin with an offer to print the work, starting cautiously with one volume at Middle Hill. In a series of brisk notes to George, he provided detailed cost estimates for paper, labor, binding, print runs, all demonstrably lower than what Catlin would have to pay a commercial printer-engraver in London. Phillipps turned huffy when Catlin failed to respond promptly, assuming—correctly, as it turned out—that George was about to decline his proposition. He gave as the reason for refusing Phillipps's offer his reluctance to burden their friendship with obligations he could not immediately repay. It's more likely, however, that Catlin was contractually bound to an earlier commercial agreement. Whatever the case, the explanation seemed to satisfy his touchy patron, and their relations continued, with Phillipps assuming an ever more fatherly role.

The problem of the printer's bills remained. Now, however, Catlin would be indebted to strangers as opposed to a friend. When George confessed to Sir Thomas that he lacked the first installment of one thousand pounds owed toward the cost of the book (obviously hoping that his patron would offer to help) Phillipps referred George to a moneylender in nearby Coventry Street; yet a short time later Phillipps warned George to stay far away from these infamous "harpies," as Clara had called them. By then it was probably too late. Catlin may not have called upon Phillipps's moneylending friend in Coventry Street, but he would soon fall into the clutches of his associates. He also ignored what these conflicting signals told him about Sir Thomas: that he was a spider of a man who patiently studied his victims' weaknesses to learn how these could work to his advantage.

ANOTHER CALLER FROM America needed no introduction. After three decades as administrator of Indian affairs in the Michigan Territory, Henry Rowe Schoolcraft now found himself out of a job, victim of a new administration in Washington. Their long acquaintance, based on a shared interest in the Indian, led him to look up Catlin shortly after he arrived in England at the end of May 1842. The two had met six years earlier, in either Mackinac or Detroit, where Schoolcraft then held the post of subagent for Indian affairs and where George, on his way east from the Pipestone Quarry, had been delayed by his injured shoulder. There Catlin discovered that he and Schoolcraft—who along with his administrative duties had dug deeply into local Indian language, culture, and history—had much to discuss.

A protégé and collaborator of Lewis Cass, Schoolcraft, a self-taught polymath specializing in geology, had rapidly acquired a vast store of knowledge of Native American life—in part owing to the resources of his half-Chippewa wife, Jane Johnson. As an administrator under Cass in the Michigan Territory through the 1830s, Schoolcraft had carried out the goal of his patron, who in turn was President Jackson's most zealous enforcer of the laws ordering Indian removal west of the Mississippi. Relations with his mentor cooled as Cass, now secretary of war, eyed a presidential bid; Schoolcraft's marriage had begun to unravel, and he found himself alone and jobless in Washington.

By 1839, the year Catlin left America, he and Schoolcraft had often been paired as "Indian experts" by their contemporaries: "Catlin may be called the red man's painter," the *Detroit Free Press* explained, "Schoolcraft his poetical historian. . . . They have done much which, without them, would, perhaps, have remained undone, and become extinct with the Indian race."

Initially both saw their work as complementary. Schoolcraft gladly provided one of the "certificates" that Catlin, increasingly sensitive to questions about the "accuracy" of both his painted and written accounts of the upper Missouri tribes, solicited from those whose names evoked distinguished scholarship or firsthand knowledge of Indian country. What may once have been true was true no longer, however. Soon their perspective on the Native American and his fate had diverged: Schoolcraft, the rationalist, the practical—and political—exponent of "progress" (which might require Indian removal), and Catlin, the artist and elegist for a vanishing race, doomed and precious, stood as polar opposites.

When Schoolcraft was fired—a Democratic casualty of the incoming Whig administration—and passed over for other patronage posts as well, he brooded bitterly about George Catlin and his seemingly unstoppable rise: He nursed a festering malice toward George's undeserved "showman's fame," seeing his success as stolen from his own hard-earned expertise. The Indian Gallery, with the artist lecturing, had been shown in every major American city, while Catlin's *Letters* from the upper Missouri, based upon two visits of several months each—had been published, excerpted, or quoted in every leading newspaper—or so it seemed. To be sure, there was *some* justice: Catlin hadn't succeeded in selling his collection to the government, but even this defeat was bemoaned by the press as a tragic loss for America. At the same time word of the impostor's triumph as the toast of London had trickled home and—most insufferable to Schoolcraft, the self-taught scholar—flattering reports were published detailing the warm reception Catlin's lectures received from Britain's foremost scientific institutions.

Out of a job and money, Schoolcraft arrived in London with an idea aimed at the English market: an encyclopedia on the subject of the American Indian, to be published in a series of eight parts, eventually to appear in two volumes. His hope was that if the serialized *Cyclopedia* caught on, a publishing contract, accompanied by real income, would follow.

The unstated goal of the *Cyclopedia*, however, was to serve as the anti-Catlin. A week after his arrival in London, Schoolcraft was invited to a reception given by Louis McLane, the U.S. minister plenipotentiary to the United Kingdom. There he encountered Duff Green, the prominent former publisher of the *United States Telegraph*, a quasi-official organ of the Jackson administration. Seizing his chance, Schoolcraft sent Green the prospectus for his *Cyclopedia*, which, he assured his compatriot, would "most effectually put at rest . . . many erroneous impressions which are entertained, both here, and on the continent." But Schoolcraft's gloves came off in his postscript: Dismissing his rival as a mere "tourist" in Indian country, he confided, "It is surely time, that something of a more substantive character than the vapid [illeg.] of our good countryman Catlin, should be brought forward. . . . By knowing nothing of *our Indian system* he has put our govt. in a shameful position."

Schoolcraft's trip to England proved a fiasco. Ponderous and pedantic, homely and awkward, he made no friends among his hosts, and found no subscribers or publishers for his *Cyclopedia*. While abroad, he received word that his wife had died of an overdose of laudanum. When Schoolcraft called at Egyptian Hall, he was told that Mr. Catlin had just taken his collection to Liverpool, at the invitation of the city fathers. Before leaving, George had instructed Clara to welcome the visitor in his absence.

Seated at tea with Clara in the garden, Schoolcraft could hardly avoid contrasting the idyllic scene at Rose Cottage—the charming hostess and mother of three blooming little girls, the discreet servants

and ample food—with his own fractured family and straitened circumstances. Meanwhile, the devoted Mrs. Catlin's apologies for her
absent husband only rubbed salt in the wounds of his own failure;
Clara could not help alluding to George's leap from triumph in London
to a lengthy engagement in Liverpool, the first of many throughout
England, Scotland, and Ireland.

Still, Schoolcraft continued sending friendly notes to his rival. From
Liverpool, two days before leaving England for home, Schoolcraft
wrote to ask whether there was any service he could render George
back in America. Catlin thanked him for the offer and expressed his
"deep regret . . . that I could not have seen more of you whilst in this
country," adding condolences from both Catlins on his recent bereavement. Then, in a lofty tone, Catlin wrote: "I am sorry to learn that
no encouragement has been offered you by Murray or others in London." He ended with a vague invitation to Schoolcraft to visit him in
Sheffield during one of his next engagements, where he could witness
George's further conquest of Britain and "where they have just completed the building of a very fine Room (12 feet in length) for my whole
Collection to be arranged on the walls."

Without seeing Schoolcraft before he sailed, Catlin was unable to
read the warning signs of an envious and angry man, and he had yet to
learn that a once-helpful colleague had become an implacable enemy.

"INDIANS! REAL INDIANS!"

L uckily for George, the expiration of the Egyptian Hall lease coincided with invitations to tour the provinces. He would never recoup his investment in self-publishing the *Letters and Notes*, but the attention the work received throughout Britain was perfectly timed to create popular interest in meeting the adventurous traveler, writer, and artist, along with his "tribe" of wild Indians.

Ticket sales had dwindled again. Catlin could never have afforded to renew the two-year lease on Egyptian Hall, the most expensive space in London. This time the drop in revenues could not be laid to the seasonal ebb and flow of the better classes in and out of town. This population of Londoners, along with others of the curious self-improving middle classes, had already seen Mr. Catlin's "Indians."

For his tour of Britain, Catlin the showman banished Catlin the artist: He packed and stored his paintings—more than six hundred canvases—the portraits, villages, games, hunts, and landscapes that had given context to the exhibition and to his own talks. In their place he re-called his Cockney "Indians"—the "old disciplined troop from the City of London": When it came to touring, however, it seems that only a few of the twenty or so original East Enders answered the call, so he had to hire and quickly train replacements. Happily, provincial audiences, like Londoners before them, failed to notice that under the quilled and beaded robes, beneath the bear claws and eagle feathers, were no "copper kings of the forest" but white, undernourished working-class men and boys.

What Catlin also carried on tour, beside his essential "Indians" and their costumes, were those objects of tribal life—especially weapons: clubs, spears, tomahawks, and scalping knives—that would lend thrills and chills to his narrative. He had a keen sense of drama, of the immediacy of things made—and used: weapons carved, polished, sharpened, then thrust into flesh, still bearing the evidence of rusted bloodstains. The other crucial prop was the Crow tent.

Twenty-five feet high, the soaring white cone made of decorated buffalo skins stood at the center of the largest room wherever Catlin showed the collection. Throughout Britain, and later on the Continent, the tent welcomed the uninitiated in the way of the familiar cathedrals nearby, a mediating structure that briefly enclosed strangers in an alien yet communal place.

Gone for the time being was the static, two-dimensional space of the picture plane. George aimed for a new mass audience: impatient, restless, hungry for novelty. Even sophisticated London periodicals had damned the original Indian Gallery with the faint praise of "informative." Now his talks, in concert with unreal Indians and real objects, would still inform but they would also excite, amaze, enchant, and even frighten his new fans.

Back in their "savage" disguise, his Indians spent the entire day in the exhibition, while twice daily, George gave a short lecture in the room, explaining the costumes and salient traits of native character; he "finished with an Indian song and gave the frightful war-whoop."

In Liverpool, George's happiest memory was the free admission of all pupils from the city's schools—both fee-paying and charity—as "in battalions and phalanxes they were passed through my room." He loved children, and he never outgrew the pleasures of childhood games and stories. Whatever he may have forgotten, his own three little girls would remind him of what kinds of tales held their attention, and he had no trouble now inventing a version of his lectures "shaped to suit their infant minds." He hadn't counted upon the limited experience of urban children who, when confronted by the "deafening war whoop" raised by Catlin's hirelings in Indian paint and brandishing terrible weapons, dived terror stricken under tables and benches, "from which they were pulled out by their feet." Over the several months of his stay, George estimated that twenty-two thousand of Liverpool's pupils (schooling then being only for boys) were given a day off from classes to attend the exhibition. With his own soul, still of a truant school-boy, Catlin boasted that "having heard me lecture, these little urchins went home, sounding the war-whoop in various parts of the town."

FOR THE NEXT two years, 1842–44, George Catlin was on the road—without his paintings. From Liverpool, he was booked for varying periods of time "in all the provincial towns of the kingdom." The march of his relentless itinerary almost demands to be illustrated by a Hollywood montage of calendar pages flying by: packing, unpacking, settling in, ironing out kinks in the exhibition rooms, hanging, lecturing, meeting and greeting the locals, then staggering to his rooms in the early morning hours to scrawl a few lines to Clara before falling into a dead sleep, fully dressed, on his bed. Then the whole weary process began again until, days later, after a few hours of rest on a night train, he arrived at dawn for the next engagement.

Looking back, he could still feel in his bones the grind of his touring days:

> My career was then rapid, and its changes sudden, and all my
> industry and energies were called into action—with twenty men

on my hands, and an average expense of twelve pounds per day
... and in the space of six months visited, with varied success ...
*Chester, Manchester, Leamington, Rugby, Stratford-on-Avon, Chel-
tenham, Sheffield, Leeds, York, Hull, Edinburgh, Glasgow, Paisley,
Greenock, Belfast and Dublin.*

Opening on April 6, 1843, Catlin's exhibition in Edinburgh proved
the turning point at which George the performer definitively buried
"Mr. Catlin the artist." He made his appearance costumed as a Crow
chief. He had dressed as a medicine man of this same tribe, covered
only in furs, when lecturing in Philadelphia's Arcade in 1838, but with
his paintings still on view nearby. Now these had been left in storage
in London: The act was the art. Traveling light and accompanied only
by "his men" and such articles as would set the stage, Catlin appeared,
according to a Scottish newspaper account, wearing "'a huge hat
encircled with a row of large war eagle feathers' fringed with scalps,
and a bear's claw necklace, and holding a shield, a bow and a quiver
of arrows." It was the moment when the lively arts replaced framed
representations of dead Red Indians, with the artist himself playing a
starring role in the transition.

On the road the letters home that Clara would have written to her
father she now addressed to her uncle Matthew Gregory, who lived
blocks from her late parents in Albany. Along with newsy reports of
her sightseeing, she reveals a deepening attachment to her religious
faith and concern for her soul's salvation. "Little *Christian* Clara"—
George's italics in seeing his wife garbed in Indian robes—points to
the universe that divided his perfunctory observance from his wife's
sustaining belief. She had always been a professing Christian and a
faithful congregant of the Episcopal Church in which she had been
baptized, confirmed, and wed, and with whose rites her infant child
had been commended to God's mercy.

Now, living abroad, separated by distance and death from many she had loved, her religious devotion and self-examination assumed an evangelical fervor; she prayed passionately for a reunion with those she had lost. To her uncle, who seems to have shared her living faith, she enumerates the friends and relatives who had been her contemporaries—all dead of tuberculosis, the "White Plague" that cruelly seemed to target the young and healthy—and she wonders why she has been spared.

With George away, Clara had too much time to ponder these dark unanswerable questions—alone. Once her household and maternal duties were dispatched, she had no friends with whom to share gossip, attend church, admire one another's children. There were few distractions from homesickness and thoughts of the dead. "Since my dear father's death—I have felt a deeper interest in the world to which he has gone," she wrote.

Then, almost miraculously, four years of exile, separation, and wandering promised to be interrupted—if not ended—with a visit home to America. George decided that, following a longer stay in Manchester, where Clara and the girls would join him, he could spare the time and money for a trip home. If all went well, their travel plans should be timed perfectly for the birth of a new baby, their fourth, due in November; several months in Manchester would allow time for Clara's lying-in, recovery, and the readiness of mother and child for the long ocean voyage.

But two weeks before the family was to leave for Liverpool where they would board ship for New York, and one week after George had advertised the exhibition in Manchester as "positively the last in the kingdom previous to embarking" for America, he received a letter. Introducing himself as "a stranger to you," Arthur Rankin made sure that Catlin would read on, promising that what he had to say "will show you a way of promoting your own interest." He went on to report that a party of nine Ojibwa Indians that "I am bringing over on speculation [was about] to be landed at Liverpool." Rankin did not explain why; having preceded the troupe in London by several weeks, he had failed to make any arrangements for them—either for working or living—in the capital.

Now he proposed that he and Catlin come to some agreement "that may promote our mutual interests." A suavely assured pitchman, he shrewdly left it to George, however, to come up with the actual terms of their partnership: "If you think of anything you could do in that way, or any advice you can give me, I shall be most happy to hear from you by return of post," And he concluded with a tribute as flattering as it was untrue: "Several persons in London conducting exhibitions have told me that they will do nothing unless they are under your management."

At twenty-seven, Arthur Rankin, a Canadian of Irish parentage and a military hero, found himself freshly demobilized (or possibly AWOL) from the Ontario militia and wondering what he could do to earn a living while still enjoying a life of adventure. According to a hazily heroicizing memoir written by Rankin's uncle, the youth had lived with a band of Ojibwa close to his home in Windsor, Ontario. It was from this group, according to his relative, that young Arthur was supposed to have handpicked the eight men and women, sending them, along with their half-breed interpreter, Alexander Cadotte, or "Strong Wind," to England. The purpose of the trip, the memoir claimed, was to obtain an annuity for the tribe from Her Majesty's Government for their loyalty to the Crown during the recent colonial uprisings in Canada. Rankin's uncle never does explain how his nephew shifted from the lofty role of advocate to that of promoter and showman, hawking the talents of a newly discovered troupe of "wild" Indians.

Catlin's reply was a classic "no-no-but-maybe": He first informed Rankin that his proposal would run "directly opposite to my present arrangements . . . as all my preparations are now made to embark for New York in . . . a fortnight from this time." Then he moved to higher moral ground: "I have always been opposed to the plan of bringing

Indians abroad on speculation."* In this case, however, he rationalized that "as they are in the country," his conscience was clear and he
could proceed both to speculate and advocate: "I shall, as the friend of
the Indians under all circumstances, feel an anxiety to promote their
views and success in any way I can," he concluded. The deal was as
good as done.

Three days after his letter was mailed, Rankin appeared in Manchester, sounding still more persuasive in person than on paper.
Although later George would insist that their brief meeting in the
exhibition rooms ended without any agreement on his part, he admitted to advising the young entrepreneur to rush to Liverpool in order to
"receive" the Indians as they landed, "with the understanding that he
would bring them to Manchester as soon as they arrived."

Always fond of the Cockney and especially of his speech, George
related with relish how, the next evening, the guard at the exhibition
rooms rushed inside to announce a "homnibus at the door quite full
of [']orrible looking folks, and ee really believed they were hindians!"
A quick look convinced Daniel. As hardheaded a promoter as Rankin
himself, he whispered to his boss, "The Ojibbeways are here, and they
are a pretty black-looking set of fellows: I think they will do."

The indispensable Daniel was now dispatched to help Rankin find
suitable lodgings for his troupe, but their efforts at discretion, in trying to keep the Indians under wraps until their opening performance,
proved futile. Possibly they had not tried that hard. After they were
turned down by one innkeeper as savages whose presence threatened
to disturb the peace, word spread. Once more Rankin, with Daniel's

---

* In a letter published in the Washington *Globe* on November 21, 1839, the secretary of war, Joel R. Poinsett, reminded his readers that under U.S. law, taking
Indians abroad for speculation constituted a crime. Thus Catlin's "feelings" about
the practice were irrelevant; as a Canadian, exploiting a tribe of Canadian Ojibwa,
Rankin did not fall under these legal restrictions.

help, herded the weary travelers back into the omnibus. This time, however, "A crowd followed the bus as it passed off, and the cry of—'Indians! real Indians!' was started in Manchester, which soon rung through the kingdom."

Defining himself as sharply and unsparingly as he would ever do, Catlin later wrote of this moment as a crossroad in his life: "[the reader would find] me turning here upon a pivot—my character changed and my occupation." Without explaining the sudden turnabout that he has undergone, or the new path he is about to pursue, he hoped, nonetheless, to share his "fresh excitement" at the transformation. We can have no doubt that Rankin, George's new business partner, was the agent of this change, coming into Catlin's life at just that moment when other possibilities, once appearing as limitless as the prairie, had evaporated. At forty-seven he was no closer to the success he had promised his father—and had once believed in himself. Exhausted by touring, suspended in a kind of limbo, George Catlin, once endlessly energetic and resourceful, was running out of both energy and resources.

Arthur Rankin appeared as the galvanizing force Catlin had been waiting for. George had never met anyone so quick to seize and to exploit opportunity. Impressed by the crowds that mobbed the Indians when they first arrived at the hotel in their omnibus, Rankin made sure that, following their reception by the mayor and "mayoress" at the town hall, another omnibus was waiting to parade the Ojibwa—without stopping—through town.

"This excursion," Catlin was quick to note, "was calculated, of course, to bring around their hotel its thousands and even tens of thousands of the excitable and excited idlers that an extraordinary 'turn out' [lock-out] had at the time thrown into the streets." Even the closed factories and mass unemployment worked in favor of Rankin's preopening publicity for his act. In order to approach their hotel, Catlin himself had to follow "in the wake of a number of police, who had

the greatest difficulty in making their way through the mass." As for
the crowds who had preceded the local constabulary to the hotel, they
remained throughout the night in a mass vigil, awaiting the reemer-
gence of their famous guests on the following day. (Not until the
Beatles returned in triumph to their native Liverpool, would England
see such an idolatrous reception for entertainers—for that is how the
Ojibwa, as managed by Catlin and Rankin, were now billed.)

While the Indians rested for a few days before their opening performance, George and his new business partner discussed the terms
of their agreement: The wily Rankin had no interest in managerial
responsibilities; he wanted to unload his valuable property at a favorable price, proposing, as Catlin recalled, "that I should take them off
his hands by paying him 100*l* per month." But Catlin wasn't buying:
He was first of all unwilling, he told Rankin, to take full responsibility for both the Ojibwa's living and working arrangements while
abroad. He had always been opposed to Indians being brought over to
be exhibited, he claimed, and he was even less inclined now to assume
any official obligations for their stay, or to release Rankin from his.
Instead George proposed to offer his Indian exhibition, with all the
prestige he had garnered for scholarship and authenticity (and with
none of the tawdry associations of ethnic "shows") as a venue for the
Ojibwa "dances." He offered to be present when they were performing,
when he would give his talks on the tribe and its way of life. He saw
the financial arrangement as "sharing equally with you all expenses
and all receipts from this day to the time they shall leave the kingdom,
expecting you to give your whole attention to the traveling and care of
the Indians while they are not in the exhibition-rooms."

As outlined by Catlin, the division of labor, expenses, and profit
sounds simple, fair, and professional: "To this proposition [Rankin] at
once agreed." George was a gentleman; he had no worries that their
agreement was "never more than a verbal one."

In Manchester, Catlin deployed all the skill with the press and with local opinion makers that had captured their London counterparts. In the few days between the arrival of the Indians and their debut performance in the Exchange Rooms, he invited the editors of *The Guardian* and the mayor to "examine" the visitors and "being much pleased with their appearance, excited the public curiosity to see them, to an impatient degree." Soon the hordes in nearby streets trying to "besiege" the hotel required a "strong party of police . . . to keep back the crowds."

As soon as the press and local eminences had left, Catlin spread buffalo robes on the floor and, lighting an Indian pipe, welcomed the troupe, introducing himself as their new manager. Democratically he sought and received their consent to performing in his rooms. He was frank in addressing their weakness for "spirituous liquor" and he exacted from each the pledge "that you will keep yourselves all the time sober."

Unaffected by the city's economic woes, the more prosperous Mancunians assured that the Ojibwa's visit would prove a wild success. Since their hotel allowed too much public access, Catlin found them new lodgings above the exhibition. On opening day hundreds waiting outside the Exchange Building were turned away. Anticipating the crowds that gathered far earlier in the evening than the announced hour, Catlin had removed the seats and erected a raised platform in the middle of the largest room. Men and women were packed as tightly on the floor as decency allowed.

"Into the midst of this mass the party dashed in Indian File . . . with war-clubs and tomahawks in hand they sounded the frightful war-whoop." With screams and yells of their own, the frightened crowd gave way and "they soon had a free passage to the platform upon which they leaped, without looking for the flight of steps prepared for them."

There were several moments of silence. The medicine man began drumming. Then he raised his voice in the war song as accompaniment to the rest of the troupe, who began to dance.

———

ON NOVEMBER 6, 1843, Clara gave birth in Manchester to their first son, George Junior. Instead of returning to America, where she had hoped to proudly introduce the two girls and boy, born abroad, to their families, she began packing for the move back to another London suburb, the village of Turnham Green, near Chiswick. Although George surely presented the voyage home as deferred rather than cancelled, the change of plans, days before the baby's birth, came as an unexpected blow to Clara. Not so George, excited about his "new occupation" of promoter. He sounds the gleeful naughty boy, proud of giving the slip to friends and family at home who daily expected news of the prodigal's return and were mystified to hear nothing.

His anxieties allayed by the partnership with Rankin, Catlin renewed the lease on Egyptian Hall for six months. For the last performances in Manchester, George continued to give his talks on Indian life, as the Ojibwa performed war and medicine dances, or mimed games and buffalo hunts. Although he still appeared in Indian costume, Catlin had moved from center stage to the place of narrator, providing continuity. From now on, his real role would be enacted behind the scenes. He was the showman, not the show.

IN LONDON, IN advance of their engagement at the Egyptian Hall, Charles Murray had secured an invitation to the Ojibwa to perform before the queen at Windsor Castle. Arriving in their rented omnibus, this one drawn by four horses, they were shown into the Waterloo Gallery, where the young queen, the queen dowager, Prince Albert, the Duchess of Kent, and Charles Murray awaited them. Catlin then introduced by name and explained the costume and weapons of each native member of the party. The queen was enchanted by the little girl, whose hands she held for a long while. Then, as the medicine man began beating his drum and singing in a low voice, the "house jarred with the leap of the War-chief . . . and after him all the party in the din of the war-dance."

Afterward the Canadian Ojibwa, as subjects of the Crown, expressed, in two short speeches—given, respectively, by the old chief, seventy-five, frail, and nearly blind, and the war chief—the tribe's joy that they had finally seen the face of their "Great Mother." The Indians then rose and performed their favorite, the high-spirited pipe dance. Back in the waiting room, a long table, which they had earlier supposed had been spread with delicacies for the royal refreshment, was now revealed to be for the guests. The plates were handed around by Murray himself, acting as surrogate host for the monarchs, who, following gracious thanks from Prince Albert, had retired.

Unhappily, as it later turned out, Murray insisted that all present must follow his example and toast the queen's health in champagne. The Ojibwa resisted, recalling to their host and managers their pledge to refuse all "spirituous liquors" while in the kingdom. But Murray, despite his familiarity with the ravages of alcohol among the tribes he visited, refused to take no for an answer. Even Catlin's quiet explanation to Murray of the gravity of the Indians' promise left him unmoved: He set a foaming glass of champagne, dubbed "*Chick-a-bob-boo*," by the guests, at the place of each of the Ojibwa, declaring that, far from being "spirituous liquor," champagne was merely "a light wine and could not hurt them." Most important, "Her Majesty's health could not be refused by Her Majesty's subjects." Still the Indians refused, but this time all eyes were "alternately upon Catlin and their filled glasses." Now, to their great surprise, the one who had exacted this pledge from them only weeks before changed his mind:

"Yes, my good fellows, drink; it will not hurt you," Catlin himself recalled telling the performers. "The promise you have made to Mr. Rankin and myself will not be broken—it did not contemplate a case like this." Then he noted, "With great delight they all joined in 'Health to the Queen' . . . as each glass was emptied to the bottom, they smacked their lips, again pronouncing the word '*Chick-a-bob-boo! Chick-a-bob-boo!*' with a roar of laughter among themselves."

The fizz of expectation and free publicity from their royal appearance sealed the Ojibwa's triumph at the Egyptian Hall. On opening night they were greeted by "roars of applause." Following the "frightful" war dance, the evening ended with the performers descending into the audience where they were showered with gifts of jewelry and silver coins. As one of the tribe's happiest recent memories, George heard them "utter the exciting word *Chick-a-bob-boo* several times." He and Rankin now decided this to be a "suitable occasion" to explain that, as their managers, they had no objection to their taking a few glasses of ale (champagne not falling within their budget) each day—one at the midday meal, and another after the evening performance. "It had never entered our heads" Catlin tells his readers, that in "binding them in the promise they had made, and so far kept," that they were to be deprived of the occasional glass of wine or ale. Under the new dispensation, their earlier pledge of abstinence shifted to one of moderation as practiced by "English fashionable people." Catlin further urged them to drink for its medicinal qualities: Not only would they enjoy the ale, but he promised that "a glass of it at dinner, and also after their night's fatigues, would give them strength and be of service to them." Indeed he had sent out for a jug of "this very fine drink" which was just now arriving at the door. Glasses were quickly emptied by each of the Ojibwa; the ale's fine taste and good effect were pronounced the equal of the queen's champagne, as shouts of "*Chickabobboo! Chickabobboo! ne-she-sheen! ne-she-sheen* (good, good) resounded through the whole house."

He and Rankin now agreed that, as of the next morning, the troupe should receive a "similar quantity" of ale every day, replacing the coffee for which, since their arrival in England, they had acquired a great fondness.

If George perceived any risks in habituating his charges to daily rations of strong English ale, he decided that the danger was small and the advantages great. Drink, together with trinkets and silver, turned "sorrowful" and homesick men and women into cheerful and tractable children.

25

GEORGE CATLIN'S WILD WEST SHOW

Showered with trinkets and money, well supplied with roast beef, and "indulged in their *chickabobboo*," the Ojibwa's run continues "to have been a very pleasant and satisfactory one," George reported. Egyptian Hall was crowded every night.

Audiences, however, were changing. For the first time some of those in attendance, according to Catlin himself, raised questions about the morality of Indians performing for profit. Earlier tribal visitors, including Ojibwa (and Tapuya from South America), had appeared in London, but they had been greeted as political delegations, presented as ethnological exhibits, or as individual curiosities, such as the "Hottentot Venus." None had been promoted as entertainers.

Catlin was ready with his defense and principal argument: He hadn't brought the Ojibwa to England. Once arrived (ostensibly, to see the queen and receive compensation for their loyal service to the Crown), they had, he claimed, begged to "make . . . a little money to carry home to their children."

There were other changes, too, in the reception of the troupe in Egyptian Hall. A different class now came to see and hear the Indian "show": No longer exhibition- or museumgoers, they were the same

Londoners who loved popular theatricals—not least for their tradition of audience participation, at once communal, expressive, even "interactive." The new "live" Indian Gallery also attracted one of the first-ever-recorded "groupies." "The Jolly Fat Dame"—Catlin never dignifies her with a name—came to every performance. A plump cream puff of a woman, she arrived early and stayed late, seeking any possible encounter with the object of her love: tall, handsome, eighteen-year-old Alexander Cadotte, the half-French translator, occasional dancer, and dandy of the troupe.

Since he rarely performed Cadotte had ample time for dalliance. If he didn't reciprocate her affections, he was vain enough to enjoy the attentions of his besotted fan. One evening, in full view of the audience, she detached one of a pair of bracelets that had circled both dimpled arms, attaching it tenderly to Cadotte's wrist; while he wore it, she announced, he would always be identified as belonging to her.

The irreplaceable Daniel, now promoted to stage manager, was quick to exploit the publicity value of the lady's passion; he placed the large lovelorn figure, "fully equipped and prepared for any emergency," leaning on the stage where she could be seen in all her ample glory, squeezed "in her *stays*, and her *poplin* and *lace* and loaded with trinkets." Overheated from her exertions and from the copious amounts of *chick-a-bob-boo* she consumed, she constantly waved a large fan. From her position at the edge of the stage, between audience and performers, she was also able to whisper to Cadotte, "whose beautifully embroidered moccasins were near to her nose when he leant forward to listen to her, with the eagle plumes and ostrich feathers of his cap falling gracefully down over his shoulders."

At this point there could be no doubt that the real show was taking place in the audience. As the "Jolly Fat Dame" covered Cadotte with kisses together with expensive adornments, her public displays of affection proved contagious. Other women in the audience followed suit: Each one held high a shiny piece of jewelry—Catlin recalled "a

beautiful bracelet . . . for the first one who should get to it." Lest anyone doubt the sexual play that guided this erotic game of "catch," hysteria now rippled from the stage through the audience: "Three or four
of the young fellows with their naked shoulders and arms, leaped with
the rapidity almost of lightening into the screaming mass."

With all the action taking place below the platform, the young and
handsome native performers yielded to temptation, remaining down
with the crowd, and it became next to impossible to get them back
onstage to resume the scheduled program of the evening: "Many
ladies were offering them their hands and trinkets: some were kissing
them, and every kiss called forth the war-whoop," George recalled,
and he admitted that, of the girls and women present, "many there
were in the room that evening who went home to their husbands and
mothers with streaks of red and black paint upon their cheeks."

In the course of that one evening in Egyptian Hall, with Cadotte
and his buxom admirer nuzzling at the edge of the stage, the Ojibwa
dancers making their erotic progress through the crowd, the women
exchanging trinkets for caresses—all boundaries dissolved between
audience and performers, between men and women, and most singular of all, between races.

WORD SPREAD ABOUT the steamy play that characterized Catlin's
"live" Indian Gallery, where half-naked Ojibwa mingled intimately
with the largely female audience at Egyptian Hall, once home to the
most sedate exhibitions in London. As the partner in charge of the
troupe when they were performing, George was pledged to protect
and uphold their sobriety and decorum. Whatever his role in the
gamey free-for-all, given his exuberant recollections some years later,
he had no regrets.

Then farce exploded into high drama: Notwithstanding his flirta-
tion with the Jolly Fat Dame, the seductive Cadotte announced that

he was madly in love with another, whom he planned to marry. It fell to Daniel to deliver the news. Sarah Haynes, the bride-to-be, was eighteen years old, daughter of a "respectable carver and gilder" and a neighbor of the troupe in George Street. A gossip sheet reported that the "beautiful Miss Haynes with her 'cherry and pulpy lips, rosy cheeks and languishing black eyes' stole Cadotte's heart."

Catlin insisted that he had no inkling of this romance—known to everyone else in the troupe. The lovesick youth had asked for—and received Rankin's consent for the couple to marry; he probably knew better than to ask for Catlin's blessing. Together with the young woman's father, George was unhappy about the match. He foresaw problems with a mixed-race union: Cadotte would never be accepted in England—by any class of society. By the same token his bride would be miserable in the Canadian wilderness, leading "a life of semi-barbarism, which . . . must result in her distress and misery at last."

Disagreement about the marriage exposed the growing rift between the partners. Rankin, as Catlin realized, had promoted the match from the beginning; in his eyes the "excitement" (George's word)—even scandal—that the union would create in London was good for business, and, as Catlin claimed to learn only later, Rankin had done everything possible to encourage the affair.

The wedding took place at Saint Martin's-in-the-Fields, the parish church of the Haynes family, on April 9, 1844. The bride wore white, with a traditional veil held in place by a wreath of orange blossoms. Her three sisters served as bridesmaids with the entire troupe of eight Ojibwa as groomsmen. Cadotte might have worn formal European dress, but he chose tribal attire instead: "a robe of blue cloth, handsomely trimmed with shells and Indian needlework, a rich headdress" and on his feet, moccasins. According to Catlin, Rankin was responsible for the advertisements that noted time and place, thereby assuring that the marriage would be a public spectacle. Indeed hordes of the curious converged upon Trafalgar Square. There Rankin had also arranged for carriages, festooned with flowers and ribbons and featuring musicians on the roofs, to parade the wedding party noisily through London's main thoroughfares.

As Rankin hoped and Catlin feared, the wedding created not only excitement but scandal: There was much clucking about good English stock being tainted by Indian and French blood. The publicity trumpeting the nuptials only added to the disgrace. *Punch*, the satiric organ of the ruling class—snobbish, racist, xenophobic, misogynist—found the marriage a made-to-order target of mockery, devoting several articles to the affair. The tribal guests, one writer observed, displayed their "fine sense of the struggles of matrimonial life by appearing in their war paint." Only "faulty female judgment" could claim that "a savage, to be considered 'quite a love' by a civilized maiden, must first be exhibited in front of the lamps [footlights]." Beyond their weakness for so-called inferior races, especially when those were also lowly performers, Englishwomen remained ignorant of the hard labor awaiting them in their new estate. The "unseemly emphasis" however, with which this bride "agreed to take her wedded husband," another article noted (with a snicker of sexual innuendo), "showed [that] she duly weighed the responsibilities of hewing and delving and shouldering the wigwam poles." And *Punch* concluded its last piece, "It is only due to MR. RANKIN the showman to observe that he managed the wedding with a fine eye to all advertising purposes."

Punch may have spared Catlin because the writer knew what the general public did not: namely, that on the morning before the wedding, Rankin had come to see George with the demand that their partnership be dissolved—immediately. He then proceeded to dictate the terms of its dissolution: After ten more days at Egyptian Hall—which George should advertise as the Ojibwa's last London performances—he, Rankin, would take the troupe on a final tour of Britain. Then, with the smooth-talking gall that always seemed to leave Catlin defenseless, Rankin announced that he had mastered George's commentary well

Albert Eckhout (ca. 1610–65), *Tapuya Men of Northeastern Brazil in War Dance*, 1641. A Dutch artist, Albert Eckhout accompanied his country's expedition to northeastern Brazil from 1637 to 1644 and documented the region's plants, animals, and indigenous peoples. His large-scale panoramic works, like this one, were widely reproduced, and Catlin could well have seen, recalled, and used a scene such as the Tapuya dancing as a source for his own work.

Tapuya Encampment, 1854/1869. Questions persist about Catlin's alleged South American voyages— for which no documentation has so far been discovered. A generic quality to his pictures of local flora, fauna, and native peoples suggests that these views could have been based upon widely reproduced works by earlier artists such as Albert Eckhout.

Wi-jun-jon, Pigeon's Egg Head (The Light) Going to and Returning from Washington, 1837–39, Assiniboine/Nakoda. Catlin had first painted Wi-jun-jon in 1831, when "the Light" was on his way to Washington, D.C., as official guest of the secretary of war. Eighteen months later, the artist depicted him on his return, when he had exchanged native clothing for a general's uniform bristling with gold buttons and epaulets. Catlin's "split screen" image has a racist element, but the tragic conclusion to the Light's conflicted identity was his murder by two fellow tribesmen.

Portrait of Joseph Chadwick, 1834. Catlin became close to nineteen-year-old Joe Chadwick in 1834, when the artist arranged for the young clerk to accompany him to Fort Gibson in Arkansas Territory to join the first dragoon regiment there. Demobilized, the friends, and possibly lovers, knew they must separate. Chadwick enlisted in the army unit sent to defend the Texas-Mexico border. He had just turned twenty-four when he was killed in the Goliad massacre at Presidio La Bahia on Palm Sunday, 1836.

Karl Girardet (1813–71), *George Catlin and His Troupe of Iowa Performing in the Tuileries before Louis-Philippe and His Family,* 1845. Fresh from a tour of Britain, George Catlin and his troupe of "live" Iowa attracted more attention in Paris than any American artist before him. Less than two weeks after their arrival in the City of Light in April 1845, the celebrities were invited to perform before the reigning monarchs in the grand ballroom of the Tuileries Palace.

Mrs. George Catlin (Clara Bartlett Gregory), ca. 1830. Painted soon after the couple's marriage in 1828, Catlin portrays his twenty-one-year old bride as a heroine worthy of the Romantic poets she loved. Her married life proved anything but romantic: shadowed by exile, money worries, and her husband's long absences. Clara was thirty-seven years old when she died suddenly of pneumonia in Paris in 1844, leaving Catlin burdened with debt and four young children.

John Neagle (1796–1865), *Portrait of George Catlin*, 1825. Long believed to be a self-portrait by Catlin, the painting has recently been reattributed to his talented contemporary John Neagle, with whom George shared a house in Philadelphia when the two young artists were newly elected Fellows of the Pennsylvania Academy of Fine Arts. Here, Neagle depicts his friend as a dandy à la Byron, with carelessly knotted cravat and carefully disarranged curls.

Photographer unknown, *Six Chippewa (Ojibwa) Indians Who Visited Europe with George Catlin*, 1851. George Henry (second from left), better known as Maungwudaus, joined Catlin in Paris in 1845 as business manager, and his appearance with a group of Ojibwa, following the Iowa's flight for home and Clara Catlin's death, gave the artist renewed hope. They had just opened in Brussels when the troupe was ravaged by smallpox. The survivors returned to America while Catlin was left to make his way back to Paris and financial ruin.

Red Jacket, 1826. Red Jacket (so named because of his early service to the British army, or "redcoats") was the most frequently painted Native American leader and the subject of Catlin's first Indian portrait, with two more to follow. This oil sketch, made when Red Jacket was about seventy years old, is the only one to survive. Although the artist described him as a pathetic drunk, his fierce will and force of character dominate this image of tattered dignity.

Mah-to-toh-pa, Four Bears, Second Chief, in Mourning, 1832, Mandan/Numakiki. Called "the most beloved chief on the upper Missouri," the veteran Mandan leader extended his famed hospitality to George Catlin, even giving him a studio where he recorded the secret O-kee-pa ceremony. When the Mandan were largely destroyed by a smallpox epidemic in 1837, Four Bears is said to have cursed the white men who had brought this scourge upon them.

Photographer unknown, *P. T. Barnum with Tom Thumb,* ca. 1850. Catlin may have been unaware that Barnum, the master showman, had masterminded the travels of the troupe of thirteen Iowa who appeared in London in 1844. Catlin showed the "live" Indians, first in Lord's Cricket Ground, then in Vauxhall Gardens. But the partnership quickly soured, with Barnum threatening Catlin with lawsuits if he did not recoup his investment. Here, America's greatest promoter is photographed with his most famous act, General Tom Thumb.

Photographer unknown, *Asher B. Durand*, 1854. Together with his friend Thomas Cole, Durand was a founder of the Hudson River School of painters, as well as being a successful engraver and, like Samuel F. B. Morse, an influential member of New York's art establishment. The loyal Durand became a friend and lifelong supporter of Catlin during the latter's expatriate years. Durand's signature appears on many "memos" to Congress urging the purchase of the artist's Indian Gallery.

Photographer unknown, *Henry Rowe Schoolcraft*, ca. 1851. Self-taught geologist, explorer, ethnographer, statistician, and administrator, Henry Rowe Schoolcraft and George Catlin were often paired as America's two great Indian "experts": "Catlin may be called the red man's painter; Schoolcraft his poetical historian" (*Detroit Free Press*). As Catlin's "showman's fame" grew, the rancorous Schoolcraft, by then a powerful bureaucrat, set out to destroy him.

Photographer unknown, *George Catlin in Brussels*, age seventy-two, 1868. "In my whole life I was never so near to starving as now," Catlin wrote to a friend from Brussels a few years before this photograph was taken. Even allowing for exaggeration, the gaunt cheeks and hollow eyes confirm this description of the artist's circumstances: He lived in furnished rooms where, isolated by his deafness, his only company was a caged family of white mice.

R. Stanley Freeman (British, dates unknown), *George Catlin*, London, 1870. Suffering from fatal kidney disease, Catlin posed for this photograph only weeks before he sailed from England to New York. The still-imperious figure in the frock coat of two years earlier is unrecognizable. The artist just managed to pack his Cartoon Collection, sail for New York, and hang his last picture show at the newly opened Smithsonian Institution in Washington, D.C., before dying on December 23, 1872.

enough to deliver all of his ex-partner's remarks himself. He even managed to convince George that his appropriation would benefit both the Indians *and* Catlin. With only a verbal agreement, however, George had no legal recourse: Rankin could do as he pleased.

One day after this conversation, when Catlin's notice of the troupe's "last" London performance appeared in all the newspapers, he was stunned to read another advertisement in the same issues, noting that Mr. Rankin "had rented the adjoining room to Mr. Catlin's, and on the same floor [of Egyptian Hall] for two months—a much finer room where ladies and others would be much better accommodated; where the lectures would be given by Mr. Rankin *himself*, who had *lived all his life* among the Indians." Rankin concluded by promising "*hereafter, the beautiful and interesting bride of the 'Strong Wind' [Cadotte], the interpreter, will make her appearance on the platform and with the Indians, and preside at the piano.*"

The new Mrs. Cadotte did not, however, appear on the platform in Egyptian Hall. There had been no such agreement. But now, along with double-dealing and duplicity on every front, Rankin revealed a vengeful streak. He told everyone in London that George had tried to cheat him by taking more than his share of the profits, and he fired Cadotte, evicting him from the rooms in George Street and leaving the young newlyweds destitute, to make their way back to Mackinac, Michigan, as best they could. (The only possession the bride salvaged of her former life was her beautiful piano, housed in an African rosewood case, sent to her by her grieving father.)

Catlin's first reaction was relief. Now that his partnership with Rankin was over, he would no longer be associated with the shoddy promoter, or with the misalliance the latter had encouraged and exploited. But George was sadly naive. In the circles that counted in London, the damage had been done. Ending the partnership did little to answer the question: How could Mr. Catlin, so recently anointed artist, explorer, and scholar of the first rank, allow his reputation to be tarnished by Rankin's low brand of showmanship? It was still George Catlin's name that appeared on the banner announcing the Indian Gallery above the portal of Egyptian Hall, which Rankin had turned into a bawdyhouse of low women consorting with half-naked Indians.

LIKE A BLOW from the diamond cutter's hammer that reveals hidden flaws in the stone, George's partnership with Rankin exposed his own deepest conflicts: the clash between opportunism and altruism toward the Indians in his care, and the contradictions that centered on the art he had abandoned for the lure of commercial success.

From the moment Rankin had appeared with the Ojibwa in Manchester, Catlin had ceded control of selling the act to his new partner: Advertisements trumpeted: "Wild Enough! Nine real Indians from N. America." In London Catlin reclaimed his usual energetic role, overseeing the distribution of handbills, placards, and broadsides, touting "chiefs, warriors, women—even a child," who would "display . . . their Dances, Songs and warwhoops, and other Ceremonies in their rudest and wildest character." Offstage he dismissed the pledge of sobriety he himself had exacted from the troupe, and saw no betrayal in keeping them cheerful and under control with champagne and ale.

As Catlin now realized, "live" Indians held the key to money and success; inevitably they would come to occupy the role played by any other "live" act—horses, elephants, or big cats; their theatrical value consisted in the illusion of danger incompletely tamed. In the process, as he also knew, the Indians had first to be uprooted and deracinated, their performances reenactments of what was lost. Their rituals and ceremonies, hunts and dances, scalping and war whoops were already acts of recovered memory. Now, as the partnership with Rankin ended, George claimed that his only concern was the well-being of the Objibwa and their safe return home—a place that no longer existed.

Prophetically Catlin had also foreseen a life of "semi-barbarism" for Sarah Haynes Cadotte. It was not the burdens of the Michigan wilderness that destroyed the young Londoner. Her husband revealed himself to be a violent drunk who often brutalized her. She ran away and, finding refuge in the church, converted to Catholicism. With the help of missionaries, she founded and taught in a school for Indian children until she died, probably in childbirth, in 1851. She was twenty-five years old.

When his lease on the small rooms in Egyptian Hall expired, Rankin returned to Canada with the Ojibwa, who individually disappear from view. Not so their former manager, however. Arthur Rankin gave up show business and took up surveying. He went into partnership with his brother, and together they made a fortune in the development of copper mining in western Canada—all before Rankin was thirty-five. Like other self-made tycoons, he followed this act by financing a successful run in politics, based on his "heroic Patriot" service in the militia. Other unsavory episodes of his past surfaced, however, leading to his early retirement from public life.

LACKING RANKIN'S LUCK, freedom from scruple, and genius for self-reinvention, Catlin was left with a blackened reputation and a pile of debts. Rankin's defection with the Ojibwa had one happy unintended consequence, declared Catlin: Without the strain of performing twice a day, and "having a little leisure, I was drawing my little children (of whom I now had four) nearer to me than ever." But the price of time with his family was also measured in George's growing financial worries: He had no earnings and greater expenses, a new baby and a new book, again "published by the Author, at Egyptian Hall," and new debts. The Catlins' only reliable income was Clara's allowance from property she had inherited from her father, along with a three-thousand-dollar cash legacy. This windfall enabled them to revive plans for a visit home to America.

Now Clara's recurrent dreams of drowning at sea, together with George's need to make money, inspired him with the idea for an incredible lifesaving invention: a floating quarterdeck that would disengage from a sinking ship to become a huge lifeboat. Once again Catlin's guilenessness torpedoed his ambition: He gave his drawings, together with 130 pounds, to a patent agent whose "research" required spending the entire amount to discover that a similar design had already been registered.

Chastened, he helped prepare for the family's return to America; this time the expatriates packed not only household possessions, but Catlin's Indian collection as well—every item from his paintings to the Crow tipi—suggesting possible one-way tickets home. "But even this *was not to be*," George recalled, "for it was announced, just then, that another party of fourteen Indians had arrived in Liverpool and were on their way to the Metropolis!" Neither George nor his family left for America.

The disembarking group of fourteen Iowa might as well each have worn name tags inscribed "George Catlin." As was true for the Ojibwa, George had already known and painted several members of the troupe when visiting nearby tribes on the Missouri. Indeed, portraits of their leaders, chiefs "White Cloud" and "Walking Rain," together with the "Fast Dancer" a famed warrior, had hung among the hundreds that, before being packed, had surveyed the empty great room in Egyptian Hall.

Led by the two chiefs who now greeted Catlin warmly by the Indian name they had given him earlier, Chip-pe-ho-la, the Iowa who arrived in London represented a splinter group of dissenters. White Cloud had unsuccessfully challenged the old guard's military leader, Neumonya ("No Heart"), who had long treated with white authority. His revolt had ended in a political stalemate and the younger man's decision to secede from the tribe, whose dwindling numbers—now about five hundred—spoke to the Iowa's diminished status.

White Cloud and his followers had been brought from their settlement on the lower Platte River in Missouri by a promoter, one with a showman's suspiciously sounding stage-name: G. H. C. Melody. In fact George Henry Curzon Melody was his real name; he and George Catlin had met during the artist's travels up the Missouri. Contradicting Catlin's later narrative, in which he casts chance as the principal player in his life story, it appears that he and Melody had stayed in touch, sealing their new business partnership before the Iowa left their Western home to make the trip east to New York, and from there to cross the Atlantic.

By 1843 Melody, a former jailer, manager of a Freemason's Lodge in St. Louis, and deeply in debt, had become a showman. Hearing that a breakaway group of fourteen Iowa might be eager to leave their settlement, he persuaded them through their restless chief, White Cloud, to come with him to England, where they would acquire advantages over their stay-at-home tribesmen, enjoying adventures and meeting distinguished Britons, all the while earning money and glory as performers. But Melody was no entrepreneur dealing on his own. The mastermind behind his newly fledged Indian act was none other than Phineas T. Barnum, for whom the former jailer and Masonic functionary was now acting as Western agent.

THE GREATEST SHOWMAN, promoter, and impresario in America, as well as one of the biggest impostors, frauds, and double-dealers, Barnum had by 1844 already achieved fame, and the beginnings of fortune, by purchasing the Peales' failing New York Museum, renaming it the American Museum. There he exhibited freaks and curiosities, from Fiji mermaids to Siamese twins, not forgetting midgets, giants, jugglers, ventriloquists, and a former female slave who he claimed had been George Washington's nurse, now more than 120 years old. These triumphs, however, had been eclipsed by the launch of Barnum's latest and greatest discovery: a perfectly proportioned thirty-two-inch high, six-year-old dancing and singing dwarf, christened Charles Stratton but promptly renamed by his new manager, "Tom Thumb." Tickets couldn't be printed fast enough; on tour thousands were turned away— or so his handler claimed; money poured into Barnum's coffers. Now, accompanied by a select entourage, including the tiny star's parents and manager, their wardrobe trunks filled with perfectly scaled replicas of historical costumes (the audience favorite being Napoleon's, with tricorne and marshal's baton), "General Tom Thumb" set sail for England.

Shrewd businessman that he was, Barnum knew better than to invest all his time and manic energy in a single act—even a blockbuster like his new star. Along with his genius for marketing and publicity, Barnum understood that success depended upon constant novelty; the next new things—and the next—had to be discovered and groomed, to make sure they were a "go"—his favorite word. He had been told of this splinter group of fourteen Iowa, ready to secede from the tribe and to leave now-hostile ancestral territory.

The Iowa had a long history of relations with nearby white settlements, mostly through land agents, including those trading in bad deals and worse whiskey. Still, Barnum had no hesitation about advertising them as "fresh" from their wild and savage state. Who better than Melody, the gentle out-of-pocket ex-jailer, to wrangle the troupe east for tryouts as performers, before they were launched abroad?

Like Barnum's other acts, the savage unspoiled Iowa tribe was an inspired fiction. They were skilled farmers and builders (some even owned houses built of brick), and Catlin had earlier been impressed by the sophistication of their chiefs; at the same time their main village "presented each day a scene of drunkenness and riot." Among other persuasive reasons for White Cloud's band of dissenters to leave: Their chief suffered from cataracts, and he hoped that an eminent European surgeon might restore his sight.

So far Barnum had been unlucky with native acts. Only the year before, in 1843, when he had featured a group of "Rocky Mountain wild I[ndians]" at his American Museum, the troupe had demanded expensive gifts and new wedding blankets for each performance of a native marriage ceremony. They also required cooking equipment and foods, which they prepared in their rooms above the theater. The cost of all this, Barnum grumbled, ate up his profits. Then, his star, billed as a beautiful Sauk maid Dohumee, died suddenly of a viral infection. Perhaps with Melody in charge, the Iowa would signal a reversal of fortune.

Barnum had another reason for optimism. As soon as Catlin's partnership was severed by the double-crossing Rankin, George had quietly entered into an agreement with Barnum, who, playing the unaccustomed role of silent partner, would sublet the large room of Egyptian Hall for the remainder of the lease. There, with great fanfare, he planned to introduce General Tom Thumb to London, while playing an invisible role in touring the Iowa, whose official managers would be Catlin and Melody.

An experienced showman, Barnum decided that his "untutored savages" were also unseasoned performers. As soon as the fourteen Iowa arrived in the East, he arranged a trial run in Hoboken. A ferry ride brought New Yorkers to a vast meadow offering a close-enough approximation of the prairie; enthralled crowds watched the Iowa reenact their games of lacrosse, buffalo hunts, medicine ceremonies, scalping and, not incidentally, allowed them to see some of the profits[*] prior to boarding the ship in New York, accompanied

---

[*] There is no record of how much the Indian performers—Ojibwa or Iowa— were actually paid, after expenses for room and board.

by a freshly killed buffalo that they would butcher and consume on the high seas.

WHILE THE IOWA were still making their way east, down the Ohio River to Cincinnati and from there to New York, Barnum and Tom Thumb and his parents set sail for Liverpool, arriving in London on January 18, 1844. There, the legendary showman met his new partner George Catlin. Leaving nothing to chance, Barnum had blanketed the capital with publicity; word of mouth did the rest. Londoners embraced the tiny American as rapturously as had his own adoring compatriots: General Tom Thumb was the spectacle to beat.

Not everyone was besotted by the latest American sensation: Francis Parkman, the proper young Brahmin who would document his Western travels in *The Oregon Trail*, to be published in 1847, arrived at Egyptian Hall primed to revisit the Plains Indians he had first seen in Boston in 1838. While Catlin's portraits still hung on the walls of the great room, darkened now by the city's greasy coal dust, he watched, repelled, as "the little wretch" beguiled his audience with impressions of the great and famous, alternating with songs and dances; Although delivered "in a voice like a smothered mouse," the tiny "general's" rendition of "Yankee Doodle" soon enjoyed the applause of Queen Victoria and her court at Buckingham Palace.

In Barnum's reports about his London stay he refers to Catlin several times, noting that the Iowa are being shown "on our joint account." In contrast Catlin's published writings about the Indians' tour never mention Barnum's name. With George's reputation in England tainted by his association with Rankin, he now heard rumblings from America of a smear campaign—probably orchestrated by Schoolcraft—attacking his veracity. In particular the embittered bureaucrat took aim at Catlin's re-creation of the Mandan O-kee-pa ceremony, claiming it was all lies. John James Audubon had replaced Catlin as the beneficiary of the American Fur Company's largesse, including free trips on their vessels. The rivalrous painter of wildlife lost no time in denouncing Catlin's writings as "trashy stuff" when not outright invention. Even as independent-minded a critic as the transcendentalist writer Margaret Fuller expressed caution about Catlin's credibility in matters of Indian life. Touring the Great Lakes in June 1843, Fuller was told that Catlin, whose *Letters and Notes* she had deeply admired, "was not to be depended on for the accuracy of his facts."

At this particular moment George was not keen to publicize his marriage of necessity with Barnum, whose name was already synonymous with the sensational, the blown-up, and the bogus. For Barnum the new partnership was a free upgrade; hoping to be burnished by the artist's cultural luster, he had only the highest praise for Catlin and even higher hopes for their profitable association: When they did meet he wrote home to say of George, "I find him a very kind, sociable and excellent gentleman, and am most happy to add he is making a fortune here." Either Barnum had been misinformed or he was puffing Catlin's success to leverage their mutual interests.

On August 2, 1844, fourteen Iowa, eight men, four women, and two children disembarked in Liverpool. Shepherded by Melody, the troupe was installed in apartments at 7 St. James's Street, the same street where George had lived before his family's arrival in London. The Iowa were accompanied by an interpreter, Jeffrey Deroin, or Doroway, son of a French father and a free black mother.

When the lease expired in July at Egyptian Hall, Tom Thumb was off on his triumphal tour of Britain. Writing from Bristol, Barnum crowed that the average daily receipts were three hundred dollars, not including publications and souvenirs.

There was no other venue big enough for the Iowa to perform with bows and arrows, to reenact war dances or play lacrosse. Barnum would have recalled how much the wide-open spaces of the Hoboken meadowlands had added to the thrilling illusion of seeing Indians in their native habitat: This seemed an opportune moment for the Iowa to move their act out of doors—to Lord's Cricket Ground, St. John's Wood. For six days a week, on the same pitch whose great annual event was the match between Eton and Harrow, mesmerized Londoners watched as male Iowa performed war dances on a raised stage, amid wigwams said to be created by squaws.

In a few weeks Lord's was reclaimed for its own native sport, but the new audiences who flocked there had voted with their feet. Their message was clear. The Indian Gallery as a museum, foregrounding Catlin's paintings, was finished: The dead had been replaced by the living. Something else had changed radically: The hidden difference between the Indians who leapt and whooped in Hoboken and St. John's Wood and the old "illustrated lectures" was money. "The new Indian show was openly for profit." There was no further mention of art.

26

DÉJÀ VU—ALL OVER AGAIN

After five years of exhibiting on and off in London's most desirable space, Catlin was out of Egyptian Hall for good. He had to find another booking for the Iowa, preferably out of doors, where they could perform. For a few weeks of glorious Indian summer, the troupe turned Vauxhall, the once-elegant Regency pleasure gardens, into the American prairie, featuring four wigwams, galloping horses, and flying arrows. Audiences and money soon disappeared with the cold, and Catlin had no choice but to repeat his earlier successful tour featuring the Ojibwa: The same bookings—Birmingham and Nottingham yielded scattered receipts; a summons lost in the mail required a quick trip to London to pay a large penalty in person. A few days each in Leeds, York, Newcastle-on-Tyne, Sunderland, and Edinburgh produced only exhaustion, not profit.

Then another legal issue loomed: Catlin received several letters from Barnum, threatening to have Melody arrested for unpaid debts. George was onto his partner's game: Knowing he would never see a shilling from the hapless Melody, Barnum decided that Catlin, vulnerable to the shaming of his associate, would pay him off. George was beside himself with rage: Theirs was a three-way partnership, and he

felt personally betrayed by Barnum's hard-nosed attitude and efforts
to shake him down for their partner's prior debts. In letters to Clara
in Turnham Green he called Barnum a "consummate blackguard"
and claimed to have fired off such a blistering reply to his attempts
at blackmail that he was confident the matter would end there. But it
was also clear that Catlin lived in fear of retaliation.

Implacable as he was about money, one can sympathize with Barnum: On the basis of receipts so far, he had given up hope that Melody
and Catlin would prove successful agents for the Iowa in Britain, and
he was trying to re-coup funds owed him. Barnum was more impressed
with the show-business flair of Burr Catlin; George's ebullient party-
loving nephew was also a "regular roarer," or go-getter, Barnum wrote
to an associate at home; he was thinking of buying the Adelaide Gallery* in London—a sort of arcade known for tawdry exhibits; if he did,
he would make Burr manager.

George had good reason to identify with the terrified Melody. He,
too, had unpaid debts—to Thomas Phillipps and to others—probably moneylenders. At the same time, he admitted to Clara, Melody's
jumbled accounts were causing him to question whether honesty or
incompetence was at issue. But he still felt responsible for his fragile
partner. Despite a history of compulsive borrowing, this time Melody
seemed on the verge of a breakdown. An arrest in England could mean
debtor's prison for the ex-jailer.

Catlin's own anxieties now took the form of hallucinatory panic
attacks. As they were boarding the train in Edinburgh for Glasgow,
Melody produced a packet of letters for George that he had received
earlier, addressed in Clara's familiar handwriting. In the predawn
darkness Catlin saw the wrapper as bordered in black and its contents

---

* In the 1850s the Adelaide Gallery became the first space in London to show
photography, thus marking a shift familiar to modernism, from the sleazy to the
avant-garde.

announcing catastrophe: He imagined several of the children fallen into the fire and burned to death; another killed by boiling water from an overturned kettle. Shaking with terror, he was too distraught to read the letters and he put the folded pages in his pocket. When morning light flooded the carriage, still trembling, he withdrew the packet. The black border he had seen on the cover was a red wax seal, and Clara's neat script conveyed the news that all four "dear little chubs" were well and happy, with baby Georgie already standing.

Touring the north of England and Scotland in February 1845, the Iowa suffered more from the bone-chilling cold and damp than the Ojibwa had earlier. Their greater vulnerability combined with a grueling schedule of travel and performances led to frequent illnesses. Most of the troupe sustained respiratory problems; the handsome and graceful Little Wolf was attacked by a recurrent intestinal infection. Catlin's meticulous listing of expenses notes frequent outlays for unspecified "medicines" required by members of the tribe. Some have assumed this to be a euphemism for spirits; they would hardly have been the first to find that whiskey and brandy made both the climate and lingering coughs easier to bear.

In Newcastle-on-Tyne, Little Wolf's son with O-kee-wee-me, three-year-old Corsair, fell ill with a high fever. On the crossing to Scotland the child died in his father's arms. His parents' anguish was beyond any grief their fellow Iowa had yet witnessed. The couple had lost two other young sons in America on the trip east. Now, when they arrived in Dundee, Little Wolf refused to give up the small body; he had heard that British graves were robbed and the corpses sold to medical students. On the boat a fellow passenger, a Quaker, promised that if they would entrust their dead child to him, he would see to its burial in the Friends' cemetery, guarded against any desecration. Little Wolf agreed, but his despair made it impossible for him to perform.

Catlin's gruesome fantasies of his own children's death did not seem to open him to the Iowa parents' devastation. On the contrary he remained defended behind fear of financial ruin, a prospect he worried would be hastened by the absence of his most popular performers. In a letter to Clara, he complained of losing

> not only the exciting interest of the tiny Ioway [*sic*] child, but also the services of the father, Little Wolf and of the wife, for [some] length of time, if not altogether. And he is the most important man of the party, taking part in all the dances and every amusement and at the *same time* is decidedly the best looking man of the lot.

Bankruptcy stared from the numbers: He was "within pences of having nothing," he confided to Clara from Dundee, "and can only be here one day."

George had talked with Barnum about next showing the Iowa in Paris. Counting the wan receipts from their recent northern tour, Catlin was reluctant to commit himself to any investment on the Continent. Another reason for holding back, he wrote to Clara, was that a booking in the French capital would once again engage him on a "joint account" with Barnum, even now amusing himself in Paris where he was making final arrangements for Tom Thumb's launch. Melody's accounting and Catlin's own finances were too shaky to risk further relations with the unforgiving Barnum. Still, Clara had always yearned to see Paris; a trip now would assuage her disappointment at the second cancellation of their visit home. So with some financial juggling, Catlin made the necessary arrangements.

The Catlins arrived in Paris by April 17, 1845; the Iowa followed with Melody a few days later, subdued once again by mourning. They had left behind, in a Liverpool grave, their beloved leader, Roman Nose, who "seemed daily to be losing flesh and strength," until he died there, in hospital, of "a pulmonary consumption."

Less than two weeks later the thirteen Iowa, accompanied by Melody and Catlin, assembled in the grand ballroom of the Tuileries Palace, adjacent to the Louvre, for an audience with King Louis-Philippe and Queen Marie-Amélie.

In contrast to the British monarchs who never issued royal invitations to the Iowa, King Louis-Philippe, having traveled through the American West from 1796 to 1800 as a youth, retained a passionate interest in Indian tribes, their ancestral lands, and the French explorers and missionaries who had preceded him into the wilderness. He knew Catlin's *Letters and Notes* well, and he was so eager to see the artist's paintings that he was among the first distinguished subscribers to the illustrated *Portfolio*, published by the author the year before.

Catlin and the Iowa's welcome at the Tuileries exceeded all expectations in warmth and enthusiasm: King Louis-Philippe's travels in the West (including a descent of the Mississippi by steamboat to New Orleans) had left him an admirer of American informality, while for their part the Iowa took the French royals to their hearts, proclaiming: "The Ojibbeways were subjects of the Queen [Victoria], but we will be subjects of Louis-Philippe."

As their gift to the king of France, they had painted the long stem of a beautiful calumet a bright blue, adding brilliant blue ribbons. The performers themselves dazzled their hosts, as "each one came out from his toilet, in a full blaze of colour of various tints, all with their wampum and medals on, with their necklaces of grizly [sic] bears' claws, their shields, and bows and quivers, their lances and war clubs, and tomahawks, and scalping-knives."

Ushered into the great reception hall of the Tuileries, the two groups moved across the gleaming parquet toward each other: their majesties accompanied by the royal entourage—the Duchess of Orleans and Count of Paris, the Princess Adelaide, the Prince and Princess of Joinville, the Duke and Duchess of Aumale, and the young Duke of Brabant; the Iowa, with chiefs in the fore, including Catlin and Melody.

Once the ceremonial requirements were dispatched, the Americans were impressed with the way the king fell into conversation with the chiefs, "in the most free and familiar manner." The royal host's welcome of Catlin and the Iowa offered a glimpse of the young Louis-Philippe—the man who had called himself the "citizen king," and who had promised to democratize an ossified monarchy—before he became hated by his people.

Waxing nostalgic for the freedom of youth and his long-ago reverse grand tour of roughing it on the American frontier, the king asked Jeffrey Deroin, the translator, to "tell these good fellows that I am glad to see them; that I have been in many of the wigwams of the Indians in America when I was a young man, and they treated me everywhere kindly, and I love them for it."

Following an exchange of gifts (medals from the king, the blue pipe from the war chief) the ceremony appeared to end, with the royal family issuing thanks and farewells and making their way from the great hall. Suddenly the king spied an Indian drum, and on being told it had been brought just in case they should be asked to perform, he excitedly summoned the queen and their party to return and proceed to the ballroom. There, to the sounds, at first soft, of singing and drumming, rose the eerie noise of "chattering whistles," so carved to imitate the noise made by the huge birds: The Eagle Dance began.

Inspired by the welcome and the setting, the Iowa threw themselves into the dance with a fervor Catlin had never seen before. All the performers seemed to live the extraordinary moment. As evidence of the once-in-a-lifetime magic of the event, the Eagle Dance was led by Little Wolf; the bereaved father emerged from mourning to play the part that was his alone: He had even created a new ending in honor of Louis-Philippe.

Raising his tomahawk above the heads of his fellow performers in a gesture that signaled them to stop, he advanced toward the king. Standing before the monarch, he declaimed, in boastful tones, of the savagery and violence with which he had killed and scalped a Pawnee warrior. He then placed in His Majesty's hands his tomahawk and the horse-whip attached to his wrist. Reminding the king that this was the very weapon, stained with his victim's blood, he had used to kill the enemy, he said: "My Father, since I have come into this country I have learned that peace is better than war, and I 'bury the tomahawk' in your hands— I fight no more."

We know nothing of Little Wolf's inner transformation from warrior chief to advocate of peace. In his recasting of the Eagle Dance, from a reenactment of killing to a plea for its enduring end, he seems to have found a lesson learned from grief and loss: He turned from mourning his own son to refusing to kill the sons of others.

CATLIN WAS LESS starry eyed about the French capital after dealing with its famous bureaucracy. Immediately on arriving he had set about finding a space big and prominent enough to house the Iowa performers and his collection, along with the audiences he hoped to draw. He settled upon the Salle Valentino, a huge hall on the fashionable rue Saint-Honoré on the Right Bank. There were delays as Catlin completed the "tedious and vexatious" paperwork and payoffs were submitted: the "poor tax" levied on all performances and the subvention of a municipal security detail to guard the collection.

In 1801, almost fifty years before Catlin introduced his Iowa to Parisians, the French began their love affair with the American West, especially with its native peoples. The spark was the publication of René de Chateaubriand's short novel *Atala*, the story of the doomed love between Atala and Chactas, two young Indians of devout yet differing beliefs.

Now Parisians were offered the opportunity to experience at first-hand a troupe of Plains Indians, reenacting the hunts, ceremonies, and battles that until now they knew only from books. It didn't hurt that artists and writers came—and came again—becoming, in their excitement, publicists for the marvels to be seen at the Salle Valentino. French writers—then as now—didn't just write; they talked—and talked. "Word of mouth" might have been invented by the Parisian *culturati* and its café denizens.

Caricature—the ultimate tribute to fame—followed, with good-natured fun poked by the leading French artists in the genre: Honoré Daumier, Paul Gavarni, Jean Ignace Isidore Gérard Grandville, and "Cham" (Amédée Charles Henri de Noé) all published in *Le Charivari*, the popular illustrated magazine for the graphic deflation of all that was fashionably overinflated. Unlike the racist barbs of *Punch*, the anti-bourgeois Parisian caricaturists positioned themselves on the side of the Indians. One strip, probably by "Cham," mocks the victims of an Iowa scalping: They may need their fashionable stovepipe hats to disguise their loss.

The most brilliant visitor to the Salle Valentino, the poet and art critic Charles Baudelaire, described nothing short of a conversion experience. Catlin's color was *terrible*, "ferocious"—he wrote—his highest praise of a fellow artist, but at the same time mysterious. The two antithetical colors: Red, "the color of blood, the color of life, harder to penetrate than the eyes of a snake . . . surges from the gloom of the Museum, to intoxicate us," while his green—"the calm, smiling, bright happy color of nature"—plays out in the painted faces of Catlin's two great portraits, both exhibited in the Salon of 1846: *Little Wolf* and the Blackfoot chief *Buffalo Bull Fat Back*. Baudelaire declared Catlin our "guide among the savages," saying, "He has brought back alive the proud, and free character of these chiefs, both their nobility and manliness."

Fourteen years after that first visit, Baudelaire evoked in one paragraph a pantheon of three landscape painters whose imaginative genius lofts a banal genre to the realm of art: Catlin, Eugène Delacroix, and Victor Hugo, for the poet's visionary pen-and-ink drawings. No coincidence that Hugo and Delacroix both made more than one visit to the vast hall on the rue Saint-Honoré.

To Delacroix, Catlin's gorgeously-attired chiefs and timeless landscapes also seemed mysterious yet familiar: an extension of his own immersion in the exotic and hidden world of Morocco. Soon he was copying Catlin's Indians, but true to the definition of genius, he didn't borrow, he stole—Delacroix never mentioned Catlin as his source.

Delacroix had been invited by a friend who soon emerged as Catlin's most ardent and influential fan in Paris. George Sand, the best-selling novelist, had begun her career as a journalist, covering for a pittance whatever story her editor at *Le Figaro* deemed worth chasing. Always needing money, she still took assignments when they came her way. Now, a commissioned article for a de luxe album, to be called *Le Diable à Paris* (The Devil in Paris) brought Sand and her son, Maurice, an illustrator, from her apartment in the rue Saint Lazare through the Right Bank snarl of horses and omnibuses, and pedestrians dodging both, to the Salle Valentino.

A keen student of history, Sand had done her homework. Before her first sight of the Iowa, she had read widely, and the article she had planned to write turned into a lengthy essay—far longer and more complex than she had intended: The Indians and their art, together with M. Catlin's, deserved more "serious" attention than topical journalism could offer, she said. Thus she became the first popular writer in France to set the stage, historically, for what Parisians were about to see: Sand established the Native Americans' history post contact—their relations with the white man's government in Washington—the way their lands were seized through his broken treaties; their ancient tribal wars made deadlier by his gunpowder; their settlements decimated by his diseases, typhoid and smallpox. She concluded with the specifics of the Iowa's hostilities with the Sauk, and the schism that had brought White Cloud to his present position of leadership in exile; she even managed to include the chief's hope of curing his cataract and improving all their lives by acquiring the advantages of a superior white civilization in Europe.

Sand's English was fluent, and she could talk to Catlin, who knew no French, without a translator. For his part George was sensitive to the honor of being interviewed, together with his star performers, by a famous writer—indeed, the most famous woman in Europe who was not a crowned head. For her next visit, when he arranged for her to meet the most prominent of the Iowa, Catlin advised her to bring gifts of red cloth, colorful beads, and other trinkets.

Artists and writers who visited the Salle Valentino invoked a state of grace; they had been present at the Creation; even "in their fallen state," Baudelaire insisted, Catlin's Indians "made us dream of the art of Phidias, and of great Homeric deeds." Also describing the Indians in classical terms, Sand likened the noblewomen in swirling tunics to the maidens in the Panathenaic frieze of the Parthenon. But it was White Cloud whom she cast as a "modern Jason." Heroic by any measure, his bronze torso, bared for the performance, linked him to warriors of antiquity. Sand's highest tribute is reserved for her fellow artist: It is Catlin's portrait of White Cloud that has quickened the Iowa chief into life: "Robed in his most splendid costume, his face gleaming with precious vermilion paint, he sits, like the prince he is, among his proud acolytes, solemnly smoking his pipe."

Sand also captured, as no one else did, the fleeting moments of the performance itself, and the way White Cloud's role of chief extended to that of choreographer, ordering,

> first, a war dance, then a gentler one of the peace pipe. He seized a tambourine or a rattle and, "in tones both sweet and guttural," joined his own voice to the chant of his colleagues. The fearsome warriors, graceful children, grave and chaste women, leapt and ran in a circle around him; occasionally he succumbed to their transports, and remembering his home, the glory of his

ancestors, and his love for his native land, he rose and joined the dance.

On her next visit George Sand went "backstage" to talk with the performers, now living in rooms behind the performance space in the Salle Valentino; and it was there that she found O-kee-wee-me. The bereft wife and mother lay on a pallet on the floor, her head pillowed by her long coiled braids. Her face was still lovely, Sand wrote, "but the tawny complexion had taken on the gray-green pallor of death." The loss of Corsair and of two children early in their voyage was known to Parisians from their newspapers. In the few months she had lived, barely visible, in mourning among them, O-kee-wee-me had become an icon of female sacrifice and suffering. Sand and others spread the word that she was dying of grief and homesickness. In fact she had contracted consumption in England, but her stricken state could have left her more vulnerable to the disease's rapid progress. Sand was moved by the devotion of her husband, Little Wolf, who "never moved from her side except when he must perform. He stroked her head as a father would his child's, showing her the gifts he has received, happy when he can make her smile." Sand would pay a final visit to the young woman, this time bringing the flower they both loved best—white cyclamen. O-kee-wee-me died on June 12, 1845. She was twenty-seven years old.

Before her death she had been converted to the Roman Catholic faith, able to receive the last rites of the church while she was fully conscious. The date of her conversion is uncertain; Sand was alone in claiming that she and her husband had both been received into the church in England, living thereafter as secret Christians, "like the recusants of old." All evidence points to her conversion as taking place in Paris, through the offices of the youthful Abbé Vattemare, son of Alexandre Vattemare, a friend of Catlin's who had been most helpful to him in Paris. The two young people had become friends as well as confessor and congregant. Fresh out of seminary, Father Vattemare's first assignment was at Notre-Dame-de-Lorette, the parish church of a neighborhood known for its large numbers of ill-paid working girls, many of whom moonlighted as prostitutes to survive. The youthful priest would have had occasion to learn that "lost" souls are more alike than different; it was their losses, whether of virtue, home, children, or health, that commended them to God.

PARISIANS HAD TAKEN to their hearts the young wife and mother, bereft in every sense and dying far from home: She became a Romantic heroine; a copper-skinned Camille or Manon Lescaut, but without the past of these iconic sinners. This outpouring of popular sympathy, together with the connections of the Vattemare family, would explain O-kee-wee-me's funeral, which took place in the Church of the Madeleine, site of the city's most fashionable obsequies. Her posthumous fame also led to a commission awarded to the noted sculptor Antoine-Auguste Préault for an elaborate funerary monument in her memory, to be placed upon her grave in Montmartre Cemetery and paid for by public subscription. The monument, in the form of an obelisk, would show scenes, carved in relief, depicting the dead woman's life on the Missouri. At the summit a portrait bust of the exile looked over Paris, which mourned the young Iowa woman as one of its own.[*]

With O-kee-wee-me's death—their third loss since coming abroad—the Iowas felt too demoralized to perform, resolving "to leave within the week." Catlin had promised that they could return to America at his expense whenever they wished, and he now arranged for the next available passage for the troupe, to be accompanied once again by

---

[*] The monument was never built due to insufficient funds. A plaster maquette of the portrait bust survived in the museum in Saint-Lô until World War II, when it was damaged beyond recognition in the bombing of the Normandy coast.

Melody. As the sailing was delayed for six days, the Iowa managed a breakfast with the noted hostess Princess Belgiojoso. Then they were gone from Catlin's life forever.

Shortly after the Iowa had moved from the Hotel Victoria into the Salle Valentino, the Catlins had taken a roomy apartment at 11 bis rue Lord Byron, a short street off the Champs-Élysses and near the Arc de Triomphe. Between settling in and finding help, Clara Catlin had only begun to enjoy the sights of Paris when a lingering sore throat turned suddenly into pneumonia. She died on July 28, 1845, at the age of thirty-seven, surrounded by her stricken family and a few friends.

Separated by six weeks, the deaths of the two women, both wives and mothers and homesick exiles, stand as a study in contrasts. White and Indian, in death they invert our expectations. The pomp of O-kee-wee-me's funeral in the Madeleine, every detail followed eagerly by the public and the press, and the obscure slipping away of Clara Catlin, recorded, as were all foreigners' comings and goings, in the weekly *Galignani's Messenger*.

As Clara would have wished, the notice of her death followed a lengthy description of her "distinguished" husband's accomplishments. But the singular qualities of the "youthful wife" manage to break through the pieties about her untimely end: Those present recalled "a moral energy never surpassed," whose effect was to allow them to hope that she might recover. In evoking Clara's most grievous disappointment, however, the writer (described as a woman friend) did not try to spare the widower's feelings: "This gentle, affectionate, intellectual being was destined never more to revisit the land of her birth, and all that was earthly of so much worth and loveliness has passed away."

Despite Clara's ardent Christian faith and the proximity of two Anglican churches, her funeral took place on August 4 in the family apartment; she remained as modest and private in death as she had been in life. Whether this reflected the dead woman's wishes or whether her husband's shock was too great to allow him to make other arrangements remains unknown. Her voyage home, always deferred, was posthumous: Clara's body was shipped to America for burial in the Gregory family plot in Green-Wood Cemetery, Brooklyn, New York.

The four children—all under ten years of age—were devastated. Their father had the distraction—indeed, the necessity—of work. On the day of Clara's death—July 28—Catlin's Musée Indienne reopened—without Indians—in the Salle Valentino, to remain there until August 20.

In early August a group of eleven Canadian Ojibwa who had been performing in London arrived in Paris. They had come with the intent of placing their act under Catlin's management. Unhesitatingly George agreed. Third time lucky? . . . With this troupe, perhaps his fortunes would change.

A FLIGHT OF ROYALS

Paris remained Catlin's base for the next three years. Despite memories of the hushed sickroom where Clara lay gasping for life, George, the four children, and their governess stayed in the apartment in rue Lord Byron. There was no reason to uproot the motherless family, and he could ill afford the costs of moving. It's likely that Clara's allowance and additional income from inherited property, upon which the expatriates depended, stopped with her death. Unless Dudley Gregory made up the difference, finances were tight.

Familiarity and routine began to act as a balm for grief. The girls continued with lessons and sightseeing; Catlin had a painting room where he worked, and where little Georgie could wander, reassured by his father's presence. Still, the pervading sadness muffled an accusing truth: The wrong parent had died. George had been home so rarely that the children, especially the younger two, hardly knew him. At bedtime Georgie sobbed inconsolably for his mama.

Besides the promise of income that he badly needed, Catlin found in the arrival of the eleven Ojibwa a welcome escape from the family's grief and from his guilt—the constant reminders of all that Clara had sacrificed of her own needs and desires, and from the endless and unaccustomed worries of the recent widower, single parent, and householder.

Like their predecessors, the second troupe of Ojibwa had come from the Great Lakes region of Canada, by way of America. This time, however, the performers' manager was one of their own.

A full-blooded Ojibwa or half-caste—accounts of his origins differ— George Henry, Maungwudaus (the name he himself chose and translated as "Great Hero"), was an English-educated Methodist missionary. Early on he gave up the Lord's work to devote himself to show business: He took this same group of Ojibwa on the road, producing Indian shows through the Great Lakes region, and then from Buffalo to New York City. Either his Christian faith or the distance between showman and performer soon erased any feelings of tribal identity: Eight years before crossing the Atlantic to England, Maungwudaus, writing in a Methodist newspaper, had compared his fellow Ojibwa to "ourang outangs, for they appeared more like them than human beings."

The Anglicized Indian promoter had long looked to Catlin as a model of how to tour Indians. He booked the troupe into Egyptian Hall, where, as master of ceremonies, arrayed in full native ceremonial wear, he introduced London audiences to twice-daily "Operations of Scalping!" Then it was on to Paris, where, Ojibwa in tow, he found the master himself, George Catlin, in the depths of mourning, needing money, and a ready mark. The new impresario had brought with him from London a young wheeler-dealer to do all the legwork, while he, Maungwudaus, assumed the loftier role of tribal chief, interpreter, and negotiator. In this latter capacity he made his offer to George of a partnership—all profits and expenses to be shared, including a percentage for the performers themselves. As George would soon learn— for the second time—"shared expenses" did not include periods when the troupe, earning nothing, still had to be housed, fed, and provided with pocket money. When not onstage, the Ojibwa, now numbering at least twelve, would be on Catlin's charge alone. (A "papoose" had been born to the chief in the same room where O-Kee-wee-me had died.) If anyone needed a business manager, it was George Catlin himself.

Grateful for the distraction provided by his new flock, George refused to peer into the future—or learn from the past. He still nursed grievances towards the Iowa for their abrupt defection: The sudden death of O-kee-wee-me had forced him to cancel a dinner given for them by Colonel Thorne, an "American gentleman of great wealth" living in Paris. A greater cause of resentment was the short notice— six days—with which they announced their departure for home, leaving no option for further shows. (It was Melody who had the "heavy responsibility . . . of taking these people back to their country at his own expense." If he could never escape his creditors, at least Melody eluded the British bailiffs and debtor's prison.) The announcement of the Iowa's departure brought a surge of Parisian interest for a final look at the *peaux-rouges*, to which Catlin added sourly: "The poor fellows enjoyed their interviews with the public to the last, and also their roast beef and beef-steaks and *chickabobboo*."

Lingering bitterness may also have led him to tout his latest stars as the greater talent: In advance of the Ojibwa's opening, he ran a notice declaring, "The dances, shooting, etc., of this party will be found to be far more exciting than that of the Ioways."

On Monday, August 18, two weeks after Clara's funeral, the Ojibwa opened at the Salle Valentino for a brief engagement: they were only booked to finish the lease of the Iowa, which ended August 30. Then came a week when George painted at home and surveyed the pile of bills—for packing and shipping the Musée Indienne to its new location just across town, for the growing expenses of his household, and for the idling Ojibwa visitors.

Three weeks later, on September 8, he was swept up in the excitement of another opening and another show, when his collection was

launched at its new location, the Galérie des Beaux-Arts, on the bou-
levard de Bonne Nouvelle, an art marketplace and exhibition hall run
on the principles of a cooperative. Its artist-managers took a modest
10 percent of sales, and it's likely that once Catlin was an exhibiter, he
could also accept commissions for copies of works on view. Occupying
the large light-filled room, created from the first floor of two combined
buildings, the Galérie was probably the most stylish setting in Paris to
see (and buy) art, but also for *le tout Paris* to see and be seen. Among
the patrons of its brilliant annual benefit gala were Louis-Philippe and
all his Orleans relations.

Catlin's growing stature, and the friendship of court artist and
marine painter Jean Antoine Théodore Gudin, brought him into the
royal inner circle, a place he had long coveted. He received an invitation "to the royal breakfast table in the palace of St. Cloud." That first
breakfast, when George was invited without his "attributes"—neither
Indians nor pictures—left him buoyed with pride. And he recalled the
occasion as "the proudest one of my wild and erratic life." A month
later, in early October, Catlin and the Ojibwa were invited to entertain
the royal family at the monarchs' country retreat near Paris. On October 5 King Leopold of the Belgians, Louis-Philippe's son-in-law, and his
queen, had arrived for a visit, so Catlin's first command performance
in a more domestic royal setting found him in the company of a quar-
tet of reigning monarchs.

The appearance at St. Cloud was followed by another invitation
for breakfast, and then another. For Louis-Philippe, facing evidence
of growing unpopularity as a ruler, it was more agreeable to start the
day exchanging anecdotes with the charming and talented M. Catlin
about the Crow and Sioux chiefs they had met, and their adventures
on horseback, and in pirogues and steamboats. As it turned out, the
monarch had not only trekked his way through Indian country in the
trans-Mississippi. He and his brother had descended the Susquehanna
River in a canoe "to a small town called Wilkesbarre [*sic*], in the valley

of the Wyoming." The king must have been astonished when his guest delightedly informed him that he was a native of Wilkes-Barre, and that "while his Majesty was there I was an infant in my mother's arms, only a few months old."

BEYOND THE FLATTERY—the invitations, the intimate breakfasts with "Two Kings and Two Queens at the table," the royal welcome as one of the family—Catlin genuinely loved and admired the French monarch. He was "wonderful," an "extraordinary" man, whose "*greatness of soul*" Catlin had occasion to see "with [his] own eyes": George the royal fan couldn't fathom how a ruler whose appealing personal qualities—simplicity, directness, kindness of heart, love of family, but also his professed sympathy for republican aspirations—traits that seemed an undistorted reflection of superior character—could be judged to have failed so spectacularly at governing his people.

Sincere as his feelings were for the king, Catlin was always drawn to powerful father figures, those who, like General Clark, possessed authority over men and events but, unlike Putnam Catlin, were able to combine a paternal affection for George with the ability to influence his success.

Just before Catlin's time was about to expire at the Gálerie des Beaux-Arts, leaving his collection homeless, the king commanded M. de Cailleux, director of all museums in France, to ready the Salle de Séances at the Louvre for the installation of the Musée Indienne, now renamed the American Museum.

This private gallery for the royal family to enjoy Catlin's collection came with an offer to the artist of a studio on the floor above. Generous though it was, the gesture was not entirely disinterested; in the course of their talks, either Catlin had proposed himself—or the monarch had commissioned him—to paint copies in larger format of fifteen of the king's favorite works from the American Museum, to be followed by a series of a twenty-five large panels depicting scenes from La Salle's explorations in the American wilderness.

If the rich are expensive friends, royalty is ruinous. Enthusiastic patronage from the king of France might appear ample compensation for the democratic indifference shown by his own nation to Catlin's art, were it not for the troubling fact that not a franc changed hands in the course of George's labors for the Orleans monarch. Louis-Philippe's imprimatur produced a shower of invitations but none of gold: The ambassador to France from the Ottoman Porte gave a soiree where Catlin and the Indians were guests of honor, lionized by a swirl of brocaded turbaned Turks, Greeks, Armenians, and Egyptians, but such grand outings produced no income, and, indeed, involved the additional expense of the right clothes. No bohemian, Catlin had the bills to prove that his tailoring would do credit to any English gentleman.

Other than arousing the envy of fellow artists—French and expatriate Americans alike—uncertainty prevails over just what breaking bread with Louis-Philippe did for Catlin. Exploiting royal favor required delicacy and indirection. When the French king told an American artist over a cozy breakfast how much he would love to own copies of his favorite Catlins, protocol forbade raising the question of money. Had Catlin expected to be paid, he would have had to go through intermediaries, such as his friend Gudin and the less friendly M. de Cailleux. An agreement might have been reached, but there would have been no more breakfast invitations.

Finances were so bleak that George could no longer afford to be genteel. He tried to enlist a representative of the New-York Historical Society, in London for research and with friends in high places, to intervene on his behalf and persuade his institution to "commission" a series depicting King Louis-Philippe's youthful wanderings in western New York and down the Mississippi and Ohio Rivers. The proposal went nowhere.

Meanwhile the Ojibwa proved a resounding flop. Some Parisians confused them with the Iowa, who, they assumed, had postponed their departure; others more cynically decided that they were Frenchmen dressed up as Indians. The troupe only wanted to return to London, and Catlin now discovered that it was his responsibility to get them there. With no money for their passage, George hatched the idea that a few weeks of touring them in Belgian cities—Brussels, Ghent, and Antwerp—and they would earn their way back to England, with some profit left for him.

In the six weeks it took to make the necessary arrangements, the Ojibwa's English manager (Maungwudaus's unnamed deputy), decamped, owing the Indians one thousand francs in back pay and eight hundred francs to Catlin for money advanced during the time that they performed in Paris—expenses that were to have been shared. George was desperate. Writing to his well-connected Parisian friend, Alexandre Vattemare, he added that during the period between the close of the exhibition and their departure from Paris, expenses had mounted to fifteen hundred francs; since leaving the city with the troupe he had paid out another seventeen hundred; it would cost a further one thousand francs to get the Ojibwa back to London and himself back to Paris. Absent from his litany of expenses for the touring troupe, were funds for the support of his own family, who remained in Paris.

In Brussels disaster struck. Before the opening performance, the entire troupe of Ojibwa came down with the dreaded smallpox. Two died in that city—one of them in hospital; a third, who had seemed in excellent health, succumbed when the group arrived back in London. After Catlin had returned to Paris and had fallen out of touch with the group, he learned that these three fatalities had been followed by another four: Maungwudaus and three of his children had perished of the same disease. The troupe had been decimated while abroad, but their fate was symbolic of the larger destiny of Native Americans at home. Of the original eleven Ojibwa who had crossed the Atlantic, only five survived to make the return voyage to America. They were the last Indians Catlin would ever show.

Deeper in debt than ever on his return to Paris, Catlin retreated to his home atelier, as he now called his painting room, to begin the enormous labor represented by the two royal commissions or gifts.

He was no longer a showman; he had returned to being the artist he had always been and to continue the writing he never stopped doing. Touring Indians had brought nothing but grief to them and to him, with not even ill-gotten gains to show for his labors. For the time being he had no plans even to show the collection. He arranged for storage of the more than six hundred portraits and landscapes, along with hundreds of tribal objects in a nearby warehouse. If he needed anything there as a model for his painting, Daniel could place it before him within hours. For once George was lucky: The secure location would save his life's work.

IT WAS A relief to free himself of the constant anxieties he had felt during his years on the road. Much as he missed Clara, he now basked in the exclusive love of his four motherless children; at ten, eight, six, and three and a half, they were "just old enough for my amusement, and too young fully to appreciate the loss they had sustained, and whose little arms were now concentrated about my neck as the only one to whom they claimed kindred and looked for protection."

If the attentions of his small daughters were gratifying, the companionship of his only son and namesake was the joy of Catlin's life: Georgie had "adopted my painting-room as his constant play-house"; there, his favorite toy drum slung around his neck, he was welcome to beat a tattoo for as long and as loud as he wanted, to the point that he soon answered to the name "Tambour Major." George moved the family to other quarters, at 21 place de la Madeleine. Without encouraging the children to forget their mother, he felt it seemed the right moment for a new beginning (at perhaps less expense).

Domestic bliss did not pay the bills. Nor did the copies George made for other clients while working on the king's fifteen commissioned works. Looking back at the losses he had suffered through this latest fiasco with the Ojibwa, he was able, for the first time, to step back and consider his own experiences in a larger perspective. His showman's swansong was also a cautionary tale about which he felt the public should be informed. In early March of the new year, 1846, Catlin was moved to write to the editors of the popular *Niles' National Register*, urging them to spread the word beyond the pages of their own publication, warning others who might contemplate bringing Indians abroad.

Niles' reminded its readers first of how "the practice of seducing the natives from our forests, for the purpose of exhibiting them as curiosities in Europe, attracted the attention of our government some thirty or forty years ago." Since then laws had been passed against shipping Indians overseas for commercial exploitation, only to be broken. Although he had himself been one of the lawbreakers, Catlin's singular honesty and professional reputation made him an exception: "No party of Indians for the last century has visited Europe for such an object with greater advantages, or been received there with more distinction, or were exhibited with more eclat than the party referred to by Mr. C.," before letting, "Mr. C.," provide in harrowing detail, arguments "to discourage any other parties of Indians from coming to England or France for the purpose of exhibition."

Leaving the moral high ground to his editors, Catlin instead opened his ledger to the page recording the recent financial disaster, the Ojibwa's

> detention in Brussels was more than a month, and my outlays
> for them since they left Paris have been more than $1,000. My

expenses in exhibiting the parties of Iowas and Ojibbeway Indians in England and France . . . during the last year, have been
quite equal to all the receipts, besides the loss of a year's time,
with much toil and a great deal of anxiety; and in that time I
have had the distress and paid the expenses of six funerals
among them.

Although he kept on working through the early spring, at home to
the cheerful rat-tat-tat of his own little drummer boy, he had become
disabused of fantasies related to the French king's patronage. After a
long silence he wrote to his irascible friend and sometime patron, Sir
Thomas Phillipps, on February 17, 1846, bringing him up to date on
Clara's death six months earlier but also proudly informing him of the
current—if temporary—home of his collection: "ordered into the Louvre, by the King, where it has been for 6 weeks, exposed to the view
of the Royal family solely." Hoping to rouse Sir Thomas's competitive
juices, he added that "the King made 4 visits to it, and has been so
much pleased as to order me to copy 15 pictures (enlarging them to
double size) and which I am now painting in an attilier [*sic*] offered
me in the Louvre." Instead of presenting himself as the Michelangelo
to Louis-Philippe's Lorenzo de' Medici, he added drily, "The compliment has been a very high one, but what the *emolument* will be I don't
yet know: probably, like all *honour*, it will be a costly article." Another
honor, if no more profitable, provided welcome validation from his
scientific peers: Later that spring Catlin was elected into the Société
Ethnologique de Paris.

More immediately, he had to move quickly on several fronts to
raise cash. He asked for Phillipps's help in selling the Indian Gallery
to the British Museum, or to an aristocratic collector, at the suggested asking price of $35,000. This seems to have been an allusion
to an offer Catlin recalled receiving for the collection at Egyptian
Hall in the course of a visit from "a Col. Fawcett (I think that was

the name)" who told the artist that "he was authorized by a noble Duke, to offer me 7000 pounds for it, which I declined. I would take this sum for it now," George concluded. It's been suggested that this "recollection" could have been a veiled offer to Phillipps himself, but given George's open pleas for loans from his friend, using his pictures as collateral, or for special commissions in return for cash "down payment," it's hard to see why he would be so coy about such an important sale now.

In July 1846, he would turn fifty. What did he have to show for the praise, the tours, the exhibitions and collections, the royal invitations and anointment by fellow artists and now, by a distinguished professional association of ethnologists? Only debts, with nothing set aside for old age, and no certainty of earnings from his present labors.

He had heard reports from home that the last fiscal year had ended with the U.S. Treasury holding a surplus of $12 million, and he recalled his own explanation for the government's rejection of his Indian Gallery in 1839: Continuing fallout from the Panic of 1837 had perpetuated a fear of "frivolous" spending on the arts, tarred with the dread word "speculation," and spooking swing votes on House resolutions of 1838, 1839, and 1840 with provisions for the government to acquire his collection. Now he felt a resurgence of his old optimism. His stars seemed to be moving into alignment, and his mind turned to renewing efforts in Washington for government purchase that he still believed to be within his gasp.

On April 21 Catlin dispatched a memorandum to Congress, reiterating his earlier offers of $65,000 for his collection: Drawing on the familiarity of some congressmen with his Indian Gallery when it had been exhibited in Washington in 1838, he was able to point to an expanded number of works; forty life-size mannequins, their heads modeled on actual chiefs, bodies used to display the costumes and weaponry, along with two tons of fossils and mineral specimens from the West. The latter collection could form the nucleus of his proposed

Museum of Mankind. With two museums for the cost of one, the same price was a bargain.

Now, at the command of the king of France, the Indian Gallery was housed in the Louvre, he reminded Congress. Lest his seven expatriate years be viewed as unpatriotic, Catlin reminded the legislators that he had only relocated abroad in the hopes of making a living from his collection while awaiting a more favorable outcome from the narrowly contested failed effort of 1839, which took place just prior to his departure.

He had been prepared to sacrifice for his patriotism. Claiming to have subsidized his own labors during these years in the amount of about twenty thousand dollars, he had rejected "several very respectable offers" for his work in Europe. His art belonged to—and thus in—America and he had been only waiting for the propitious day when the artist and his elected representatives joined together in this belief to give his work a permanent home.

On June 5 Catlin's memorandum was presented to the Senate, and three days later to the House, where it was referred to the Committee on the Library. In his seven years in the desert of exile, with its attendant griefs and burdens, Catlin had learned to seek the right kind of help from diverse expatriate communities: sympathetic artists, businessmen, and diplomats. This time he had orchestrated a campaign on his own behalf with three well-timed petitions (one presented before Catlin's own memorandum had been introduced) signed by "Fifteen American citizens living in London." Identifying themselves as defenders of the American past, with "a deep interest in the collection, preservation, and protection of works of art, of literature, records, and whatever may illustrate the early history of our country," the signatories declared that Catlin's Indian Gallery was the perfect example of a national treasure at risk of sale, dispersal, or worst of all, finding a more appreciative home abroad: They had heard that this artist's American Museum bade fair to become the jewel in the Historical

Gallery of Versailles. Against such a loss, the collection should first return to American ground and ownership, with the artist retained as steward to "enlarge and perfect it." Two weeks later Lewis Cass, now a Democratic senator from Michigan, presented a document signed by eleven artists living in Paris: Signers included the star of federal patronage, John Vanderlyn, and such reassuringly establishment figures as William Morris Hunt and John Kensett. The portraitist George P. A. Healy, a friend from the Catlins' London days, and Samuel F. B. Morse sent separate supporting letters.

Dazzled by royals, perhaps, Catlin never mentions those artist compatriots and friends living and working in France at this time. Nonetheless the Paris petitioners raised a stirring chorus of peer solidarity, making the case that "interesting to our countrymen generally" as Catlin's collection was, "it is absolutely necessary to American artists." "As the Vatican was to the Italian, artifacts of the ancients Gauls in the Louvre to the French, and the armor and weapons in the Tower of London to the British, so Catlin's Indian Gallery was to the American historical painter, an invaluable repository of material."

A Whig senator from Delaware and future secretary of state, John M. Clayton, introduced a petition signed by fifty-two artists from New York City, including once again Asher B. Durand, who as president of the National Academy of Design was best placed to make the case, as phrased by Clayton, that acquisition of Catlin's lifework was "a matter of high national importance" as it would reverse the Republic's disgraceful record of failed responsibility to the arts.

On July 24, two days before Catlin's fiftieth birthday, the Library Committee reported back in favor of purchase. The members endorsed all the arguments put forth by the petitioners, both artists and other citizens, adding its own tribute to the "Americanness of his work." Indeed the "Americanness" of the legislators rang out in the committee's assurance that the nation would be getting the deal of the century: Within a few years of Catlin's return home with his collection, he would have completed the work needed to "double it in value and extent."

Most promising of all, a bill had just been passed by the House of Representatives establishing the Smithsonian Institution. Included was the institution's charge of providing "for the increase and diffusion of knowledge among men"; it was also to include a gallery of art. "No productions, your committee believe, at present exist, more appropriate to this gallery than those of Mr. Catlin, or of equal importance." The committee further recommended that the freshly enacted bill establishing the Smithsonian be amended to meet Catlin's asking price, $65,000, payable to the artist in annual installments of $10,000.

For once, every piece was in place: Support—political and cultural—was assured from all the strategic redoubts. Nothing was missing this time except the motor: Congress failed to act before the session ended in May.

In the end, however, it was more than inertia or even philistinism that killed his latest campaign—the best planned and orchestrated to date. This time he was also the victim of colliding ironies. In the following session of Congress the determined Senator Clayton tried another tack. Having failed to amend the Smithsonian bill to include the purchase of Catlin's collection, he now proposed another omnibus amendment making provisions for the government's diplomatic and civil expenses. This vaguely worded proviso could embrace a "Welcome Home" to Catlin and the purchase of his collection, providing only that the Smithsonian could "find a place" for the six hundred paintings, which, he hardly needed to remind his colleagues, "had found unqualified approbation" in Paris.

But not at home. Senator James D. Westcott, Jr., of Florida declared that he "would not vote a cent" for portraits of savages, but the particular savage he had in mind was Osceola, hero of the Seminole Wars, smoked out of hiding before being imprisoned by the U.S. government, and murderer of Senator Westcott's Florida settlers. It was these white martyrs who should be immortalized in the new Smithsonian, not a lawless Seminole.

Osceola had died hours after Catlin painted him, but he had already become a folk hero, the subject of epic poems, a political cause célèbre, and a moral stain on the national character. The artist who exploited his death agony for profit became part of this dark narrative. Now the purchase of Catlin's collection was, in effect, subverted for the opposite reason: In the very act of taking Osceola's final likeness, "Indian-lover Catlin" had painted himself into the wrong corner yet again.

IN PARIS HIS rich acquaintances, collectors, or those artists and bureaucrats with court connections appeared to be doing better than ever, but what he saw in the streets told a different story; disastrous potato and wheat harvests of 1845 and 1846 had wrought havoc in the French economy, urban as well as rural: Class hatred and revolutionary rumblings were evidence of the widening chasm between rich and poor. Blame, along with popular rage, targeted Louis-Philippe's favorite minister, François Guizot, whose support of a free-market economy was his religion, and whose credo, *Enrichissez-vous* ("Get Rich!") came inevitably to stand for Louis-Philippe and his entire regime.

In pursuit of patrons among newly minted millionaires, Catlin failed, but not for want of trying. The rich bankers and speculators of the period sought flattering portraits of wives and mistresses, or sexed-up Greek mythology—not American "*sauvages.*"

George divided his time between his home studio and the Louvre, finishing the king's "honorary" commission and beginning work on the La Salle paintings. Intended for the Marine Gallery at Versailles, the series, eventually to number twenty-nine paintings, had the official backing of the royal arts establishment and supposedly, a more collaborative role for Louis-Philippe. Artist and patron together chose the scenes that Catlin would illustrate from the king's own copy of La

Salle's *Voyages*. It is not clear that a fee was ever agreed upon for this commission either; still, the involvement of royal officialdom and the evaluation of three thousand dollars that George later placed upon the collection (one hundred dollars a picture) suggests a more professional arrangement this time.

THROUGH THE HARSH winter and icy spring of 1847, Catlin worked, cocooned by a new sense of contentment: "The days and nights and weeks and months of my life were passing on whilst my house rang with the constant notes of my little girls and my dear little 'Tambour Major,' producing a glow of happiness in my life . . . which I never before had attained to." But in late April the silence of the sickroom muffled all happy noise. His eldest daughter, Libby, was sent home from school with fever and an inflammation of the lungs "so violent," her father wrote, that he was "in great distress for her safety." Her two sisters fell sick with the same illness and, along with their brother, were ordered to bed, where they remained for the next month. The girls recovered, but Catlin's adored only son and namesake, his "Tambour Major," died on June 1 of "dropsey of the brain."

He had always been a frail child, and there is something haunting and haunted about him. He seems more motherless than his older sisters, as he follows their father into his studio, solitary and silent but for his constant drumming. Georgie had suffered two attacks of "brain fever" earlier, suggesting seizures or possibly a tubercular meningitis that ultimately proved fatal.

No one else would know the absolute love Catlin felt for his son or the depth of his pain—"my whole soul," he wrote, "was set upon this dear and pretty boy," his "lovely flower." Two weeks passed and the child's body was still at sea, bound for burial next to his mother, and Catlin was still too stricken to tell his daughters. He seemed to feel a guilt he had sloughed off at Clara's death, one month short of two years ago. He had "introduced an influenza into the house"; or he had failed to seek specialized medical advice for the boy's earlier symptoms; it may be that the child's health had deteriorated during George's long absence in Belgium, and his father, distracted by other worries, had failed to notice.

Like the Victorian dynamo he also was, Catlin retreated into work, flogging himself to finish the La Salle pictures; of equal importance, he had to keep M. de Cailleux happy; the Louvre director and dispenser of royal arts patronage was not known to be an enthusiast of the artist or of his project. By midsummer the *Voyages of La Salle* were sufficiently advanced for the artist to give Cailleux a private showing, when he also felt confident enough to announce its completion by early 1848.

Whatever he may have expected in payment at the end was still six months away. Money was tighter than ever, with recent medical, funerary, and transportation bills added to his other expenses. He made a trip to London, on October 4, when he wrote to Sir Thomas Phillipps from Gregory's Hotel, telling him of Georgie's death (Clara's passing, on July 28, 1845, is never mentioned in Catlin's surviving letters). Every thought of his child racked his heart with fever. He laid open his grief to Phillipps, he wrote, as he could do only with one who was also a father. But George never grasped the fathomless depth of Sir Thomas's ego. Phillipps replied that he had experienced the same loss: When his daughter married without seeking his permission, she was the same as dead to him. Whatever he had hoped to find in London, from Sir Thomas or others, George returned to Paris empty handed.

At the end of February 1848, three days before he was to show the twenty-seven LaSalle paintings to Louis-Phillippe, the monarchy was toppled and the king, along with most of the royal household, fled to England.

In later years Catlin liked to compare his flight from Paris to that of the monarch himself: He had just time to seize his daughters and flee for his life to London. In fact, with his ties to the court and his works hanging in a private viewing room of the Louvre, he was warned, with ample time to move his girls and household to England a week before the 1848 Revolution. Returning to Paris six weeks later, Catlin found his worst trial to be moving his collection from the warehouse where he had prudently stored it more than a year earlier, and accompanying the vast assemblage of paintings and objects through a city that had become an obstacle course. His progress was slowed by barricades constructed of the famous paving stones, tree trunks, furniture, and broken crockery—everything that could impede or halt the movement of authority—until they had made their way to the Channel and safety. Only Catlin's paintings of La Salle were left behind. Crated by a faithful museum functionary, the evangelizing French explorer—saving souls and staking royal title to New France in the wilderness of Canada—was spared. Fortunate to be out of sight of enraged men and women—bent upon vengeance, slashing their way through palaces, private houses, and museums, stepping over corpses of workers and police, royals and revolutionaries, piled in the streets—La Salle waited, in pristine state, for Catlin's return.

28

"A THING BELONGING TO US"

In Paris, Catlin had felt tossed between extremes of brilliance and darkness. *Grandeurs et misères*—the title of Balzac's cycle about the rise and fall of courtesans, published in these same years—could apply to an artist-courtier.

Still, he had hobnobbed with kings and pashas, and his paintings had been exalted by critics, poets, novelists, and journalists in a city where opinions mattered as nowhere else. Baudelaire, the greatest critic of the age, had placed Catlin next to Veronese as an inventor of landscape. How many self-taught American artists could claim such company?

Now the drabness of London in February enveloped him like the fog he had managed to forget. At least he had fled Paris in good company. "By the way, I am going in a few days to visit the poor old King & Queen" he wrote airily to Sir Thomas Phillipps. "What do you think they will say? I can't imagine."

In most ways, though, his life had contracted. When he returned to Paris at the beginning of March to retrieve his Indian Gallery, he found that, six weeks after the Revolution, the main thoroughfares were still barricaded with rubble and the railroads destroyed.

Whatever he had saved toward relocation was fast disappearing. Back in London, he moved with the girls and their governess first to a house in the Edgeware Road on the margins of suburbia, while he looked for a more central location. Early in 1849 he found a modest suite of rooms at 6 Waterloo Place,* actually the termination of Nash's Regent Street and just off Pall Mall. The elegant Georgian facade of their new home hid small dingy rooms that had to serve as living quarters, studio, and exhibition space. For the latter he had no choice but to charge admission—one shilling—supposing that anyone still wanted to come and see his work.

In Catlin's four years of absence, his earlier London social world had moved on without him. The Hon. Charles A. Murray, his erstwhile friend who provided introductions to everyone who counted, had been appointed minister to Persia. In the hopes of exploiting his Old World adventures, Catlin sweated a two-volume sequel to *Letters and Notes.* The new work, *Adventures of the Ojibbeway and Ioway Indians . . . Being Notes of Eight Years' Travels and Residence in Europe . . .* was almost unanimously panned as a potboiler but sold respectably. Trying to be helpful (when it didn't cost him anything) Sir Thomas Phillipps urged Catlin to do a second volume of the beautiful *North American Indian Portfolio.* For once good sense prevailed. He was still paying off creditors for the first one, which had not earned back its expenses in sales.

He had neither money nor time to make a home—normally a wife's role—and the girls, older now, needed a mother who could smooth their welcome in the proper circles. Where most widowers would have sought to re-create a family, Catlin does not seem to have cultivated friendships, or any other liaisons, with women.

In Paris, Catlin had been hampered by his inability to learn French; this obstacle was almost certainly related to a more serious problem

---

* Now the Sofitel St. James's, number 6, along with two adjoining houses, has retained its original facade.

whose worst symptoms emerged in London. Catlin's hearing had
deteriorated. He mentions only suffering from tinnitus, a frequent
consequence of the influenza from which he had recovered, but the
deafness worsened.

Loss of hearing increased his isolation. Once, George's lively conversation had burnished his celebrity and he was a prized guest at London's best tables. Now the effort to disguise his deafness made social
life an ordeal for him and awkward for hosts and fellow guests.

Still, his optimism seemed indestructible, surviving revolution,
financial blows, and repeated rejection: By the new year of 1849, he
had readied yet another campaign in Washington. He amassed a vast
dossier of previously submitted documents: memoranda, letters, petitions, the favorable Library Committee report to the last Congress,
plus a new up-to-date catalog. He enlisted an old friend and longtime
Washington insider to make certain that, this time, he would not fail.

An ordained Presbyterian minister, Ralph Randolph Gurley, had
never led a congregation; His true religion was the cause of black
repatriation to Africa. Settling in Washington fifty years before, he
devoted his life to the American Colonization Society and its founding goals: the emancipation of the slaves and their repatriation to an
African nation of their own—Liberia. In principle this was a separate-
but-equal plan carried to a geographical extreme: Slaves or free, the
Colonization argument held, blacks could never rise in a white America; only within their own culture could they escape the demeaning
perception of their inferiority. Whatever the high-flown rhetoric,
the reality could not be disguised: To separate meant to get rid of
unwanted people of color.

For all that divided Catlin and Gurley in the actualities of sepa-
ratism and removal, they were united by a romantic primitivism: a
determination to run the clock in preserving the unique culture of
the savage races before these disappeared. They could not envision
assimilation without destruction. A further bond was Gurley's admira-

tion for Catlin. He was a true believer in the man and his art. Known and respected on both sides of the contentious slavery problem, Gurley appeared as the man of the moment to steer Catlin's fresh effort in Congress.

Soon after seeing the Indian Gallery in Egyptian Hall in the early 1840s, Gurley took pen in hand: "I should be mortified beyond expression could I believe there was a single enlightened man in this country who would not rejoice to see Congress add these memorials of the Indian race to the National Museum," he wrote. For the rest of the decade Gurley discreetly lobbied his political connections. Then, rolling up his sleeves, he took on the clerical donkeywork for Catlin's 1849 campaign; the artist's own petition, along with lists and letters from sponsors, are all in his friend's handwriting.

Besides his confidence in Gurley's politically savvy support, Catlin drew hope from the triumphalist wave of success the Republic was now riding at home. While Europe was routing monarchies and shedding more blood in deciding who represented the "People," America was vanquishing all obstacles to the course of empire. Boundaries with Britain had been established peacefully in Oregon at the 49th parallel. The Mexican War, in which Catlin's beloved friend Joe Chadwick had given his life, had been settled through immense land concessions: The prize being the annexation of Texas, vast swaths of California, and the Southwest up to the "Mormon Zion" in the Great Basin—a booty of half a million square miles—and below the Rio Grande into Mexico itself. Catlin's optimism conflated a successful expansionist policy with an expansive view of the arts as national patrimony.

Like many others, he failed to see the serpent of slavery coiled and ready to strike within the new Eden of freshly annexed territories; battlegrounds-in-waiting, they would be the political spoils of either slave or free states. Deadly fissures widened beneath the miles of "free soil"—the name of the new third party uniting those opposed to slavery in the expanded nation.

He picked up further Whig support in early August 1849, in the form of a joint resolution. But despite fresh eloquence from the Library Committee, the session ended with no action taken.

Refusing to give up, Catlin regrouped over the long London summer. In late August 1848, he had written Phillipps, asking for a loan of six hundred dollars, offering 6, 7 or even 10 percent interest, with the Indian Gallery as security. In Catlin's smoke-and-mirrors calculations, telling the U.S. government first that his collection was already "encumbered" and thus in danger of being lost to his own country, and at the same time that it was "*conditionally* sold in England, would be the thing to cause American Congressmen & the Press to make the proper move."

Phillips, the "*conditional*" buyer of his tale, turned him down, but the other piece of his representation to Congress was most likely all too true; the Indian Gallery was "encumbered" to a lender or lenders unknown.

Four days into the New Year found him firing off another letter to Congress, "the last [I] could possibly make," he insisted, but there is a cocky tone to his threat. Seven weeks later, on February 27, 1849, Senator William Dayton, a Whig of New Jersey, moved for an amendment to the Civil and Diplomatic Appropriation Bill—the same under-the-radar ploy that had been tried earlier—inserting five thousand dollars as the first payment to Catlin of a projected fifty-thousand-dollar purchase price of the collection. Probably to the senator's surprise, the proposal sparked spirited debate.

Following Dayton's speech supporting purchase, Daniel Webster rose to speak. The hero of two generations of Catlins, Webster was still a Whig power to reckon with; within two years he would add secretary of state to his public offices. Now he laid the case for federal patronage of the arts on principle before moving to Catlin as exhibit A in his argument: "I do think that the preservation in this country of such a gallery as Catlin's pictures is an important public policy," he declared. "A policy contributing to our knowledge, but more important, our self-knowledge as a nation . . . I go for this as an American subject; as a thing belonging to us—to our history; to the race whose lands we till, and over whose obscure graves and bones we tread every day."

Geography, in this case, was destiny: Dissent came from southern state's rights advocates, fearful that expansion of the federal presence would act as a wedge for ever-greater control from Washington—and the diminishing power of slaveholders: "I perhaps should have felt less interest in this matter had it stood alone," warned Representative Robert M. T. Hunter, of Virginia. "But I think I have seen evidences . . . of a design to commit this Government, by precedent, at least, to a general encouragement of the Arts and Sciences."

For Catlin the most heartbreaking words came from Senator Jefferson Davis of Mississippi, whose presidency of the Confederacy still lay in his future, but whose past, as an officer of the regiment attached to Fort Gibson, bound him to Catlin as only extreme circumstances can do. Davis had been twenty-six and a freshly commissioned dragoon officer when he waved off into Comanche country the doomed expedition from which so few men returned; among the lucky ones were Catlin and Joe Chadwick. Davis now recalled "for the record" Catlin's bravery, the risk he took with his talent, laid humbly in the service of his authentic subject, and not a studio portrait: "He has painted the Indian as he lives, unfettered by art, untamed and [not] degraded by the contact of the white man."

But it was Davis who also spearheaded the defeat of the proposal for purchase; generally he seconded Hunter's objections, but his emphasis was on the scale of Catlin's collection. Too big to be "displayed in any room, it would require a gallery, an institution for fine arts." Citing the "departure from the simple republican character of the Government," Davis voiced fears that the purchase of Catlin's work would open the floodgates to a new and radical era when "Congress becomes the patron of art, the caterer to the tastes and refined pleasures as well as the law-makers of the people."

In the event, Davis's exhortation ended the debate: The amendment was defeated by a vote of 25 to 23. The close count encouraged Senator Dayton to try again the following evening, but by then, fears raised by the Southern speakers had spread. The second and final vote dramatized the finality of defeat: 21 to 15.

Not even George could turn fantasy into fact, or talk about liens on his collection as "conditional" sales: Brinksmanship was irrelevant if the votes weren't there. Finances were desperate. As Catlin owned no other property, the collection was his only asset and the only collateral he could offer to borrow money. Like a house topheavy with mortgages, he began to encumber his collection "in earnest." His art would never belong to him again.

ON MAY 8, 1849, two months after this defeat, Catlin transferred twenty paintings from his collection to Sir Thomas Phillipps. Four years and many due notes later, in 1853, George reclaimed the pictures, but not for cash—which he never had in hand: Shrewd and obsessive collector that he was, Phillipps exacted payment "in kind"; exchanging art he already owned for new commissions, he avoided extending further credit and the likelihood of a further series of defaults. He extracted the commitment of fifty copies in oil of works by Catlin that he, Phillipps, would choose, in specified dimensions of eleven by fourteen inches. But other anonymous British lenders took a traditional percentage of the collection. Either way one hundred pounds, more than ninety-nine hundred dollars in today's terms, plus dribbles of unspecified cash disappeared with alarming speed. He needed a reliable source of income, a big killing—or both.

Then, in 1848, President James K. Polk's address to Congress officially confirmed a wild rumor. Panning in a stream, Capt. John Sutter, a prospector, saw gold nuggets glinting among the pebbles. This was the beginning of a strike of boundless yellow treasure. The gold rush was on. Soon the forty-niners themselves formed a human stream, clawing their way west in any conveyance they could find. Most would be doomed to failure and worse poverty than they had left behind.

George Catlin was the perfect victim: "I wish you or I had a deed for a hundred or two acres in the gold mines of California," he wrote wistfully to Phillipps. Then the offer arrived. Better than acreage, he would soon become a paid agent for two recently merged companies, the principal ones promoting English settlement in Texas: the Universal Emigration and Colonization Company and the United States Land Company.

When touring the Midlands with Catlin, the Ojibwa had noticed Manchester's huge darkened "mansions" that turned out to be shuttered factories. The lecture that launched Catlin's dubious new career was delivered to wide-eyed workingmen in Manchester's Free Trade Hall on January 5, 1849, and was called "The Valley of the Mississippi and its Advantages to Emigration, with an Account of the Gold Regions of California." For live and painted Indians, Catlin now substituted a huge map of the American West and, using an authoritative pointer, directed his listeners' gaze to those regions, as unfamiliar to his audiences as they were to George, where gold had been found. Should anyone present wish to go, he was available to advise them.

A voyager in imagination as much as in fact, Catlin was a travel artist: From where he had actually been and what he had seen there, it was the smallest leap to describe a place unknown to him as though he were long familiar with its every flowering shrub. So from the meanders of the Sacramento and San Joaquin Rivers, site of the "gold diggings," his pointer now moved eastward, circling the region between the Great Salt Lake, the Sierra Nevada, and the Rockies. Giving his audience to believe that his horses' hooves had galloped this same route, he declared, based upon firsthand observation, that far from the arid desert others had described, this was "beautifully variegated, fine and fertile" land. To confirm the truth of his pitch, he had seen Iowa and Comanche Indians, wearing "lumps of gold" for necklaces, gathered, they told him, "seven days' ride west." Only a bilious fever had prevented their accompanying him to the site.

Catlin also imparted one piece of practical advice: It behooved his audience to think of emigrating as a group or "colony" in order to benefit from the economies of scale that his employers dangled before the unwary. In a northern Texas carpeted with wildflowers, he would direct them to where they could "together obtain, at half the cost to individuals, a large tract of good land, with undoubted title" for five shillings an acre. A fertile farmland upon which to live and raise families, it was there that they would find "the real, true and best gold region of the North American continent."

The showman's zest reemerged, adorned with the full-fledged skills of the slickest "land shark," denounced in editorials everywhere in America for encouraging the naïve—or desperate—to part with their savings and set out for "the Big Rock Candy Mountain" that "turns out to be either a sand-hill or a swamp." For his success in recruiting "colonists" following his lectures through the British Midlands in 1850, Catlin was promoted to superintendent of the merged companies' Texas department.

In his defense, George, as desperate as his audiences, proved to be just as credulous. Hired to lead the first party of colonists sailing from Liverpool, on September 3, for a fee (on arrival) of fifteen hundred dollars, he resigned just before departure under stormy circumstances. He had also invested twelve hundred dollars of his own in the business, which collapsed within a year. He never recovered a penny.

HE WAS BANKRUPT, and despite evidence that he believed his own fairy tales of new goldfields, his reputation in England suffered fur-

ther. If Catlin expected sympathy from Phillipps, his patron and
creditor clearly saw the recent disaster as yet another example of
Catlin's poor judgment: "I am extremely sorry to hear of your bad
success," he wrote, "but I always thought it was a wild goose chase."
The cycle of grandiose dreams floated by deeper debt justified Phillipps in his insistence upon repayment—no matter how degrading
the terms: With no possibility of repaying his one hundred pound
loan from his patron, George had little choice but to copy away at
two pounds a picture, plus a few shillings for the frame and canvas.
He tried to lure cash from Phillipps by lofting still more grandiose
"partnerships." For a new loan of five hundred pounds, he could
finally publish the long-awaited sequel to the *North American Indian
Portfolio*; from the sure-fire profit from sales, he would first repay the
one hundred pounds he still owed, and next redeem himself from
the toil of copying the fifty pictures still part of his debt. Thus lib-
erated from forced labor, he could personally assure the sale of his
collection to the government by going to Washington and building
a two-hundred-foot-long temporary structure in which to display his
entire collection. In this setting or in the halls of Congress, he could
lobby representatives to a triumphant change of heart and vote. Phillipps declined, replying, no doubt truthfully, that he was himself in
debt over his head with costly new purchases of books and had no
ready cash at hand.

There was no returning to the Indian Gallery—with either live or
painted exhibits, Indian "shows" were passé. And with George's out-
standing debts, it was impossible to raise money toward new publications, no matter how bright their potential for future profits. In those
dire straits he succumbed to that most terrible despair described by
Dante—the remembrance of past happiness. Recalling the talk he had
given—to great excitement and much applause—ten years earlier at
the Royal Institution, he now relaunched his idea for a floating ethnological exhibit.

In March 1851, before the London Ethnological Society, he delivered an embellished form of his earlier pitch for a Museum of Mankind. His latest form of grandiosity would, in the eyes of its inventor, redeem the small-time showman who had once shilled for Barnum. Now his Museum would be, literally, showboated in a two-hundred-foot steamer and feature a panorama of native peoples, displaying the scale upon which both invention and salesmanship could flourish.

Catlin's fantasy had something of a "Flying Dutchman" (or ultimate escape artist) appeal, with the museum reconceived as a two-way educational project—albeit a vastly entertaining one for all concerned. Western visitors would experience aboriginal peoples in the process of displaying their indigenous cultures; they would then repair to the ship's grand saloon for lectures by noted experts. The native peoples, meanwhile, would receive the civilizing benefit of a smattering of Anglo-European education from an aborigines' school.

The Ethnological Society obviously saw the Museum of Mankind for the strange hybrid it was: tourism and entertainment with tidbits of adult education to keep it serious, but whose costs—of building, maintenance, dry-docking in winter—could never hope to turn a profit for any investors. Politely calling the proposal "of great advantage to Ethnology," the society tried, in a resolution passed a month after Catlin's talk in April, to focus flatteringly on the artist's own contribution to the proposed museum: "Under any circumstances, the Council trust that Mr. Catlin's valuable *Collection* will not be lost to this country, but will find its way to the Ethnological department of the *British Museum*."

ONE CAN ONLY marvel at the energy—even if fueled by despair—that always seemed to galvanize George to greater efforts. Dressing up life-size wooden figures to resemble colorfully arrayed braves and squaws, he now bumped his way in a wagon over London cobble-stones, to Hyde Park where Paxton's Crystal Palace, the wonder of the Victorian Age, rose before him.

The first in a series of world's fairs, organized throughout the nine-teenth century to showcase the modern industry and technology of developed nations—and to foster healthy competition—the Great Exhi-bition of the Works of Industry of all Nations, or Crystal Palace Exhibi-tion, as it came to be known, was the special project of Prince Albert. The U.S. government was never persuaded of the importance of this "world stage" to publicize American manufacture, commerce, and industry. As the daily average of 43,000 visitors to Hyde Park filed past the American exhibit, they saw little more than a lonely replica of a huge golden eagle, wings spread over the most famous sculpture ever carved in America: Hiram Powers's *Greek Slave*. The London press lost no time in twitting this "desert" of a display—like the unpopulated prairie itself! Not only were the Americans thinly represented but, as the *Illustrated London News* observed, "Aboriginal manufactures were underrepre-sented throughout the exhibition."

For once Catlin's offer was quickly and gratefully accepted; his Indian models were welcomed as representing the authentic racial character of native peoples, and for the beauty and skill of their exqui-site workmanship. Catlin's brilliantly clad figures were prominently displayed on a raised catwalk spanning the exhibit, a (nearly) living advertisement for the Museum of Mankind. The press enthusiastically greeted these additions to the sparse American offerings, and their remarks boosted George's arguments for his new museum: "These Indians and their works suggest a powerful motive for making the Exhibition *permanent*." Given its educational value, such examples from Catlin's collection should be purchased and displayed in desig-nated "ethnographical galleries." From there, as Catlin was already fantasizing, it was but a short leap across a gangplank to floating gal-leries at anchor, especially for those not likely to get to Hyde Park.

As he often did, George tried to press his luck: He managed to find a group of Iroquois whose visit to the exhibition would garner still more positive press. But while the Native Americans greeted their facsimiles with whoops of recognition, a native Londoner, drunk, disorderly, and female, had climbed up to attack the costumed Indian figures, knocking them to the ground, where they lay, smashed to pieces. Angered visitors loudly berated the drunken woman, and their threatening shouts quickly attracted crowds. The bright prospects for his museum faded into silence. And once again his efforts to generate publicity had left him poorer. George was forced to repeat the pleas he had first broached to Phillipps in July: He desperately needed five to six hundred pounds. "I *must* keep my collection together," he wrote. In fact Catlin's collection *was* together materially; in terms of ownership, however, it was already so encumbered as collateral that he could no longer borrow against it, or for that matter, against any of his notes. He had exhausted his credit—in England as nowhere else, a dire situation.

Another unexpected blow had fallen in January 1851. The Treasury Lords informed Catlin that the exemption from duties on works of art granted to his Indian Gallery would extend only through the next exhibition season, "at the expiration of which the collection will be taken from this country." The collection had to leave England or incur enormous duties. A sale of the entire Indian Gallery was the only hope of retaining ownership; with his paper worthless, any future loans would require the transfer in whole or in part to the lender.

For the last time he banged on Congress's door, beginning once again the melancholy gathering of bona fides, affidavits, earlier petitions, and favorable reports from the Library Committee, accompanied by Catlin's own letters to each member of that legislative body; he showered Daniel Webster with paper, not realizing that the aged gentleman was secretary of state and no longer the great Whig orator of the Senate. As Catlin knew, Webster, too, had seen his career clouded by debt and dubious transactions, and he poured out his desperation to what he hoped was a sympathetic listener: "I have been led into unfortunate speculations which have brought my affairs to a most trying and alarming state," he wrote to Webster on April 4, 1852. As always, he characterized himself as a passive victim, but he also suggests losses beyond those he incurred in the Texas colonizing scheme. "I actually tremble for the security of my works. I am fighting at this moment with the most unfeeling wretches, which the civilized world I have just learned is made up of, to protect my Collection for my country."

Barely had Catlin launched this last campaign when his worst fears became fact: His creditors (moneylenders by trade certainly among them) got wind of the rumor that he planned to leave for America with his collection. Once on the high seas, both the borrower and any possibility of repayment or repossession would have slipped their grasp. All the authorities needed was a hint of a planned getaway. Bailiffs arrived at Waterloo Place. Catlin was taken to jail and his collection (but for the contents of a small separate studio) seized and put up at auction, handbills with the particulars being posted all over London.

His next letter to Webster, two weeks later, was headed "Queen's Bench *prison!*" There was neither reason for—or possibility of—discretion: "I am filled with sorrow and shame that I must address you from such a place as this—but so it is, and I am only induced to confess it in the hope that something may yet be done to save my Collection, the labour and the ambition of my life."

He enclosed a placard from the Auctioneer, where "advertised to be sold" was Catlin's collection, "in the hands of and at the mercy of, [his] creditors": "I have not the power to save it—but the Congress of my Country has, provided their action is quick. I believe the sale can be delayed some 5, or 6 Weeks. And within that time it can be saved."

Catlin's evangelical tone confirms that he had come to see his art, in the sense of "my Collection," as something separate from the artist. Purchased or not, "my Collection" and "my Country" were one.

> If nothing is voted for *me*, for Heaven's *Sake*, for our *Country's honour's sake*, let the Collection be redeemed and kept together. . . . I have never had an office, or a perquisite or a shilling in any way from our Government, nor asked it—I will give them the works of my life if they will pay my liabilities, and save them— e.g. if they are not willing to vote me the price I have asked for my Collection.
>
> You can imagine me *unhappy*.

HE DID NOT have to spend long in debtor's prison. On hearing of his arrest, his brother-in-law Dudley Gregory seems to have booked the first available passage, arriving sometime at the end of April or beginning of May. Before sailing, Gregory, possibly together with other well-off American friends, wired the funds required for payment of George's most pressing debts, setting in motion the bureaucratic machinery to expedite his earliest possible release.

Gregory is often portrayed as the Victorian heavy, swooping down upon Waterloo Place and, in the presence of their weeping father, bundling his little nieces back to Jersey City and respectability. In fact the brothers-in-law had always gotten along well; the Reverend Gurley was a friend of both men, and Dudley Gregory had been a partner in business ventures with Richard Catlin—George's only successful brother. They would have discussed the girls' future, their need for a stable home, religious education (The Dudley Gregorys were pillars of their church and the parents of fourteen children), and the opportunity to make good marriages. Threatened constantly by financial disaster, by obsessive anxiety about losing his collection, by the need to pull up stakes and start over, Catlin's life had been a series of crises, ending with his stay in prison. It's easier to see their father's relief in the girls' assured future as one less worry in his distracted, chaotic existence.

The collection was safe—along with the artist, for the time being. But there were other creditors out there—the "harpies," whom Clara had so early and presciently identified—waiting for notes to fall due, when they too would pounce. Moving to the Continent did not carry the same risks as leaving for America. And with the girls gone, even the pokey rooms at Waterloo Place suddenly seemed too big. On May 8 Catlin was writing to Daniel Webster from Paris, where he was lying low "for a few days 'till I can hear the result of my last application to Congress." A free man—in all senses—he girded for battle—yet again, exhorting Webster to see through with him this last push. "And in the mean time, I am endeavouring to obtain an audience of the Prince Napoleon with the view of offering him my Collection in case the Congress do nothing effectual for me."

29

MAGICAL MYSTERY TOURS

F rance had long been the favored refuge for the better class of English fleeing creditors and debtor's prison. Boulogne harbored a colony of Regency aristocrats who could never go home. Beau Brummell, the immaculate dandy, had died in Caën in 1840, a drunken, disheveled pauper.

Catlin had no interest in joining a community of outcasts. He may have lost everything, but he was also traveling lighter than he had ever done, and he felt stirrings of his old buoyancy. In London the bailiffs had seized the entire contents of Waterloo Place, except for the separate studio where, using a camera lucida,[*] George had managed to make images of some of the Indian portraits before they were taken away, and had begun copying the others from memory. The collection itself, the six hundred paintings and countless marvels of Indian manufacture, was packed and waiting for the auctioneer's hammer to fall, dispersing his lifework to the four winds.

---

[*] An optical device used as a drawing aid by artists, it projects the subject being viewed upon the surface where the artist is drawing. The resulting process becomes a form of tracing.

Then, out of Russia, there rode to the rescue a self-made millionaire, art collector, and fellow Pennsylvanian. Joseph Harrison's passion was steam—the source of power rendered most visible in paintings of the nineteenth century's favorite structure: the railway station. Harrison had been experimenting since he was a boy growing up on the wrong side of the tracks in Philadelphia, and the locomotive was his laboratory. He trained as a mechanical engineer, and by the time he was thirty, Harrison's entrepreneurial genius had made him one of the richest industrialists in his native city, but his fame had spread far beyond America. The vastness of Russia made it inevitable that the czar would be eager to entice and enrich those whose skill lay in bridging distances—moving people and goods faster and more economically across thousands of frozen miles. Now, in 1852, at the age of forty-two, Harrison was returning home after almost a decade spent overseeing the design and construction of the first Russian rolling stock—the cars and locomotives for the railway line that would link St. Petersburg to Moscow. Lavishly rewarded by Czar Nicholas, Harrison was passing through London on his way back to America. Along the way he was burnishing his claim to return in glory as Philadelphia's foremost patron of art—and more exceptionally, American art. Harrison had earlier joined other investors in lending Catlin money, taking a part interest in the collection as security. Then, at a creditors' meeting in London, he dramatically rose and offered to buy out all the other principal holders of liens on Catlin's collection on the eve of its auction.

Now, with a stroke of Harrison's pen, George's largest debts were cleared, and his collection, intact down to every feather, was shipped and stored in a warehouse of the Harrison Boiler Works in Philadelphia. Though Catlin preferred to exalt Harrison as a patriot and high-minded benefactor, in fact the arrangement had more in common with a pawnshop than with philanthropy: He had simply consolidated his creditors. His debt to Harrison would continue to grow: The principal, consisting of eight to ten thousand dollars, compounded by interest. George could only redeem his collection when Harrison was paid—in full. The Indian Gallery would remain unclaimed, unpacked, and unseen (except by vermin) for the next twenty years.

For the moment, though, George felt safe, if not entirely out of danger. If he returned to England, smaller "harpies" could descend and land him back in prison. Still, being a fugitive in Paris was no terrible thing. Harrison had "saved" his life along with his collection. Catlin saw this as a sign: He would start over somewhere else; he would reinvent himself and his art. A new life beckoned.

Meanwhile there were real bills to pay in the present. So there he was, once again reduced to begging, apologizing, temporizing, and promising about funds needed and work still owed to Sir Thomas Phillipps: the fifty copies of paintings at ten dollars each (with five more for which he was to be paid a supplement) to be chosen by Sir Thomas from the collection. Haggling extracted about two dollars more apiece for frames and canvas. After complaining about the long labor involved, Catlin managed to complete the contracted work, only to have the paintings seized from his premises and through, error or oversight, shipped to New York together with Harrison's crates containing the original collection. Presumably the copies remained there when the rest had gone off to Philadelphia. Until it was safe for him to reappear in England, Catlin wrote to Phillipps, and to expedite their return in person, there was scant hope of uniting Sir Thomas with his commissioned works. This last remark was clearly intended to stir Phillipps's self-interest, if not his generosity: "I am now impatient, as I wrote you, to get away from here," George lamented, "but am out of money, and have incurred a small Bill at my hotel & some other trifling items which must be paid, and I have no means that I yet know of by which I can raise it here."

Reality ambushed his daydreams. He was trapped in the Hôtel des

Étrangers—the name alone a mockery of his fallen state: *étranger*—foreigner, stranger, alien. Comfortable and cheap, the hotel was favored by Anglo-American travelers on a budget,* but its location on the rue Tronchet, practically within sight of the place de la Madeleine where little Georgie used to play, suggests that Catlin clung to the past, needing the assurance that what he had once possessed could be his again. Still, every day he was forced to contrast his present life, a solitary fugitive hiding out in the same city where, a few streets away and a lifetime ago, he had been the head of an adoring family and breakfasted with kings.

Ultimately, however, his fear of angering the irascible Phillipps trumped Catlin's terror of a second arrest in England. Besides, for the twenty pictures that he had earlier produced for his patron, Sir Thomas owed *him* money for a change. Scraping together the francs to pay his Paris hotel bill, he made his way to Folkestone and from there managed to locate the fifty-five paintings and expedite their shipment from New York to Sir Thomas's Gloucestershire estate, Middle Hill, where they were delivered on November 7, 1853. Aware, finally, of the financial disaster that had engulfed his friend, Phillipps produced another helpful offer that would cost him nothing while enhancing his reputation as a collector: Catlin should stay at Middle Hill as lecturer in residence. His host would give him a "Bedroom Kitchen and large Room for the Gallery gratis." There he could lecture on his art, using Sir Thomas's twenty copies as examples: "Charge the moderate price of 1 shilling and I think you will get many to come & see them," Phillipps wrote. George declined. Middle Hill's infamous "squalor" and its owner's need to control everyone around him made poverty look less painful and freedom more alluring than ever. By way of apol-

---

* There were several hotels by that name, one catering to rich American travelers on the rue Vivienne, and Catlin's more modest establishment.

ogy Catlin sold Sir Thomas seventy watercolors for the fire-sale price of forty pounds.

BEFORE LEAVING PARIS, George had found a perfect escape from the hotel—a splendid refuge to read and dream that was free to visitors. The Imperial Library, home to the former royal collections, was now France's great repository of early printed books and manuscripts. He found himself drawn to illustrated accounts of early European travelers' explorations of Central and South America: From Guiana to Tierra del Fuego, it seemed that some expeditions, often including an artist, had wandered this territory.

The familiar lust for travel, for *leaving*, seized him when a new friend—never named—now appeared to gild Catlin's free-floating fantasies with tales of gold. In the mountains and riverbeds of South America lay glittering metals and precious stones in blinding, dazzling quantity. Peering at ancient maps, George's friend described the horde accumulated by Spanish miners working the Tumuc-Humac or Crystal Mountains three hundred years earlier. According to his informant, they had buried their treasure of "gold dust and nuggets" in the adobe walls of their dwellings. Massacred in their houses or driven from the country by attacking Indians, the surviving miners had fled, leaving their riches behind. Catlin was hooked: Great adventure and greater riches could both be his.

Like his father, George was always susceptible to get-rich-quick schemes—whether involving land or treasure buried beneath. With his "occupation gone" and "less than half a life, at best, before me . . . my thoughts tended toward Dame Fortune," he said. Less poetically, he confessed himself driven by "cupidity" and thus "easily led" into "one of the eccentric adventures of my chequered life"; he could even joke—later—about the chimera that drew him on: "The wealth of London was to be at my command if I succeeded."

———

THERE WAS NO gold in the Crystal Mountains, or, at least none that was ever found by George Catlin. By his account he had set out from Le Havre in May 1854, with a first stop in Havana; from there he sailed to Caracas, then, "to the Orinoco and to Demerera [today Georgetown, Guyana], ascended the Essequibo, crossed the Tumucamache [sic] . . . to the headwaters of the Trombutus, which I descended in a pirogue to the Amazon at Obidos." And that was only the first voyage.

During the years between 1854 and 1860, Catlin claimed to have made three separate trips to South and Central America—one of them included the passage from the Atlantic to the Pacific—and a journey along the Pacific Northwest of North America as far as the Aleutians.

In two books he evokes a travel itinerary of adventures more fabulous than any tale of treasure retrieved. These trips have been—and remain to this day—subject to debate. The best efforts of historians, biographers, and anthropologists to find evidence confirming his travels have proved fruitless. Catlin's trail—if there ever was one—has gone cold: There are no records of his transit through customs in port cities or his presence in remote jungle outposts. Archives—from Ostend to Buenos Aires—have been sifted for a ticket or passport, diary, or agenda of anyone who might have encountered him; there are no passenger manifests nor name scribbled in a guest book—his passage or presence more elusive than El Dorado itself. Beyond the absence of documentation, larger questions await answers: Where did a man who couldn't pay "a small Bill at [his] hotel," find the cash—or credit—to sail from Liverpool to Havana; back to Europe—to Paris and Berlin—then, back again to South America, with another return to the Continent, and from there a third and last voyage to Argentina. But that is where our pursuit begins, following a slight quicksilver shadow through the "lost years," in whose adventures—real or invented—Catlin found himself.

We have only two sources for these disputed travels, Catlin's own writings and his paintings: more than three hundred small oil sketches on Bristol board or cardboard—most of them the size of Canaletto's smaller views of Venice—like enlarged postcards. All that we know of his travels is what George Catlin shows and tells us, in exuberant, sometimes manic, or fevered prose—about where he has been and what he has seen: Mapping these journeys almost twenty years later, he sounds as breathless as if he had just returned, pursued by man-eating tribesmen—of which, in fact, he met none.

When there wasn't a glint of gold in the Crystal Mountains, Catlin claimed he was cured of "nugget fever"; but he relapsed. "From Para, I took a steamer to the Barra, to Tabatinga, and Nauta," he recalled of his second voyage:

> From Nauta I descended the Amazon to Obidos, one thousand miles in a cupola boat. . . . I afterwards ascended the Amazon again, and went on a gold-hunting expedition to the Acarai mountains. . . . Returning to the Amazon, I took a . . . steamer to Nauta, ascended the Yucayali to the Connibos, four hundred miles, and made a tour on horseback to the "Pampas del Sacramento," to the base of the eastern sierra of the Andes . . . crossed the mountains by the mail route to Lima, steamed to Panama, to San Diego and San Francisco, and took a sailing vessel to the mouth of the Columbia, to Nootka Sound, Queen Charlotte's Inlet . . . to Liska in the Aleutian Islands, to Kamskatka, to Sitka.

Then, descending the coast by steamer, the same way he had come, down the Rio Grande del Norte, "in a 'dug-out' steering with my own paddle," he arrives at Matamoros, via El Paso, a distance of some eight hundred miles.

Those who have tried to map his coordinates; to fit time frames to place-names, (including two return trips to Europe), track schedules of transport, and above all compute miles covered, have come up empty. There are the distances Catlin himself describes, in retracing for us his progress, mileage stated, and distances covered on foot, horseback, canoe, pirogue, down the Essequibo from Guiana, up the Amazon, down the Orinoco across the Tumuc-Humac and Andes. Then, hardly conceivable in its vastness (and unmentioned by most writers on Catlin), there is the immensity of the continent itself: the hundreds of thousands of square miles that separate the mere thousands Catlin claimed to have covered in his stated itineraries.

He reels off the indigenous peoples he encountered, intoxicated in the telling by their sheer numbers. Visible and invisible, hidden in the green darkness, he invokes their names—all phonetically transcribed—in an ecstatic quest for completeness. From the Amazon at Obidos, he claims to have sighted "Carribees, Gooagives, Arowaks, Wayaways, Macouchies, Tarumas, and Zurumatis." On his second descent of the Amazon alone—a distance of one thousand miles—he has seen "thirty of the one hundred tribes of Indians said to inhabit the shores of that river." Along the Yucayali and on the pampas, he adds the Remo, Papacrui, Connibo, Chetibo, and Sepibo. Steaming around the shores and inlets of the Pacific Northwest, he is greeted by Klaho-quat, Hyda, Naya, Chippewyan, Stone, Dogrib, Athapasca, Esquimaux Aleutian, and Koriak.

Then there's something suspicious in the skillful way Catlin deflects suspicion. Before he is questioned he has a ready alibi: With seemingly artless candor he recalls that he had traveled using a false British passport, hinting that it just *might* have been issued to a "Mr. Smythe," a traveling companion for part of his journey. (Needless to say, no trace has ever been found of this traveler.) He tosses us a vague explanation: Hostilities between Paraguay and Brazil made a British passport the most useful at the border.

As for money, he claims to have paid his way by working as an itinerant portrait painter, immortalizing the families of his colonial

Spanish hosts while staying on their *estancias;* one such gentleman, a mysterious "Señor L. M.," guided him across the Crystal Mountains. A visit with the family of a beautiful young half-Auca girl revealed that her parents had misunderstood his painterly tribute as an offer of marriage or purchase. But not a single portrait has survived that can be attributed, even provisionally, to the artist, amid a vast inventory of eighteenth-and nineteenth-century colonial images of regional grandees, their families, priest, and patron saints.

George Catlin published two accounts of his travels through South America and up the coast of the Pacific Northwest: *Life Among the Indians: A Book for Youth* (1861) and *Last Rambles Amongst the Indians of the Rocky Mountains and the Andes* (1868). Taken together they provide evidence, hidden in plain sight, of the way the author may have seen these travels. The clue lies in Catlin's intended audience: Both were written, as the subtitle of the first states, for "youth," a category not to be confused with today's "young adult" market of consumers, which had yet to be invented. Until the twentieth century "youth" defined older children. In signaling the young reader, Catlin gave himself permission to cast or recast his travels as fictions: fairy tales, adventure stories.

If he wasn't the hero with a thousand faces, Catlin deliberately hid his real one. Somewhere along the way he also abandoned his story about the faked passport. He traveled incognito, he tells us grandly, "as kings and emperors sometimes do." As do also the heroes of myths and legends.

Three—the magic number and familiar trope of fairy story and quest narrative is strategically repeated—starting with the number of the voyages themselves. Even before he sets sail, Catlin tells us, he must submit to three delays as tests of perseverance. Waiting for money from Phillipps to arrive at Le Havre, he misses his sailing twice. He can finally buy a ticket on the third steamship (unnamed) to leave for Latin America. He was to have been one of three traveling companions; the other two had left without him.

When he finally reaches Havana in early May 1854, he catches up with the two scientists who preceded him; only one, a German doctor, accompanied Catlin to Venezuela and on to Guiana. Then, in Demerara he, too, disappears.

In Havana, George finds a guide. Caesar Bolla is a maroon, or runaway slave, and a "first-rate Negro man." Over six feet two inches in height, Bolla stood a head taller than George, and was so broad that he not only carried Catlin's supplies in a large portfolio strapped to his back but willingly served as a human easel, allowing a blank canvas to be stretched across this same expanse of flesh and muscle, flat enough to permit Catlin to draw and paint on its surface. For four or five weeks Catlin and Caesar, aided by a team of small naked Indians, navigated the Xingu River, where he painted the tribe of that name.

Whether he saw, read about, or imagined what he described, Catlin evoked his progress in the Amazon with a painterly eye and the voice—matter-of-fact and dreamlike at the same time—of magic realism that seems to come with the territory: The "emperor George" traveling incognito could have been Werner Herzog's Fitzcarraldo, feverishly claiming the crocodile-infested empire for his own:

> In the fresh air and sunshine at the tops of trees, which we can never see, there is a busy chattering neighborhood of parrots and monkeys, but all below is a dark and silent matted solitude, in which a falling leaf, from want of wind, may be a month in reaching the ground, and where a man may be tracked by the broken cobwebs he leaves behind him.

Their looping journey through Brazil was cut short by a letter Catlin claimed to have received "*actually ordering* me home as quick as possible," which he attributed to a sudden change of mind on the part of Congress; that body, he asserted, had (out of the blue and with no debate or vote) appointed a committee at its last session to negotiate purchase of the Indian Gallery. This may not be the first instance in which Catlin embedded one fantasy within another. Then, in mid-November 1854, after nearly six months of travel, he fetched up at Le Havre; from Southampton on November 27 he wrote to Phillipps asking for the return of the twenty oils he was still owed; in exchange he had brought his friend the gift of some sketches he had made along the Amazon.

Catlin would never get to Washington. For want of a gold hoard, his brief return to Europe (locations unknown) lasted only from late November 1854 to late February or early March 1855, and suggests that if he did make any of these South American voyages, he came back only to seek fresh funding for his next trip.

IT WAS IN September 1855, between the second and third of his declared voyages to South and Central America, that Catlin arrived in Berlin, at the invitation of Baron Alexander von Humboldt. He had sailed, he recalled, from Sisal in Yucatán, where he visited the ruins of Uxmal and painted the local Maya and then from Sisal to Le Havre, stopping in Paris before appearing in the Prussian capital.

Catlin's visit to Humboldt is well documented: But even this trip within Europe has the eerie glow of legend: The hero, lost and in danger, travels a great distance to pay homage to the ancient wise man, seeking instructions that will end his puzzlement and his quest.

At eighty-five Humboldt indeed occupied a place between myth and monument. The most famous savant of his day, he towered, a colossus of scientific knowledge, bestriding two centuries and two streams of thought and belief—at once a child of the eighteenth-century Enlightenment and its rational classifying drive, and of the mystical Romantic embrace of nature as key to the unifying secret of creation.

Humboldt also had the good fortune to have lived in the last era before "specialization," when it was possible—at least for a genius—to make of all branches of scientific knowledge his own holistic study, natural and physical: geology, climatology, biology, zoology, physics, statistics, ethnology, and even linguistics. His five-volume work *Cosmos*, published in 1845, was the summa of his synthesizing vision, but his research pushed even further: Without Humboldt's early studies of avian mutation within species over time, Darwin acknowledged that he would never have set out for the Galápagos.

Humboldt himself refused to be confined to the library or laboratory: Starting in 1799, he began his exploratory travels in Latin America. Among the scientific discoveries made possible by these journeys were his revolutionary proposition that the lands bordering the Atlantic Ocean—notably Africa and South America—were once joined, leading to theories of migrations since accepted as accurate, while his pioneering work on volcanoes of the New World would inspire Catlin to write his own study: *The Lifted and Subsided Rocks of America, with Their Influences on the Oceanic, Atmospheric, and Land Currents, and the Distribution of Races* (1870), a tribute to his mentor's synoptic vision.

In his younger days Humboldt had chafed at the obligation to live in provincial Berlin and play the courtier at Sans Souci, the royal palace at nearby Potsdam, and he made sure that his work required him to travel as often as possible. There was another reason for Humboldt's restlessness at home. Whenever he could flee civilization and especially his role of royal scholar on display, Humboldt seized the chance to pursue the homosexual life for which colonial outposts were even then the favored destinations. On his South American travels, a devout traveling companion reported the scientist frequenting houses where "impure love reigned," of befriending "obscene dissolute youths," and indulging "shameful passions of his heart." At home or abroad his deepest attachments seem to have been for men; in Catlin, Humboldt found a fellow explorer of mutual scientific interests and, possibly, one with a shared need for escape into the wild to accommodate sexual adventures that, at home, would take place only in the shadows.

On his constant travels Humboldt had seen the Indian Gallery in London at Egyptian Hall in 1842 and in Paris in 1845, when he and Catlin probably met. Omnivorous reader that he was, he knew Catlin's *Letters and Notes* well before they began corresponding in 1855, shortly before George's Berlin visit.

Catlin remained in Berlin for most of September, staying at the Crown Prince Hotel. One reason for his visit at this particular moment appears to have been his hope that despite Humboldt's advanced age, the great scientist and traveler could still be persuaded to accompany him on this next journey: With his years of experience navigating rivers, climbing volcanoes, bushwhacking through rainforests and jungles, and his discovery of tribes on the verge of extinction, he would have made the ideal travel companion. With regret Humboldt admitted that at eighty-five he was too old for such arduous travel. Instead, over the weeks of George's stay in the Prussian capital, his host arranged (despite many royal changes of plan) a visit to the king and queen at Sans Souci, and offered much useful advice on Catlin's forthcoming Argentine itinerary, providing letters of introduction to his French friend Aimé Bonpland, now living in Santa Ana on the Uruguay River. They discussed one of Humboldt's pet theories—that the Toltec were ancestors of the Crow (the German was fixated on the presence or absence of aquiline noses as a measure of racial origins). Geological formations were another of their shared interests. The older man was much impressed by Catlin's analytic descriptions of the Pipestone Quarry, along with the catlinite he had discovered, and offered suggestions for promising fieldwork in Colombia. He also sat to Catlin for his portrait in pencil, presented by the artist to Sir Thomas Phillipps in hopes of another infusion of cash from his "only patron."

Nearly a year after Catlin's visit to Berlin, Humboldt wrote to him, in care of an associate in Uruguay (possibly Bonpland), to alert his American friend to an attack upon his honesty and integrity. The aggressor was none other than Henry Rowe Schoolcraft, whose remarks, dismissing the accuracy of Catlin's description of the Mandan O-kee-pa ceremony, had appeared in the fifth and next-to-last volume of his magnum opus, *Historical and Statistical Information Respecting the History, Condition and Prospects of the Indian Tribes of the United States.*

Since leaving London in 1842, his career and personal life in shambles, Schoolcraft had made a comeback that refutes the cliché about there being no second acts in America. He settled in Washington, where his connections, productivity, and relentless self-promotion resulted in his ascent to the status of official expert on all matters related to the Indian.

In fact both Catlin and Humboldt already knew about Schoolcraft's denigrating references to George's published account of the Mandan O-kee-pa ceremony, made four years earlier. What George did not know was that Humboldt had also been the target of an attack by Schoolcraft—or more precisely, a counterattack. An 1853 article in the *North American Review* attributed to Humboldt the view that Schoolcraft's multivolume work was "a crude and worthless compilation, and his great surprise that it should be allowed to appear with the sanction and at the expense of the government of the United States." After waiting—in vain—for Humboldt to repudiate these remarks attributed to him, Schoolcraft took his revenge, and in volume 5 he implied that *Cosmos* trafficked in generalities, noting especially, considering its author's particular area of expertise, that "we look in vain for anything that may be used to solve the question of Indian origin."

Too grand to defend himself, Humboldt's insistence that Catlin go after Schoolcraft has been seen as the older man's use of his acolyte

as a stalking horse. There's a nasty whiff of Humboldt goading Catlin to declare war on the powerful bureaucrat: Surely his esteemed
younger friend could not allow Schoolcraft to get away with saying
that his Mandan discoveries were "contrary to facts; and that they are
the works of your imagination, etc." This charge, Humboldt insisted,
was "calculated, not only to injure your hard-earned good name, but
to destroy the value of your precious works, through all ages, unless
you take immediate steps with the Government of your country to
counteract its effects." No one has ever seen the original of this letter,
cited by Catlin and dated by him June 1856, but his efforts to heed
its advice came to nothing: The damage had been done—and published. Subsequent testimonials as to Catlin's character and scholarly
bon fides, even from such eminent supporters as Benjamin Silliman
and Humboldt himself, were no match for the authority of the government's official expert on the Indian. Still more galling, Schoolcraft had
leveraged the principal illustrator of his work, Capt. Seth Eastman, to
the role of preeminent painter of Native American life. Known as the
"soldier-artist of the frontier," Eastman, garrisoned at Fort Snelling
through the 1830s, produced a pictorial record of the local tribes well
suited to reproduction.

WHEREVER CATLIN WAS to be found—Uruguay, Paraguay, Argentina—or somewhere in Europe, when Humboldt's letter arrived for
him, in care of another younger Humboldt colleague in Paraguay, he
wasn't there to read it.

By now, though, we're used to the shadowy elusive gringo, a disappearing act that Catlin perfected but that has since taken on a literary
life of its own. This time George supposedly left Berlin, setting out
directly for Rio and Buenos Aires. If his journey seems to have a more
purposeful sense of direction, it may be that, exceptionally, our voyager found himself on firmer financial ground: The sale of "real prop-

erty" in New York brought him a windfall of three hundred dollars, he
reported, more travel funds than he had ever seen before.

THEN, OUT OF the blue Samuel Colt, the manufacturer of firearms,
commissioned Catlin to make a series of twelve paintings based
upon his South American adventures. Once engraved and endlessly reproducible, they would feature the dramatic use of a Colt
gun—in most images deployed by the dashing artist-explorer-hunter
himself—shown shooting flamingoes and buffalo, frightening the
natives, along with the many other uses to which a Colt firearm
might be put.

Colt and Catlin had met at the Great Exhibition where, in contrast to
the disaster of Catlin's shattered wooden Indians, Samuel Colt's display
of revolvers drew excited crowds to the Crystal Palace, one of the few
articles of manufacture to uphold the reputation of American know-
how. Colt's primary goal—beside selling his guns to the English—was
to persuade the U.S. Army to adopt his mass-produced weaponry. To
that end, and as a further example of Yankee ingenuity, he was among
the first to exploit "product placement" as a form of subliminal advertising: Catlin's paintings would illustrate the use of his guns "in the
field." The exact terms of their arrangement are unclear—even which
Catlin expedition (if any) Colt's commission helped underwrite, but we
can assume that if George traveled in fact as well as in his imagination,
to any of the places he described, he was well supplied with firepower
along with some cash. He became so attached to his favorite rifle that
he called the gun "Sam," in honor of its maker. A publicity coup for
both parties was a reproduction in the *Illustrated London News* after a
painting, *A Mid-Day Halt on the River Trombutas, Brazil,* showing a figure on a boat, shooting a wild animal about to devour his companions
asleep on the shore. Another image, designed to appeal to less intrepid
hunters, is a self-portrait of the artist in the act of mowing down an

entire population of nestling flamingoes. One wonders whether Catlin, the early environmentalist, ever reflected upon the irony that his only subsidy came from promoting the principal weapon of mass destruction of native peoples and wildlife.

Beside such evidence of better-financed travel, Catlin's third and final trip differs from the earlier two because part of the itinerary he describes, namely his travels in northeastern Argentina, has been recently tracked by an Argentine-American anthropologist, Edgardo Krebs. Armed with historical and geographical familiarity with much of the terrain Catlin claimed to have covered, ethnological training, and knowledge about the tribes the artist declared that he saw and painted, Krebs was able to compare Catlin's account of events with those of others who left written evidence of their observations and experiences: He, too, found no record of this particular passenger's arrival in the port of Buenos Aires; nor did Catlin note—as have almost all other visitors coming by sea at the time—the singular peculiarity of disembarking in Buenos Aires: The harbor was so shallow as to require a horse-drawn wagon to carry passengers from their ship to the dock. But in defense of Catlin as a firsthand observer, Krebs confirms weather conditions on the Rio Plate in late January and February—"the insupportable heat of summer led to the thinning of the water and the resulting dangerous rapids," and other phenomena such as the presence, just outside of Corrientes of a "tent city" of wigwams, where Indians who came to trade from as far away as Brazil, set up transient settlements. Krebs points to mistakes that would be particularly troubling to an anthropologist: confusions in identifying tribes and uncertainties about gender distinctions; whether the men or women whom he observed wore lip disks, while acknowledging that these errors could be made by an observer as well as someone who read and quoted the erroneous accounts of others.

Catlin tells us that soon after his arrival in Buenos Aires, he accepted an invitation to stay with someone he identifies only as "my friend Thomas." Krebs raises the possibility that George's host may have been L. Thomas Jefferson Page, commander of the *Water Witch,* a small side-wheel steamer. Page was on assignment from the U.S. Navy, charged with exploring tributaries of the Rio Plata. If Catlin was his houseguest, he could also have accompanied his friend on the *Water Witch,* as a volunteer or paid crew member, observer—or spy. His name does not appear in the ship's manifests in any capacity.

Among the doubts that stalk Catlin on all of these journeys, along with the distances involved, is the question: How could one Anglo-European, who claimed often to travel alone, with severe hearing problems and knowing neither Spanish nor any native language, ever have survived? Here Krebs reminds us of Catlin's proven self-sufficiency and long experience on the frontier. Since boyhood he had honed essential survival skills: He knew his way around firearms; he was a skilled hunter who could kill and dress a variety of game; he knew how to make fires, a fishing pole, shoot rapids. And probably most important, George Catlin, then sixty years old, communicated an openness and warmth that led strangers to want to help him.

No less ambiguous is the evidence of the paintings themselves: Called his "cartoon collection" by the artist, they survive as more than three hundred small oil sketches on Bristol board, some subsequently bound into albums for sale to collectors.

THE MOST DRAMATIC difference between Catlin's paintings of Indians on the upper Missouri and his images of tribal peoples he claims to have encountered on his South American travels is the absence of any individual portraits. Arranged in groups, vaguely pyramidal in composition, his tribal subjects are seen from a consistent middle-distance perspective, suggesting that Catlin, if he indeed painted from life, worked from the water. Struggling to capture his subjects onshore while maintaining his balance of hand and seat, this "paddle-by" challenge explains the artist's compensatory "adjustment" to produce static images—even of groups engaged in dance.

Such individuals as do emerge are differentiated from one another by details of dress, leading one art historian to describe Catlin's representations of South American tribal people as generic.

In contrast his landscapes evoke visionary, dreamlike vistas of swans, flamingoes, and trees whose large silvery leaves will soon shiver in frenzy at an approaching storm. Devoid of their summarily rendered human inhabitants, these landscapes—beaches lapped by transparent lagoon waters, savannas of tall grass—offer a prelapsarian world. Of such an Eden before the Fall, Catlin re-created its delights for our own reveries.

For those who believe these travels to be the invention of the artist, there are sources suggesting that Catlin could have borrowed, stored, and embroidered images of the people and places he painted during these years. His days of escape in the Imperial Library might well have introduced him to colored prints by the fascinating Dutch artist Albert Eckhout. As a court painter in Brazil for seven years between 1637 and 1644, Eckhout produced portraits, still lifes, and "natural curiosities" for the Dutch-German count Johan Maurits van Nassau. Was Catlin recalling Eckhout's close-up *Tapuya Dance* when he peopled his *Tapuya Encampment* with dancers? It would be easier to fix Eckhout's oil portrait of a *Lesser Anteater* than to catch the creature on the hoof as Catlin tries to do in his maurauding version of the same beast. Recently, scholars have questioned whether Eckhout himself actually painted what he saw firsthand in Brazil, adding yet another layer to the problem of whether Catlin filtered his images through other artists.

Considering "notions of 'truth' and 'falsehood' in early European depictions of places and objects of the Americas," Edward J. Sullivan, the leading historian of Latin American art from the precolonial period to the present, writes, "To this should be added the category of 'relative truth.' . . . Many early modern 'traveler-artists' had never crossed the ocean and thus relied on the images of those who had. . . . Their work can be considered in the light of 'partial fictions' created through intimate contact with observed things."

Closer to home, Catlin's contemporary and acquaintance, the explorer and administrator Sir Robert Hermann Schomburgk, directed the artwork for a "hand-colored" lithographic series *Twelve Views in the Interior of Guiana,* published in 1841, whose scale and perspective suggest that Catlin knew this popular album.

TRAVEL WRITING HAS always been a shape-shifting genre bender. It's anything the author wants it to be—and can persuade us to read— scholarly documentary, extreme adventure, mysticism, fantasy, drug-induced hallucinations—as long as these don't take place at home. We feel privileged to shadow Captain Cook, Lady Hester Stanhope, Lawrence of Arabia, Jack Kerouac; Paul Theroux, following the interplay of observer and observed. The least important question, after all, may be: Is it true?

The great travel writers have always been inventors of real places. In our own time, development, urbanism, pollution, and erosion have changed many actual sites into memories. Bruce Chatwin's Patagonia is as unrecognizable as George Catlin's. Before his death from AIDS in 1982, Chatwin wrote wistfully of plans for a future journey: "One day I want to make a really long and slow trip right across Asia, by the most obscure frontier posts and along the least frequented routes," he told his friend the filmmaker James Ivory. "I would write the whole thing into a semi-imaginary picaresque journey." Not Chatwin's most striking phrase, "semi-imaginary" seizes, nonetheless, that unstable mix of fantasy and phenomenon, reality and seductive mirage of "the obscure frontier post" that never ceased to beckon George Catlin. And a good story trumps facts anytime.

We'll never know whether Catlin made any of these journeys or all of them; neither can the opposing argument be proved: that he never set foot on South or Central American soil. Like his thrilling evocations of Mount Chimborazo, which we know he never actually saw, his writings on Latin America, as much as his well-documented *Letters and Notes* from the upper Missouri confirm what his paintings declare: Recording, copying, borrowing, imagining, or simply making it all up, George Catlin was an artist.

"NOW I AM G. CATLIN AGAIN, LOOK OUT FOR THE PAINT!"

Wherever George had roamed, in reality or in his imagination, by 1860, he declared his days of adventure and exploration over. He had returned from South America, he said, with a large cache of minerals and semiprecious stones, predominantly amethysts and agates, and he settled in Brussels, possibly because of its proximity to Antwerp, center of the commerce in gems: cutting, polishing, buying and selling. He may have hoped for income from occasional sales. In any case he preferred the European atmosphere of Brussels to that of medieval Antwerp with its incomprehensible Flemish speech or the guttural Low German spoken by its clannish Jewish community of diamond cutters. Loud street sounds were the only ones that George could hear. He was now almost completely deaf.

Brussels beckoned as the cheapest capital in Europe, with few American or English visitors of the sort George might want to avoid. He found affordable space in a *hôtel garnis*—furnished rooms with minimal amenities—a bed, a chair, a table, a fireplace, much-mended linen. Still, the Hôtel Duc de Brabant, located on the street of that name near the railway station, compensated for its austerity by providing George with the luxury of two separate rooms—one for painting, the other for sleeping and eating.

Downstairs the corner café became his club. Every day he bought the London and Paris papers for news of America, which he read there "by a good gas light." By late afternoon, when it was too dark to paint, George would be drawn by the café's warmth, assured by the heat of bodies crowded together, the locals drinking beer and playing dominoes. Hearing nothing, George wrote.

And he drew and painted. Solitude, deafness, isolation, neglect—endured over the course of nearly a decade—might have sapped others of energy and ambition and hope. Instead Catlin now saw his life and career in the process of rebirth. Troubles only toughened him. He seems to have escaped the depressive suicidal strain in his generation of Catlins; if anything, his mind and spirits appeared eerily focused on the task at hand, on what he wanted—no, what he *must* accomplish—in the time he had left.

Earning money was, as always, the first order of business. One steady and quick source of income was copies, and sometimes copies of copies. He churned out albums of line drawings based upon paintings of his North or South American scenes; a number of these boasted the misnomer *Album Unique*; others were *Souvenir Albums*. His great project and the vehicle of his planned "comeback" would be what he called his "Cartoon Collection." With the help of his unclouded memory (at least for his art), aided by the useful camera lucida, Catlin had earlier begun a picture-by-picture reconstruction of the hundreds of his Indian portraits, scenes of native life, and landscapes—copies of the work of thirty years. He called these drawings "outlines." (Confusingly, this linear version of the Indian Gallery had its own "double"; at the same time that George was drawing his outlines, he was also working on color facsimiles of the same collection, painted on Bristol board instead of canvas, which he planned to add to his South American scenes and images from the Pacific Northwest in the same thinned oil pigment.)

He had begun this consuming labor of drawing in London, probably in anticipation of the originals being seized, but before he knew of their "rescue" by Joseph Harrison. The artist had been spared a price on his head, but the price of his first Indian Gallery, George suspected, would place it beyond his reach for the foreseeable future.

THE CARTOON COLLECTION remains a unique phenomenon in the history of art. On the cusp of the age of mechanical reproduction, George Catlin, in the absence of originals to reproduce mechanically, had sought to reproduce by hand, Indian by Indian, buffalo by buffalo, his entire collection. Strangely, the nature and meaning of this prodigious act of memory—as existential reinvention, as retrieval of the artist and his art from nothingness—have never been examined. Or rather the process and, still more remarkable, its completion have been taken for granted. Living anonymously in the shadows in Brussels, Catlin created a shadow collection, one that would ultimately compete and play hide-and-seek with its inaccessible source, the "real" Indian Gallery. Presciently he had intimations of the way the very act of drawing pointed to a more abstract definition of the object. Planning a new portfolio containing a selection of the "cartoons," he wanted it "to be executed in lines," he said, "in the best style of modern art."

Finishing his Cartoon Collection was only part of a day's work at the Hôtel Duc de Brabant: He also saw to the publication of the two books of South American travels, intended for youth: *Life Among the Indians*, and *Last Rambles*. While he had his young readers mesmerized by his adventures, from Tierra del Fuego to the Yucatán, he tried to enlighten them about the moral issues that had moved him to write these books in the first place: to record, for a new generation, the shameful deletion of Native Americans from their rightful place in their country's history. The government's aim had been the Indians' "rapid decimation and final extinction," and he urged his young readers to reflect on the question "Who is the *savage*, and which the *brute?*" He pointed out to them the cruel paradox of recent history: The emancipation of the slaves, "giving *freedom* and rights of citizenship to two million, of Africans, now at the point of the bayonet, to *disenfranchise* and *enslave* a *free* and *independent* people—to *disinherit* her 'red children.'"

PHYSICALLY CATLIN WAS failing on several fronts. Disembarking at Ostend, he experienced "burning and bursting" sensations in one knee, likely symptoms of arthritis. From there, in April 1861, after nine years of silence, he wrote to his youngest daughter. In an apology of sorts, he explained that the labors of the dedicated artist must excuse the failures of a father: "If my life had been thrown away in idleness or dissipation during these long years of absence, there would be no excuse for me, I would be a *monster*, and I would have no right to ask forgiveness of my dear little angels, but I have been constantly at work, and still am so, even when lying on my back, or hobbling about on crutches."

More serious, if less painful, was the shortness of breath that stopped him as he climbed the steep narrow stairs to his room. Both had the effect of curtailing movement out of doors, while the first made standing before an easel for hours a painful test of endurance. His preoccupation with breathing as key to health revived an old hobbyhorse. Based upon his observations of Indians at rest, George had become convinced of the crucial benefits of lying on the back and sleeping with closed lips. His short book, *The Breath of Life, or Mal-respiration*, was published, first in America, by J. Wiley, George Putnam's former partner, in 1861; then it appeared in England where it was called, *Shut Your Mouth and Save Your Life!* The title could account for the book's critical neglect, if it was seen as another of the crank cures between covers that rolled off the presses at just this period. But its robust sales and many printings boosted Catlin's precarious finances and pointed to legions of converts,* among them an Oxford professor of mathematics, Charles Lutwidge Dodgson, better known as Lewis Carroll.

George also hadn't given up on his lifesaving device for ocean-going vessels. Realizing that he had been the victim of fraudulent representation in England, he tried, through connections, to promote the design in America as Catlin's "Steamship Slipper," but ships were deemed safer now and his invention found no traction at home.

Still, despite urging by friends, he was unwilling to consider returning until he could do so in triumph. And that dream required that he finish his Cartoon Collection. To this end, however, he also realized that the groundwork must be laid before his arrival, and by others.

He had never stopped brooding over Schoolcraft's slanderous attacks on his honesty. Before returning to America, he wanted vindication; he wanted to see his enemy unmasked and his hate campaign revealed for the vendetta it was. Schoolcraft had targeted Catlin's account of O-kee-pa as "evidence" of his rival's unreliable invention, bearing little relation to fact, and sensationalized for the purpose of selling books. This "expert" critique, disseminated under government sponsorship, George believed, had effectively doomed his last efforts to secure the sale of his collection to Congress. From Brussels, George arranged for a new publication of *O-kee-pa*, in the form of a small free-standing monograph describing the Mandan torture ceremony, with engravings based upon the four scenes he had painted earlier and which constituted a "narrative" of the events. He followed the text with new bona fides and affidavits from such authorities as Humboldt and Prince Maximilian of Wied-Neuwied, attesting to the author's scholarship, honesty, and credibility—including an "old" imprimatur from Schoolcraft himself, dating from the days when he was trying

---

* Native American practice and Catlin's faith in its health-giving properties have been vindicated by recent research suggesting that placing infants on their backs to sleep will prevent the mysterious and fatal SIDS, Sudden Infant Death Syndrome.

to woo Catlin as a collaborator. Published in London in 1867, *O-kee-pa* sold few copies. Either Schoolcraft had gotten there first—among those interested in such issues—or Catlin and the Mandan were no longer an alluring subject to readers.

In his original account, published in London, the author Catlin had omitted rituals of phallic worship. Taking place outside the torture lodge, these ceremonies were based upon the expectation that observers would become participants. Beyond the issue of his readers' sensibilities, George did not want to have to reveal whether he had accepted this invitation. Now, however, he decided on yet another edition, a *folium reservatum* "for gentlemen only," in which the phallic rituals would be reinstated, including the women's pursuit of the mocked male "villain" with his huge, hydraulically operated dildo. As a "limited edition," the numbers of copies sold would say little about the venture's success. Politically, however, publishing *O-kee-pa* in the form of erotica provided Schoolcraft and his allies in Congress with a new weapon to be used against the artist. It was not one of George Catlin's better ideas.

DESPITE MOUNTING EVIDENCE to the contrary, Catlin remained convinced that his country would still see the light—and purchase his collection after all. If the Congress could not arrange with Harrison to redeem the original Indian Gallery from his boiler works, there was now the Cartoon Collection on offer. Essential to George's recharged ambitions, however, was the reasonable belief that Americans, along with their legislative body, had to be visually reminded of what they had nearly lost.

Pondering how to pave the way for his triumphal return from the wilderness, George had a revelation: Reconnecting with relations, reclaiming his role of brother and father was the indispensable prelude to his welcome home as a citizen and artist. He couldn't just reappear after thirty years and, following a tearful embrace, expect to be swept into the family circle. He wrote to his daughters, now young women (and was apparently surprised not to receive an immediate reply).

His brothers, Francis and Richard, and nephew Burr—now a grandfather—were another, happier story. Whatever Dudley Gregory may have decided to tell the girls about their father, George knew that his own family, his late sisters especially, had long believed him dead. Both his brothers and nephew, George rightly surmised, could only be pleased to hear that he was alive, reasonably well, and wanted to see them.

George decided that Francis, now living in Wisconsin, should come to Brussels for a long visit. He had great plans for his youngest sibling: He would make Francis his partner, agent, and advance man for the varied projects that would insure his triumphant return home.

Francis had never been to Europe. In fact, he had only been out of Lockport, New York, to migrate to Hudson, Wisconsin, where he joined his sisters and their families. He had never managed to prosper on his own, scrambling to feed his children, always a summons away from bankruptcy court. Almost fifty and a widower now, with his sons graduated from dependency, the wide-eyed provincial was thrilled by the prospect of a midlife adventure.

He had last seen his older brother as a handsome, fine-featured thirty-five-year-old, a new husband, and, as befitted a public figure, the glass of gentlemen's fashion. George had then seemed born to wear velvet-collared overcoats and doeskin trousers. Now gray haired and limping in pain, he was as shabby as Francis himself, but for the immaculate collars and large collection of fine ties that his little brother remembered from the old days. Among the shocks came the realization that George couldn't hear a thing his brother said. Francis soon learned that howling was not the answer, and they communicated in writing.

At home, they had all counted on George as their master of revels: He teased his adoring sisters and sisters-in-law; poured forth endless anecdotes of Indians, traders, military brass, and important political players; he returned to boyhood pleasures of "rod and gun" with whoops of childlike joy. It seemed incredible that such a social animal as his brother had withdrawn into silence and solitude. George had not been out in society for two years, Francis reported to his journal. He worked "from early light till dark every day."

His brother's visit lasted almost two months, every day and evening spent together. Francis became ever more matter-of-fact about George's eccentric and marginal life; his only companions a cage of white mice. The pets' lives were precarious: Each day witnessed a scene of dismemberment. "Just discovered how the mice tails grow shorter," he confided to his journal. "George has an hour amusement every day with his da—— nasty little mice. An Outsider [that is, a resident hotel mouse] gets at their tails sticking through the wires of the cage and bites them off." He did not try to explain George's amusement at the mutilation of his mice.

The highlight of Francis's visit was the brothers' invitation to a lavish Thanksgiving at the home of the Hon. H. S. Sanford, American minister to Brussels, replete with splendid turkey and vintage wines. Nevertheless the glamour of Francis's trip soon began to fade.

Either Francis had failed to ask their brother, Richard, to help with the costs of his visit or the latter had refused; he had nothing but his fare home. With no possibility of sightseeing or travel elsewhere in Europe, which George had earlier promised (on the assumption that his brother would pay his own way), Francis was getting restive: The cold and gloomy rooms, the futile effort to catch the attacker mouse— the charm of foreign travel was over: "Here we sit in our dungeon, raining, fearfully dark."

GEORGE TOO WANTED Francis gone—but not because he had tired of his brother's company. He had been overjoyed to draw closer to the one family member from whom he was never estranged. But he had made plans for their partnership, and he needed Francis home in America right now to organize George's comeback: If all went well, his brother reminded him, there would be a small fortune there for him too.

On arriving in Washington, Francis was, first, to set up the purchase by subscription of his new "portfolio" with the highlights of the Cartoon Collection. He had provided his brother with a prospectus he was to place before every member of Congress. To make the case, simultaneously, for the sale of the large "outline" copies of the original Indian Gallery, including 120 full length portraits, he charged Francis with securing a hall in the Capitol itself; George was specific about dimensions. The space had to be eighty feet long and readily accessible to lawmakers during any short recess. Exhibiting the new collection would require the construction of about twenty screens, each eight feet high and about twenty five feet long, along with four more to run the length of the four walls. (He provided Francis with a scale model). The screens were to be completely covered with the drawings, each one two by two and one half feet edge to edge (George had even given him detailed instructions on just how the paste should be brushed on the backs). Members of Congress would thus have available, in the most convenient form, line drawings in the same size as the originals of the Indian Gallery they had declined to purchase many times before.

With the help of Ambassador Sanford, Catlin had assigned Francis power of attorney together with supporting documents that would legally authorize him to act in any commercial venture on his brother's behalf. (Collectors and art patrons, the Sanfords felt a particular sympathy for Catlin's woes. The minister, moreover, appears to have been a diplomat worthy of the name: Before Francis arrived to be designated his brother's agent, Sanford had tactfully dissuaded George from any thoughts of going to Washington to make his case in person: "He constantly told me," Catlin recalled, "it would be time & money

lost to try anything there during this Session troubled with impeachment [of President Andrew Johnson] & I have postponed my application there, until the opening of next Session." George's deafness,
however, was tacitly understood as a good reason to "postpone" any
personal appearances in Congress.)

It was in view of this next session, however, that George now
nudged his bemused brother to act quickly—on all fronts: "Push it
Francis—Push it!" he urged. At the same time that he was to apply
for permission to set up his screens near the congressional chambers,
George tasked Francis—who, in all probability had never been to
Washington, or dealt with any legislator save at the most local level—
to prepare the usual memorandum with letters from fellow artists,
scientists, trappers, and traders confirming the veracity, authenticity, and importance of his collection to the nation, and to make certain that each member of the House, but especially members of the
Committee on the Library (to whom Francis was to present a letter of
introduction from Ambassador Sanford) had copies, including recent
documentation. George also exhumed a scale model of his "patent of
Invention" the Steamship Slipper and made a present of it to Francis
and Burr, jointly, to exploit as they wished, together with the joint
assignment of ownership of the drawings, and a percentage of all
exhibition and sales proceeds—all *on the condition* that Francis, having received his marching orders in Brussels, would "run them Barnum fashion."

All this had been explained to Francis before he embarked for the
United States; when these arrangements were made, it may be that he
found it too confusing or fantastic to take seriously. But at that point
George had convinced himself and led Francis to assume that he would
be working with the more experienced Burr, with the backing of their
successful brother, Richard Catlin and perhaps even Dudley Gregory
as silent partners. As soon as Francis arrived home from Brussels,
he found himself bombarded, as often as the speed of packet ships

allowed, by still-more-feverish directives, instructions, warnings, and new ideas from George. By now he also knew that he was in it alone and without a cent to bring any of these plans to pass.

Cozily settled in his usual café in Brussels, George found that news from home—the bloody progress of the Civil War as reported by London and Paris papers—reverberated but faintly, like the music he could sometimes barely hear on the street. Francis's son had returned miraculously unscathed, from fighting on the Union side, giving the hostilities a human face.

Postwar America, paradoxically, seemed a foreign country. George had been away for thirty years; memories of his native land had blurred with time. In the seven years since Appomatax, upheavals on every front—economic, political, and social—had exacerbated old fissures and seemingly created new ones: In 1869, twenty-nine states had ratified the Fifteenth Amendment, giving the vote to black Americans, including former slaves. Two years later—on the eve of Catlin's return, Congress enacted the Indian Appropriations Act, nullifying all Indian treaties and making all Native Americans wards of the nation; the U.S. Army followed suit by suppressing the Apache tribe, forcing them onto reservations in New Mexico and Arizona. Those who resisted began attacking white settlements. It was now open season on Indians. Too many demobilized soldiers, used to killing and unsuited to civilian life, had reenlisted. They had fewer compunctions about torching entire Indian settlements and all their inhabitants than had the prewar volunteer militias.

Other betrayals, still in progress, would have been hard for any recently returned expatriate to track—especially a deaf, solitary, impoverished artist: Reconstruction in the South, the claw back of Emancipation's promises; the scandals of the administrations of Grant and Andrew Johnson, leading to the latter's impeachment in 1868.

Then, there were shining portents of progress whose dark shadows were slow to emerge. The gold spike that joined the Union Pacific and

Central Pacific railroads in 1869, two years before Catlin's return, effectively closed that frontier for which George could never have imagined any boundary but the Pacific Ocean itself.

Consolidating the country's vastness also began a process of concentrating the nation's wealth. This last change was so immense as to be impossible to grasp except as a kind of atmospheric corruption. "There was money in the air," said Henry James, with uncharacteristic brevity, returning to America after twenty years' absence. But it was a different kind of money than James or Catlin knew, rising now from big business and a market economy. Mergers, monopolies, and trusts created interlocking juggernauts, starting with railroads, themselves, and soon to include mining, shipping, cattle, banking; resources natural and man-made led to the creation of wealth on a scale and with a political power that few citizens, certainly not those who had lived abroad for decades, could begin to fathom.

When George instructed Francis about how to exhibit his Cartoon Collection in Washington, to make it "readily accessible to lawmakers during any short recess," he was still living with memories of the young republic and its statesmen politicians: De Witt Clinton or William H. Seward had readily found an hour to drop by and see Catlin's Indians. Their successors would be likelier to spend "any short recess" seeing railroad "men" or mining or banking "interests." Now, he was both mystified and crushed to learn from Francis that, despite his best attempts to carry out his brother's instructions, Congress showed not the slightest interest in his new collection: No room was available for the screens or the subscription books. Legislators who hardly remembered the name of George Catlin could see no reason why valuable space should be given to hundreds of drawings of Indians, and non-too-skillful examples of the draftsman's art at that. The best Francis could do in Washington was to find a smaller room, far from the Capitol, where some of George's drawings, pasted carefully to their screens, remained for several weeks only, visited by a few curious souls more by chance than by design. Silent indifference greeted the prospectus for George's portfolio, and his model of the steamship slipper. Crossing the Atlantic was a faster and safer proposition now; while passengers slumbered peacefully steamships knifed through towering waves; the notion that these vessels could turn into lifeboats would only undermine confidence in the craft, its crew, and its captain. In this, as in all of his fantastic schemes hatched in exile and solitude, George was a half century out of date.

However, a misunderstanding between the brothers might have led to the one successful venture among a string of failed plans. Under the illusion that George had assigned physical ownership of the Cartoon Collection to him, Francis entered into dealings to publish it with the help of yet another brother-in-law of Dudley Gregory, one Henry Steele. (Gregory himself had wisely decided to steer clear of any business projects involving George Catlin.) The new arrangement was to involve a partnership with Ezra Cornell and the new university that bore his name. With three parties in negotiations, George now saw the publication of his collection as excluding him. Informing Francis that he, George Catlin, still owned the collection—to the extent of having the right of refusal of any reproductions—he promptly exercised his veto power. As he grandly informed his desolate brother: "If you are disappointed in the fate of the 'great work,' there will be this advantage, it will not be 'donated' to the College, and it is still your property, and certainly will be enhanced in value by *not ever being published*."

Masters of self-destruction can always count on help. In late summer of 1870 Catlin's outlines in oil, the parallel Cartoon Collection that he had been working on since Paris, were now "before the world," covering "every inch of the walls" in an airy hall in Brussels. "Unfortunately," the artist reported, "on the very day that I opened, commenced the public excitement of the first bloodshed in the awful battles about Metz." The Franco-Prussian War had begun.

————

THERE WAS NOTHING left for Catlin in Europe. News of resurgent hostilities and revolutionary violence aroused painful memories of 1848,
evoking all the losses he had suffered in Paris. He was seventy-five, his
health ebbing, his limp and shortness of breath more pronounced with
every passing day. Packing up his few belongings, mostly pictures and
art supplies, he boarded a ship bound for New York. It had been thirty-
one years since George—accompanied by Burr, Daniel, the grizzlies,
with eight and one-half tons of his Indian Gallery in the hold—had set
forth in disappointment but with the feisty "I'll-show-them" spirit that
was also part of his flinty Catlin heritage.

The man that his daughters, Libby, Clara, and Louise, remembered
had been an elegant figure of erect, almost military bearing. Now they
had to call upon their best manners to disguise the shock they felt on
meeting an old man, a gray and stooped stranger, stone deaf and dragging one leg, who held out his arms stiffly to embrace them. If they
couldn't immediately summon feelings of affection, they were moved
to pity. He belonged with his family; they hoped he would come home
with them to Jersey City for a long visit.

Thanking them, he refused. He had managed, probably with Francis's help, to find a space in New York willing to exhibit his collection
of color "outlines."

Catlin's Indian cartoons opened with a private viewing at the Somerville Gallery on October 23, 1871. A respected venue for the exhibition
and sale of established American artists, the gallery was well known
to collectors, and Catlin felt justified in restricting invitations to "the
'Press' & 'Big Bugs'—and Millionaires," as he had earlier advised Francis to do in Washington. The press, at least, came, urging others to
follow suit—especially schoolchildren: "It is truly like a visit to the red
man to get among Catlin's pictures, for we feel at once that all is simplicity and truth," advised the *Herald* in one of Catlin's kiss-of-death
accolades. Schoolchildren may indeed have come (or more likely been

taken) but millionaires, 'Big Bugs' and the general public stayed away. The ghostly colored drawings evoked bleached palimpsests of Catlin's dimly recalled original Indian Gallery. His successors, painters of the West such as Seth Eastman, John Mix Stanley, and Charles B. Russell, working close to the dramatic narrative style of magazine illustration, portrayed the red man and woman as raider, scalper, daring horseman, or mourning maiden. Catlin's Indian Cartoons closed early in December, with the familiar story that rent had exceeded receipts.

One of the few visitors at the Somerville Gallery was an assistant to the director of the newly opened Smithsonian Institution, Dr. Joseph Henry. A physicist and noted pioneer in the science of electromagnetic induction, Henry's discoveries had laid the groundwork for Morse's telegraph. Following a teaching career at Princeton, he was an obvious choice for the Smithsonian's first secretary. Henry was also an admirer of Catlin's art. On November 7, 1871, he wrote to offer the artist an exhibition in the new building's great hall. Catlin's reply was noncommittal; he would only be permitted to sell the catalog, but not the drawings there, and he was, as usual, desperate for cash. A year of more failed schemes passed before he acknowledged that he had run out of options in New York. On February 13, 1872, he accepted the Smithsonian's offer, and two days later, his collection crated, he was on his way to Washington.

On February 27, 1872, Catlin's last show, his Cartoon Collection, arranged on screens he had prepared himself, opened in the Smithsonian's exhibition hall. When he and Henry had finally met during the days of preparation, the secretary's admiration for Catlin's art immediately extended to affection for the artist. As soon as the show was hung, he helped George prepare what would be his last petition to Congress for the purchase of his collection.[*]

---

[*] On December 13, 1873, a year after Catlin's death, Henry himself wrote to the Committee on the Library, urging the purchase of Catlin's collections by the Congress.

———

AS LONG AS the pictures were on view, Catlin suffered himself to remain in Washington—"this horrible place," as he called it, and never more so than during the infamous summer months. Twice a day he trudged, gasping in the "intense heat of that season," more than a mile each way from his boarding house to the Smithsonian.

When Henry returned from his holiday in late September, he took one look at George Catlin and saw that he was dying. A visit from his own physician confirmed what Henry suspected. Besides the malfunctioning heart revealed by difficulty in breathing, George's kidney's were failing: Bright's Disease, then the general term for renal shutdown, was diagnosed.

Acknowledged by all who knew him to be the kindest of men, Henry tactfully suggested that the artist consider moving into the unoccupied tower of the Smithsonian's distinctive red sandstone building to be closer to his work. Initially Henry had shielded George from the bleak medical prognosis. He tried to cheer his frail tenant with hopes that at the "next" session of Congress, victory would be theirs. He was also in communication with Joseph Harrison, he told Catlin, to try and secure the original, now-legendary Indian Gallery, from the basement of his boiler works, for the Smithsonian, where it belonged.

Within days George could no longer leave his bed. His mind, however, was clear, and Henry decided that respect and affection dictated telling him the truth; he needed to plan for the end of his life and the disposal of his work. Henry asked for and was given permission to inform the Catlin daughters and their guardian, Dudley Gregory, of his condition. With no very warm feelings toward the dying man, Gregory, nonetheless, did his Christian duty: On the evening of November 2, George was helped down from the tower and into a waiting carriage headed for Jersey City.

Most accounts place George Catlin's last hours within the context of that favorite Victorian scene: the dying father's farewell when, surrounded by a weeping family, he raises his hand in benediction. According to Elizabeth, the eldest, her father spent his last days sitting upright, stoic as an Indian, his face averted from those offering comfort and sympathy. His only sign of suffering came in the anguished question: "What will become of my gallery?"

His death did not take place at home among his family. Charity had its limits. Dudley Gregory, onetime U.S. senator and mayor of Jersey City, was also a successful developer of commercial real estate. He was able to provide his brother-in-law with comfortable rooms in one of his properties, the D'Arcy Hotel. There George Catlin died at 5:30 in the morning of December 23.

He was buried in the Gregory family plot, located on a small hill with a view, in Green-Wood Cemetery, Brooklyn, near Clara and their son; Catlin's grave was once marked by a small blank stone, but that has been missing for years, and no one is sure anymore of his precise burial place.

Joseph Harrison wanted all the money owed him by Catlin as the price Dr. Henry would have to pay to acquire the Indian Gallery for his institution. It was unaffordable. Following her husband's death in 1874, Harrison's widow donated the entire collection to the Smithsonian. What Congress, for almost half a century, had refused to buy from the artist became a gift to the nation from his late creditor.

Because Catlin had died there—and because Dudley Gregory was a leading figure in the community—Jersey City claimed George Catlin for its own. After all, he had no other home: The *Jersey City Times* waxed more indignant than any other newspaper about the rejection of his collection: He had labored, "unaided, nay, discountenanced by the United States government, which should have fostered and aided him." His remains, the writer dared hint, received scarcely more respect, but his soul, the *Times* declared with confidence, would soar "to the grand Elysian Hunting grounds," where he would be received by the vanished Indians as one of their own.

———

CATLIN'S INDIAN PORTRAITS have merged with their subjects. The millions of visitors to his Indian Gallery, fractionally recreated in the Smithsonian's National Portrait Gallery, gaze up in immediate recognition. They experience the images—the rows of warriors, wives, and children, elders and teenage boys, somber and accusing, prideful or tender, with the sense of encountering not painted representations, but "the real thing." In that regard George Catlin was too successful. In an age just beginning to exalt individualism as an American birthright and the artist as celebrity, he disappeared into his art.

ACKNOWLEDGMENTS

Traditionally, writers use the language of indebtedness to acknowledge those who have helped us. With our published thanks (and a copy of the book) we hope to repay what our work owes to others. Now, with a few more titles and years to show for the writing life, I see all that I've been given—by friends, fellow writers, researchers, archivists, librarians, collectors—not as a debt, but as a gift.

The collegial generosity and bracing friendship of Dr. Joan Carpenter Troccoli, a ranking scholar of the art of the American West, and of George Catlin in particular, touched every aspect of my work. A transplanted westerner, she acted as cicerone to this easterner with everything to learn. Her network produced another incomparable guide, Calvin Grinnell ("Running Elk"), cultural preservation resource specialist of the Mandan, Hidatsa, and Arikara Nation, who, leading me backward in time to both Indian and Catlin country, revealed the Great Bend of the Missouri, seemingly unchanged from the artist's great painting of this site, a visit warmed by the hospitality of his New Town, North Dakota, community.

My thanks to Dr. Stephen Aron, executive director of the Institute for the Study of the American West, for a welcoming visit and introduction to the porous borders separating the real and the mythic West through the collection of the Autry National Center.

For those of us who work alone, record keepers become our colleagues. Roy Goodman steered me to the marvels of the American Philosophical Society. I gratefully recall the guidance, over many days spent at the Archives of American Art, of Marisa Bourgoin and Elizabeth Botten. Thanks also to David Kessler, the Bancroft Library, University of California, Berkeley; Dr. Katherine Manthorne, City University of New York; and David Maxey, Esq., historian and former trustee of the Historical Society of Pennsylvania, who directed me to that institution's wealth of Catlin material. I'm grateful for help from Cheryl Liebold, the Pennsylvania Academy of the Fine Arts; Barbara Rimkinas, Exeter (N.H.) Historical Society; Linda Hocking, Litchfield Historical Society; Christopher Gray, Office for Metropolitan History, New York; Molly Kodner, Missouri Historical Society; Nancy Anderson, National Gallery of Art; Dr. Roberta J. M. Olson, New-York Historical Society; Alex Pezzati, University of Pennsylvania Museum; Betty Smith and her former colleague Dawn Augenti, at the Susquehanna Valley Historical Society; and Dr. Jonathan King, at the British Museum, who provided timely references to the little-known partnership of Catlin and P. T. Barnum. Thanks are also due Russell A. Flinchum, the Century Association Archives Foundation; Kenneth Cobb, Department of Records, the City of New York; Deborah McKeon-Pogue, United States Military Academy at West Point; and Regina Rush, University of Virginia Library. A brief talk with Dr. Brian W. Dippie illuminated all my Catlin readings, as did every page of his own great work, *Catlin and His Contemporaries: The Politics of Patronage.*

Scholars and amateurs pursuing related interests were generous in sharing them. I gratefully acknowledge the expertise of Emily Randall, Gregory family descendant and genealogist, and that of Alex Hovel, on Asher B. Durand; Dane and Carol Deleppo, on other Catlin family members in Connecticut; and Joseph Goddu, on Audubon. It's a pleasure to note the help of friends and sometimes the merest acquaintances who were forthcoming with invaluable information about museum and private collections, auctions, exhibitions, and publications: Stuart P. Feld, Mary Libby, Adelaide de Menil, Linn Cary Mehta, Charles Millard III, Jenny Lawrence, John Snyder, Joyce Seltzer, Eric Zafran, and Rosella Mamoli Zorzi. Dr. Kenneth Kolarsky thoughtfully analyzed descriptions of the Catlins' baby's death for possible causes.

In the course of an inspiring conversation, Edgardo Carlos Krebs diverted me from seeking answers to Catlin's problematic South American travels and toward asking different questions. On the same vexed subject, the distinguished scholar of Latin American art Dr. Edward J. Sullivan,of the Institute of Fine Arts at New York University, kindly took time to look at Catlin's paintings from this period and pointed me toward earlier artists and the flow of visual information between the Old and New Worlds.

Among the great rewards of my life over many years has been the friendship of those who have ably represented my interests. First always among these is Gloria Loomis. The deaths of Mary Kling and of Abner Stein, also longtime friends and agents, inflicted a double loss. Ever more appreciated is Mary Luria's wise counsel and constant support.

Through the good offices of my friend Brenda Wineapple and of Patricia O'Toole, both biographers of distinction, I was the recipient of a Hartog Fellowship, a shared bounty administered by the Columbia University School of the Arts that pairs a nonfiction writer with a researcher of similar interests: my able "prize," Brook Wilensky-Lanford, followed by Josh Garrett-Davis, now themselves published writers, pushed several Catlin projects forward. Other researchers whom it's a pleasure to recall are Elizabeth Martin, Jillian Russo, and Justine Taylor.

Home base through forty years of research and writing, the New York Society Library's staff has changed, but never its unique spirit. Nothing ever seems too much to ask of the gracious and knowledgeable professionals who are there to help: former head librarian Mark Piel; his successor, Mark Bartlett; Sara Elliot Holiday; Steven McGuirl; Patrick Rayner; Brandi Tambasco, who dexterously juggled interlibrary loans; Carolyn Waters; Andrew Corbin; and Ingrid Richter.

For anything I may have learned about computers, and for all I will never master, reassurance and help is always provided by Steven Rattazzi.

Crucial to survival are salutary diversions bestowed—and sometimes demanded—by friends and family: Rachel Adler, Halcy Bohen, Frederick Brown, Hester Diamond, Wendy Gimbel, Stephen Haas, Molly Haskell, Phyllis LaFarge Johnson, Caroline Kelly, Woodruff Price, Stacy Schiff, Anne Umland, and, irreplaceably, by Colin and Rachel Eisler and Geoffrey, Harry, and Leah Genth. Sometimes, survival is no metaphor—a difference that will be appreciated by Dr. Valery Lanyi.

The long march from proposal to publication has been shepherded by a talented group at Norton: Catlin benefited as much by the novelist's sense of style as by the sure editor's hand of Starling Lawrence. In trimming a longer text, Patricia Chui wielded the surgeon's scalpel while keeping the patient alive. Sue Llewellyn leavened the copyeditor's skills at questioning and scolding with the rewards of her taste and wit. It's hard to imagine *The Red Man's Bones* becoming a book without assistant editor Ryan Harrington.

Rhys Conlon appeared more than halfway through the writing of this long life. Her skills, resourcefulness, and fidelity could never be contained by the job description of researcher or assistant. The generosity she brought to every task, her spirit of collaboration and friendship, sustained and inspired me.

NOTES

ABBREVIATIONS

AAA: Archives of American Art, Smithsonian Institution, Washington, DC

CC: Charles Catlin

CGC: Clara Gregory Catlin

FC: Francis Catlin

GC: George Catlin

HSP: Historical Society of Pennsylvania, Philadelphia

JC: Joseph Chadwick

LHS: Litchfield Historical Society, Litchfield, CT

MHS: Missouri Historical Society, St. Louis

NARA: National Archives and Records Administration, Washington, DC

NYCA: *New York Commercial Advertiser*

NYHS: New-York Historical Society, New York

NYPL: New York Public Library, New York

PAFA: Pennsylvania Academy of the Fine Arts, Philadelphia

PC: Putnam Catlin

PSA: Philosophical Society of America, Philadelphia

ROEHM: Marjorie Catlin Roehm, *The Letters of George Catlin and His Family: A Chronicle of the American West* (Berkeley: University of California Press, 1966)

SVHS: Susquehanna Valley Historical Society, Montrose, Pennsylvania

UVA: Special Collections, University of Virginia Library, Charlottesville

PROLOGUE: OPENING CEREMONY

1 " 'a great *medicine white man* '": George Catlin, *Letters and Notes on the Manners, Customs and Conditions of the North American Indians*, 2 vols. (London: Egyptian Hall, Piccadilly, 1841). Unless otherwise indicated, all subsequent quotations from George Catlin are based upon this edition. For the context of the ceremony, observations of earlier witnesses, and the history of Catlin's several publications devoted to the subject, see a contemporary scholar's recent edition, George Catlin, *O-kee-pa: A Religious Ceremony and Other Customs of the Mandan*, ed. John C. Ewers (New Haven, CT: Yale University Press, 1967).

4 who had repaid his friendship with death: This version of the suicide of the stricken Four Bears, along with his curse, is one version of the chief's death; Catlin, however, reported that Four Bears, "to whom I became so much attached," survived the smallpox epidemic of 1837–38, but after watching "every one of his family die about him, his wives and his little children . . . wept over the final destruction of his tribe" before he starved himself to death.

CHAPTER 1: HOMECOMING

6 the first Wild West show: Paul Reddin, *Wild West Shows* (Urbana: University of Illinois Press, 1999) 4, 43, 51–52. The same point is made in a history of English taste for "primitive" performers, Richard D. Altick, *The Shows of London* (Cambridge, MA: Belknap Press, 1978).

8 "First Artist of the West": Joan Carpenter Troccoli, *First Artist of the West: George Catlin, Paintings and Watercolors from the Collection of the Gilcrease Museum* (Tulsa, OK: Gilcrease Museum Association, 1993).

9 "the endless mountains": Geologically, these formations are not mountains but a dissected plateau, a region in northeastern Pennsylvania that includes Bradford, Sullivan, Susquehanna, and Wyoming Counties. Thomas F. Gordon, *A Gazetteer of the State of Pennsylvania* (1832; reprint, New Orleans: Polyanthos, 1975).

9 Pennamite-Yankee wars: For the background of settler hostilities, see James H. Merrell, *Into the American Woods: Negotiators on the Pennsylvania Frontier* (New York: W. W. Norton, 1999).

10 first of the family to leave England: *The History of the Town of Litchfield, Connecticut, 1720–1920*, compiled for the LHS by Alain C. White (Litchfield, CT: Enquirer print., 1920), 90ff.

10 set out for a part of Pennsylvania: George B. Kulp, *Families of the Wyoming*

Valley: Sketches of the Bench and Bar of Luzerne County, Pennsylvania, vol. 3 (Wilkes-Barre, PA: E. B. Yordy, printer, 1890), 1051–107.

11 Putnam's nineteen year-old bride: Kulp, *Families*, vol. 1, 213.

11 anti-Indian hate propaganda: Peter Silver, *Our Savage Neighbors: How Indian War Transformed Early America* (New York: W. W. Norton, 2008). For the Wyoming Valley Massacre as instigated by arsonists working for the illegitimate, Connecticut-based, Susquehanna company, see Daniel K. Richter, *Facing East from Indian Country* (Cambridge, MA: Harvard University Press, 2001), 199–200.

11 soon replaced by native languages: Silver, *Savage Neighbors*, 119.

12 the scam of the century: Rebecca Geoffroy, *Asylum*, *"A Paris in the Wilderness,"* Unearthing the Past: Student Research on Pennsylvania History, at http://libraries.psu.edu/digital/pahistory/folder_6//psgr;1.html; *A French Asylum on the Susquehanna River*, Pennsylvania Historical and Museum Commission, at www.phmc.state.pa.us.ppet/French page1.asp?secid=31; Alexander D. Gibson, "The Story of Azilum," *French Review* 17 (December 1943), 92–98.

13 "interested parties": PC to John Nicholson, July 10, 1798, Asylum Company Papers, 1786–1803, Box 1, HSP, quoted by permission. The author wishes to thank David Maxey, Esq. for calling my attention to the employment of Putnam Catlin by the Asylum Company and its principals, which helped explain the family's flight from Wilkes-Barre and subsequent failure of Catlin senior's political ambitions.

14 "where Indians from the south": Lawrence M. Hauptman and George Hamell, "George Catlin: The Iroquois Origins of his Indian Portrait Gallery," *New York History: Quarterly Journal of the New York State Historical Association* 84 (Spring 2003), 135–51.

17 a little over thirty miles north of Scranton: Betty Smith of the Susquehanna Valley Historical Association established the precise location of Putnam Catlin's payment in land from the Wallace family.

17 a surviving copybook: SVHS Collection.

CHAPTER 2: AWAY

19 "You are now placed more favorably for study": PC to GC, August 4, 1817, Roehm, 15.

20 "Will you be a man": CC to GC, July 12, 1817, ibid.

20   "My new business keeps me": PC to GC, August 2, 1817, ibid., 16.

21   "The gratitude you express": PC to GC, August 4, 1817, ibid., 15.

21   "Wilkes-Barre is stupid": CC to GC, January 3, 1818, ibid., 18.

21   Lyman Beecher, called from East Hampton: White, *History*; *The Autobiography of Lyman Beecher*, ed. Barbara M. Cross (Cambridge, MA: Harvard University Press, 1961).

22   Catlin, the exile, wrote to him: GC to Lyman Beecher, October 18, 1853, Vattemare Papers, NYPL.

22   The Tapping Reeve School of Law: White, *History*, 107ff.

23   "You must therefore get as much legal science": PC to GC, January 21, 1818, Roehm, 20.

24   Anson Dickinson was Litchfield's master: Mona Leithauser Dearborn, *Anson Dickinson: The Celebrated Miniature Painter* (Hartford, CT: Connecticut Historical Society, 1983).

25   "Lay down the world! you little arrant thief": The first stanzas of the poem George Catlin inscribed and illustrated with watercolors. Litchfield Female Academy Collection, Series 2, Folder 70, Mansfield, Mary (Peck) Friendship Album, LHS, Helga J. Ingraham Memorial Library, Litchfield, CT. Quoted by permission.

26   "Luzerne and adjoining counties": There is a short lag (possibly due to holiday adjournment of the court) between December 1818, when Catlin was admitted to the practice of law at "Wilkesbarre," and Catlin's documented admission to the bar of Luzerne County, Pennsylvania, dated January 4, 1819. Kulp, *Families*, vol. 1, 1103.

26   He had never before seen such ingenious variety: A fine selection of portraits, including miniatures, of Litchfield's leading families, along with a full display of decorative arts made in the area, is on view in the Museum of the Litchfield Historical Society.

CHAPTER 3: GEORGE CATLIN, ACADEMICIAN

29   In George's only recorded court appearance: Luzerne County Court of Records, quoted in Loyd Haberly, *Pursuit of the Horizon: A Life of George Catlin, Painter and Recorder of the American Indian* (New York: Macmillan, 1948), 23.

29   A series of fifteen sheets: Collection of the Green Bay (WI) Historical Society.

30   "very deliberately resolved to convert my law library": Roehm, 23; cited by

Thomas Donaldson, *The George Catlin Indian Gallery in the U.S. National Museum, Smithsonian Institution, 1885 with Memoir and Statistics* (Washington, DC: Smithsonian Institution, 1886), 717.

30 "I am pleased that you at length resolved": PC to GC, March 26, 1821, Shelf V, 30H, Box 1, AAA.

31 Declared by foreign visitors: Auguste Levasseur, *Lafayette in America in 1824 and 1825; or, Journal of a Voyage to the United States*, trans. John J. Codman, MD, vol. 1 (Philadelphia: Carey and Lea, 1829), 157–58.

32 In 1821 the academy's fortunes: *Board Minutes of the Pennsylvania Academy of the Fine Arts, 1821–1824*, PAFA.

32 George Catlin had four miniatures accepted: Peter Hastings Falk, ed., *The Annual Exhibition Record of the Pennsylvania Academy of the Fine Arts, 1807–1870* (Madison, CT: Sound View Press, 1989), 45.

32 Born in Boston in 1796: Robert W. Torchia, *John Neagle, Philadelphia Portrait Painter* (Philadelphia: Historical Society of Pennsylvania, 1989).

33 "The said Neagle and Catlin": Signed by Matthew Carey, George Catlin, and John Neagle, October 21, 1822, John Neagle Papers, PSA.

34 manly art of pugilism: John Neagle, "Blotter Folio," John Neagle Collection, Case 59, HSP.

34 When the latter was in London: Thomas Sully Diaries, 1821–1827, "Journal," vol. 1, Dreer Collection, HSP, 175.

35 Among the latter were two arresting likenesses: Neagle's page with a double portrait of Big Kansas and Sharitarische, chief of the Grand Pawnee, and the other of Petalesbarro, Knife chief of the Pawnee Loup, in the collection of the Historical Society of Pennsylvania, is presently on loan to the Atwater Kent Museum in Philadelphia.

35 "I always thought I resembled": Torchia, *John Neagle*, 112.

36 At the 1824 meeting: *Board Minutes of the Pennsylvania Academy of the Fine Arts, 1821–1824*, "Wed. Feb 1824," PAFA.

36 "two cultures": The formulation of British novelist C. P. Snow concerning the widening chasm between science and humanism in twentieth-century discourse.

36 "a world in miniature": Edgar P. Richardson, Brooke Hindle, and Lillian B. Miller, *Charles Willson Peale and His World* (New York: H. N. Abrams, 1983), 83.

37 "Indian costumes, leggings": Ibid., 158; Chares Coleman Sellers, *Mr. Peale's*

Museum: Charles Willson Peale and the First Popular Museum of Natural Science and Art (New York: W. W. Norton, 1980), 187.

38 Along with the costumes and artifacts: Ibid., 260.

38 "Indian and European scalps": Ibid.

38 "the most complete ever seen": Ibid., 258.

38 While there he completed a miniature: Comment on copy of Catlin portrait used in "Memorial" at Tyler's death, SVHS Collection.

39 Putnam urged George not to "in any degree": PC to GC, July 25, 1824, Roehm, 28.

40 rose to the height of the building's eaves: Levasseur, *Lafayette in America*, 141.

40 "Never could it be more truly said": Ibid.

40 Passing before thousands of cheering spectators: John Thomas Scharf and Thompson Westcott, *History of Philadelphia, 1609–1884*, vol. 3 (Philadelphia: L. H. Everts, 1884), 2083.

41 "Most of the travelers who have visited": Levasseur, *Lafayette in America*, 157.

CHAPTER 4: A JOURNEYMAN ARTIST

42 Collier-Lewis clan: Loren Wilson Hall, "Portrait of a Mind: A Psychological-Intellectual Biography of George Catlin," PhD diss., Emory University, 1987, 47–48.

43 The graceful mansion on the corner: Dorothie Bobbe, *De Witt Clinton* (New York: Minton, Balch, 1933), 218ff.

45 the official souvenir book: William L. Stone, *Narrative of the Festivities Observed in Honour of the Completion of the Great Erie Canal*, included as an appendix in Cadwallader D. Colden, *Memoir, Prepared at the Request of a Committee of the Common Council of the City of New York* (New York: Corporation of New York, 1825), 296.

45 "superbly fitted up for the occasion": Ibid.

45 "classical emblematic production": Ibid.

45 "in the foreground is a full-length portrait": Ibid.

47 "I am very glad I did": Mrs. Mabel Seymour to Delia Seymour, March 5, 1825, Beckwith Collection, Box 10, LHS.

47 "Sent to George Catlin": John Neagle Papers, "Blotter Book," October 30, 1825–December 20, 1854, HSP.

48 Neagle also settled: Ibid.

48 "The distinctive quality of New York City": Thomas Bender, *New York Intellect: A History of Intellectual Life in New York City from 1750 to the Beginnings of Our Own Time* (New York: Knopf, 1987), 57.

49 Even his subsequent election: Thomas S. Cummings, *Historic Annals of the National Academy of Design: New York Drawing Association, etc. with Occasional Dottings by the Way-side, from 1825 to the Present Time* (Philadelphia: G. W. Childs, 1865), 80.

50 "with many handsome private dwellings": Robert T. Augustyn and Paul E. Cohen, *Manhattan in Maps: 1527–1995* (New York: Rizzoli, 1997), 112.

51 "the unusual proportion of pretty girls": JC to GC, June 5, 1828, AAA; Roehm, 36.

52 the council "read and accepted": *Minutes of the Common Council*, May 21, 1827, vol. 14, 314.

53 "The 'Commission' named": GC to William L Stone, January 7, 1827, Ayer Collection 146, Newberry Library, Chicago, IL.

54 to "alter or retouch": *Minutes of the Common Council*, March 17, 1828, vol. 17, 304.

54 writing under the name "Demon": Cummings, *Historic Annals*, 80.

54 "What induced him to prefer painting": William B. Dunlap, *A History of the Rise and Progress of the Arts of Design in the United States*, vol. 3 (Boston: C. E. Goodspeed, 1918), 172.

55 a "big noise": Roehm, 30.

56 "For the first time": Cummings, *Historic Annals*, 80.

58 "unavoidable dread of steamboats": PC to GC, May 30, 1928, Roehm, 33.

58 "Take good care of Clara": Ibid., 34.

58 "I will anticipate seeing you very happy": Ibid.

CHAPTER 5: WANDERERS

60 A fisherman reported: "Obituary: An Ill-fated Artist," *Rochester Daily Advertiser*, September 22, 1828.

61 "haven in a heartless world": See Christopher Lasch's cultural study of middle-class domesticity, *Haven in a Heartless World: The Family Under Siege* (New York: Basic Books, 1977).

61 The average cost of a boardinghouse: Ellen Nicolay, *Our Capital on the Potomac* (New York: Century Company, 1924), 289.

62 "weak lungs": Roehm, 59.

62 "Every new building": Nicolay, *Our Capital*, 129.

62 Bad weather caused so much sickness: Ibid., 190.

63 In the forefront of the capital's leading artists: Herman J. Viola, *The Indian Legacy of Charles Bird King* (Washington, DC: Smithsonian Institution Press, 1976).

64 "Their destiny as a race, is sealed": See Brian W. Dippie, *Catlin and His Contemporaries: The Politics of Patronage* (Lincoln: University of Nebraska Press, 1990), 281, 497 n. 32; Thomas McKenney to ———, March 20, 1851, in "Stanley's Indian Gallery," *New Haven Palladium*, March 23, 1851; Stanley Scrapbook, AAA, 38.

66 In the equivalent of a cold call: GC to Peter B. Porter, February 22, 1829, Buffalo and Erie County Historical Society.

69 They worked through the fall: The convention was adjourned in the spring of 1831.

70 According to an earlier undocumented account: Haberly, *Pursuit of the Horizon*, 34.

71 "We hereby agree to associate ourselves": Ms., 1825, Century Association, New York. With thanks to Russell Finchum, archivist, for informing me of the existence of these minutes.

71 To oversee the project on the spot: GC to General Lafayette, May 4, 1832, and June 20, 1833, Cornell University Library; cited by Dippie, *Catlin*, 444 n. 30.

CHAPTER 6: A FREE MAN

75 "secure peace and friendship": William N. Fenton, *The Great Law and the Longhouse: A Political History of the Iroquois Confederacy* (Norman: University of Oklahoma Press, 1998), 15.

75 they "came marching in straggling order": Haberly, *Pursuit of the Horizon*, 27ff.

76 a full-length biography: William Leete Stone, *The Life and Times of Red Jacket, or Se-go-ye-wat-ha; Being the Sequel to the History of the Six Nations* (New York: Wiley and Putnam, 1841). See also Jadviga da Costa Nunes, "Red Jacket: The Man and His Portraits," *American Art Journal* 12 (Summer 1980), 5–20.

78 not as "gruesome": William H. Truettner, *The Natural Man Observed: A Study of Catlin's Indian Gallery* (Washington, DC: Smithsonian Institution Press, 1979), 86.

79 Auguste-Marie Chouteau: Shirley Christian, *Before Lewis and Clark: The Story*

of the Chouteaus, the French Dynasty That Ruled America's Frontier (New York: Farrar, Straus and Giroux, 2004).

79   On the cobblestone streets above the wharves: For a lively history of St. Louis's rise as the "gateway to the West," see Ernest Kirschten, *Catfish and Crystal* (Garden City, NY: Doubleday, 1960).

79   "birchbark sacks of maple sugar": Ibid., 21.

80   the one grand hotel in town: Ibid. 34.

81   A six-footer from the age of fifteen: For a balanced and brilliant life of the extrovert of this mythic pair, see Landon Y. Jones, *William Clark and the Shaping of the West* (New York: Hill and Wang, 2004).

82   he felt forced to earn money: Ibid., 209, 237, and 290–91.

83   "in which they agreed to relinquish": Ibid., 84.

84   his terse late journal entries: Ibid., 332. The view of Clark as "conflicted" derives from the many self-justifying comments about his own role in the four hundred treaties he concluded with tribes and their often catastrophic consequences. But it's also possible to see these same remarks as "setting the record straight" for posterity.

84   But Catlin would have already seen: Sellers, *Mr. Peale's Museum*; Richardson et al., *Charles Willson Peale*.

CHAPTER 7: SAVAGE AND CIVILIZED TRIBES

86   "a man of primitive and heroic character": Jones, *William Clark*, 237.

89   "humane and considerate attention": Ibid., 295.

89   "exchange public land in the West": Ibid.

90   They now signed away: Ibid., 167

94   Even the sitter's hands: Truettner, *Natural Man*, 209.

97   "We can hardly conceive": PC to GC, January 21, 1831, Roehm, 50.

98   "detailed descriptions of Indian dress": Truettner, *Natural Man*, 65.

99   "was a veritable museum": John C. Ewer, "William Clark's Indian Museum," in *A Cabinet of Curiosities: Five Episodes in the Evolution of American Museums*, ed. Walter Muir Whitehill (Charlottesville: University Press of Virginia, 1967).

CHAPTER 8: BORDER CROSSINGS

100   In his published letters: These appeared erratically in the *New York Commercial Advertiser* before Catlin self-published them in *Letters and Notes* in London.

101 In letters to his older sister: Papers of the Kilham and Chadwick Familes, 1794–1864, Accession Number 3230, UVA. Quoted with kind permission.

102 All St. Louis was on holiday: Donald Jackson, *Voyages of the Steamboat* Yellow Stone (New York: Ticknor and Fields, 1985), 2.

104 A new law limited: Ibid.

113 "eye of the geologist": Truettner, *Natural Man*, 67.

CHAPTER 9: THE FUR FORTRESS

114 To the terrified natives the *Yellow Stone*: Jackson, *Voyages*, 118.

116 "King of the Upper Missouri": Hiram Martin Chittenden, *The American Fur Trade of the Far West*, vol. 1 (Lincoln: University of Nebraska Press, 1986), 383.

116 One of the traders: Charles Larpenteur, quoted in *Fort Union Trading Post*, "National Historic Structure Report, Part 2; Historical Data Section, Part 1: A Chronological Structural History of Fort Union Trading Post, 1829–1867," Historical Data Section, chapter 4, 1, at www.nps.gov.archve/fous/hsr1-4.htm.

CHAPTER 10: "WHITE MEDICINE MAN"

124 "mountain sheep skin dress": George Catlin, *Adventures of the Ojibbeway and Ioway Indians in England, France, and Belgium; Being Notes of Eight Years' Travels and Residence in Europe with His North American Indian Collection*, vol. 1 (London: published by the author 1852), 264.

126 Almost all cohabited with Indian women: "National Historic Structure Report, Part 2," chapter 2, 20.

126 The first Anglo-European female: Noted by Edwin Denig, a later bourgeois, or chief clerk, of the fort, as reported by visiting Swiss artist Rudolph Kurz in *Journal of Rudolph Friederich Kurz* (Washington, DC: U.S. Government Printing Office, 1937); "National Historic Structure Report, Part 2," chapter 5, 3.

CHAPTER 11: A STRANGER IN PARADISE

131 Everything about the Mandan: The literature on the Mandan is vast, but useful overviews, along with examination of particular issues, are found in the following: Raymond W. Wood and Lee Irwin, "Mandan," in *Handbook of North American Indians: Plains*, ed. R. J. DeMallie, vol. 13, part 1 (Washington,

DC: Smithsonian Institution, 2001), 94–114; *South Dakota Historical Collections: Fort Tecumseh and Fort Pierre Journals and Letter Books*, abstracted by Charles Edward De Land, notes by Doane Robinson, vol. 1, "The Mandans" (Pierre, SD: Hipple Printing Company, 1918), 103–6; Alfred W. Bowers, *Mandan Social and Ceremonial Organization* (Chicago: University of Chicago Press, 2004); Marshall T. Newman, "The Blond Mandan: A Critical Review of an Old Problem," *Southwestern Journal of Anthropology* 6 (Autumn 1950), 255–72; and Gwen A. Williams, *Madoc, the Making of a Myth* (London: Eyre Methuen, 1979).

132 George's new friend: "National Historic Structure Report, Part 2"; "James Kipp," at www.mman.us/kippjames.htm. See also Kurz, *Journal*, July and August of 1851, for a vividly acerbic portrait of Kipp, but one written almost twenty years after Catlin's visit.

138 "beauty touched by strangeness": In slightly varied formulations, this phrase has been attributed to Francis Bacon, Edgar Allan Poe, and John Ruskin.

CHAPTER 12: O-KEE-PA

139 O-kee-pa's fearful secrets: See Catlin, *O-kee-pa*, for the context of Catlin's three versions (and editions) of his firsthand account of O-kee-pa and its role in his professional fortunes.

148 "White men are always": The description of this public sexual exchange, the start of the Buffalo Calling Ceremony, is based upon the notes of Nicholas Biddle, first editor of Lewis and Clark's journals, initially published in English in *Letters of the Lewis and Clark Expedition with Related Documents, 1783–1854*, ed. Donald Jackson (Urbana: University of Illinois Press, 1962), quoted in Catlin, *O-kee-pa*, 9.

149 "During this short separation": Catlin, *O-kee-pa*, 9.

150 "attached, by a small thong": Ibid., 82.

CHAPTER 13: "PROBLEMS OF SHADE, SHADOW AND PERSPECTIVE"

154 "providing for the extinguishment": Jones, *William Clark*, 167.

154 he asked his sister Elizabeth: JC to EC, January 25, 1832, Papers of the Kilham and Chadwick Familes, 1794–1864, UVA.

155 now imprisoned at Jefferson Barracks: Kirschten, *Catfish*, 107, 161.

157 "When Mr. Catlin, the artist": Samuel Gardner Drake, *Book of the Indians*, book 4 (Boston: antiquarian bookstore, 1841), 163, quoted in Donaldson, *George Catlin Indian Gallery*, 33.

158 Washington Irving, last heard: Jones, *William Clark*, 319.

158 *"Let no one see this"*: JC to EC, February 26, 1833, Papers of the Kilham and Chadwick Familes, 1794–1864, UVA.

158 "I have almost everything": Ibid.

159 Catlin's text as it appeared: GC to Pierre Chouteau, Jr., January 29, 1833, P. Chouteau Maffitt Collection, MHS. All but the first paragraph of the letter is printed in Francis A. Chardon, *Chardon's Journals at Fort Clark, 1834–1839*, ed. Annie Heloise Abel (Freeport, NY: Books for Libraries Press, 1970), 222 n. 74; Dippie, *Catlin*, 450.

160 "they can afford to drink but little": GC, letter dated "4th ——— 1833," NYCA, June 20, 1833; Dippie, 450 nn. 20, 21.

CHAPTER 14: A MAN WHO MAKES PICTURES FOR A TRAVELING SHOW

163 His eulogist did not mention that Hook: "Interments in the Historic Congressional Cemetery," *National Intelligencer* (Washington, DC), December 9, 1841.

163 young painter of Indians, Peter Rindisbacher: *St. Louis Beacon*, December 12, 1829.

164 "fancifully decorated with Indian arms": Dippie, *Catlin*, 32

164 "Such facilities as Government": GC to Thomas L. Smith (Cass's assistant), September 4, 1833, Letters Received, Records of the Headquarters of the Army, RG 108, NARA; Dippie, *Catlin*, 446 n. 45.

166 "Nowhere in the world": Michel Chevalier, *Society, Manners and Politics in the United States: Letters on North America* (Gloucester, MA: P. Smith, 1967), 166–67.

166 "Mr. Catlin will endeavor to entertain": *Pittsburgh Gazette*, April 19, 1833.

167 "the wildest tribes in North America": Ibid.

167 "His collection of portraits is destined": Ibid.

169 at a cost of fifty-one dollars: October 26, 1833, George Catlin Papers, Financial Records, Account and Receipt Book: 1826–1838, Box 2, AAA.

169 "There is now in this city": James Hall, "Mr. Catlin's Exhibition of Indian Portraits," *Western Monthly Magazine and Literary Journal*, November 1833, 2, 11.

CHAPTER 15: "WE ARE INVADERS OF A SACRED SOIL"

172 "feel willing to aid me": GC to Maj. Thomas L. Smith, September 1833, Dippie, *Catlin*, 32–33.

173 George's request to Cass stipulated: Roehm, 72.

174 The "Comanche Empire," as it has recently been called: Pekka Hämäläinen, *The Comanche Empire* (New Haven, CT: Yale University Press, 2008).

174 "like a pot of boiling water": David Walker Lupton and Dorothy Ruland Lupton, "A Dragoon in Arkansas Territory in 1833," *Arkansas Historical Quarterly* 45 (Autumn 1986), 224.

174 "Sometimes you may travel": Ibid.

181 "Six litters [of sick]": Harold McCracken, *George Catlin and the Old Frontier* (New York: Dial Press, 1959), 144.

CHAPTER 16: "CATLIN ENCAMPED,
WOLVES IN THE DISTANCE"

187 "'Roslin Castle'": "Fifty-Five Marches for the Militia," in *National Tune Index: Early American Wind and Ceremonial Music, 1636–1836*, ed. Raoul F. Camus (New York: University Music Editions, 1989), 723.

188 "foundations had been laid": Fairfax Downey, *Indian Wars of the U.S. Army, 1776–1865* (Garden City, NY: Doubleday, 1963).

192 "thick stagnant stuff": Christopher Benfey, *Degas in New Orleans* (New York: Knopf, 1997), 3.

193 "taken with the ague": Polly Catlin to FC, February "18305 [sic]," Roehm, 79.

193 "A plan of railroad": "Letter—No. 36, Pensacola, West Florida," NYCA. See also Henry Gardner Cutler, *History of Florida: Past and Present*, vol. 1 (Chicago: Lewis Publishing, 1923), 376. From the context, the author makes it clear that Catlin's letter was made available to investors in the railroad for use as a prospectus.

194 according to Catlin's account: GC to Henry Ward Beecher, October 18, 1853, Vattemare Papers, NYPL. In the same letter cited earlier, where Catlin recalled Lyman Beecher's Litchfield sermons, he tells his son of his visit to Rossville, Georgia, with John Howard Payne, and his subsequent audience with President Andrew Jackson to protest John Ross's imprisonment there and the forced Cherokee removal from that state. There is no evidence that either of these events took place.

CHAPTER 17: FLIGHT PATHS

197 "The great world": Dippie, *Catlin*, 185.

203 "The little child got to bleeding": GC to FC, n.d., Roehm, 91.

204 "It has been impossible": Ibid., 90.

204 a mass execution of American troops: Accounts of the attack on the garrison stationed at the Presidio La Bahia under the command of Colonel Fannin and known as the Goliad Massacre are found in Kathryn Stoner O'Connor, *The Presidio La Bahía del Espíritu Santo de Zúñiga, 1721 to 1846* (Austin, TX: Von Boeckmann-Jones, 1966), and Barbara Rimkunas, "Joseph March Chadwick and the Massacre at Goliad," at www.seacoastonline.com/apps/pbcs.dll/article?aid=/2009.

205 In his hometown of Exeter: *Exeter News-Letter*, July 10, 1836; *St. Louis Bulletin*, July 1, 1836.

205 "They were the glory of the race of rangers": Walt Whitman, "Song of Myself," quoted in Lois Burkhalter, " 'My Real Friend, Joe,' " *American Heritage* 16 (April 1965), 44.

206 He acted, his mother declared, "as though he was crazy": Polly Catlin in a postscript to letter from PC to FC, September 11, 1836, Roehm, 95.

CHAPTER 18: THE PIPESTONE QUARRY

210 of that same tribe of Santee Sioux: For the essential account of the Sioux role in westward expansion and growth of the Northern Plains, see Richard White, "The Winning of the West: The Expansion of the Western Sioux in the Eighteenth and Nineteenth Centuries," *Journal of American History* 65 (September 1978).

211 pyrophyllite, diaspore, and quartz: Jackson's findings were published in Benjamin Silliman's *American Journal of Science*, series 1, vol. 35 (1839), 388. A report by Catlin followed that same year in vol. 38, 138. For a history of publications on the subject and conclusions about the mineral itself, see Ernest L. Berg, "Notes on Catlinite and the Sioux Quartzite," *American Minerologist* 23 (April 1938), 259–68.

212 "most too *poor* to do *anything*": GC to FC, December 29, 1836, Roehm, 102.

212 "public letter": NYCA, August 3, 1836. Not reprinted in *Letters and Notes*.

212 "she could not bear the thought of his going": PC to FC, September 11, 1836, Roehm, 94.

213 "Great Rail Road": GC to FC, December 29, 1836, Roehm, 102.

CHAPTER 19: A "GO-A-HEAD" ARTIST

214 "Dissolving Tableaux" . . . "Pyric [*sic*] Fires": *Daily Albany Argus*, June 17, 1837.

215 the Panic of 1837: See Stephen Mihm, *A Nation of Counterfeiters: Capitalists, Con Men, and the Making of the United States* (Cambridge, MA: Harvard University Press, 2007).

216 "rebellions and revolutions": Allan Nevins and Milton Halsey Thomas, eds., *The Diary of George Templeton Strong*, abridged by Thomas J. Pressley (Seattle, WA: University of Washington Press, 1988), 63. See also page 4 for a discussion of the Panic of 1837 by Pressley.

217 a novel attraction like vaudeville: Sean Wilentz, *Chants Democratic: New York City and the Rise of the American Working Class, 1788–1850* (New York: Oxford University Press, 1984).

217 the Ravels: "The principal attraction was the Ravel French company of rope dancers and pantomime actors. These personages, as usual, were advertised as the *very first* rope dancers in Europe." *New York Mirror*, August 11, 1832, 43. For more on the Ravels, see Don B. Wilmeth, ed., *The Cambridge Guide to American Theatre*, 2nd ed. (Cambridge, UK: Cambridge University Press, 2007), 544.

217 "CATLIN'S INDIAN GALLERY": *NYCA*, September 23, 1837.

218 "intensely interesting": George Catlin, *Adventures*, appendix, 215–16.

218 "set lectures": *NYCA*, September 25, 1837.

218 "spontaneous oral explanations": Ibid.

218 "the highest respect": William H. Seward to GC, October 4, 1839, George Catlin Papers, Reel 5824, Frame 68, AAA. See also Dippie, *Catlin*, 147.

219 "spoke entirely too vehemently": McCracken, *George Catlin*, 184.

220 "sins of our Government": Ibid., 184–85.

223 "Mr. Catlin's great collection": *The Diary of Philip Hone, 1828–1851*, ed. Allan Nevins (New York: Dodd, Mead, 1936), 290.

223 "had seldom witnessed so interesting an exhibition": Ibid., 291.

224 "patriot heroes": Alvin M. Josephy, *The Patriot Chiefs: A Chronicle of American Indian Resistance* (New York: Penguin, 1993), 177.

225 "very strange": GC to Carey A. Harris, January 31, 1838, Record Group 75, Letters Received, 1824–1880, Office of Indian Affairs, Florida Emigr., C535, M234. Roll 290, NARA.

225 "construed it into a compliment": Ibid. See also Dippie, *Catlin*, 90.

226 "that their modes of life": GC to Carey A. Harris, January 31, 1838, Record

Group 75, Letters Received, 1824–1880, Office of Indian Affairs, Florida Emigr., C535, M234. Roll 290, NARA.

226 "worth much more dead": PC to FC, March 18, 1838, Dippie, *Catlin*, 117. See also Roehm, 127.

226 "as I presume": Thomas Hartley Crawford to GC, November 15, 1838, Record Group 75, Letters Sent, 1824–1880, Office of Indian Affairs, Florida Emigr., M21, Roll 25, NARA.

CHAPTER 20: "WITHOUT FORTUNE AND WITHOUT PATRONAGE"

229 "I have never been acquainted": PC to FC, January 21, 1838, Roehm, 126.

230 "it becomes painful": PC to FC, May 4, 1838, Roehm, 129–30.

230 "receipts will much more": Ibid.

231 "to ascertain from Mr. Catlin": Dippie, *Catlin*, 65.

233 "Mr. George Catlin": Henry Clay to Earl Selkirk, July 7, 1838, George Catlin Papers, Reel 5824, Frame 43, AAA.

233 Catlin had printed 2,500 copies: *Catalogue of Catlin's Indian Gallery of Portraits, Landscapes, Manners and Customs, Costumes &c. &c.: collected during seven years' travel amongst thirty-eight different tribes, speaking different languages* (New York: Piercy and Reed, 1837).

234 "one car load": McCracken, *George Catlin*, 188.

234 "There is not in our land": Catlin, *Adventures*, vol. 2, 229.

235 "sinister rumors": *The Liberator*, June 22, 1838.

235 "A crime is projected": Ibid.

236 "If your seal is set": Ibid.

236 "his collection makes a fine show": CGC to Abigail Sayre Catlin, September 29, 1838, Roehm, 139.

237 "I wish you could see George": Ibid., Roehm, 138.

237 "The ladies here": CGC to Abigail Sayre Catlin, September 29, 1838, Roehm, 139.

237 "his time": Ibid., 140.

238 "extremity of the season": PC to James Catlin, January 4, 1839, Roehm, 142.

238 "suitable rooms": Ibid.

238 "leisure": Ibid.

238 "write what he has": Ibid.

238 "he will be fast spending": Ibid

239 "pretty full convinced": GC to Joel Roberts Poinsett, [February] 27, 1839, Reel P20, Frame 438, AAA. See also Dippie, *Catlin*, 111, 462 n. 25.

240 "dressed himself each evening": *Philadelphia Saturday Courier*, May 25, 1839.

241 "the public houses": GC to Theodore "Burr" Catlin, August 18, 1839, George Catlin Papers, Box 1, Folder 2, Reel 5824, Frames 60–61, AAA.

242 "Keep your brush": GC to Theodore "Burr" Catlin, September 2, 1839, George Catlin Papers, Box 1, Folder 2, Reel 5824, Frames 64–65, AAA.

CHAPTER 21: THE GREAT AND THE GOOD

244 "I was suddenly thrown upon my back": GC to Benjamin Silliman, November 24, 1839, HSP.

244 "an abcess [*sic*] formed": Ibid.

244 "entirely defer the promise": Ibid.

246 "the most awkward part of my freight": Catlin, *Adventures*, vol. 1, 2.

247 "they were not much larger than my foot": Ibid., 32.

247 "clawed and chewed": Ibid., 3.

247 "The circumstance of sixty passengers": Ibid., 9.

247 "Ragamuffin children": Ibid., 12.

248 "an unsuspecting old lady": Ibid., 14.

248 "breakfast and a clean face": Ibid., 16.

251 "complete with house and reindeer": Altick, *Shows*, 273–74.

251 costly repairs: For specifics on the costs of repairs to Egyptian Hall, see Catlin's account book, George Catlin Papers (originals), Box 2, AAA.

253 "most conspicuous": Catlin, *Adventures*, vol. 1, 35.

254 "philosophical enquirer": *Literary Gazette and Journal of Belles Lettres, Arts, Sciences, &c*, February 1, 1840, no. 1202, 77; see Catlin, *Adventures*, vol. 1, appendix, 207.

254 "work of deep and permanent interest": *Art-Union*, 1840; see Catlin, *Adventures*, vol. 1, appendix, 208.

254 "Mr. Catlin's avowed object in visiting": "Catlin's *Indian Gallery*," *Quarterly Review* 65 (London: John Murray, 1840), 420; see Catlin, *Adventures*, vol. 1, appendix, 206.

255 "As I was daily growing richer": Catlin, *Adventures*, vol. 1, 45.

257 "He loved me too much": Ibid., 50.

257 "Her Most Gracious MAJESTY": Ibid., 51.

258 *"Three Notices, Twenty-five Columns"*: *Literary Gazette and Journal of Belles Lettres, Arts, Sciences, &c*, October 2, 1841, no. 1289, 633; see Catlin, *Adventures*, vol. 1, 53–54.

258 "This is a remarkable book": *Westminster Review*; see Catlin, *Adventures*, vol. 1, 53.

258 "free and easy conversational style": *Morning Chronicle* (London); see Catlin, *Adventures*, vol. 1, 55.

258 "loud & repeated cheers": GC to PC and Polly Catlin, February 17, 1840, Roehm, 157.

258 "clearness—for self-possession": Ibid.

259 He wrote home proudly: GC to PC and Polly Catlin, January 10, 1840, Roehm, 155.

259 "32,500 visitors": Inscription by GC on back of letter sent by Theodore "Burr" Catlin to FC, Roehm, 207.

CHAPTER 22: HIGH SOCIETY

261 "several living figures": Catlin, *Adventures*, vol. 1, 61.

261 "for many years": Ibid.

261 "contain and perpetuate": Ibid., 62.

261 "Great Britain has more": Ibid.

262 "For the occupation of a new country": Ibid.

262 "literary and scientific men": Ibid., 64.

263 "I was here at once": Ibid.

263 "their kilts, and with the badges": Ibid., 66.

264 "He took especial pains": Ibid., 69.

264 "lady Patronesses": Ellen Moers, *The Dandy: Brummell to Beerbohm* (New York: Viking Press, 1960), 43–60.

265 "the most brilliant and splendid": Catlin, *Adventures*, vol. 1, 70.

265 "make a *sensation*": Ibid., 69.

265 "finest costumes . . . along with weapons": Ibid., 70.

265 "with a bold and Indian outline of face": Ibid.

266 "denoting his readiness": Ibid.

266 "bold daubs of vermilion": Ibid., 72.

267 "flourishing his enormous headdress": Ibid.

267 "The introductions I had": Ibid., 74.

267 "magnificent bracelet": Ibid., 76.

268 "violent exertions": Ibid., 77.

268 "a flow of perspiration": Ibid.

268 "It was now past sunrise": Ibid., 78.

268 "gaze and grin at each other": Ibid.

270 "I wish really": GC to PC and Polly Catlin, June 3, 1840, Roehm, 171.

270 "We who are younger": Ibid.

271 "well-attended & fashionable": Ibid.

271 "Oh what feelings": Ibid.

271 "I felt now as if": Catlin, *Adventures*, vol. 1, 60.

272 "Clara has seen but little": GC to PC and Polly Catlin, June 29, 1840, Roehm, 174.

272 "more familiar faces": Journal entry, July 27, 1840, Asher B. Durand Papers, Journals, 1840, Reel N20, Box 6, page 54, NYPL.

272 "multitude of the representative faces": Journal entry, June 27, 1840, Asher B. Durand Papers, Journals, 1840, Reel N20, Box 6, page 21, NYPL.

272 "glad to learn": Ibid.

273 another Catlin venture: George Catlin, *Manners, Customs and Condition of the North American Indians. A Descriptive Catalogue of Catlin's Indian Gallery: Containing Portraits, Landscapes, Costumes, &c. and Representations of the Manners and Customs of the North American Indians* (London: published by the author, Egyptian Hall, Piccadilly), 1840.

273 "is an extremely interesting man": George Palmer Putnam to Victorine Haven, October 18, 1840, Herbert Putnam Collection, Family Correspondence, Folder: "Victorine Haven Putnam (mother) 1840–41," Manuscript Division, Library of Congress.

273 "I think I shall go": Ibid.

274 "Would to God": GC to PC, September 30, 1840, Roehm, 193.

275 "full value": CGC to PC and Polly Catlin, October 29, 1840, Roehm, 196–97.

275 "But they little know": Ibid.

275 "But we are here": Ibid.

CHAPTER 23: "TABLEAUX VIVANS"

277 "That big chief": Catlin, *Adventures*, vol. 1, 88.

277 "My dear little *Christian* Clara": Ibid.

277 "one of the prettiest": Ibid.

278 "in the wake": Ibid., 89.

278 "This, in the street": Ibid.

278 "The idea was so ridiculous": Ibid.

278 "about 20 American gentlemen": George Palmer Putnam to Victorine Haven, November 1, 1840, Herbert Putnam Collection, Family Correspondence, Folder: "Victorine Haven Putnam (mother) 1840–41," Manuscript Division, Library of Congress.

281 "narrowly escaped with her life": GC to PC, November 3, 1841, Roehm, 221.

281 "He is an honest, hearty, famous fellow": Charles Dickens to Mrs. S. C. Hall [Anna Maria Hall], December 2, 1841, in *The Letters of Charles Dickens*, vol. 2, ed. Madeline House and Graham Storey (Oxford, UK: Clarendon Press, 1969), 438. See also Kate Flint, "Dickens and the Native American," in *Dickens and the Children of Empire*, ed. Wendy S. Jacobson (New York: Palgrave, 2000), 95.

281 "howling, whistling, clucking": Charles Dickens, "The Noble Savage," *Household Words* 7 (June 11, 1853). See also Altick, "Noble Savage," in Altick, *Shows*.

282 "an accurate survey": Catlin, *Adventures*, vol. 1, 98.

282 "accuracy and execution": Ibid.

282 "a handsome silver medal": Catlin won a silver medal "for a model of Niagara Falls, Indian dress, and specimens of minerals and pipe clay" in 1839. *Journal of the American Institute* 4 (September 1839), 673.

283 "for whose rights they said": Catlin, *Adventures*, vol. 1, 98.

283 "afflicting intelligence": GC to PC, April 3, 1842, Roehm, 243–44.

283 "No one, my *dear, dear* parent": Ibid., 244.

284 "beautiful little 'Rose Cottage'": Ibid., 245.

284 "I wish to have one copy": Nicholas Basbanes, *A Gentle Madness: Bibliophiles, Bibliomanes, and the Eternal Passion for Books* (New York: Henry Holt, 1995), 120–21.

287 "Catlin may be called": *Detroit Free Press*, June 21, 1839, quoted in Henry R. Schoolcraft, *Personal Memoirs of a Residence of Thirty Years with the Indian Tribes of the American Frontiers: With Brief Notices of Passing Events, Facts, and Opinions A.D. 1812 to A.D. 1842* (Philadelphia: Lippincott, Grambo, and Company, 1851), 654.

287 "certificates": See Dippie, *Catlin*, 52.

287 "showman's fame": Ibid., 293.

288 "most effectually put at rest": Ibid., 79.

289 "deep regret": Ibid., 94.

CHAPTER 24: "INDIANS! REAL INDIANS!"

290 "old disciplined troop": Catlin, *Adventures*, vol. 1, 100.

292 "shaped to suit their infant minds": Ibid., 99.

292 "deafening war whoop": Ibid.

292 "having heard me lecture": Ibid.

292 "in all the provincial towns of the kingdom": Ibid., 100.

292 "My career was then rapid": Ibid.

293 "'a huge hat encircled'": *The Scotsman*, April 8, 1843; see Robert M. Lewis, "Wild American Savages and the Civilized English: Catlin's Indian Gallery and the Shows of London," *European Journal of American Studies* 1 (2008), at http://ejas.revues.org/2263.

294 "Since my dear father's death": CGC to Matthew Gregory, n.d., George Catlin Papers, Missouri History Museum Archives, St. Louis.

294 "positively the last": Catlin, *Adventures*, vol. 1, 100.

294 "will show you a way": Ibid., 101.

295 "that may promote": Ibid.

295 hazily heroicizing memoir: The memoir by Rankin's maternal uncle C. Stuart, published in London in 1844, is entitled *Description of the Ojibbeway Indians Now on a Visit to England*. See also Altick, *Shows*, 276–78.

295 "directly opposite to my present arrangements": Catlin, *Adventures*, vol. 1, 101.

295 "I have always been opposed": Ibid.

296 "with the understanding": Ibid., 102.

296 "homnibus at the door": Ibid.

296 In a letter published: The letter from Secretary of War Joel R. Poinsett, which first appeared in the *Globe* (Washington, DC) on October 21, 1839, was subsequently reprinted in *Niles' National Register*, November 2, 1839, 150.

297 "A crowd followed the bus": *Adventures*, vol. 1, 102.

297 "[the reader would find] me turning": Ibid., 103.

297 "This excursion": Ibid., 112.

298 "sharing equally with you": Ibid., 106.

298 "To this proposition": Ibid.

299 "being much pleased": Ibid., 106–7. See also "Visit of the Ojibbeway OQ Chippeway Indians of North America to Mr. Catlin's Exhibition," *Manchester Times and Gazette*, November 11, 1843, and "A Party of North American Indians in Manchester," *Manchester Guardian*, November 11, 1843.

299 "spirituous liquor": Catlin, *Adventures*, vol. 1, 107.

299 "Into the midst of this mass": Ibid., 114.

300 On November 6, 1843: George Junior's date of birth is based on an announcement in the *Liverpool Mercury*, November 17, 1843.

300 "house jarred with the leap": Catlin, *Adventures*, vol. 1, 137.

301 "Great Mother": Ibid. See also "Presentation to Her Majesty of the Ojibbeway Indians," *Morning Post* (London), December 22, 1843; "Windsor—Wednesday," *Standard* (London), December 21, 1843; "The Ojibbeway Indians," *Essex Standard* (Colchester, UK), December 22, 1843; and "The Ojibbeway Indians," *Illustrated London News* 3 (December 23, 1843), 401.

301 "a light wine": Catlin, *Adventures*, vol. 1, 139.

301 "Yes, my good fellows": Ibid.

302 "roars of applause": Ibid., 143. See also *Lloyd's Weekly London Newspaper* (London), February 18, 1844.

302 "frightful": Catlin, *Adventures*, vol. 1, 144.

302 "utter the exciting word": Ibid., 148.

302 as practiced by "English fashionable people": Ibid., 149.

302 "a glass of it at dinner": Ibid.

302 "similar quantity": Ibid.

CHAPTER 25: GEORGE CATLIN'S WILD WEST SHOW

304 "indulged in their *chickabobboo*": Catlin, *Adventures*, vol. 1, 167.

304 "Hottentot Venus": Altick, *Shows*, 269–73.

304 to "make . . . a little money": Catlin, *Adventures*, vol. 1, 154.

305 "The Jolly Fat Dame": Ibid., 156.

305 "fully equipped and prepared": Ibid., 162.

306 "a beautiful bracelet": Ibid., 168.

306 "Many ladies were offering": Ibid.

306 "many there were in the room": Ibid., 169.

307 "respectable carver and gilder": *Illustrated London News* 4 (April 13, 1844), 228.

307 "beautiful Miss Haynes," *Adventures*, vol. 1, 181, 187.

307 "a life of semi-barbarism": Ibid., 184.

307 "excitement": Ibid., 187.

307 "a robe of blue cloth": "An Indian's Marriage in London," *New World* 8 (May 25, 1844), 650.

308 "fine sense of the struggles": "The 'Strong Wind' in St. Martin's Church," *Punch* 6, 173.

309 "had rented the adjoining room": *Adventures*, vol. 1, 187.

310 "Wild Enough!": Reddin, *Wild West*, 35.

311 a life of "semi-barbarism": See "Sarah Haynes—The Indian's Wife," *New York Sun*, reprinted in *Western Literary Messenger* 18 (August, 1852), 255. See also "Sad End of a Romance," *The Republican*, June 16, 1852.

311 Arthur Rankin gave up show business: See Patrick Brode, "Arthur Rankin," *Dictionary of Canadian Biography Online*, vol. 12, University of Toronto / Université Laval, 2000, at www.biographi.ca/009004-119.01-e.php?&id_nbr=6388. See also "Colonel Arthur Rankin, 1816–1893 Historical Marker," at http://detroit 1701.org/Rankin%20Marker.html.

311 "having a little leisure": *Adventures*, vol. 1, 197.

312 He gave his drawings, together with 130 pounds: Ibid., 200.

312 "But even this *was not to be*": Ibid., 202.

313 The greatest showman, promoter, and impresario: See A. H. Saxon, *P.T. Barnum: The Legend and the Man* (New York: Columbia University Press), 1995.

314 "presented each day a scene of drunkenness and riot": U.S. Indian Agent Andrew Hughes to Superintendent of Indian Affairs Henry Doge, May 12, 1837, Letters Received, Great Nemaha Agency, M234, Roll 308, Records of the Bureau of Indian Affairs, RG 75, NARA; cited by Joseph B. Herring, "Selling the 'Noble Savage' Myth: George Catlin and the Iowa Indians in Europe, 1843–1845," *Kansas History: A Journal of the Central Plains* 29 (Winter 2006–2007), 233.

315 "Rocky Mountain wild I[ndians]": *Selected Letters of P.T. Barnum*, ed. A. H. Saxon (New York: Columbia University Press, 1983), 14.

315 wedding blankets: Joel Benton, *A Unique Story of a Marvellous Career: Life of Hon. Phineas T. Barnum* (New York: Union Publishing House, 1891), 137.

315 Dohumme: Ibid.

315 "untutored savages": Ibid., 135.

316 "the little wretch": Parkman quoted in *The Journals of Francis Parkman*, ed. Mason Wade, vol. 1 (London: Eyre and Spottiswoode, n.d.), 222–23 (entry for May 1844). See also Dippie, *Catlin*, 102–3.

316 "on our joint account": See Phineas Taylor Barnum, *Life of P.T. Barnum* (London: Sampson Low, Son, & Co., 1855), 346; A. H. Saxon, *P.T. Barnum: The Legend and the Man* (New York: Columbia University Press, 1995), 369 n. 3; Dippie, *Catlin*, 104.

317 "trashy stuff": Audubon quoted in Dippie, *Catlin*, 59–60.

317 "was not to be depended": Fuller quoted in ibid., 60.

317 "I find him a very kind": Barnum quoted in Philip B. Kunhardt, Jr., Philip B. Kunhardt III, and Peter W. Kunhardt. *P.T. Barnum: America's Greatest Showman* (New York: Knopf, 1995), 62.

318 "The new Indian show": Dippie, *Catlin*, 101.

CHAPTER 26: "DÉJÀ VU—ALL OVER AGAIN"

320 "consummate blackguard": GC to CGC, n.d., George Catlin Papers, Reel 5824, Frame 102, Box 1, Folder 4, AAA.

320 "regular roarer": P. T. Barnum to Moses Kimball, August 18, 1844, included in Saxon, *Selected Letters*, [letter] nos. 20, 28.

320 Catlin saw the wrapper: For Catlin's anxiety-ridden response to Clara's packet of letters, see George Catlin Papers, Reel 5824, Frame 102, AAA.

321 "dear little chubs": Ibid.

322 "not only the exciting interest": George Catlin Papers, Reel 5824, Frame 100, Box 1, Folder 4, AAA.

322 "within pences of having nothing": Ibid.

322 "seemed daily to be losing flesh": *Adventures*, vol. 2, 175.

323 "The Ojibbeways were subjects": Ibid., 210. See also insightful articles in *Galignani's Messenger*, April 22 and 28, 1845.

323 "each one came out from his toilet": *Adventures*, vol. 2, 211.

324 "in the most free": Ibid.

324 "tell these good fellows": Ibid., 212.

324 "chattering whistles": Ibid., 214.

325 "My Father, since I have come": Ibid., 215.

325 "tedious and vexatious": Ibid., 210. According to *Galignani's Messenger* of May 10, 1845, the exhibition opened on May 8, 1845, not June 3, 1845, as often noted.

326 Honoré Daumier . . . "Cham": "L'Année Prochaine Illustrée," *Le Charivari*, December 31, 1845.

326 "the color of blood": Author's translation of Charles Baudelaire, "Peintres et Aquafortistes," in *Oeuvres Completes de Charles Baudelaire*, vol. 2 (Paris: Gallimard, Bibliothèque de la Pléiade, 1976), 634.

326 "guide among the savages": Ibid.

328 "in their fallen state": Author's translation of Charles Baudelaire, "Salon de 1859," in *Oeuvres Completes*, vol. 2, 802.

328 "modern Jason": Author's translation of George Sand, "Relation d'un Voyage chez les Sauvages de Paris (Lettre à un Ami)," in *Le Diable à Paris: Paris et les Parisiens à la Plume et au Crayon*, vol. 2 (Paris: J. Hetzel, 1846), 186–212.

328 "Robed in his most splendid": Ibid.

329 "but the tawny complexion": Ibid.

329 O-kee-wee-me died on June 12, 1845: On June 13, 1845, *Galignani's Messenger* reported: "The Ioway Indians have sustained a severe loss. O-ke-our-mi [*sic*], the wife of Little-Wolf, died yesterday of an affection of the lungs, brought on by grief for the death of her young child in London."

329 converted to the Roman Catholic faith: On June 14, 1845, *Galignani's Messenger* reported O-kee-wee-me's conversion to Christianity. See also *Niles' National Register*, June 14, 1845.

329 "like the recusants of old": Benita Eisler, *Naked in the Marketplace: The Lives of George Sand* (Berkeley, CA: Counterpoint, 2006), 5.

330 an elaborate funerary monument: For information on the funerary monument to O-kee-wee-me, see Charles W. Millard, *Auguste Préault: Sculpteur Romantique, 1809–79* (Paris: Réunion des musees nationaux, 1997), 24, 162; Charles W. Millard, Préault Papers, J. Paul Getty Research Institute and Library, Special Collections, 29 Boxes, No. 990025, consulted with the kind permission of Charles W. Millard and the J. Paul Getty Library, Los Angeles, CA.

330 "to leave within the week": Dippie, *Catlin*, 107. See also *Adventures*, vol. 2, 273, and *Galignani's Messenger*, July 5, 1845.

331 "a moral energy never surpassed": *Galignani's Messenger*, July 30, 1845. See also *Galignani's Messenger*, August 4, 1845, for the funeral notification and July 28, 1845, for the reopening of the exhibition at Salle Valentino.

CHAPTER 27: A FLIGHT OF ROYALS

334 "ourang outangs, for they appeared": Maungwudaus quoted in Donald B. Smith, "Maungwudaus Goes Abroad," *Beaver* 307 (Autumn 1976), 4.

335 "American gentleman of great wealth": *Adventures*, vol. 2, 272.

335 "heavy responsibility": Ibid., 273.

335 "The poor fellows enjoyed": Ibid., 274.

335 "The dances, shooting, etc.": *Galignani's Messenger*, August 19, 1843.

335 its new location: For the move to the Galérie des Beaux-Arts, see *Galignani's Messenger*, September 8, 1845.

336 "the proudest one": *Adventures*, vol. 2, 282.

336 "to a small town": Ibid., 284.

337 "while his Majesty": Ibid., 285.

337 "Two Kings and Two Queens": Ibid.

337 *"greatness of soul"*: Ibid., 319.

338 "commission": Dippie, *Catlin*, 122. See also GC to Alexandre Vattemare, January 12, 1846, Vattemare Collection, NYPL.

340 "just old enough": *Adventures*, vol. 2, 312.

340 "adopted my painting-room": Ibid.

341 "the practice of seducing": *Niles' National Register*, March 7, 1846, 2. Catlin's letter was dated January 30, 1846.

341 "detention in Brussels": Ibid.

342 "ordered into the Louvre": GC to Sir Thomas Phillipps, February 17, 1846, George Catlin Collection, Thomas Gilcrease Institute of American History and Art, 1840–1860, Part 6, Reel 3277, Frames 532–34, 3876.622, AAΛ, transcription in A. N. L. Munby, *The Formation of the Phillipps Library from 1841 to 1872*, Phillipps Studies No. 4 (Cambridge, UK: Cambridge University Press, 1956), 54–55.

342 "a Col. Fawcett": Ibid.

344 "several very respectable offers": "Memorial of George Catlin," Sen. Doc. No. 374, 29th Cong., 1st Sess. See also Dippie, *Catlin*, 110–11, 461–62 n. 24.

344 "Fifteen American citizens": Dippie, *Catlin*, 111.

344 "a deep interest in the collection": Ibid., 111–12.

345 "enlarge and perfect it": Ibid., 112.

345 "interesting to our countrymen": Ibid.

345 "it is absolutely necessary": Ibid.

345 "a matter of high national importance": Ibid., 113.

345 "Americanness": Ibid.

345 "double it in value": Ibid.

345 "for the increase": Ibid., 114.

345 "No productions": Ibid., 113.

345 "find a place": *Congressional Globe*, 29th Cong., 2nd Sess., 529. See also Dippie, *Catlin*, 114.

345 "would not vote a cent": *Congressional Globe*, 29th Cong., 2nd Sess., 529. See also Dippie, *Catlin*, 115–16.

348 "The days and nights": *Adventures*, vol. 2, 323.

348 an inflammation of the lungs "so violent": GC to John Howard Payne, [April 1847], Vattemare Collection, NYPL; Dippie, *Catlin*, 118.

348 "dropsey of the brain": GC to Alexandre Vattemare, June 15, 1847, Vattemare Collection, NYPL; Dippie, *Catlin*, 119.

348 "brain fever": Dippie, *Catlin*, 465 n. 43.

348 "my whole soul": GC to Alexandre Vattemare, June 15, 1847, Vattemare Collection, NYPL; Dippie, *Catlin*, 119.

349 "introduced an influenza": Dippie, *Catlin*, 464–65 n. 43.

349 he wrote to Sir Thomas Phillipps: GC to Sir Thomas Phillipps, October 4, 1847, George Catlin Collection, Thomas Gilcrease Institute of American History and Art, 1840–1860, Part 6, Reel 3277, Frames 555–56; 3876.632, AAA. For Phillipps's response, see draft of letter, October 8, 1847, written on GC letter to Sir Thomas Phillipps, October 4, 1847. See also Joan Carpenter Troccoli, "George Catlin and Sir Thomas Phillipps: A Nineteenth-Century Friendship," *Rare Books & Manuscripts Librarianship* 10 (March 20, 1995), 14.

CHAPTER 28: "A THING BELONGING TO US"

351 Baudelaire, the greatest critic of his age: *The Mirror of Art: Critical Studies by Charles Baudelaire*, ed. and trans. Jonathan Mayne (Garden City, NY: Doubleday, 1956), 49, 72–73 ("The Salon of 1846), and 268, 289 ("The Salon of 1859"); cited by Dippie, *Catlin*, 465 n. 47. See also Robert N. Beetem, "George Catlin in France: His Relationship to Delacroix and Baudelaire," *Art Quarterly* 24 (Summer 1961), 29–44.

351 "By the way": GC to Sir Thomas Phillipps, March 29, 1848, George Catlin Collection, Thomas Gilcrease Institute of American History and Art, 1840–1860, Part 6, Reel 3277, AAA.

354 "I should be mortified": Ralph Randolph Gurley to Francis Markoe, Jr., corresponding secretary of the National Institute for the Promotion of Science, September 22, 1841, reprinted from "National Institute," *Newark Daily Advertiser*, September 28, 1841; Dippie, *Catlin*, 129.

355 "encumbered": Dippie, *Catlin*, 132.

355 "*conditionally* sold in England": GC to Thomas Phillipps, August 25, 1848; transcription in *Phillipps Studies*, no. 4, 56–57.

355 "the last [I] could possibly make": GC to Hon. Sir, January 4, 1849, Papers of John M. Clayton. See Dippie, *Catlin*, 132.

355 "I do think": Daniel Webster, *National Intelligencer*, March 5, 1849. *Congressional Globe*, 30th Cong., 2nd Sess., 603.

356 "I perhaps should have felt": Robert M. T. Hunter, *National Intelligencer*, March 5, 1849. See also Dippie, *Catlin*, 133.

356 "displayed in any room": Jefferson Davis, *The Papers of Jefferson Davis*, vol. 4, ed. Lynda L. Crist et al. (Baton Rouge: Louisiana University Press, 1983), 14–17; cited by Dippie, *Catlin*, 135.

357 "in earnest": Dippie, *Catlin*, 135.

357 exacted payment "in kind": GC to Sir Thomas Phillipps, May 8, 1849, George Catlin Collection, Thomas Gilcrease Institute of American History and Art, 1840–1860, Part 6, Reel 3277, Frames 586–87, 3876.645, AAA.

357 eleven by fourteen inches: Troccoli, "George Catlin and Sir Thomas Phillipps," 17.

358 "I wish you or I": GC to Sir Thomas Phillipps, December 30, 1848, George Catlin Collection, Thomas Gilcrease Institute of American History and Art, 1840–1860, Part 6, Reel 3277, AAA. See also Dippie, *Catlin*, 136.

358 "The Valley of the Mississippi": *Manchester Guardian*, January 7, 1849; cited by Dippie, *Catlin*, 136, 469 n. 75.

358 "gold diggings": Ibid.

359 "seven days' ride west": Dippie, *Catlin*, 137.

359 "together obtain": *Manchester Guardian*, January 7, 1849; cited by Dippie, *Catlin*, 137, 469 n. 75.

359 "land shark": See Dippie, *Catlin*, 138 and 470 n. 77, which references "American Land Agency Swindlers," *Times* (London), June 10, 1851.

359 He had also invested: Regarding these financial losses, see GC to Sir Thomas Phillipps, December 14, 1850, George Catlin Collection, Thomas Gilcrease Institute of American History and Art, 1840–1860, Part 6, Reel 3277, Frames 593–94, 3876.645, AAA. See also Dippie, *Catlin*, 138–39, and Troccoli, "George Catlin and Sir Thomas Phillipps," 16.

360 "I am extremely sorry": Sir Thomas Phillipps to GC, December 20, 1850, George Catlin Collection, Thomas Gilcrease Institute of American History and Art, 1840–1860, Part 6, Reel 3277, Frames 595–96, AAA. See also GC to Sir Thomas Phillipps, April 15, 1851, ibid.; GC to Sir Thomas Phillipps, July 10, 1851, ibid.; Sir Thomas Phillipps to GC, July 12, 1851, ibid.; and GC to Sir Thomas Phillipps, November 27, 1851, ibid.

361 "of great advantage to Ethnology": Dippie, *Catlin*, 141, 470–71 n. 83.

362 "Aboriginal manufactures": Ibid., 142.

362 "These Indians and their works": *Illustrated London News* 19 (August 23, 1851), 254–55.

363 a group of Iroquois: Ibid., 234.

363 "I *must* keep": GC to Sir Thomas Phillipps, November 27, 1851, George Catlin Collection, Thomas Gilcrease Institute of American History and Art, 1840–1860, Part 6, Reel 3277, Frames 608–9, AAA.

363 "at the expiration of which": Quoted in Dippie, *Catlin*, 143.

364 "I have been led": GC to Daniel Webster, April 4, 1852, NYHS, Roehm, 441–43.

364 "Queen's Bench *prison!*": GC to Daniel Webster, April 15, 1852, Morristown National Park, Morristown, NJ; Dippie, *Catlin*, 145, 472 n. 91. See also *North American Miscellany and Dollar Magazine* 4 (July 1852), 271.

365 "If nothing is voted for *me*": GC to Daniel Webster, April 15, 1852, Morristown National Park, Morristown, NJ; Dippie, *Catlin*, 145, 472 n. 91.

366 "for a few days": GC to Webster, May 8, 1852, Morristown National Park, Morristown, NJ; Dippie, *Catlin*, 146.

CHAPTER 29: MAGICAL MYSTERY TOURS

369 "I am now impatient": GC to Sir Thomas Phillipps, January 23, 1853, George Catlin Collection, Thomas Gilcrease Institute of American History and Art, 1840–1860, Part 6, Reel 3277, Frames 629–30, AAA.

369 Hôtel des Étrangers: For information on the Hôtel des Étrangers on rue Tronchet, see Zadock Thompson, *Journal of a Trip to London and Paris and the Great Exhibition in 1851* (Burlington, VT: Nichols and Warren, 1852), as well as *Bradshaw's Continental Monthly of 1853*.

370 "Bedroom Kitchen and large Room": GC to Sir Thomas Phillipps, November 7, 1853, quoted in Troccoli, *First Artist*, 29. See also Munby, *Formation*, 60–61. In addition to the seventy watercolors that Catlin sold to Phillipps in 1853, Phillipps purchased a copy of George Catlin's *Souvenir of the North American Indians as They Were, in the Middle of the Nineteenth Century* (1849), a collection of fifty watercolors, now in the Gilcrease Museum. See Troccoli, *First Artist*, 21–22, and Troccoli, "George Catlin and Sir Thomas Phillipps," 16–19.

371 "gold dust and nuggets": George Catlin, *Episodes from "Life among the Indians"*

and "Last Rambles," ed. Marvin C. Ross (Norman: University of Oklahoma Press, 1959), 10.

371 "occupation gone": Ibid.

372 "to the Orinoco": Catlin, "Itinerary," in *Episodes*, appendix B, 344.

372 "a small Bill at [his] hotel": GC to Sir Thomas Phillipps, January 23, 1853, George Catlin Collection, Thomas Gilcrease Institute of American History and Art, 1840–1860, Part 6, Reel 3277, Frames 629–30, AAA.

373 "nugget fever": Catlin, *Episodes*, 12.

373 "From Para, I took a steamer": Catlin, "Itinerary," *Episodes*, appendix B, 344–45.

374 "Carribbees, Gooagives": Ibid., 344.

374 "thirty of the one hundred": Ibid.

374 "Mr. Smythe": Catlin, *Episodes*, Ibid., 11.

375 "Señor L. M.": Ibid., 13.

375 "as kings and emperors": Ibid., 11.

376 "first-rate Negro man": Ibid., 12.

376 small naked Indians: Ibid., 14.

376 "In the fresh air": Ibid., 16.

376 "*actually ordering* me home": GC to Sir Thomas Phillipps, November 27, [1854], George Catlin Collection, Thomas Gilcrease Institute of American History and Art, 1840–1860, Part 6, Reel 3277, Frames 664–66, AAA.

378 "impure love reigned": Cited by Robert Aldrich, *Colonialism and Homosexuality* (London: Routledge, 2003), 27.

379 when he and Catlin probably met: While Catlin had hoped to meet Humboldt in London in 1842 (Roehm, 234), judging from correspondence and Catlin's summary of their 1845 meeting, it sounds as though they did not meet one another until Paris. See *Adventures*, vol. 2, 246. See also letters 228–35 in *Alexander Von Humboldt, und die, Vereinigten Staaten von America, Briefwechsel*, ed. Ingo Schwarz (Berlin: Akademie Verlag, 2004), 353–61.

380 Humboldt wrote to him: This original letter, no. 249 in Schwarz, *Alexander Von Humboldt*, has not been found.

380 "a crude and worthless": *North American Review* 77 (July 1853), 262.

380 "we look in vain": Schoolcraft quoted in Dippie, *Catlin*, 342.

381 "contrary to facts": Humboldt quoted in Ibid., 338.

381 "calculated, not only to injure": Ibid.

381 "real property": Ibid., 352.

382 "in the field": Ibid., 347.

383 "the insupportable heat": Edgardo Carlos Krebs, "George Catlin and South America: A Look at His 'Lost' Years and His Paintings of Northeastern Argentina," *American Art Journal* 22 (Winter 1990), 439.

384 "my friend Thomas": Catlin, *Episodes*, 73.

385 "To this should be added": Edward J. Sullivan, *The Language of Objects in the Art of the Americas* (New Haven: Yale University Press, 2007), 34, 36.

386 "One day I want to make": Bruce Chatwin to James Ivory, December 8, 1969, *Under the Sun: The Letters of Bruce Chatwin,* ed. Elizabeth Chatwin and Nicholas Shakespeare (London: Jonathan Cape, 2010), 149.

CHAPTER 30: "NOW I AM G. CATLIN AGAIN,
LOOK OUT FOR THE PAINT!"

389 "by a good gas light": FC, diary on his trip to Belgium, November 23, 1868, Roehm, 360.

390 "to be executed in lines": Roehm, 348.

390 "rapid decimation and final extinction": George Catlin, *Last Rambles amongst the Indians of the Rocky Mountains and the Andes* (London: Sampson Low, Son, and Marston, 1868), 358.

391 "Who is the *savage*": Ibid., 339.

391 "giving *freedom* and rights of citizenship": Ibid., 340.

391 "If my life had been thrown away": GC to Louise Catlin, April 22, 1861, George Catlin Papers, Reel 5824, Frames 178–79, AAA.

392 "evidence": Dippie, *Catlin*, 374.

393 "for gentleman only": George Catlin, *O-kee-pa: A Religious Ceremony; and Other Customs of the Mandans* (Philadelphia: J. B. Lippincott, 1867). See also Dippie, *Catlin*, 368–69.

395 "from early light till dark every day": FC, diary, November 21, 1868, Roehm, 359.

395 "Just discovered how the mice tails grow shorter": FC, diary, November 30, 1868, Roehm, 367.

395 "Here we sit in our dungeon": FC, diary, December 5, 1868, Roehm, 368.

396 "He constantly told me": GC to FC, June 7, 1868, Roehm, 346–47.

397 "Push it Francis—Push it!": GC to FC, n.d., Roehm, 375.

397 "patent of Invention": GC to FC, September 9, [1868], Roehm, 350.

397 "run them Barnum fashion": GC to Theodore "Burr" Catlin, September 9, 1868, Roehm, 350.

400 "If you are disappointed in the fate": GC to FC, February 5, 1870, Roehm, 394–95.

400 "before the world": GC to FC, August 29, 1870, Roehm, 402.

401 "It is truly like a visit to the red man": Dippie, *Catlin*, 419.

403 "this horrible place": Ibid, 425.

404 According to Elizabeth: See Donaldson, *George Catlin Indian Gallery*, 716–17.

404 "What will become of my gallery?": Dippie, Catlin, 427. See also Roehm, 411.

404 Catlin's grave was once marked: On July 26, 2012, a bronze statue by the American sculptor John Coleman was unveiled in Green-Wood Cemetery, near Catlin's simple gravestone of 1961. Coleman's sculpture is an "interpretive" representation of "The Greeter," the name given to Black Moccasin. Known to both Lewis and Clark, as well as to George Catlin, this long-lived Hidatsa chief was chosen to symbolize the historical span of Indian-white friendship that coexisted with the legacy of suffering and violence.

404 "unaided, nay, discountenanced": "George Catlin," *Jersey City Times*, December 24, 1872.

ILLUSTRATION CREDITS

COLOR INSERT

The Cutting Scene, Mandan O-kee-pa Ceremony, 1832.
  Denver Art Museum, The William Sr. and Dorothy Harmsen Collection,
  2001.456. Photograph: © Denver Art Museum.

Medicine Man, Performing His Mysteries over a Dying Man, 1832.
  Blackfoot/Siksika: Smithsonian American Art Museum, Gift of Mrs. Joseph
  Harrison, Jr. Photograph: Smithsonian American Art Museum, Washington,
  DC / Art Resource, NY.

Osceola, the Black Drink, a Warrior of Great Distinction, 1838, Seminole.
  Smithsonian American Art Museum, Gift of Mrs. Joseph Harrison, Jr. Photo-
  graph: Smithsonian American Art Museum, Washington, DC / Art Resource,
  NY.

Interior View of the Medicine Lodge, Mandan O-kee-pa Ceremony, 1832.
  Courtesy of American Museum of Western Art—The Anschutz Collection.
  Photograph: William J. O'Connor.

The Last Race, Mandan O-kee-pa Ceremony, 1832.
  Courtesy of American Museum of Western Art—The Anschutz Collection.
  Photograph: William J. O'Connor.

Ru-ton-ye-wee-ma, Strutting Pigeon, Wife of White Cloud, 1844, Iowa.
  Smithsonian American Art Museum, Gift of Mrs. Joseph Harrison, Jr. Photograph: Smithsonian American Art Museum, Washington, DC / Art Resource, NY.

Sha-kó-ka, Mint, a Pretty Girl, 1832, Mandan/Numakiki.

> Smithsonian American Art Museum, Gift of Mrs. Joseph Harrison, Jr. Photo-graph: Smithsonian American Art Museum, Washington, DC / Art Resource, NY.

Kee-o-kuk, the Watchful Fox, Chief of the Tribe, on Horseback, 1835, Sauk and Fox.

> Smithsonian American Art Museum, Gift of Mrs. Joseph Harrison, Jr. Photo-graph: Smithsonian American Art Museum, Washington, DC / Art Resource, NY.

Dying Buffalo, Shot with an Arrow, 1832–33.

> Smithsonian American Art Museum, Gift of Mrs. Joseph Harrison, Jr. Photo-graph: Smithsonian American Art Museum, Washington, DC / Art Resource, NY.

Niagara Falls, View of Table Rock and Horseshoe Falls, from Below, 1828.

> Private collection.

Prairie Meadows Burning, 1832.

> Smithsonian American Art Museum, Gift of Mrs. Joseph Harrison, Jr. Photo-graph: Smithsonian American Art Museum, Washington, DC / Art Resource, NY.

Shon-ta-yi-ga, Little Wolf, a Famous Warrior, 1844, Iowa.

> Smithsonian American Art Museum, Gift of Mrs. Joseph Harrison, Jr. Photo-graph: Smithsonian American Art Museum, Washington, DC / Art Resource, NY.

William Fisk (1796–1872), *George Catlin* (1796–1872), artist, 1849. Oil on canvas, 127 x 101.6 cm.

> Transfer from the Smithsonian American Art Museum. Gift of Miss May C. Kinney, Ernest C. Kinney, and Bradford Wickes, 1945. NPG.70.14. National Portrait Gallery, Smithsonian Institution / Art Resource, NY.

BLACK-AND-WHITE INSERT

Albert Eckhout (ca. 1610–65), *Tapuya Men of Northeastern Brazil in War Dance*, 1641.
> Nationalmuseet Copenhagen, Denmark. Photograph: Nationalmuseet Copen-hagen, Denmark / The Bridgeman Art Library.

Tapuya Encampment, 1854/1869.
> National Gallery of Art, Washington, Paul Mellon Collection.

Wi-jun-jon, Pigeon's Egg Head (The Light) Going to and Returning from Washington, 1837–39, Assiniboine/Nakoda.

Smithsonian American Art Museum, Gift of Mrs. Joseph Harrison, Jr. Photograph: Smithsonian American Art Museum, Washington, DC / Art Resource, NY.

Portrait of Joseph Chadwick, 1834.

Present location unknown.

Karl Girardet (1813–71), *George Catlin and His Troupe of Iowa Performing in the Tuileries before Louis-Philippe and His Family*, 1845.

Chateaux de Versailles et de Trianon, Versailles, France. Photograph: © RMN-Grand Palais / Art Resource, NY.

Mrs. George Catlin (Clara Bartlett Gregory), ca. 1830.

The Metropolitan Museum of Art, Fletcher Fund, 1938. Photograph: Image copyright © The Metropolitan Museum of Art. Image source: Art Resource, NY.

John Neagle (1796–1865), *Portrait of George Catlin*, 1825.

Gilcrease Museum, Tulsa, OK.

Photographer unknown, *Six Chippewa (Ojibwa) Indians Who Visited Europe with George Catlin*, 1851.

Chicago History Museum.

Red Jacket, 1826.

Gilcrease Museum, Tulsa, OK.

Mah-to-toh-pa, Four Bears, Second Chief, in Mourning, 1832, Mandan/Numakiki.

Smithsonian American Art Museum, Gift of Mrs. Joseph Harrison, Jr. Photograph: Smithsonian American Art Museum, Washington, DC / Art Resource, NY.

Photographer unknown, *P. T. Barnum with Tom Thumb*, ca. 1850.

Library of Congress.

Photographer unknown, Asher B. Durand, 1854.

Collection of The New-York Historical Society.

Photographer unknown, Henry Rowe Schoolcraft, daguerreotype, ca. 1851.

Library of Congress.

Photographer unknown, George Catlin in Brussels, age seventy-two, 1868.

George Catlin Papers, Archives of American Art, Smithsonian Institution, Washington, DC.

R. Stanley Freeman (British, dates unknown), George Catlin, London, 1870.

Virginia Museum of Fine Arts, Richmond. Paul Mellon Collection. Digital photograph: Katherine Wetzel, © Virginia Museum of Fine Arts.

INDEX